W9-AAW-668

What readers are saying about *Mastering Dojo*

I'm so glad to see this book released. Dojo has a lot of power, but there's also a lot of complexity to knowing which API methods to use when, and how to use them, and this book goes beyond just explaining the Dojo API to explaining what developers need to know to use it effectively.

> ► **Bill Keese**
> Project lead for Dijit
> IBM, Emerging Technology Group

Mastering Dojo will teach you how to build an Internet application that will impress your end users and delight you while you're writing it. The book also explains Dojo's JavaScript underpinnings, both for newcomers and for refugees from other languages.

> ► **Ian Dees**
> Software engineer

The book really rolls out the red carpet for Dojo to emerge with guns blazing! The authors show you how easy it is to use impressive widgets without installing a thing. I was amazed to discover that JavaScript is not just a toy language, how Dojo is built on top of it, and how both are invaluable in any web development project. Buy this book. It's the next best thing to having the authors working at your side.

> ► **Brian C. Reeve**
> Application developer, bluecomIT.com

Mastering Dojo is an understandable, in-depth guide to learning the Dojo Toolkit. It's a great supplement to the Dojo Toolkit's online documentation.

> ► **Steve Orvell**
> Senior Engineer, WaveMaker Software

Mastering Dojo

JavaScript and Ajax Tools
for Great Web Experiences

Mastering Dojo

JavaScript and Ajax Tools
for Great Web Experiences

Rawld Gill

Craig Riecke

Alex Russell

The Pragmatic Bookshelf

Raleigh, North Carolina   Dallas, Texas

Many of the designations used by manufacturers and sellers to distinguish their products are claimed as trademarks. Where those designations appear in this book, and The Pragmatic Programmers, LLC was aware of a trademark claim, the designations have been printed in initial capital letters or in all capitals. The Pragmatic Starter Kit, The Pragmatic Programmer, Pragmatic Programming, Pragmatic Bookshelf and the linking *g* device are trademarks of The Pragmatic Programmers, LLC.

The Browser Application Framework code is Copyright © 2000-2008, Vista Information Technologies, Inc., and released under the BSD license.

Every precaution was taken in the preparation of this book. However, the publisher assumes no responsibility for errors or omissions, or for damages that may result from the use of information (including program listings) contained herein.

Our Pragmatic courses, workshops, and other products can help you and your team create better software and have more fun. For more information, as well as the latest Pragmatic titles, please visit us at

http://www.pragprog.com

Printed in the United States of America.

ISBN-10: 1-934356-11-5

ISBN-13: 978-1-934356-11-1

Printed on acid-free paper with 50% recycled, 15% post-consumer content.

P1.0 printing, June 2008

Version: 2008-6-1

Contents

*Oh Kate, nice customs curtsy to great kings. Dear Kate, you
and I cannot be confined within the weak list of a country's
fashion. We are the makers of manners.*
► William Shakespeare, **Henry V**

Chapter 1

Introduction

There's a new king in town.

Over the past couple of years we've seen new technologies redefine the
rules of server-side web app development. It's the client's turn. Get
ready to throw out your current "customs" of client-side development.
With Dojo, we're entering a new era of browser-based applications.

Dojo is a set of tools that helps you build better browser-based applications. Dojo is built mostly using client-side JavaScript, and it expands
the capabilities of the modern browser (and even Internet Explorer) far
enough that the line between local, native applications and browser-
based applications has all but disappeared.

This is a pretty significant statement. It means that browser-based
(and, therefore, web-based) user interfaces can be made indistinguish-
able from those included with the best local, native applications. And it
means that the user interface of local applications can be implemented
in the browser rather than through one of the heavy, platform-sensitive,
and complex native GUI frameworks (Windows, Tk, Qt, Fox, AWT, SWT,
Swing, Cocoa, and the rest).

The ubiquitous browser becomes the user interface platform. It no
longer matters where the back end lives: on a network of distant HTTP
servers or in a small local program that implements the HTTP protocol.

Unfortunately, the "modern" browser provides an incomplete, inconvenient, and incompatible programming environment. You could get
around these problems using a plug-in such as ActionScript, but this
breaks an important rule: locally installed software is strictly forbidden.

Although it may be OK to break this rule for a local application, it is certainly not OK to break it for a web-based application.[1] Enter Dojo.

Dojo fixes browser defects such as browser incompatibilities and memory leaks, and it adds important capabilities such as HTML user interface controls and DOM querying. Although many JavaScript libraries are available, most focus on one particular idea. Some include effects libraries, others concentrate on perceived core JavaScript omissions, and still others implement one or more HTML widgets (user interface controls). In contrast, Dojo addresses all of these functional areas—and many others—extensively. In this respect, we say that Dojo has breadth and depth unlike any other open source solution.

For example, looking at Dojo's depth, Dojo normalizes the event system among the popular browsers (Internet Explorer does not implement the W3C event model, and it leaks memory; most other browsers do the opposite). If you want to connect to a click event in Dojo, you can write the following:

```
dojo.connect(myButton, "click", myFunction);
```

This code will work perfectly on any supported browser. You can include a tree control on a web page by writing this:

```
<div dojoType="dijit.Tree" label="Order" id="ordTree" store="ordJson" ></div>
```

This is quite a bit easier than what's required in many native frameworks.

Dojo also has incredible breadth. It includes some forty user interface controls, a graphics framework, cometd support,[2] a packaging system, and much more. Today, Dojo stands alone in its vast capabilities.

You may be concerned that all of this capability implies increased complexity. We think the opposite it true—at least if you compare apples to apples. Dojo is organized into a hierarchy of functionality. This allows you to focus on just the area you need for the current work at hand. As your needs change and expand, Dojo will be ready to answer those needs precisely because of its breath and depth. Contrast this to a smaller, less-ambitious library. Although such an alternative may be

---

1. In the corporate world, installing anything on company computers is a big deal. If you eliminate this road block, you can instantly open markets that were previously untouchable.

2. Cometd is a low-latency communications technique that allows the server to push data to the browser. See http://cometd.com/.

> **Buzzwords**
>
> The terms *Ajax*, *Web 2.0*, and *Rich Internet Application (RIA)* are so popular these days that sometimes it is not completely clear what they mean. Given what we can do with modern browser programming techniques, Ajax has come to mean "the way we do modern web apps." That's the way we use it. *Web 2.0* is as much a business strategy as a technical term. We'll avoid it. Finally, a local, browser-based application that communicates with an on-host HTTP server is usually considered an example of an RIA, yet such a program isn't an Internet application. But the word is pervasive, so we'll use it. When we do, we mean a *mostly* single-page, browser-based application. Ahh, precision.

easier to digest on day one (and we dispute even this), three or six months later when you need a capability that the library does not provide, you are left with either learning another library or implementing something yourself. Both of these choices imply much more complexity and cost than using Dojo from the beginning.

Further, one of the core values of the Dojo contributor community is "beat down complexity." All key attributes of Dojo's design have been vigorously debated, implemented and reimplemented, tested, and used with this value in mind. Rather than ignore defects and build beautiful new buildings on sinking swamp land, the Dojo community has mixed the mature, rational, even skeptical engineer's approach with the fast-moving forward thinking of the young hacker. There is real substance behind these words: the community spent most of 2007 refactoring the core system. This is surely a sign of commitment to excellence and professionalism, which can sometimes be missing in open source projects.

Finally, you should know that Dojo is not an academic project. It's being used in hundreds of projects at hundreds of companies. Navigate to http://www.myaol.com, and hit View Source. Dojo is there. IBM is a major contributor to the Dojo foundation—and is using Dojo in its WebSphere stack. BEA and Sun ship Dojo with their products. With this kind of Fortune 100 usage and sponsorship, you can be sure that Dojo is here for the long haul.

1.1 Key Aspects of Dojo

Let's survey the broad landscape that is Dojo.

Not Just a Library—A Toolkit

Dojo is a collection of static, client-side JavaScript scripts. There is no client-side plug-in or server-side components. It includes the following:

- A design and implementation that normalizes the browser, allowing the same source code to work in several browsers (no more browser/feature sniffing and resulting browser-dependent code).

- Functions/libraries that abstract the sometimes-obtuse, arcane, and inconvenient W3C DOM programming model into a convenient, parsimonious, efficient interface.

- Functions/libraries that fix several gross browser errors such as memory leaks; others that provide functionality likely to be available natively in the browser in a few years—today!

- A library of arguably the largest single set of HTML widgets available today.

- A module system coupled with a build system that lets you divide code into small, manageable chunks during development and later package the release system for optimal download performance—without any modifications to the source code. The build system even lets you slice and dice Dojo itself in a way that's optimal for your project.

- Independent libraries (that is, you can load them on demand) that implement several other advanced capabilities.

Several of the libraries result in frameworks for the following:

- Building custom HTML widgets

- Internationalization (i18n)

- Localization (l10n)

- Accessibility (a11y)

Dojo also includes a utility application called the *build system* that packages large projects that may include hundreds of files into small, optimal sets of compressed files for deployment on production servers.

At the time of this writing, Dojo officially supports Internet Explorer (6+), Firefox (1.5+), Safari (3+), and Opera (9+, Dijit doesn't support Opera).

Since Dojo is pure JavaScript, it can be used in nonbrowser, Spider-Monkey-embedded, and Rhino-embedded environments. Of course, much of Dojo—anything that leverages HTML, CSS, and/or XHR—is not applicable in these environments. Still, there is an inner core of functionality that is useful. The loader, language extensions, asynchronous programming, object-oriented programming, and Common Locale Data Repository functionality depend upon nothing but JavaScript and can be used in these nonbrowser environments.[3]

Dojo Targets a Wide Audience

Dojo aggressively targets a broad range of users, from designers of simple web sites through enterprise application developers. This is a very tough requirement to get right since design decisions that are optimal for one group are often less so for another. Most "web design" tasks can be accomplished by simply loading the script dojo.js. In this respect, Dojo is as lightweight and easy to use as the best competing libraries. On the other hand, larger projects require more. Dojo includes machinery to load different function families upon demand. This design gives Dojo users the luxury of digesting exactly as much complexity as they need to solve the problem at hand.

Dojo Targets the Future

The state of the browser-based programming environment is another major force behind Dojo's philosophy and content. If the browsers were standards-compliant (or, at least compatible), if JavaScript and the DOM API fixed some glaring shortcomings, and if HTML included user interface controls more modern than 1989, then much of Dojo wouldn't be required. The architects of Dojo recognize that, eventually, these defects will be fixed. And when native functionality becomes available, you'll want to use it rather than a scripted alternative. Dojo was created to solve key defects in the browser-based programming environment so that modern, highly capable programs (indeed, programs rivaling native applications) can be targeted to the browser—while preparing for a forward upgrade path as the native browser environment improves.

---

3. Using Dojo outside the browser is beyond the scope of this book.

Since browsers won't be fixed in a single flash, Dojo's modular design can hook into these facilities directly—on a per-facility/per-browser level—as they become available. In short, Dojo provides a stable, browser-based programming environment, even as we enter the next round of browser wars.

Dojo Is Open Source

The source code is free and available. It is dual-licensed under either the terms of the modified BSD license or the Academic Free License version 2.1. The BSD license is very friendly to commercial products; it allows you to use or modify Dojo in your own commercial products without any requirement to open source anything that you do. Naturally, you can change whatever you want for such products. (Heck, under the BSD license, you could sell unmodified copies of Dojo.)

The development process is rigorous and open. Source code is maintained in an SVN repository; defects and enhancements are tracked by Trac. Anonymous access is available to both. Coding style guidelines are enforced, and code must be accompanied by unit tests prior to inclusion in the key release sets.

There are avenues of free support through forums and mailing lists as well as companies that provide for-fee services.

Unlike many open source projects, Dojo is backed by a foundation. The Dojo Foundation is a 501(c)(6) nonprofit organized to help promote the adoption of Dojo and to provide a healthy environment for JavaScript engineering of every stripe. One of the key benefits that the foundation affords is the ability to insulate users from hidden liabilities (for example, patent or copyright infringement) regarding the use of the code.

All things Dojo discussed here start at http://dojotoolkit.org/.

Dojo Is Divided Into Three Projects

Dojo includes three projects:

- *Dojo*: The foundation upon which everything else is built. Altogether, it includes about fifty JavaScript scripts and several other resources that handle browser normalization, JavaScript modularization, extensions to the core JavaScript library, extensions to the W3C DOM API (including a parsing and querying the DOM), remote scripting, Firebug Lite, drag and drop, a data store API, localization and internationalization, and a few other miscellaneous functions.

- *Dijit*: The Dojo widget framework and built-in widgets (about forty HTML user interface widgets).

- *Dojox*: Dojo extensions. This includes everything from the grid widget to graphics libraries. Dojox is the Wild West of Dojo—there are some very sophisticated and stable libraries that are currently deployed in real-world, for-profit systems as well as some completely experimental systems. Each library includes a readme that describes the project.

Each of these three projects resides in its own source code tree. Typically Dojo and Dijit coordinate releases; so far, Dojox has released with Dojo and Dijit, but this may change in future releases. We'll cover Dojo and Dijit exhaustively in this book while only touching on a couple Dojox projects.

Dojo Has a High Degree of Conceptual Integrity

Despite the size of Dojo, the design and implementation possess a high degree of conceptual integrity. In Fred Brooks' classical software engineering tome *The Mythical Man-Month* [Bro95], Brooks postulates that conceptual integrity (the ratio of functionality to complexity) is the most important attribute of any programming project. This is a well-established and frequently missing attribute of long-lived software. We already noted that beating down complexity is one of the Dojo project's core values. Further, the Dojo and Dijit project trees are each managed by a single individual who guides and coordinates project evolution. This fulfills another of Brooks' requirements to achieve conceptual integrity—designating a single system architect. Finally, as we explore Dojo, you'll see that it just feels right. It seems to surprise the least...to be natural.[4] All of these are attributes of high conceptual integrity.

1.2 Using the Book

Here are a few last preliminary remarks that will help you maximize the value of the book.

---

4. Although Dojo is mature, like any significant software system, it isn't perfect. We'll occasionally point out weaknesses.

Assumptions

We assume you have at least some minimal web programming experience. Dojo builds on top of standards-based technologies, most notably, (X)HTML, CSS, DOM, and JavaScript. Although we'll often provide a few orienting remarks on an underlying technology when discussing a particular Dojo functional area, we will not attempt to teach these technologies—that's at least four more books! In case you are fairly new to all of this, here are some recommendations:

- Yahoo has published an excellent set of lectures about JavaScript and DOM programming by Douglas Crockford.[5]

- The canonical JavaScript reference is *JavaScript: The Definitive Guide* [Fla06]. It also includes a very good DOM tutorial and reference.

- CSS is often arcane and obtuse. *Cascading Style Sheets: The Definitive Guide* [Mey06] makes a good attempt, but there are several other references with different strengths and weaknesses.

- On the other hand, HTML is fairly simple to grasp. *HTML and XHTML: The Definitive Guide* [MK08] is a nice reference, but any number of free, online references are also probably sufficient.

JavaScript is a great language. Contrary to popular—and very misinformed—belief, it is closer to Lisp than BASIC. It allows you to express very powerful ideas quickly and with elegance. Dojo pushes JavaScript hard; so will we.

The Example Code

We've constructed real, working examples throughout the book. We've tried to find a good balance between including enough code in line with the narrative so that you can understand the code but not so much that the flow is interrupted with pages of code. If you find that a particular code fragment is missing some detail that you find perplexing, you can find the complete working examples online at http://www.pragprog.com/titles/rgdojo/source_code.

---

5. http://yuiblog.com/blog/2007/01/24/video-crockford-tjpl, http://yuiblog.com/blog/2006/11/27/video-crockford-advjs/, and http://yuiblog.com/blog/2006/10/20/video-crockford-domtheory/

Debugging

Web programming is a very dynamic activity. Typically, you'll write a few lines, hit Refresh in your browser, and see what happens. Still, a good debugging environment is critical to maximize programmer efficiency. Since Firefox + Firebug are among the best options (and they're free!), we use them in the narrative. If you're using something other than Firefox (for example, Internet Explorer), then you probably already have a good debugging environment scoped out. If not, Dojo includes the Firebug Lite console that you can use with any browser. See the *Alex Says...*, on page 73 for more debugging advice from Alex.

The Plan

The book is divided into four parts. Part I demonstrates how Dojo helps you build powerful apps quickly and easily. These chapters include complete details on the examples they present, but they intentionally do not dissect the areas of Dojo they touch. Part II gives an extensive exploration of Dojo Core—the foundation upon which all things Dojo are built. Part III covers Dijit, the Dojo widget system, and Part IV demonstrates how to construct a Rich Internet Application.

1.3 Acknowledgments

Above all, the three of us would like to recognize and thank the Dojo contributors. Without such a dedicated and truly talented community Dojo simply wouldn't be. We hope this book reflects well upon their herculean efforts. We also owe special thanks to Bill Keese, Adam Peller, Ian Dees, and Brian Reeve for taking the time to read and critique the manuscript. Nearly every page includes improvements recommended by these experts. Finally, a tip of the hat to the folks at Pragmatic Programmers—clearly a publisher by programmers for programmers. Thanks for giving us the opportunity and all of the support along the way. —Rawld, Craig, and Alex

I would like to especially thank my coauthors, Craig and Alex, and the development editor, Jackie. What a wonderful set of people to work with, each highly skilled in completely different ways, all helping me get out a better product. —Rawld

At the risk of sounding like a long Academy Awards speech, I would like to thank my writing teachers Carolyn Goodwin, James Alsop, Gerry Shapiro, and Judith Sornberger. They encouraged me to keep writing, even though the last thing the world wants is another writer. And to Kathy, thank you for the Starbucks card, your love, and your limitless patience that made this book possible. If life were fair, the first published book between us would've been yours. —Craig

First, I'd like to thank Craig and Rawld, whose book this really is. Their dedication, talent, and willingness to plumb the deepest depths of Dojo has produced a book whose quality and clarity will be an asset to Dojo developers for years to come. I feel lucky to have had the opportunity to contribute in the small ways that I have to this effort. Rawld, Craig, and Jackie Carter have made the process easier than I could have possibly imagined. My humblest thanks to them.

I'd like to thank the contributors and committers who have made Dojo the outstanding achievement that it is. They have given their time and astonishing efforts to the project without any expectation of material reward, and I am lucky to lead and work in such a team. Their boundless optimism, perseverance, and dedication have pushed the open Web forward in ways that many often wrote off as impractical. Their work has improved the lives of millions of users every day. My particular thanks go to Dylan Schiemann, Tom Trenka, Bill Keese, David Schontzler, Paul Sowden, Eugene Lazutkin, Adam Peller, Becky Gibson, Pete Higgins, James Burke, Brad Neuberg, and Owen Williams. I owe so much to so many.

My deepest thanks go to my wife, Jennifer, who has supported me and inspired me in so many ways. Her help, advice, and patience have been boundless. She has not only made Dojo possible but has made me a better person. —Alex

Part I

Ajax the Dojo Way

Chapter 2

Powerful Web Forms Made Easy

Approximately five minutes after JavaScript was invented, people began messing around with their web forms. They split long forms into tabbed pages, wrote validators to check input, and developed easy-to-use controls such as date entry calendars. These features are so prevalent now that users don't think twice about them. But you do. They're still not native features in HTML, so you must either write your own components or shoehorn someone else's into your application.

There's an easier way. Dijit, the widget system built on Dojo, can do the heavy lifting for you. A *widget*, also called a *Dijit component*, is a user interface control built from HTML and JavaScript. You create one by adding a simple dojoType= attribute to an HTML tag. It's a remarkably simple way to add form functionality.

dojoType= is nonstandard HTML, but Dijit uses the attribute to endow special features onto the enclosing tag. This is called a *declarative* widget because you write no actual code for it. But you can create the same widgets through JavaScript, a subject we'll touch on in Chapter 12, *Scripting Widgets*, on page 317. These are called *programmatic widgets*. For the next couple chapters, we'll use only declarative widgets because of their simple learning curve.

There are widgets to control layout and validate input. There are widgets that emulate native application controls such as sliders, tooltips, and progress bars. There are widgets to model complex data such as hierarchical trees and tables. Dijit comes with more than forty prepackaged widgets, and many work well without a stitch of extra JavaScript!

In this chapter, we will take a traditional fill-and-submit form and turn it into a more functional, intuitive, and feature-rich form. We'll "super-size" the regular HTML controls into Dijit components, adding tons of useful functionality with almost zero programming. When we're done, you'll have a form that's so neat and functional that you'll want to tape a copy of it to your refrigerator.

Dijit components solve common web design issues, and you can drop them in and make them work in a matter of minutes. And that's good, because you have a problem form on your hands...

2.1 What Customers Are Saying About Your Form

So, let's talk about *that* web page. You know the one. It's where subscribers change their address, look up their order information, manage their subscription preferences, and so on. It's called Account Preferences or My Account or something like that.

You know that page? Well... people hate it.

No one told you? Of course not. It's easier to mutter under your breath than send a comment to "Contact Us." Here's what they're saying:

- *Customer Looking for Their Order History*: "OK, phone number, phone number. Where is it? [scroll, scroll, scroll, scroll] Oh, here it is. Way down at the bottom. Nice."
- *Customer Service Representative*: "Oh, great. Someone typed Rover as their email address. Stupid web server. Doesn't it know all email addresses have an @ sign?"

Hmmm. Your form has an attitude problem. Fortunately, Dijit is here to help. Its layout, verification, and user interface elements will solve these problems, and the overall design will be much prettier to boot. So, what are we waiting for? The sooner we get it installed, the sooner we can get started!

2.2 Installing Dojo on Your Own Server

Dojo is a client-side JavaScript toolkit, and its heart lies in some well-tuned JavaScript scripts. In a Dojo-based web application, you create small bits of HTML and JavaScript that call the Dojo toolkit code.

Technically, Dojo doesn't need a web server. You can install Dojo into any directory, build Dojo-based web applications, and load them all with the file:// protocol. But a web server lets you do more interesting things such as proxying (introduced in the sidebar on page 41) and partitioning (in Section 10.3, *Partitioning with QueryReadStore*, on page 269). For that reason, we recommend installing a web server first—and here, you can choose any one that fits your needs. Dojo is stubbornly server-agnostic. There are no special procedures for serving it from a Windows, Linux, or Mac OS X server.

You can download the latest Dojo package from http://dojotoolkit.org. It comes bundled with Dojo, all the Dijit components, the extension components of Dojox, and utilities such as the DOH unit tester and the ShrinkSafe source code compressor.[1] Follow the directions for expanding the .zip or .tar.gz file on your computer. If you know what you're doing, you can pick any directory you want for installation. This book's example code assumes the files are in the /dojoroot directory on your web server. The Dojo archive file contains four directories: dojo, dijit, dojox, and util.

Finally, if you're picky about such details like "Did I install it right?" then simply hit the URL http://yourserver.com/dojoroot/dojo/tests/runTests. html. This will run Dojo through a battery of unit tests.

We should note here that for serving dynamic content from your own data sources, you'll need to use a server-based programming language such as PHP, ASP, or JSP. Since our focus here is Dojo, the examples in this book are server-agnostic. Instead, we'll hook either to third-party data sources, such as Yahoo, or to static files that emulate dynamic data sources.

2.3 Adding Dojo and Dijit to a Page

Dojo and Dijit act much like other JavaScript libraries. You add a few statements to the top of each page, and these statements transfer the Dojo/Dijit JavaScript code to the browser. Below those statements, you can call Dojo methods and/or use Dijit components. Dijit components rely on Dojo methods, but the loading processes handle all the dependencies for you.

You must add a few statements to the *<head>* and *<body>* sections of each page to accomplish that. Fortunately, the statements are fairly

---

1. This is the "binary distribution" of Dojo. You can also download the entire source version, which allows you to do custom builds. We explain the other differences in Section 4.2, *Getting the Source*, on page 71.

boilerplate. You can add these statements to a text editor template file, a macro, or a snippet within easy reach. Or, if your site uses a standard include file, you can place the boilerplate in that file. In short, you need to do the following:

1. Add the standard Dojo headers to the <head> section.
2. Set the class for the <body> tag to a Dijit theme.
3. Add dojo.require statements for the components you need.

If you are using Dojo without Dijit, some of these steps can be eliminated or reduced. We'll note where you can do this. But there's no harm, except for a small increase in load time, in including all of them. So, let's begin.

Step 1: Add the Standard Dojo Headers

The following statements load the Dojo toolkit and style sheets from your server:

```
advanced_forms_made_easy/hello_dojo_world.html

<style type="text/css">
    @import "/dojoroot/dijit/themes/tundra/tundra.css";
    @import "/dojoroot/dojo/resources/dojo.css"
</style>
<script type="text/javascript" src="/dojoroot/dojo/dojo.js"
        djConfig="parseOnLoad: true"></script>
```

The @import rule loads the standard Dojo styles and the theme Tundra. In Dijit terminology, a *theme* is a set of fonts, colors, and sizing settings for components so they look good together. Three themes come prepackaged with Dijit—Tundra, Soria, and Nihilo—and you can develop your own themes as well, a process we describe in Chapter 16, *Dijit Themes, Design, and Layout*, on page 427. You must always import dojo.css, but if you're using Dojo without Dijit, you can omit the theme style sheet import.

The <script> tag pulls the Dojo code from your server. The djConfig="parseOnLoad:true" attribute is required to use Dojo elements declaratively. The declarative vs. programmatic distinction in Dojo is one we'll cover throughout the book, but for now we'll be using just declarative widgets because they're easier to learn. If you can't wait for the details, see the sidebar on the facing page.

Declarative vs. Programmatic: A Preview for the Impatient

You can create Dijit widgets declaratively or programmatically. In a nutshell, declarative widgets are nestled in HTML like this:

advanced_forms_made_easy/declarative_vs_programmatic.html

```
<div dojoType="dijit.layout.ContentPane"
    href="http://www.yahoo.com" ></div>
```

Programmatic widgets are built from JavaScript like this:

advanced_forms_made_easy/declarative_vs_programmatic.html

```
var programmaticPane =
    new dijit.layout.ContentPane(
        { href: 'http://www.yahoo.com' }
    );
```

Declarative widgets use nonstandard HTML attributes such as dojoType=. Although this may bother purists, the utility of declarative widgets makes them an acceptable trade-off.*

So, with that said, declarative is the easiest method for using Dijit and the one we'll use for most of the book. In Chapter 12, *Scripting Widgets*, on page 317, we'll see programmatic Dijit components. If you use only programmatic Dijit or use plain Dojo without Dijit, you don't need dojo.parser or djConfig="parseOnLoad:true". Omitting them makes the page load a smidge faster.

---

*. Not convinced? See the *Alex Says...*, on page 75 for an explanation of nonstandard attributes and their role in Dojo.

Step 2: Set the Class of the Body

Next, you set the class of the body to match the theme. In our case, we're using Tundra, so we add the following:

advanced_forms_made_easy/hello_dojo_world.html

```
</head>
<body class="tundra">
```

The class name will match the theme name in lowercase: tundra, soria, or nihilo. (The a11y theme is autoapplied under certain conditions that you'll learn about in Section 16.3, *A11y and Themes*, on page 439.)

You might ask, "Why do I need to specify my theme here? I loaded it in the style sheet." The biggest reason is that Dojo doesn't perform "magic." Simply including something in the page shouldn't have huge side effects, and every modification of your page should be at your control. By scoping theme rules to the tundra (or other theme-appropriate) prefix, Dijit puts you in control. Second, placing the theme in the <body> tag partitions the styles into a neat namespace hierarchy. We'll show you how this works in Section 16.1, *Theme Structure*, on page 427.

The theme is used for Dijit components only. If you're using Dojo without Dijit, you can omit loading it.

Step 3: Add dojo.require Statements

Dojo and Dijit components, like big treasures, come in small packages; they're called *modules*, and you will need to include a dojo.require for each module referenced in your page. dojo.require acts like require_once in PHP or **require** in Ruby.

You add code like this to the <head> section:

advanced_forms_made_easy/hello_dojo_world.html

```
<script type="text/javascript">
   dojo.require("dojo.parser");
   dojo.require("dijit.layout.ContentPane");
</script>
```

The dojo.parser module is required for all pages using declarative Dijit. (See the sidebar on the previous page for details.) Then you load the dijit.layout.ContentPane module, required to draw Dijit content panes. Dojo modules correspond roughly to JavaScript files under /dojoroot. For example, requiring dijit.layout.TabContainer loads the JavaScript script /dojoroot/dijit/layout/TabContainer.js. The story is more complex, as we'll see in Chapter 4, *Dojo In Depth*, on page 65, but this is the general idea.

dojo.require is one of the most important functions in Dojo. But how do you know which modules to include? In this book, we'll always introduce a new component or Dojo API, say the Date API, with its module name, for example, dojo.date. These module names are also shown in the Dojo online API guide at http://dojotoolkit.org/api.

You will be applying these three steps to every page using Dojo or Dijit. Once the browser loads the theme style sheet and executes the Dojo script, processes the dojo.require statements, and sets the <body> class, you're ready to roll. Meanwhile back on our Account Preferences form, we have problems to solve.

First Name: _____

Last Name: _____

Middle Initial: ▢

Address Line 1: _____

Address Line 2: _____

City: _____

State: ▢

Postal Code: _____

Country: _____

Date of Move to this
Address: _____

Home Phone: _____

Work Phone: _____

Cell Phone: _____

Figure 2.1: OUR FORM BEFORE ADDING DIJIT

2.4 Laying Out the Form

In Figure 2.1, you can see Account Preferences as it exists now. The form is too long, and users hate scrolling through it. It would be easier to use if the fields were presented in logical groups. We will do that by using the Dijit components dijit.layout.ContentPane, a widget that separates parts of a page, and dijit.layout.TabContainer, which adds tabs to them.

Tabs along the top will group the form into sections: Personal Data, Address, and so on. Only one tab shows at a time. Clicking a tab label on the top brings the corresponding section to the front. It looks like a file cabinet—intuitive and friendly.

Preparing the Page

To get to the tabbed interface, we must first add Dojo and Dijit to the page, as outlined in the previous section.

First, add the *<style>* and *<script>* tags:

```
advanced_forms_made_easy/form_with_dijit.html

<!DOCTYPE html PUBLIC "-//W3C//DTD HTML 4.01 Transitional//EN"
    "http://www.w3.org/TR/html4/loose.dtd">
<html>
<head>
<meta http-equiv="Content-Type" content="text/html; charset=UTF-8">
<title>Account Preferences With Dijit</title>
<style type="text/css">
    @import "/dojoroot/dijit/themes/tundra/tundra.css";
    @import "/dojoroot/dojo/resources/dojo.css"
</style>
<script type="text/javascript" src="/dojoroot/dojo/dojo.js"
        djConfig="parseOnLoad: true"></script>
```

(The lines marked with a triangle in the margin are the ones we added.) Then, add the *<body>* class for the theme, which is tundra in our case.

```
advanced_forms_made_easy/form_with_dijit.html

<body class="tundra">
```

Finally, add the dojo.require statements. In this case, the page needs the dijit.layout.TabContainer and dijit.layout.ContentPane components:

```
advanced_forms_made_easy/form_with_dijit.html

<script>
    dojo.require("dojo.parser");
    dojo.require("dijit.layout.ContentPane");
    dojo.require("dijit.layout.TabContainer");
</script>
<style>
.formContainer {
   width:600px;
   height:600px;
}
label {
   width:150px;
   float:left;
}
</style>

</head>
```

The styles will line up the labels and textboxes we will add in a second. With the preliminaries out of the way, we can now add our Dijit components.

Organizing the Form with Tabs

In Dijit, "adding a component" really means "adding the dojoType= attribute to an HTML tag." Dijit components nestle right inside your HTML code. Most components begin life as <*div*> tags, but others are built on <*input*>, <*span*>, or other tags.

The two components we need, again, are as follows:

- A dijit.layout.ContentPane, which holds one "tabful" of data. Each ContentPane has a label that appears on the tab.

- A dijit.layout.TabContainer, which holds a group of ContentPanes.

To turn a form fragment into a ContentPane, just surround it with <*div*> tags and specify a dojoType= of dijit.layout.ContentPane, like this:

advanced_forms_made_easy/form_with_dijit.html

```
<div dojoType="dijit.layout.ContentPane" title="Personal Data">
    <label for="first_name">First Name:</label>
    <input type="text" name="first_name" id="first_name"
        size="30" /><br/>
    <label for="last_name">Last Name:</label>
    <input type="text" name="last_name" id="last_name"
        size="30" /><br/>
    <label for="middle_initial">Middle Initial:</label>
    <input type="text" name="middle_initial" id="middle_initial"
        size="1" /><br/>
</div>
```

Then repeat this for all the tabs:

advanced_forms_made_easy/form_with_dijit.html

```
<div dojoType="dijit.layout.ContentPane" title="Address">
    <label for="address_line_1">Address Line 1:</label>
    <input type="text" name="address_line_1" id="address_line_1"
        size="30" /><br/>
    <label for="address_line_2">Address Line 2:</label>
    <input type="text" name="address_line_2" id="address_line_2"
        size="30" /><br/>
    <label for="city">City:</label>
    <input type="text" name="city" id="city"
        size="30" /><br/>
    <label for="state">State:</label>
    <input type="text" name="state" id="state"
        size="2" /><br/>
    <label for="postal_code">Postal Code:</label>
    <input type="text" name="postal_code" id="postal_code"
        size="15" /><br/>
    <label for="country">Country:</label>
    <input type="text" name="country" id="country"
        size="30" /><br/>
```

```
        <label for="date_move">Date of Move to this Address:</label>
        <input type="text" name="date_move" id="date_move"
               size="11" /><br/>
▶  </div>
▶  <div dojoType="dijit.layout.ContentPane" title="Phones">
        <label for="home_phone">Home Phone:</label>
        <input type="text" name="home_phone" id="home_phone"
               size="30" /><br/>
        <label for="work_phone">Work Phone:</label>
        <input type="text" name="work_phone" id="work_phone"
               size="30" /><br/>
        <label for="cell_phone">Cell Phone:</label>
        <input type="text" name="cell_phone" id="cell_phone"
               size="30" /><br/>
▶  </div>
```

Wrap up these panes in a *<div>* with dijit.layout.TabContainer:

```
advanced_forms_made_easy/form_with_dijit.html
```

```
<div class="formContainer" dojoType="dijit.layout.TabContainer"
     style="width:600px;height:600px">
```

Notice the height style on the TabContainer. That's required, and if you leave it off, the tabs will not appear at all. (Consider yourself warned!) The width, on the other hand, is optional.

So, let's get this party started! Download the code, and place it into a new directory called dojobook/advanced_forms_made_easy. Fire up your favorite browser, and hit the URL http://yourserver/dojobook/advanced_forms_made_easy/form_with_dijit.html. Up pops your tabbed form, which should like Figure 2.2, on the facing page.

It looks and works great! Click a tab, and the data pops out in front. The Tundra theme makes the design elements look good. It acts like you'd expect. What would have taken you hours to code in JavaScript takes just a few *<div>* tags and two JavaScript statements.

Something Wrong?

Things happen. The most common novice problem is seeing no formatting appear so that our form looks more like the form we started with—see Figure 2.1, on page 19. If this is you and you're using Internet Explorer, you probably also saw a script error pop up or a Script Error icon in the browser's lower-right corner. If you're running Firefox with the JavaScript console open, you probably saw the error there. But when things go wrong, you could use some industrial-strength help.

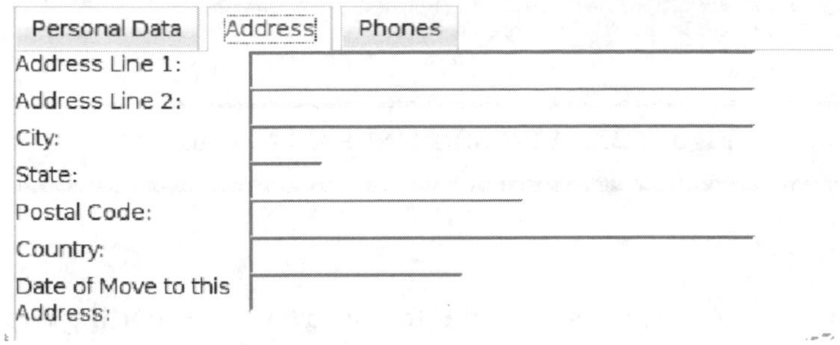

| Personal Data | Address | Phones |

Address Line 1:

Address Line 2:

City:

State:

Postal Code:

Country:

Date of Move to this
Address:

Figure 2.2: A TABBED CONTAINER

Enter Firebug. Firebug is a combination debugger, DOM viewer, console logger, and profiler. The full version is an open source Firefox extension, and to install it in Firefox, simply visit http://www.getfirebug.com and click the Install button.

But if you use Internet Explorer or Safari, never fear! Dojo comes packaged with Firebug Lite, which includes the more useful features of Firebug. To turn on Firebug Lite, simply change your script-loading statement to the following:

```
<script type="text/javascript" src="/dojoroot/dojo/dojo.js"
    djConfig="parseOnLoad: true, isDebug: true"></script>
```

Firebug Lite will appear in the browser window unlike Firebug, which keeps itself hidden. So, you'll want to turn the isDebug flag off in production apps.

When running Firebug or Firebug Lite, you get a bit more information on the console, as shown in Figure 2.3, on the following page.

Here, it looks like whatever statements are referencing dijit.layout. TabbedContainer are wrong. Taking a quick look into the directory /dojoroot/dijit/layout, you see TabContainer.js, not TabbedContainer.js. That's the problem. We're trying to use *Tabbed*Container instead of TabContainer.

If there is still no formatting but no errors in the console either, check these things:

- Make sure your dojoType= attributes are correct. Case matters here.

- Double-check the <*body*> tag to make sure it has class="tundra".

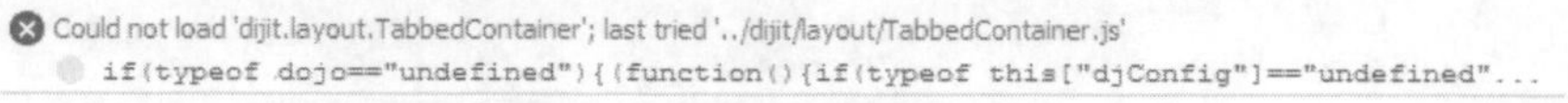

Figure 2.3: Firebug finds the problem.

- Double-check the *<style>* tag to ensure you're loading the Tundra CSS from the correct place.

Once you have that working, step back and take a look at your new tabbed form. It cuts a very fine figure, indeed! And easy to use? Absolutely! And this is only the beginning.

2.5 Improved Form Controls

Getting back to our problem form, one issue concerns bad data. A little behavioral psychology on the user will help: make the good choices easy to pick and the bad choices difficult. Unfortunately, HTML controls go for the lowest common denominator, leaving choices wide open. Dijit's validation controls can fix that. Controls like dijit.form.ValidationTextBox flag the unacceptable choices immediately. Finally, input helpers such as dijit.form.DateTextBox make choosing dates very easy.

Validating Fields

Client-side data validation is win-win: it helps you by keeping the data clean and helps the user by giving immediate, targeted feedback. In fact, validation is so useful that it was one of JavaScript's first and most popular applications. Dijit goes one step further by making popular validations available via HTML attributes with no visible JavaScript.

We need some data cleanliness, so let's start with the fields on the Personal Data tab. First start with a regular *<input>* or *<textarea>* tag. Add a dojoType= attribute of dijit.form.ValidationTextBox. Then add validations and field-cleansing attributes:

advanced_forms_made_easy/validating.html

```
<label for="first_name">First Name:</label>
<input type="text" name="first_name" id="first_name"
   dojoType="dijit.form.ValidationTextBox" trim="true"
   propercase="true" required="true" size="30"
   missingMessage="You must enter your first name" /><br/>
```

Alex Says...

Debugging Tools

If I were allowed to give but one piece of debugging advice, it would be this: start with Firebug (get it at http://www.getfirebug.com/). For a long time the development tools for doing development in a browser were so poor as to be laughable. Luckily, Firebug has almost single-handedly dragged the state of the art forward by a tremendous amount. As a response to Firebug, new versions of Internet Explorer, Opera, and Safari are all beginning to include improved debugging facilities. Despite this renewed arms race for developer mind-share, Firebug remains the gold standard.

Perhaps the most compelling feature of Firebug is its JavaScript console. Firebug exposes APIs for logging events from pages that you may be interacting with, but the console builds on that to let you type or paste in some JavaScript and execute it on-the-fly. This lets you "poke around" the environment fluidly, often drastically shortening the time it takes to prototype a new feature or debug a problematic one. Firebug's DOM tree, CSS style, and layout exploration tools are so convenient that they frequently eliminate the need to dump messages and objects to the console or to programmatically change properties and styles. Finally, Firebug sports a full-featured JavaScript debugger with complete stack and variable inspection, breakpoint, and stepping functionality. In fact, we're so enamored of Firebug that Dojo includes a beefed-up version of "Firebug Lite" as part of the toolkit to give you a console on browsers that otherwise wouldn't provide one.

And don't forget to add dojo.require to the header:

advanced_forms_made_easy/validating.html

```
dojo.require("dijit.form.ValidationTextBox");
```

These extra attributes do an incredible amount of work:

- required="true" makes the field required, of course. When the field is blank, the background is colored yellow, as is the case with any erroneous fields.
- trim="true" automatically removes leading and trailing spaces in the input. So when you type a string and tab out of the field, the spaces are trimmed.
- propercase="true" is similar to trim. When the box loses focus, the first letter is capitalized, and the rest are lowercased.

In a similar vein, we can validate the email address with Validation-TextBox's regular expression option:

advanced_forms_made_easy/validating.html

```
<label for="email">Email:</label>
<input type="text" name="email" id="email" size="30"
    dojoType="dijit.form.ValidationTextBox" regExp=".*@.*"
/>
```

Here you have the full power of JavaScript regular expressions. In our case, .*@.* matches all strings with any prefix (including an empty string), then @, and then any suffix.

ValidationTextBox has many other kinds of validation, which we'll cover in Chapter 15, *Form Controls*, on page 393. As powerful as Dijit validation is, however, it should always be backed up with server-side validations. That way, bad people cannot introduce bad data by merely turning off JavaScript.

Easier Date Entry

How many ways can you specify a date? No one really knew until HTML forms were invented—evidently, the answer is "millions of ways." Of course, we'd much rather have consistently formatted dates, and users would rather have easier ways to pick them.

With Dijit, you use dijit.form.DateTextBox to turn any textbox into a widget with a calendar. First, add it to the header:

advanced_forms_made_easy/validating.html

```
dojo.require("dijit.form.DateTextBox");
```

Figure 2.4: DIJIT DATETEXTBOX

Then, add it to the textbox:

advanced_forms_made_easy/validating.html

```
<label for="date_move">Date of Move to this Address:</label>
<input type="text" name="date_move" id="date_move" size="11"
       dojoType="dijit.form.DateTextBox" /><br/>
```

By clicking the textbox, the user can unfold a calendar underneath. In Figure 2.4, you can see the DateTextBox in its open state.

DateTextBox also respects the value= attribute of the textbox, provided it is in ISO date format, which we'll cover in Section 15.4, *Standard Form*, on page 409.

2.6 Wrapping It Up

Well, that was a rush! Here's the form source code we've built bit by bit:

advanced_forms_made_easy/finished_form.html

```
<!DOCTYPE html PUBLIC "-//W3C//DTD HTML 4.01 Transitional//EN"
         "http://www.w3.org/TR/html4/loose.dtd">
<html>
<head>
<meta http-equiv="Content-Type" content="text/html; charset=UTF-8">
<title>Account Preferences Final Form</title>
<style type="text/css">
    @import "/dojoroot/dijit/themes/tundra/tundra.css";
    @import "/dojoroot/dojo/resources/dojo.css"
</style>
<script type="text/javascript" src="/dojoroot/dojo/dojo.js"
        djConfig="parseOnLoad: true"></script>
```

```html
<script>
    dojo.require("dojo.parser");
    dojo.require("dijit.layout.ContentPane");
    dojo.require("dijit.layout.TabContainer");
    dojo.require("dijit.form.ValidationTextBox");
    dojo.require("dijit.form.DateTextBox");
</script>
<style>
.formContainer {
    width:600px;
    height:600px;
}
label {
    width:150px;
    float:left;
}
</style>

</head>
<body class="tundra">
<div class="formContainer" dojoType="dijit.layout.TabContainer">

<div dojoType="dijit.layout.ContentPane" title="Personal Data">
    <label for="first_name">First Name:</label>
    <input type="text" name="first_name" id="first_name"
        dojoType="dijit.form.ValidationTextBox" trim="true"
        propercase="true" required="true" size="30"
        missingMessage="You must enter your first name" /><br/>
    <label for="last_name">Last Name:</label>
    <input type="text" name="last_name" id="last_name" size="30"
        dojoType="dijit.form.ValidationTextBox" trim="true"
        propercase="true" required="true" length="30"
        missingMessage="You must enter your last name"/><br/>
    <label for="middle_initial">Middle Initial:</label>
    <input type="text" name="middle_initial" id="middle_initial"
        size="1" /><br/>
    <label for="email">Email:</label>
    <input type="text" name="email" id="email" size="30"
        dojoType="dijit.form.ValidationTextBox" regExp=".*@.*"
    />
</div>
<div dojoType="dijit.layout.ContentPane" title="Address">
    <label for="address_line_1">Address Line 1:</label>
    <input type="text" name="address_line_1" id="address_line_1"
        size="30" /><br/>
    <label for="address_line_2">Address Line 2:</label>
    <input type="text" name="address_line_2" id="address_line_2"
        size="30" /><br/>
    <label for="city">City:</label>
    <input type="text" name="city" id="city" size="30" /><br/>
    <label for="state">State:</label>
```

```
    <input type="text" name="state" id="state" size="2" /><br/>
    <label for="postal_code">Postal Code:</label>
    <input type="text" name="postal_code" id="postal_code"
        size="15" /><br/>
    <label for="country">Country:</label>
    <input type="text" name="country" id="country" size="30" /><br/>
    <label for="date_move">Date of Move to this Address:</label>
    <input type="text" name="date_move" id="date_move" size="11"
        dojoType="dijit.form.DateTextBox" /><br/>
</div>
<div dojoType="dijit.layout.ContentPane" title="Phones">
    <label for="home_phone">Home Phone:</label>
    <input type="text" name="home_phone" id="home_phone"
        size="30" /><br/>
    <label for="work_phone">Work Phone:</label>
    <input type="text" name="work_phone" id="work_phone"
        size="30" /><br/>
    <label for="cell_phone">Cell Phone:</label>
    <input type="text" name="cell_phone" id="cell_phone"
        size="30" /><br/>
</div>
</div>
</body>
</html>
```

This form is easier to navigate, is easier for adding data, and is patient but firm about accepting good data. Yet it takes only a few lines of JavaScript and some extra HTML attributes. Dijit is a very powerful thing indeed! Out of the entire Dijit catalog of more than forty widgets, you now know four of them:

- dijit.layout.ContentPane creates boundaries around content to place in containers.

- dijit.layout.TabContainer stacks ContentPanes on top of one another and lets the user choose one with tabs on the top.

- dijit.form.ValidationTextBox performs validations on individual controls.

- dijit.form.DateTextBox adds a pop-up calendar to a textbox.

All of this takes place without any extra server communication. In the next chapter, we'll leave Dijit for a bit and see how Dojo can create small, chatty conversations with servers—your own or someone else's.

Chapter 3

Connecting to Outside Services

In the previous chapter, we used Dijit to improve the user-to-browser experience. Now we're going to go the other direction: from the browser to the server. Ajax, or Asynchronous JavaScript and XML, uses this communication path to free the browser from the shackles of form submission and the tedium of constant page redrawing. This, in turn, improves the user interface, making web apps look and behave more like regular programs.

3.1 Dojo Remote Scripting

Google Maps was to Ajax what Elvis Presley was to rock 'n' roll. Unlike the popular map programs of the time such as MapQuest, Google Maps could scroll in any direction, zoom in, and place markers all without the flicker of a page submit. Users loved it! Developers, eager to please users and show their prowess, immediately dug into the details of Xml-HttpRequest, or XHR.

But here's the thing: *XHR is hard!* Or more accurately, XHR is easy to use naively but hard to use *correctly*. Some of its many weirdisms include the following:

- An unfamiliar syntax. Many developers simply copied and pasted XHR code snippets but had no idea what the code was doing. That makes debugging. . . ehhhhh, not so fun.

- Poor handling of content types. Though XHR is supposed to speak XML fluently, you could hand back valid XML from the server and still get a head-scratching "Not valid XML" message from XHR.

- No help in creating the parameter string. You had to do all the URL encoding yourself, or perhaps you didn't do it at all. . . and the first & in a textbox broke your application.

But don't worry. XHR may have saved the Internet, but Dojo will save you from XHR!

Dojo's *remote scripting* facilities enable a client-side script to communicate with a server without a page reload. Remote scripting's easy-to-use XHR and pseudo-XHR APIs extend the walls of the application, reaching out to services from your own server and beyond. And Dojo does all this without excessive JavaScript on your part. Dojo and Dijit provide control and data translation services layered on top of XHR, making it easy to use. In this chapter, we'll look at three Dojo techniques for service connections:

- dojo.data is an API specification like JDBC or ODBC. A dojo.data driver implements this specification and responds to requests from your data-enabled widgets or JavaScript code. Traditionally, each driver is in charge of a different data provider format, for example, JavaScript Object Notation (JSON) or XML. But it could also abstract a web service or an in-memory JavaScript object. You use common APIs to read or write the data, no matter what the source and format is.

- The dojo.io.script method accesses JSON with Padding (JSONP) services in other domains.[1] XHR must follow the same-origin rule— you can call only those services housed on the same server as the outer page. JSONP removes this restriction in a clever way by using *<script>* tags. More and more web services from Yahoo and Google are available in JSONP format, and dojo.io.script calls them in a way that mimics XHR.

- The dojo.xhrGet, dojo.xhrPost, dojo.rawXhrPost, dojo.xhrPut, dojo.rawXhrPut, dojo.xhrDelete, and dojo.xhr methods are the lowest-level remote scripting services. These methods, collectively called dojo.xhr*, don't provide the common API layer and translation services that dojo.data does. They also require a server-side *proxy* to call services outside your domain. But dojo.xhr* works without writing a compatible dojo.data driver, and they can use data in any format. They are best for off-site services that don't support JSONP.

---

1. The acronym JSONP was proposed by Bob Ippolito in http://bob.pythonmac.org/archives/2005/12/05/remote-json-jsonp/. Many providers use the JSONP technique for servicing cross-domain requests, but do not call it JSONP. Yahoo, for example, calls it "JSON with callbacks."

Generally, dojo.data is the most sophisticated of the three. Its drivers are built on the dojo.io.script and dojo.xhr* methods. If you're already used to XHR, the latter two methods will feel more familiar. All of these methods require fluency with less-common JavaScript idioms such as hashes and function literals, so we'll take a slight detour to learn those first. Then we'll build three working examples: a grid of wish-list entries, a list of Yahoo Search matches, and a web service for gathering reviews.

3.2 JavaScript Idioms for Calling XHR

Before we plunge into calling web services, we need to look at some JavaScript features that are used in Dojo XHR but are less common in the real world. They may look unfamiliar to you even if you have used JavaScript for a while. But they will be extremely useful here and down the road.

Literals and Hashes

A *literal* is a notation for a fixed value in source code. So in JavaScript, "Foo" is a string literal, 1 is a number literal, and [1, 2, 3] is an Array literal. Literals are the atoms of a particular JavaScript type.

A *hash* is a collection of name-value pairs called *properties*. Each property name can be used only once in a hash. So, you can have the properties ("bun", "wheat") and ("burger", "beef") in the same hash, but not both ("bun", "wheat") and ("bun","white"). This concept is probably familiar to you already—in Perl it's called a *hash*, in PHP it's an *associative array*, and in Java it's a *Map*. Or if you like to think in relational database terms, properties are two-column rows with the property name acting as a primary key. Fair enough.

In JavaScript, any instance of the type Object is a collection of properties. Although we'll see objects can be used for much more than simple collections of properties, sometimes just bundling some properties together in one place is all you need. When an object is used like this, we'll call it a *hash*; if the object happens to be a literal, we'll call it a *hash literal*. The general form is as follows:

```
{
    «propertyName1»:«value1»,
    «propertyName2»:«value2»,
    ...
    «propertyNameN»:«valueN»
}
```

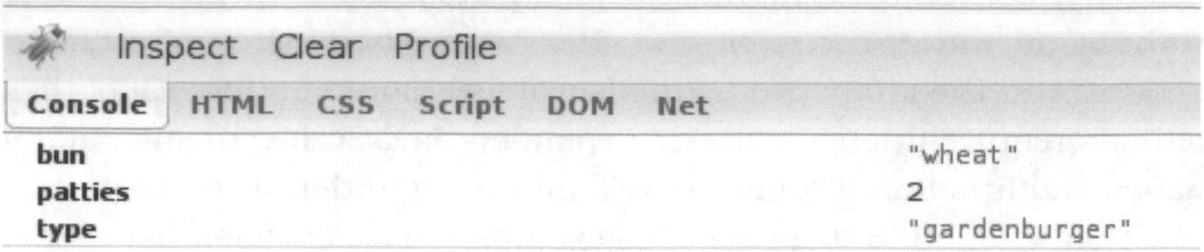

Figure 3.1: A HASH PRINTED WITH CONSOLE.DIR

One important note: you should *never* end the last property-value pair with a comma. Firefox is forgiving about this, but other browsers are not. It's better to be on the safe side.

The following code assigns a hash literal to a variable:

```
var burger = {patties: 2, type: "gardenburger", bun: "wheat"};
// displays the object structure in the Firebug console
console.dir(burger);
```

That console.dir statement looks interesting. This method, along with console.debug, console.log, and console.error, is your passport to Firebug and Firebug Lite's logging mechanism. If you have spent your web life debugging JavaScript with alert boxes, you'll find this a welcome change of pace.

The console.dir method prints the hash properties on the log, similar to Figure 3.1. It's also handy for printing objects, arrays, and all kinds of complex data structures. Its low-power cousin console.debug prints strings, numbers, and other primitives. Finally, console.log and console.error do the same thing as console.debug, but with different message levels and different icons appearing in the console. You can filter messages by these different levels in Firebug.

So, now back to hash literals. Like array literals, these are a nice syntactic shortcut. Just as var a = [2, 4]; is equivalent to a[0] = 2; a[1] = 4;, so is the hash literal example equivalent to the following:

```
var burger2 = {};
burger2.patties = 2;
burger2.type = "gardenburger";
burger2.bun = "wheat";
// Should be exactly the same as previous example
console.dir(burger2);
```

Here we have three properties named patties, type, and bun with values 2, "gardenburger", and "wheat", respectively.

Many documents (including the Dojo API documentation) don't use the word *hash*. We find it useful because it says, no matter its origin, "It's an object that's just being used to bundle up some properties—nothing more, nothing less."

We'll have lots more to say about objects and classes in Chapter 9, *Defining Classes with dojo.declare*, on page 221, but for now we'll concentrate on plain ol' hashes and their usefulness in Dojo.

Hash literals can contain other literals, including array literals and other hash literals:

```
var burger3 = {
    // an array literal
    patties: ["gardenburger", "bocaburger"],
    toppings: {
        cheese: "American",
        meat: "bacon"
    },
    bun: "wheat"
};
console.dir(burger3);
```

(The fact that you can mix a vegetarian patty with a nonvegetarian topping proves JavaScript is *very* loosely typed!) Notice the formatting here—when we nest hashes with more than a few properties, it helps to indent them inward like structured code. The extra whitespace reveals the structure at a glance.

For the property-value pairs, the property name can be placed in quotation marks, so "patties":2 is the same as patties:2. The right sides of the colon can be any expression: numeric and string literals, array literals, nested hash literals, function calls, or object constructor calls.

Hash literals are important in Dojo because they make function calls more readable. Take, for example, dojo.io.script.get, a Dojo function we'll use later in this chapter for Yahoo Search.

Even without knowing dojo.io.script.get, the parameters here are clear and readable:

```
dojo.io.script.get({
    // URL for Yahoo Search
    url: "http://search.yahooapis.com/WebSearchService/V1/webSearch",
```

```
    // Send search term parameters:
     content: {
         appid: "DEMO",
         query: searchTerms,
         output: "json"
     },

     // If the response takes longer than 10000ms (= 10 seconds), error out
     timeout: 10000,

     // Yahoo API requires you to send the callback function name in the
     // parameter "callback"
     callbackParamName: "callback"

     // The full call will have load and error parameters too
     // ...
});
```

All of the data is passed as one hash with properties url, content, and so forth. This could be simulated with individual primitive parameters, but there are big advantages to doing it with a hash literal:

- The hash literal is more descriptive than a set of parameters. To replace dojo.io.script.get with dojo.io.script.get(1, 'someNode', ...), we'd have to review the API documentation to learn what "1" refers to. Put another way, though JavaScript has only positional parameters, you can simulate named parameters by passing a hash.

- You can reorder or skip properties in a hash literal with no penalty. This is especially important in dojo.io.script.get, where a normal call specifies only about half the possible parameters.

- Finally, let's suppose you call a function several times with the same parameters. Building a hash and then passing it to the function over and over is more efficient than parsing the arguments each time.

You can create complex hashes with many levels of nesting, all by separating elements with commas and wrapping hashes with braces. This is handy in XHR and other Dojo APIs and is indispensable in declaring class structures. We'll see an example of the latter in Chapter 9, *Defining Classes with dojo.declare*, on page 221.

Function Literals

Unlike hash literals, which make a good deal of sense, function literals might throw you for a loop.

Before diving into function literals, you need to understand JavaScript's idea of "functions as data." In JavaScript numbers, strings, hashes, arrays, objects, and multitudes of other types of data can be assigned to a variable or passed to a function or method. That's nothing special. But in JavaScript, *functions* can be assigned to variables and passed to functions too. The function name represents a function *definition*, not a function call.

This technique makes your code shorter, simpler, and more expressive. An example will clarify. Suppose you have an array of hashes that you'd like to make into a list. Each hash has a few properties, each of which will be made into a hyperlink, like so:

```
// Assume there's a <ul id="listOfUrls"></ul> present.
var listNode = document.getElementById("listOfUrls");

// You want to turn this:
var urls = [
    { url: "http://www.yahoo.com", title: "Yahoo" },
    { url: "http://www.ask.com", title: "Ask" },
    { url: "http://www.google.com", title: "Google" }
];

/* into this:
    <li><a href="http://www.yahoo.com">Yahoo</a></li>
    <li><a href="http://www.ask.com">Ask</a></li>
    <li><a href="http://www.google.com">Google</a></li>
*/
```

Your first shot at it looks like plain ol' procedural JavaScript:

```
for (var i=0; i < urls.length; i++) {
    var listItem = document.createElement("li");
    listItem.innerHTML =
        "<a href='"
        + urls[i].url
        + "'>"
        + urls[i].title
        + "</a>";
    listNode.appendChild(listItem);
}
```

Bluggh! That middle assignment statement is nasty looking. Are the quotes balanced right? Are the subscripts off? You have to look awfully close to find out. So, we use a trick from dojo.string:

```
for (var i=0; i < urls.length; i++) {
    var listItem = document.createElement("li");
    listItem.innerHTML =
        dojo.string.substitute("<a href='${url}'>${title}</a>", result);
    listNode.appendChild(listItem);
}
```

That's much better. The dojo.string.substitute method takes the hash in oneResult and applies the properties to a template. This template uses ${...}-style placeholders. So, ${url} is replaced with oneResult.url, and ${title} is replaced with oneResult.title.

Now about that **for** loop. How many times have you used i only to find it was being used by some other inner or outer loop? OK, you don't have to admit it. But isn't there a better way to loop through arrays?

Dojo has a similar method, dojo.forEach, with an interesting signature. You pass an array and a function—not a function call, an actual function. This function must define one parameter: an item. Here's what we mean: the following function mirrors the inside of the previous example's **for** loop:

```
var listNode = document.getElementById("listOfUrls");
function appendNewListItem(oneResult) {
    var listItem = document.createElement("li");
    listItem.innerHTML =
        dojo.string.substitute("<a href='${url}'>${title}</a>", oneResult);
    listNode.appendChild(listItem);
}
```

You pass the name of this function to dojo.forEach:

```
dojo.forEach( urls, appendNewListItem );
```

Your fingers will instinctively reach for the parentheses when typing appendNewListItem. Don't do it! You're not passing the *result* of the function call; you're passing the function itself. Amazingly, dojo.forEach calls appendNewListItem(urls[0]); and then appendNewListItem(urls[1]);, and so on. Hmmmmm. That saves you an entire **for** loop. Now we're getting somewhere!

And now we can talk about function literals. Just as you can use a hash literal in place of a hash, you can use a *function literal* in place of a function. Their general form is as follows:

```
function(«parameters») {
    «body»
}
```

Function literals are sometimes called *anonymous functions* because they look like a function definition without a name. So, you can write the previous code using a function literal.

```
var listNode = document.getElementById("listOfUrls");
dojo.forEach( urls, function(oneResult) {
    var listItem = document.createElement("li");
    listItem.innerHTML =
        dojo.string.substitute("<a href='${url}'>${title}</a>", oneResult);
    listNode.appendChild(listItem);
});
```

We'll see plenty more examples of function literals, but here's what we need to know for Dojo XHR: XmlHttpRequest calls are asynchronous, meaning they return control to the JavaScript program immediately while they work in the background. We need to tell XHR, "This is what you do when the result comes back." That's perfect for a function literal, because most often the function is used only for that XHR call. Defining a named function to call it only once feels like too much overhead. A function we pass to an asynchronous request is called a *handler*, or equivalently a *callback*. We want the process to "call back" our function when it's ready.

The functions-as-data concept of JavaScript turns out to be extremely useful. Dojo uses it in XHR and also in surprising places such as animations and declaring subclasses. We'll discuss those later, but for now let's dig into the first project.

3.3 A Wish List with dojo.data and dojox.grid.Grid

The Justa Cigar Corporation is overhauling its web site, and we've just won the contract to write it. Customers on the Justa site are gung ho about cigars, and Justa wants to help them connect to each other, share information, and (Justa hopes) purchase cigars.[2]

Each Justa customer has a wish list of cigars with brand names, sizes, country of origin, and other information. The execs want to list this in a scrollable table and give the customer the ability to add, delete, and edit cigars in place without leaving the page. In Figure 3.2, on the next page, you can see the "cocktail napkin" view of what Justa wants. Already this is impossible with the old web technology because of the don't-leave-the-page requirement. We're going to need XHR to send add, delete, and edit requests to the server.

---

2. Just for the record, we don't condone such carcinogenic activities. The point is you can use the same techniques for finding ice cream, cross-country skis, or flat-screen televisions. Whatever floats your boat. Dojo will not judge you.

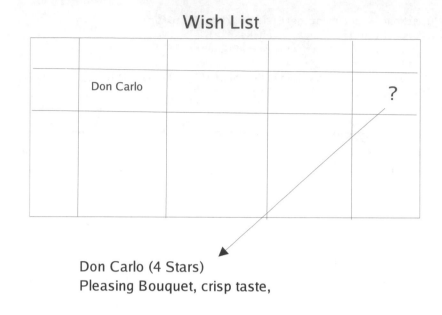

Don Carlo (4 Stars)
Pleasing Bouquet, crisp taste,

Figure 3.2: WISH-LIST USER INTERFACE DESIGN (COFFEE STAIN OMITTED)

dojox.grid.Grid is a good fit for the user interface part. Grid acts like a mini-spreadsheet where you can view, sort, filter, and edit tabular information. dojo.data provides plumbing between Grid and server-based data. Together they'll form the backbone of the wish list.

Because Justa controls the web site and database, its IT department can write web services in any format we want. These web services will read from the wish-list database, translate the data to the right format, and send. Writing these server-side scripts is beyond the scope of this book, but Dojo can generally work with any server-side language and any database because they communicate over HTTP. If this notion is foreign to you, the sidebar on the facing page gives you some help on where to start.

Fortunately, we can stub out the web services while writing the client. After all, XHR simply sends a request to a URL and gets data back in some standard format. A plain old text file will suffice—it has a URL, and we can write it in some format. That makes the job small and easier to manage. But we still need to pick a data format. dojo.data has drivers for commonly used data formats such as XML, comma-

<u>**Server-Side Options**</u>

Dojo enables a significant architectural shift. When scripting fill-and-submit pages in a middle-tier language such as PHP, ASP, or JSP, both the navigation and HTML generation rest mostly in that language. With Dojo, more code executes on the client and less on the middle tier. But you still need some middle-tier code for the following:

- Connecting to a database and passing the results in a format Dojo understands
- Proxying calls to external web services

PHP is a particularly adept language for these calls because proxying is a one-line call and JSON support is built in (at least to 5.2 and newer). But any language that can talk to HTTP servers and use databases will work.

Alternatively, you can use an enterprise service bus (ESB). This software is made for proxying and translation, and many require declarative configuration in lieu of programming. Many ESB products are large and expensive, but Apache Synapse is an open source, lightweight ESB that's a good match for Dojo.

separated variables (CSV), JSON, and HTML tables. Seeing this list, you might think XML is the way to go. But hold up a minute!

JSON, the Language

JavaScript Object Notation is a better choice for sending the wish-list data in our example. If you haven't seen or used it before, you might wonder why we'd pick JSON over XML. After all, practically every programming language and every browser on Earth speaks XML. It's self-descriptive, standardized, and mature.

But in browsers, XML suffers from two problems. First, browsers don't implement XML standards uniformly. Second, and this is the deal-breaker, browser-based XML implementations are slow. That's a problem because the more interactive you want your interface, the chattier you have to be with the server, and the faster your data interchange format must be.

Enter JSON. In a nutshell, JSON data looks like the right side of a JavaScript assignment. For comparison, here is a snippet of XML data from our Justa wish lists:

```
<wishListItem>
    <wishId>4455</wishId>
    <description>Don Pepin Garcia Delicias</description>
    <size>7-50</size>
    ...
</wishListItem>
```

This is equivalent to the following JSON:

```
"wishListItem": {
    "wishId": 4455,
    "description": "Don Pepin Garcia Delicias",
    "size": "7-50",
...
}
```

This looks suspiciously like a hash literal. And it is! However, JSON has more restrictions placed on it:

- All strings, including the names on the left side of the colon (:), must be quoted. (Hash literals are not as strict.)

- Nested hashes and arrays are allowed on the right side of the colon. But the only primitive data allowed are single- or double-quoted strings, numbers, the boolean constants **true** and **false**, and the constant null. No expressions or variable names are allowed.

It's really that simple. Dojo feeds the data to a JavaScript eval, gets back a hash, and gives it to you. But it also enforces the JSON quoting rules behind the scenes, and that's an important security feature. Otherwise, someone could type in a wish-list item named while(1); and lock up someone's browser.

If you're given the choice of web service output to consume by Dojo, JSON is usually preferable to XML. It's expressive, flexible, and easy to manipulate in JavaScript. Adapters for popular server-side languages are plentiful, as you can see at http://www.json.org. And it's fast, fast, fast! Some studies have clocked it at 100 times faster than XML in a browser. This makes sense because JSON is "closer to the metal" of JavaScript and requires less translation. When you need cigar data, those extra clock cycles count!

A Stub Data Source

dojo.data has its own terminology, which we will cover completely in Chapter 10, *dojo.data*, on page 257. But here's enough to build our test wish-list data. A *data source* is the URL from which the data comes. In our test case, the URL will be very simple: services/cigar_wish_list.json. When we fill out the stubs, we'll probably send parameters along with it, as in services/cigar_wish_list.php?userid=99555. A *data store* is the corresponding dojo.data object that holds the data. Finally, an *item* is one data object. An item is like a database record but can have a more complex structure.

So, here's a snippet from our data source, in services/cigar_wish_list.json:

xhr_techniques/services/cigar_wish_list_abbrv.json

```
{
    "identifier": "wishId",
    "label": "description",
    "items":
    [
        {
          "wishId": 4455, "description": "Don Pepin Garcia Delicias",
          "size": "7-50", "origin": "Nicaragua", "wrapper": "Corojo",
          "shape": "Straight"
        },
        {
          "wishId": 4456, "description": "601 Habano Robusto",
          "size": "5-50", "origin": "Nicaragua", "wrapper": "Natural",
          "shape": "Straight"
        },
        {
          "wishId": 4457, "description": "Black Pearl Rojo Robusto",
          "size": "4 3/4-52", "origin": "Nicaragua", "wrapper": "Natural",
          "shape": "Straight"
        },
        /* ... */
    ]
}
```

The structure may look complex on first glance. Judicious use of whitespace makes things a bit easier—here we use a style similar to a JavaScript program, lining up brackets and indenting common levels. Working from the inside out, a wish-list item...

xhr_techniques/services/cigar_wish_list_abbrv.json

```
{
    "wishId": 4455, "description": "Don Pepin Garcia Delicias",
    "size": "7-50", "origin": "Nicaragua", "wrapper": "Corojo",
    "shape": "Straight"
},
```

is a simple hash literal following the JSON rules. The brackets surrounding these hashes create an array of wish-list objects:

xhr_techniques/services/cigar_wish_list_abbrv.json

```
[
    {
      "wishId": 4455, "description": "Don Pepin Garcia Delicias",
      "size": "7-50", "origin": "Nicaragua", "wrapper": "Corojo",
      "shape": "Straight"
    },
    {
      "wishId": 4456, "description": "601 Habano Robusto",
      "size": "5-50", "origin": "Nicaragua", "wrapper": "Natural",
      "shape": "Straight"
    },
    {
      "wishId": 4457, "description": "Black Pearl Rojo Robusto",
      "size": "4 3/4-52", "origin": "Nicaragua", "wrapper": "Natural",
      "shape": "Straight"
    },
    /* ... */
]
```

Finally, this array becomes the items property of the data source, as we saw earlier:

xhr_techniques/services/cigar_wish_list_abbrv.json

```
{
    "identifier": "wishId",
    "label": "description",
    "items":
    [
        {
          "wishId": 4455, "description": "Don Pepin Garcia Delicias",
          "size": "7-50", "origin": "Nicaragua", "wrapper": "Corojo",
          "shape": "Straight"
        },
        {
          "wishId": 4456, "description": "601 Habano Robusto",
          "size": "5-50", "origin": "Nicaragua", "wrapper": "Natural",
          "shape": "Straight"
        },
        {
          "wishId": 4457, "description": "Black Pearl Rojo Robusto",
          "size": "4 3/4-52", "origin": "Nicaragua", "wrapper": "Natural",
          "shape": "Straight"
        },
        /* ... */
    ]
}
```

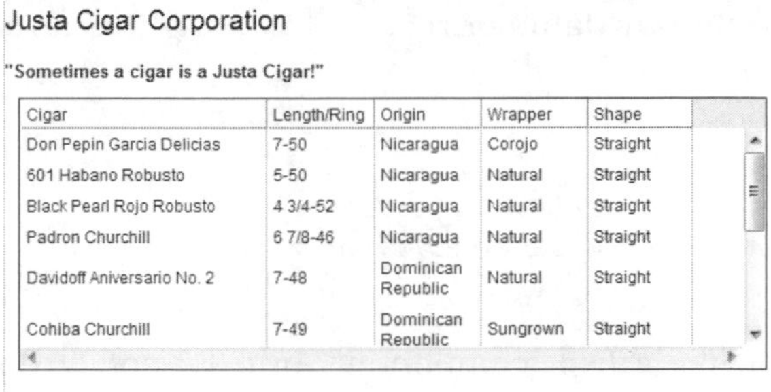

Figure 3.3: THE WISH LIST: SCROLLABLE, SORTABLE, AND FULL OF TASTY CIGARS

We are then going to feed this into the dojo.data driver dojo.data. ItemFileReadStore. This driver expects JSON data in a specific format with the following properties: identifier is the field containing an item's ID; label is the field with the human-readable identifier; and items is the data itself, which is an array of hashes. Not all dojo.data drivers are this restrictive: CSV and XML data sources do not require an identifier field, for example.

The IT people at Justa will write a server-side component that reads database records and writes the data into this format. But this fixed data source will do for now.

The Data-Enabled Widget, dojox.grid.Grid

Grid widgets are very familiar to GUI designers. A grid is a spreadsheet-like "supertable" that allows editing, sophisticated display, and a well-structured event system. Grids are unfamiliar to most web programmers, though, because they're difficult to construct from scratch.

The Dojox grid component is the state-of-the-art in web-enabled data grids, and it gives client-server grids a run for their money in features, performance, and stability. You can pipe dojo.data data stores into it with just a few lines of code.

The goal is to get to Figure 3.3. It looks pretty sophisticated, but every journey begins with a small step, so let's begin.

Every grid needs data. A grid's *model* is the set of data that is feeding the grid, named after the *M* in MVC architecture.

We've already built our data source, and making this a model requires just one *<div>* tag:

```
<div dojoType="dojo.data.ItemFileReadStore"
    jsId="wishStore" url="services/cigar_wish_list.json">
</div>
```

This looks a lot like a Dijit component, but it's not. It doesn't display anything—which is usually a tip-off that it's not from Dijit. And the dojo-Type= value does not begin with dijit. (In Section 12.1, *What Exactly Is a Widget?*, on page 317, we'll learn the full story.) Instead, it acts more like an assignment statement. The jsId= attribute declares a JavaScript variable to hold the object. You can use these variables in your own JavaScript code, or, as we do here, feed the contents of one object into another. So, this tag sets up a dojo.data.ItemFileReadStore, a data store using JSON in the special format we used for cigar_wish_list.json.

With the model taken care of, we can define the grid itself:

```
<table id="grid" dojoType="dojox.grid.Grid" store="wishStore"
    query="{ wishId: '*' }" clientSort="true">
    <thead>
        <tr>
            <th field="description" width="15em">Cigar</th>
            <th field="size">Length/Ring</th>
            <th field="origin">Origin</th>
            <th field="wrapper">Wrapper</th>
            <th field="shape">Shape</th>
        </tr>
    </thead>
</table>
```

Hmmm, that sure looks like an HTML *<table>*. . . although there's a few extra attributes. But those extra attributes wield tremendous power. First, dojox.grid.Grid takes in the data store wishStore, defined earlier. The grid can apply sorting and filtering to the data store, designated by the attributes clientSort= and query=. The former is straightforward. The latter involves another hash literal defining filter criteria. In this case, { wishId: '*' } means "Match every item that has a wishId property." In our case, that's all the records in the store.

Inside the *<table>* tag, it looks like a table with exactly one row. For our simple two-dimensional table type of grid, all we need are a few *<th>*

tags, each of which define column characteristics. The field property points to a field in our data source. (You'll learn more about that later.) And the body of the tag is used as the column header.

Let's step back, review our work, and fold in some last-minute touches. Here's the full script:

`xhr_techniques/wish_list_grid.html`

```
Line 1  <!DOCTYPE html PUBLIC "-//W3C//DTD HTML 4.01 Transitional//EN"
   -           "http://www.w3.org/TR/html4/loose.dtd">
   -    <html>
   -    <head>
   5    <meta http-equiv="Content-Type" content="text/html; charset=UTF-8">
   -    <title>Justa Cigar Wish List</title>
   -    <style type="text/css">
   -        @import "/dojoroot/dijit/themes/tundra/tundra.css";
   -        @import "/dojoroot/dojo/resources/dojo.css";
   10       @import "/dojoroot/dojox/grid/_grid/tundraGrid.css";
   -    </style>
   -    <script type="text/javascript" src="/dojoroot/dojo/dojo.js"
   -        djConfig="parseOnLoad: true"></script>
   -    <script>
   15       dojo.require("dojo.parser");
   -        dojo.require("dojo.data.ItemFileReadStore");
   -        dojo.require("dojox.grid.Grid");
   -
   -    </script>
   20   <style>
   -    #grid {
   -        border: 1px solid #333;
   -        width: 550px;
   -        margin: 10px;
   25       height: 200px;
   -        font-size: 0.9em;
   -        font-family: Geneva, Arial, Helvetica, sans-serif;
   -
   -    }
   30   </style>
   -
   -    </head>
   -    <body class="tundra">
   -
   35   <h1>Justa Cigar Corporation</h1>
   -    <h3>"Sometimes a cigar is a Justa Cigar!"</h3>
   -
   -        <div dojoType="dojo.data.ItemFileReadStore"
   -            jsId="wishStore" url="services/cigar_wish_list.json">
   40       </div>
   -
```

```
        <table id="grid" dojoType="dojox.grid.Grid" store="wishStore"
            query="{ wishId: '*' }" clientSort="true">
          <thead>
45          <tr>
              <th field="description" width="15em">Cigar</th>
              <th field="size">Length/Ring</th>
              <th field="origin">Origin</th>
              <th field="wrapper">Wrapper</th>
50            <th field="shape">Shape</th>
            </tr>
          </thead>
        </table>

55  </body>
  </html>
```

There are two things to note here. First, we must add an extra style sheet to make the Grid match the Tundra theme, which you see at line 10. Second, the two dojo.require calls starting at line 16 load the Grid and ItemFileReadStore components.

Run this script, and the grid pops up, as shown in Figure 3.3, on page 45. And dig the functionality! The grid has the following characteristics:

- *Alternately striped*: Odd/even colors are automatically applied for easy reading.

- *Scrollable*: Scroll bars automatically appear if needed for horizontal or vertical scrolling.

- *Column sizable*: Point between columns on the top, and drag left or right.

- *Row-selectable*: Just click anywhere on a row to select it. The row changes color.

- *Sortable*: Just click a column header to sort by that field. Click again to switch the sort direction.

If you have the Firebug debugger installed in your browser, you can watch the XHR packets go over the network, as shown in Figure 3.4, on the next page.

dojo.data and dojox.grid provide a quick way to get XHR up and running against your domain's web services, but what if you want to use services outside your network? You can write your own proxy in a server-side language that calls the outside service on your behalf. But for some specially written web services, there's an even easier way.

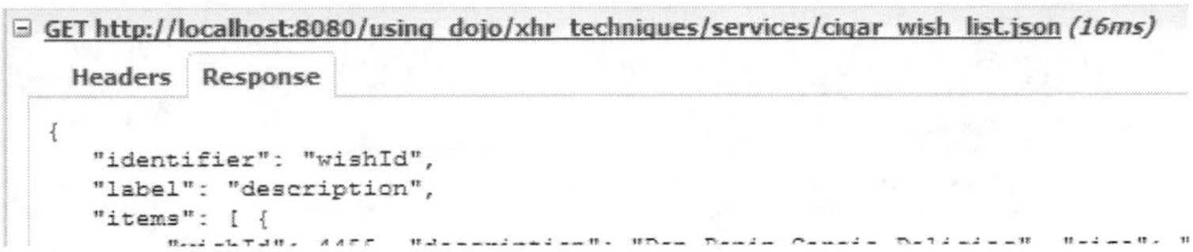

```
⊟ GET http://localhost:8080/using_dojo/xhr_techniques/services/cigar_wish_list.json (16ms)
   Headers  Response

   {
     "identifier": "wishId",
     "label": "description",
     "items": [ {
```

Figure 3.4: FIREBUG VIEW OF GETTING THE WISH LIST OVER XHR

3.4 Researching Cigars Using JSONP

The second part of the project adds lists of cigar-specific hyperlinks from Yahoo Search. Yahoo publishes its Search API through a JSONP-based web service, and we'll use dojo.io.script to stitch it to the application. The user clicks a cigar name; Dojo calls the Yahoo web service, gets the hyperlinks, and displays them in a list underneath the grid. Clicking another cigar name erases the previous list and displays results for the new cigar. The results look like Figure 3.5, on the following page.

http://developer.yahoo.com is a good starting place for researching Yahoo web services. From there, the Search API documentation is a few clicks away at http://developer.yahoo.com/search/web/V1/webSearch.html. For this example, we'll use the most current API at the time of this writing, version 1. Yahoo is very good about keeping old APIs running for backward compatibility, so all the techniques here should work even if updated APIs are available.

Once there, we find the following information about Yahoo Search. You need a Yahoo web application ID, for which you fill out a form at http://search.yahooapis.com/webservices/register_application. Under the terms and conditions, you are not obligated to keep this application ID protected. This is important to know for JSONP services, because the application ID must be sent down to the client browser.

Yahoo Search uses the HTTP GET command and a query string to pass parameters individually. This is called a REpresentational State Transfer (REST) protocol. The interesting parameter for us is query, which defines the search terms. The output can be returned in one of three formats: XML, serialized PHP, and JSON, depending on which output parameter you send. Obviously we want JSON here, but other situations may call for other formats.

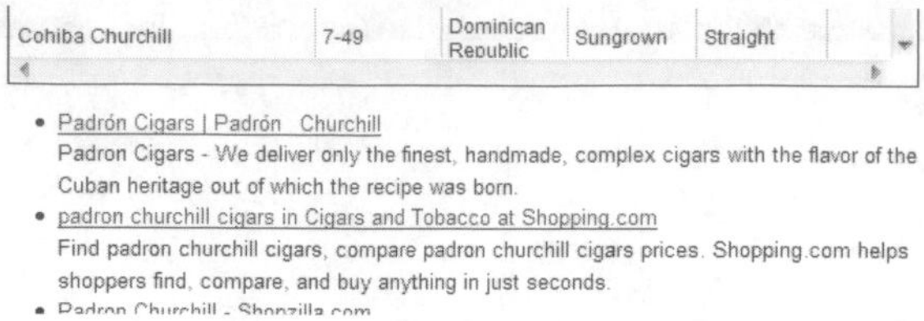

Cohiba Churchill		7-49	Dominican Republic	Sungrown	Straight		

- Padrón Cigars | Padrón Churchill
  Padron Cigars - We deliver only the finest, handmade, complex cigars with the flavor of the Cuban heritage out of which the recipe was born.
- padron churchill cigars in Cigars and Tobacco at Shopping.com
  Find padron churchill cigars, compare padron churchill cigars prices. Shopping.com helps shoppers find, compare, and buy anything in just seconds.
- Padron Churchill - Shopzilla.com

Figure 3.5: CLICK A CIGAR, GET A FREE SEARCH.

Generally, to use a web service, you need to know the following:

- *What URL do you call?*
- *Where are the input parameters?* For this service, we need the search terms, which are available in our grid. dojo.io.script functions can send an entire HTML form, a hash literal, or both. For JSONP services, the form field names or the hash literal property names must match the web service parameters exactly.
- *How long should Dojo wait for a response?* Since the Dojo XHR calls are asynchronous, you must define a comfortable waiting period before an error occurs.[3]
- *For JSONP services, which input parameter names the callback function?*
- *What should be done when the answer arrives? And what if there's an error?* Dojo handles these through callbacks—JavaScript functions called when an asynchronous function completes.

The first four metadata items—url, timeout, content, and callbackParam-Name—are fairly straightforward, so let's tackle those. From the API documentation, we find the Yahoo Search URL is http://search.yahooapis. com/WebSearchService/V1/webSearch. We set the timeout to ten seconds initially—during the testing phase, we may increase or decrease this time depending on the speeds we observe. For content, it seems we need three parameters for the call to succeed. Two of them—appid and output—are constants we fix in the program. The other parameter, query, needs to be extracted from the grid. We'll put a placeholder there for the time being.

---

3. Dojo can perform XHR calls *synchronously* as well. But because synchronous calls may fail to connect and cause the browser to lock up, they are generally not recommended. This is not Dojo's fault *per se*; it's a problem with any toolkit calling the browser's XHR implementation.

Finally, JSONP requires you to send a function name with the request, which it will use as the callback. Yahoo Search requires the callback function name to be sent in the callback parameter. Other JSONP services may require it in a different parameter, such as callthis. The callbackParamName variable of dojo.io.script.get serves this purpose, so you can specify "callback" for Yahoo Search (as we've done here), "callthis", or whatever the service requires.

Here's what we have so far:

`xhr_techniques/yahoo_remote_script.html`

```
dojo.io.script.get({
    // URL for Yahoo Search
    url: "http://search.yahooapis.com/WebSearchService/V1/webSearch",

    // Send search term parameters:
    content: {
        appid: "DEMO",
        query: searchTerms,
        output: "json"
    },

    // If the response takes longer than 10000ms (= 10 seconds), error out
    timeout: 10000,

    // Yahoo API requires you to send the callback function name in the
    // parameter "callback"
    callbackParamName: "callback",

    // The load and error functions will be filled in here
});
```

Just as we saw in Section 3.2, *Literals and Hashes*, on page 33, dojo.io. script.get takes just one parameter, which is a hash with many properties. This makes it easy to read and understand. But... that searchTerms variable from the Yahoo Search API is bugging us. We need a good way to get it.

The Grid and Events

It looks easy enough. You click a grid row, the row highlights, and you extract the search term from the list. But where do you start? Is the grid a table? Do the cells have IDs?

Luckily, you don't have to piece together the cigar name by "screen-scraping." Remember that grids have a model. The model has all the unprocessed data in it. If you could just get the clicked row and map it to an item in the model, you could easily get the value you need.

Fortunately, the Grid widget provides hooks for you called *events*. You are probably already used to HTML's familiar events such as onClick or onMouseOut. These are the DOM level 0 events. Grid events are similar and are named things like onRowDoubleClick or onCellHover. As we'll learn in Section 6.2, *Connecting to User-Defined Events with Dojo*, on page 111, these are Dojo user-defined events that carry rich event information to functions we provide.

We'll save most of the information for later. But for now, let's just dive right into an event function for onRowClick:

```
xhr_techniques/yahoo_remote_script_demo.html
```

```
<table id="grid" dojoType="dojox.grid.Grid" store="wishStore"
    query="{ wishId: '*' }" clientSort="true">
    <script type="dojo/connect" event="onRowClick" args="evt">
        var searchTerms = this.model.getRow(evt.rowIndex).description;
        console.debug(searchTerms);
    </script>
    <thead>
        <tr>
            <th field="description" width="15em">Cigar</th>
            <th field="size">Length/Ring</th>
            <th field="origin">Origin</th>
            <th field="wrapper">Wrapper</th>
            <th field="shape">Shape</th>
        </tr>
    </thead>
</table>
```

That *<script>* tag looks strange. Generally, *<script>* tags have type= "text/javascript", right? Browsers, upon finding a type= they don't recognize, will simply skip over it. That's good for us. We don't want the browser to simply execute this code on page load. Making the type "dojo/connect" tags this script for use only by Dojo.

The args= attribute takes a list of JavaScript variable names and matches these up with the signature parameters. You can consider them the formal parameters of the method. So when Dijit calls the handler code, it will put the event object into the variable evt, which you can then use in the body of the handler. (Recall that *handler* is synonymous with *callback*.)

Let's work from the inside out on that assignment statement. Events such as onRowClick send useful information through the argument, in our case evt.

One of the properties in evt is rowIndex, which contains the 0-based index of the row we just clicked. That's useful. Then this.model.getRow (**this** meaning the grid) gets the row hash, which looks exactly like the hash in our model. For example, this.model.getRow(2) is just the following:

```
{
"wishId": 4457, "description": "Black Pearl Rojo Robusto", "size": "4 3/4-52",
"origin": "Nicaragua", "wrapper": "Natural", "shape": "Straight"
}
```

We just grab the description property, and we're done!

That's pretty elegant. The method is defined right in the tag that needs it, and a lot of the infrastructure is there for you. So, where do you find these events? And how do you know the event data passed back? One way is to consult the online guide at http://www.dojotoolkit.org, which lists all the event method signatures. As far as grid goes, we'll be talking a lot about events in Chapter 14, *Grid*, on page 365 as well.

XHR Callbacks

Now, back to the business at hand. We have most of the properties ready for dojo.io.script.get except for the two meatiest ones: load and error. These two properties are callbacks—functions that run after an asynchronous event completes.

What do those functions look like? Here's the rest of our dojo.io.script.get call:

xhr_techniques/yahoo_remote_script.html

```
    // Function runs when Yahoo returns with the answer
    load: function(searchResult) {
      // Zero out the current list
      listNode = dojo.byId("resultUl");
      listNode.innerHTML = "";

      dojo.forEach(searchResult.ResultSet.Result, function(result) {
          var listItem = document.createElement("li");
          listItem.innerHTML =
            dojo.string.substitute(
                "<a href='${Url}'>${Title}</a><br/>${Summary}",
                result
            );
          listNode.appendChild(listItem);
      });
    },
```

```
      // And this is the callback used when a web service communication error or
      // timeout occurs.  Note that errors returned from Yahoo in the response
      // are still handled with load()
      error: function(text) {
         alert("An error has occurred.");
         return text;
      }
});
```

We'll go over the code inside load and error in a minute, but for now let's concentrate on the form of these callbacks. load and error are called when the XHR answer arrives at the client PC. The browser calls either one or the other, but never both. The notion of callbacks may look a little strange at first. Your natural inclination might be to call dojo.io.script.get like this:

```
// WRONG!  response won't hold the value you think
var response = dojo.io.script.get(...);
// Do something with the response
```

Well, that sure *looks* easy, but it's incorrect.[4] It's also not desirable. To guarantee a value in response, the JavaScript interpreter in the browser would have to *block*, that is, pause at this statement until the XHR message arrives. Remember, the Internet is involved. We can't guarantee a response from the web service—their server might die, the Internet connections may be slow, and so on. That wouldn't be so bad except Internet Explorer and Firefox both lock up waiting for an answer—their implementations of XHR, on which Dojo must rely, synchronously block the entire browser process. Your user is stuck. The Stop button won't even work—killing the browser process is the only option.

The dojo.io.script.get method returns immediately, before the server has responded. When the response does come back, Dojo calls the load or error callback you specified in dojo.io.script.get. In Figure 3.6, on the next page, you can see a good overview of the process.

Let's take the error callback first since it's the easiest. error must be a function with the signature function(someVariable), where the text of the error message is send back through someVariable. In our example, we call it simply text.

---

4. If dojo.io.script doesn't return a response, what *does* it return? It returns a dojo.Deferred object, which we'll see in Section 6.4, *Managing Callbacks with dojo.Deferred*, on page 117. With dojo.Deferred, you can chain callbacks to load and error, as in "When you're done with all the successful callbacks, also do this one." This allows for easy reuse of callbacks among XHR requests.

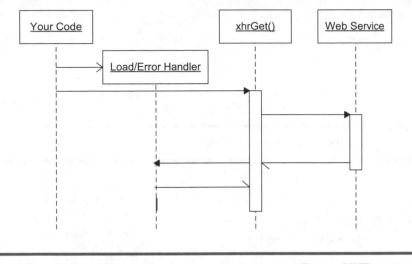

Figure 3.6: UML SEQUENCE DIAGRAM OF A DOJO XHR CALL

Note that error is called only when the process of sending or receiving fails. An incorrect URL, a bad Internet connection, or a slow response time (longer than our timeout property) will cause this to fire.

However, it will not be called if the web service itself returns an error. For example, an address verification web service could return an <error> tag if the address is not legal, but this is not considered an error by Dojo.

load is the most important callback. This is where we can first view the response, which Dojo places in the searchResult parameter. But how do we extract the stuff we need from searchResult? Here's where Firebug is really useful. The call console.dir(searchResult); dumps the entire contents of searchResult to the debug log. From there, as pictured in Figure 3.7, on the following page, we can view its structure.

We see that searchResults contains a ResultSet property, which in turn houses a Result array of hashes, each with the interesting properties title, url, and summary. Pay dirt!

And now it's clear why we did that example back in Section 3.2, *Function Literals*, on page 36. It's easy to write a dojo.forEach loop that creates list items from these results and puts them in the list at the bottom. dojo.require ends the prologue.

```
⊟ Result                                    [ Object Title=Padrón Cigars / Padrón_ Churchill,  Object,  Object Title=P...
  ⊟ 0                                        Object Title=Padrón Cigars / Padrón_ Churchill
    ⊞ Cache                                  Object
      ClickUrl                               "http://uk.wrs.yahoo.com/_ylt=A9iby4m49SxHwawAFD_dxMwF;_
      DisplayUrl                             "www.padron.com/cigar_show.php?cigar=churchill"
      MimeType                               "text/html"
      ModificationDate                       1200211200
      Summary                                "Padron Cigars - We deliver only the finest, handmade, c
                                             he..."
      Title                                  "Padrón Cigars | Padrón_ Churchill"
      Url                                    "http://www.padron.com/cigar_show.php?cigar=churchill"
                                             Object
```

Figure 3.7: FIREBUG SHOWING THE STRUCTURE

xhr_techniques/yahoo_remote_script.html

```
dojo.require("dojo.io.script");
```

And when we run the app and click a grid row, the search results pop out at the bottom, as shown in Figure 3.5, on page 50. Click a new row, get another list, and so on.

All in all, that was fairly painless XHR. With one small server-side component and one call to dojo.io.script.get, you have extended the reach of your application quite far. On-the-fly searches like this were unthinkable just a few years ago.

JSONP services are nice, but not all web services are built on it. By far the most common web services use REST and XML. But even that isn't so hard, as we'll find out.

3.5 Reviews with dojo.xhrGet

Justa has a great opportunity. The magazine *Cigars Unlimited* now offers its world-renowned cigar reviews via a web service. Justa pays a small fee each time the service is called, but it will make up that money easily by selling more cigars. The company wants an icon added to the grid, which the user will click to fire the request and put the reviews in a list.

It would be nice to connect Dojo and JavaScript directly to the *Cigars Unlimited* web service. But there are two issues:

- *Cigars Unlimited*'s web services, like most web services, don't use JSONP. They use plain-vanilla REST and XML. We must call them with XHR, but an XHR request must obey the *same-origin policy* of browser-based JavaScript. That is, JavaScript can send XHR requests only to the same server from which it was loaded.

- The terms of the web service agreement stipulate that you can request reviews only from a fixed IP. If every Tom, Dick, and Mary could access the service from their client PC, *Cigars Unlimited* would make no money.

At the time of this writing, browser producers are discussing options for relaxing the same-origin policy. But even if that problem is solved, that service agreement stipulation is the showstopper.

This is a common Ajax problem, and a common solution is a *proxy service*. If the browser can't communicate directly with the service, it can communicate with the proxy, and the proxy will communicate with the service. After all, your server-side language—be it PHP, JSP, ASP, Ruby on Rails—has no same-origin policy.

Since this book concentrates on Dojo, a client-side toolkit, we won't discuss how to write the proxy. There are many options for this, and the sidebar on page 41 gives a few of them. Instead, we'll use the same technique as in Section 3.3, *A Wish List with dojo.data and dojox.grid.Grid*, on page 39 and just place a sample XML file on the server. This will simulate the output of *Cigar Unlimited*'s web service:

```
xhr_techniques/services/ratings.xml
<?xml version="1.0" encoding="UTF-8"?>
<rating>
    <numerical>4</numerical>
    <descriptive>
        Rolled in an aesthetically pleasing
        reddish-brown wrapper, this cigar smokes well
        exuding a pleasant aroma. The smoke has a buttery,
        leathery quality with tea and cocoa bean notes,
        and a long, pleasant finish.
    </descriptive>
</rating>
```

But how do you get the data from the server? Dojo provides low-level functions dojo.xhrGet, dojo.xhrPost, and others for this purpose. Fortunately, they share many characteristics with dojo.io.script.get, so learning them will be a snap.

One more thing: we need to deal with XML and its APIs, which are less elegant than JSON's. Dojo is heavily skewed toward using JSON and provides almost no facilities for helping out with XML. In our case, we will use the native DOM APIs to read XML data. There are other options: you can use a third-party JavaScript XML toolkit like Google's or do a server-side translation of XML to JSON before hitting the client.

Using dojo.xhrGet

First we'll gather the web service information, as we did in the previous example:

- *URL*: services/ratings.xml, which is our stub data source. We call it with HTTP GET.
- *Input parameters*: The *Cigars Unlimited* web site uses a query parameter, and we also use that parameter to the proxy. Of course, our stub data source, since it's not a program, will ignore this.
- *Timeout*: Ten seconds.
- *Content type*: XML. Note that JSONP services do not need this parameter, but dojo.xhr* functions do.

Also unlike dojo.io.script.get, there is no callbackParamName. But like dojo.io.script.get, the load and error callbacks are required.

Dojo's four low-level XHR methods—dojo.xhrGet, dojo.xhrPost, dojo.xhrPut, and dojo.xhrDelete—correspond to the four HTTP commands GET, POST, PUT, and DELETE. The method you use is determined by the web service, but most of the time it's GET or POST.

So, let's start coding! First we'll place a blank <p> tag above the search result list to hold the rating description:

xhr_techniques/ratings_xml.html

```
<p id="ratingP" style="width:550px"></p>
<ul id="resultUl" style="width:550px">
```

Then we'll add to our onRowClick handler. Since the script is getting a little large, we delegate this code to a JavaScript function:

xhr_techniques/ratings_xml.html

```
var searchTerms = this.model.getRow(evt.rowIndex).description;
getRating(searchTerms);
```

The calls to dojo.io.script.get and dojo.xhrGet will use the same error handler. So, we wisely refactor this into a separate function:

xhr_techniques/ratings_xml.html

```
// Share this error function
function commonError(text) {
  alert("An error has occurred.");
  return text;
}
```

And finally, there's the meat and potatoes of the rating system:

`xhr_techniques/ratings_xml.html`

```
function getRating(searchTerms) {
    dojo.xhrGet({
      // URL for our proxy that calls the rating service
      url: "services/ratings.xml",
      content: { query: searchTerms },
      timeout: 10000,

      // Set this to parse response into XML
      handleAs: "xml",

      // Function run when web service returns with the answer
      load: function(ratingResult) {
        // Make an object out of the dynamic data for substitute.
        var reviewObj = { name: searchTerms };

        var ratingNodes = ratingResult.getElementsByTagName("numerical");
        reviewObj.numerical = ratingNodes[0].firstChild.nodeValue;

        var reviewNodes = ratingResult.getElementsByTagName("descriptive");
        reviewObj.descriptive = reviewNodes[0].firstChild.nodeValue;

        var reviewPara = document.getElementById("ratingP");
        reviewPara.innerHTML =
            dojo.string.substitute(
                "<b>${name}</b>: ${numerical} stars<br/>${descriptive}",
                reviewObj
            );
      },

    error: commonError
  });
}
```

Much of the code is similar to the Yahoo Search lookup. The differences
are as follows:

- You must specify the handleAs parameter as XML. Other values
  you can use here are json and text.
- The load callback extracts data as parsed XML. Note the use of
  document.getElementsByTagName, which is standard JavaScript. It
  is rather inelegant compared to JSON's rating.numerical equivalent,
  but it does the job.
- There's no dojo.require needed for dojo.xhr*. This and the other low-
  level XHR methods are part of Dojo Core.

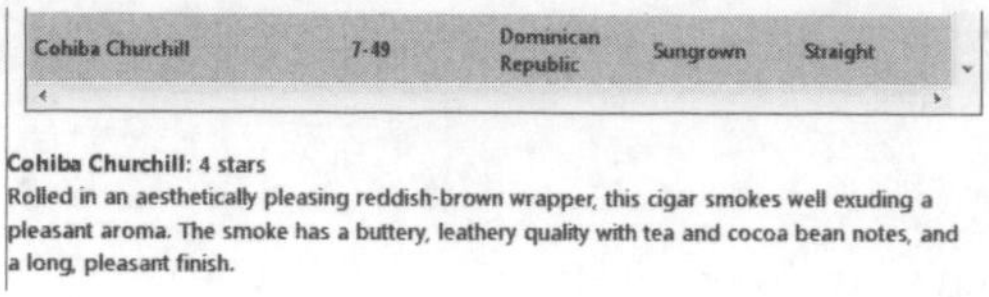

| Cohiba Churchill | 7-49 | Dominican Republic | Sungrown | Straight |

Cohiba Churchill: 4 stars
Rolled in an aesthetically pleasing reddish-brown wrapper, this cigar smokes well exuding a pleasant aroma. The smoke has a buttery, leathery quality with tea and cocoa bean notes, and a long, pleasant finish.

Figure 3.8: GETTING A CIGAR RATING

So, now we're ready to roll. Pull up the page, click a row, and the rating appears between the Grid and the search result list, as pictured in Figure 3.8.

3.6 Errors and Debugging

In both of our examples, the error callback is admittedly somewhat meager. Unlike standard submit-and-redraw web processing, XHR happens behind the scenes and will not display an error by default. Without adequate feedback, the user will not know anything has gone wrong. Still, an alert box is Draconian. Consider the effect if multiple errors happen at once and the user is bombarded with annoying feedback.

A lightweight alternative to alert() is the Toaster widget, also known as dojox.widget.Toaster. A Toaster widget is a box that pops up in the corner of the browser and then waits for a mouse click or simply fades out. It's a good way to draw attention without being modal. We show one in Figure 3.9, on the facing page.

Toaster comes from Dojox, the Dojo extension package. So, let's toast that error! First we add dojo.require:

xhr_techniques/ratings_xml_with_toaster.html

```
dojo.require("dojox.widget.Toaster");
```

The Toaster widget usually works best at the bottom of the web page. It's not displayed until invoked, so in theory it could go anywhere. But placing it outside all other code keeps the DOM straight:

xhr_techniques/ratings_xml_with_toaster.html

```
<div dojoType="dojox.widget.Toaster" duration="0"
    messageTopic="xhrError" positionDirection="tr-left" />
```

positionDirection= specifies tr-left, meaning "in the top-right corner, moving in from the left." messageTopic= is the topic that the Toaster

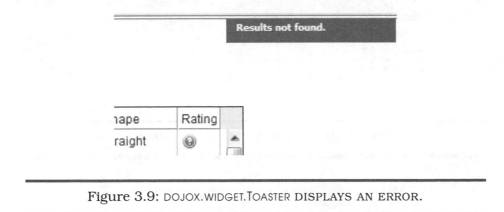

Figure 3.9: DOJOX.WIDGET.TOASTER DISPLAYS AN ERROR.

widget listens to for a message. *Topics* are part of Dojo's publish-sub-scribe event system, which we'll cover in great detail in Chapter 6, *Asynchronous Programming*, on page 95. But for now, think of a topic as a magazine subscription where one publisher sends out magazines to a list of interested subscribers. Here the magazine is xhrError, the error handler is the publisher, the Toaster is the subscriber, and a particular error message is a magazine issue.

```
xhr_techniques/ratings_xml_with_toaster.html

function commonError(text) {
  dojo.publish("xhrError",
      [{ message: text, type: "error", duration: 0 }]
  );
  return text;
}
```

And once again, hash literals swoop in to save the day. The publish-subscribe system passes messages of many different formats between components. Toasters understand message hashes with the properties message=, type=, and duration=. A duration= of 0 means keep the message displayed until the user clicks it. Toaster widgets stay in the corner of the screen, even as you scroll up and down the page. To test it, simply change the XHR URL to a file that doesn't exist:

```
xhr_techniques/ratings_xml_with_toaster.html

url: "services/file_doesnt_exist.xml",
```

Of course, errors are sometimes debuggable, and you need a good tool to see the XHR communication in the background. Firebug is a great tool for that. To see XHR traffic, open Firebug, and make sure the

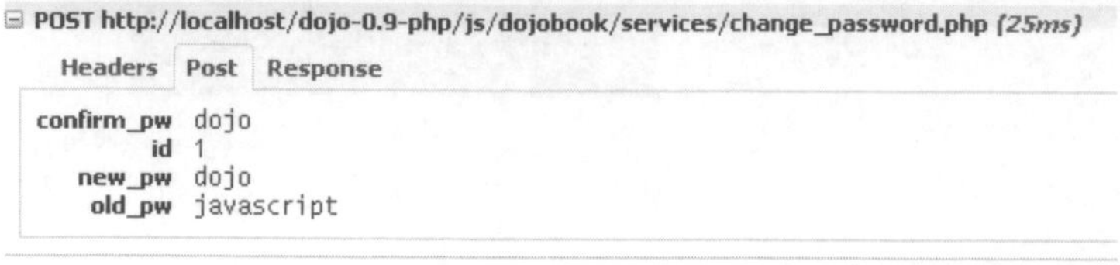

POST http://localhost/dojo-0.9-php/js/dojobook/services/change_password.php *(25ms)*

| Headers | Post | Response |

confirm_pw	dojo
id	1
new_pw	dojo
old_pw	javascript

Figure 3.10: XHR REQUEST TAB IN FIREBUG

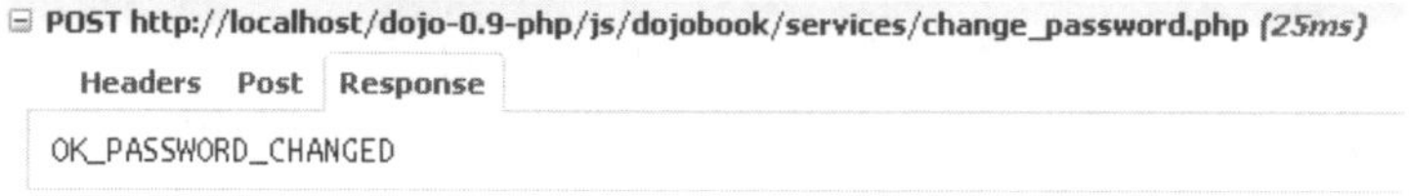

POST http://localhost/dojo-0.9-php/js/dojobook/services/change_password.php *(25ms)*

| Headers | Post | Response |

OK_PASSWORD_CHANGED

Figure 3.11: XHR RESPONSE TAB IN FIREBUG

Console tab is showing. When you fire off an XHR request of any kind, the Headers tab tells you the endpoints of the communication and any HTTP status codes. In Figure 3.10, you can see the parameters sent, nicely parsed, and displayed. In Figure 3.11, you can see the actual data received. It looks like this particular request was successful.

Dojo XHR does a lot with a little bit of code on your part. It handles cross-browser support, asynchronous processing, constructing query strings, and parsing the output all in the background. You provide the metadata for calling the service, and you provide the input data. By using JSON, when available, you can write efficient, easy-to-read output processors in a few lines of code. What better way to plug your web applications into the vast network of services?

Part II

The Dojo APIs

Chapter 4

Dojo In Depth

Now that you've had a taste of what Dojo can do, we're going to take a step back and explore Dojo in depth. Like any well-designed system, Dojo layers higher-level functionality on top of lower-level functionality. We're going to start at the bottom and work our way up. This chapter sets the table for our journey. It covers a few foundational details that you'll use in every Dojo application you write: how Dojo is organized, how to get a development copy, and how to load and initialize Dojo in your web pages.

4.1 Modularizing JavaScript

Dojo is implemented through static, client-side JavaScript scripts together with a few supporting HTML templates and CSS style sheets. No server-side processing is required other than sending a static file, just as there's no browser-side extension or plug-in.

Between Dojo and Dijit, there are about 150 scripts.[1] Since Dojo is strictly a client-side toolkit, you must somehow load the particular script that contains the functionality you want to use. Further, since JavaScript does not include any formal concept of modules, namespaces, or source file composition, the sheer size of Dojo could lead to unmanageable complexity. How do you know which script to load to get a particular function? Do scripts depend on each other? How do you avoid loading the same script more than once? What about performance?

---

1. This number should stay fairly constant. Although existing scripts are undergoing constant refinement, most new features are developed in Dojox.

These problems are addressed by organizing the various Dojo function families into a hierarchy of modules. The term *module* is used loosely since JavaScript does not formally define the concept of a module. A Dojo module manifests itself as a JavaScript object; we'll term this object the *module object*. All JavaScript objects (functions and data) that are members of a particular module exist as properties of that module object. Some of these properties may be other module objects—this results in a hierarchy of modules.

A Dojo module object is defined (that is, a JavaScript object variable is instantiated) by one JavaScript source file; we'll term this file the *module primary script.*[2] When a module primary script is loaded, it may cause other scripts to load (see Section 11.2, *The Dojo Loader*, on page 287). In this sense, a module may be decomposed into several source files, but exactly one of these files is responsible for defining the module object. Finally, module primary scripts and module names reflect each other:

- The files that make up all the modules are stored in a directory tree so that the path/filename of a module primary script gives the module name. For example, the Dojo drag-and-drop manager module dojo.dnd.manager is stored at *dojo-module-path*/dnd/manager.js (*dojo-module-path* gives the absolute path to the dojo module).

- For the most part, when a module primary script is loaded into your JavaScript program, all JavaScript objects defined by that module, with the exception of child module objects, are created as properties of the module object.[3] Continuing the example, all public objects defined by the module dojo.dnd.manager are created as properties of the JavaScript object dojo.dnd.manager. The root module in any such hierarchy of modules is defined in the global scope. So, dojo is a global variable.

Here's another way to look at the design: the module primary script filename *implies* the module name, which *implies* the JavaScript object name that holds all JavaScript objects defined by the module. The converse equation is also true.

---

2. *Module primary script* is not an official Dojo term but rather a device we're using to explain how things work.
3. There are a few exceptions to this rule. Some module primary scripts create additional objects that are not part of the module. For example, the Dijit module dijit.form.Button creates dijit.form.DropDownButton, dijit.form.ComboButton, and dijit.form.ToggleButton in addition to dijit.form.Button.

The source code directory tree defines the hierarchy of JavaScript objects that hold the Dojo function families. You can visualize these objects as a hierarchy of nested namespaces. This design allows for extremely flexible organization. Here's what the dojo/ tree looks like (we opened only the subdirectories dnd and io—the other subdirectories are not empty):

```
Line 1   /dojo
   -        /_base----------------->names that begin with a leading underscore
   -        /_firebug               are considered private (for internal use)
   -        /cldr
   5        /data
   -        /date
   -        /dnd
   -            autoscroll.js
   -            Avatar.js
  10            common.js
   -            Container.js
   -            Manager.js-------->defines the module "dojo.dnd.Manager"
   -            move.js             which happens to be a constructor function
   -            Moveable.js
  15            Mover.js
   -            Selector.js
   -            Source.js
   -        /io
   -            iframe.js--------->defines the module "dojo.io.iframe"
  20            script.js           which is a regular module object
   -        /nls
   -        /resources
   -        /rpc
   -        /tests
  25        _base.js
   -        AdapterRegistry.js
   -        back.js
   -        behavior.js
   -        colors.js
  30        cookie.js
   -        currency.js
   -        date.js
   -        DeferredList.js
   -        dojo.js-------------->the entry point for the toolkit
  35        fx.js                   must be loaded first by a script tag
   -        i18n.js
   -        NodeList-fx.js
   -        number.js
   -        OpenAjax.js
  40        parer.js
   -        regexp.js
   -        string.js
   -        tests.js
```

The tree shown here calls out a few conventions used throughout the toolkit. First, if a module defines a single constructor function, then its name is capitalized to indicate that the module defines a class.[4] Second, a few scripts and modules have names that begin with an underscore. These are considered private and are used internally by other modules. Since they will be automatically included if you need them, you can pretty much ignore them.

The breadth and depth of Dojo is one of its greatest strengths, but Dojo *is* big. Classifying functions into smaller and smaller subgroups makes such a large system easier to digest than a single massive list of functions. Needless to say, the reference manual (see http://api.dojotoolkit. org/) is organized along the same hierarchy. This is nothing but good design—reassuring, if not terribly novel.

Furthermore, we *don't* have to download the entire, massive toolkit in order to get just a few key functions. Since the toolkit is divided up into small chunks, we are required to download only the parts that we actually use and then only when we actually need them.

Let's take it one last step. Since the script filename can be deduced from the module name, why not write some JavaScript code to manage the whole script downloading process for us? This is the function of the Dojo loader, which we'll discuss in Section 11.2, *The Dojo Loader*, on page 287. Further, once all the development is done and we're ready to release our new application to production, why not package several modules together so they can all be sent to the browser in a single JavaScript file? This is the function of the Dojo build system (see Section 11.3, *Optimizing Deployment with the Dojo Build System*, on page 296).

Consider the implications of the last two features taken together. Dojo divides source code up optimally from the programmer's point of view while suffering no performance penalty when it comes time to publish the application on the Web (serving lots of little script files would result in sluggish performance). And you can use Dojo's module, loader, and build system when developing and deploying your own code. Although this functionality is necessary for large applications, it can be com-

---

4. JavaScript doesn't explicitly include the concept of a class as do other languages. But, most aspects of the class concept *are* available in terms of constructor functions and prototypal inheritance. We'll discuss these concepts in detail in Chapter 9, *Defining Classes with dojo.declare*, on page 221.

pletely ignored if all you need is some basic Ajax or browser normalization functionality. Just load the modules you need, and forget about the loader and the build system.

4.2 Dojo Source Code Organization

The module decomposition (and therefore the source code) for the Dojo toolkit is divided into three trees:

- *Dojo*: The core toolkit that includes libraries that are useful in nearly any program; the contents of this tree is referred to as Dojo Core.

- *Dijit (Dojo widgets)*: A framework for building HTML user interface controls (widgets) as well as a library of many prebuilt widgets. Dijit depends on Dojo.

- *Dojox (Dojo extensions)*: Projects that may not be needed in every single app or may not be 100% stable yet because they're pushing on the edge of what's possible in browsers today (say, GFX). Many of the projects in Dojox would be considered highly mature in the context of other toolkits. But Dojo sets the bar so high for Core (API documentation and tests) and Dijit (API documentation, tests, a11y, and i18n) that it's easier in many cases for projects to continue to mature as extensions. Each project in Dojox includes a readme file that explains the state of the project. We'll look at the occasional Dojox module, but most of Dojox is beyond the scope of this book.

The root directory of the dojo/ tree includes the file dojo.js; a script element must load it before you do anything else with the toolkit. dojo.js is the module primary script for the module dojo. When dojo.js is evaluated, the global variable dojo (an object) is created, and properties are added to it that make up the minimal runtime system defined by Dojo.

In addition to dojo.js, the root of the dojo/ tree defines several other modules. Each of these is a child to the dojo module (remember, modules can contain other modules). For example, the module primary script number.js is located in the root directory of the dojo/ tree and defines the module dojo.number. In this sense, dojo.js is different from any other file in the root: dojo.js causes the module dojo to be created; all other siblings to dojo.js cause modules that are children of dojo to be created (for example, dojo.number). Similarly, the root directory of the Dijit tree includes the file dijit.js, which serves as the entry point for Dijit and exhibits the same kind of special behavior.

As far as possible, the directory trees capture dependencies. So, for example, it is always true that for some imaginary modules dojo.x and dojo.x.y, dojo.x.y depends on module dojo.x. There is nothing to be gained by learning all of the module dependencies. Each module will ensure that its prerequisite modules are loaded.

The Catalog of Dojo Modules

Now that we've seen how Dojo is organized, let's see what's actually in it. First and foremost, there is the module dojo that includes the following functionality:[5]

- *Environment properties*: A small set of variables that indicate various properties of the runtime environment (for example, browser version and capabilities).
- *Language extensions*: Functions that fill in a few elements missing from the core JavaScript library (see Chapter 5, *JavaScript Language Extensions*, on page 77).
- *Asynchronous programming*: Functions for programming events and asynchronous callbacks (see Chapter 6, *Asynchronous Programming*, on page 95).
- *DOM programming*: A library of functions that makes programming the DOM more pleasant (see Chapter 7, *DOM Utilities*, on page 135).
- *XHR programming*: Functions for communicating with the server via XHR objects (see Chapter 8, *Remote Scripting with XHR, script, and iframe*, on page 173).
- *Object-oriented programming*: A function for creating powerful, flexible class hierarchies (see Chapter 9, *Defining Classes with dojo.declare*, on page 221).
- *The Dojo loader*: Functions that load JavaScript scripts and Dojo modules (see Chapter 11, *The Dojo Loader and Build System*, on page 283).

The dojo/ tree includes several other modules that are *not* loaded automatically as a result of loading dojo.js in a script tag; you must thus

---

5. Most of the dojo module is implemented in the scripts contained in the directory _base. But this is an implementation detail that doesn't affect the typical user.

explicitly load them with a dojo.require function call, which we'll see in Section 4.3, *dojo.require*, on page 74. They include the following:

- dojo.back: Back button functionality for browser applications that don't navigate by loading new URLs
- dojo.behavior: "Behaviors" attachable to sets of nodes
- dojo.cldr: A Common Locale Data Repository (CLDR) implementation; works in concert with dojo.i18n
- dojo.colors: Convenient CSS color manipulation functions
- dojo.cookie: Simple HTTP cookie manipulation
- dojo.currency: Parse, format, and i18n functions for currency data
- dojo.data: Functions to access a generalized data source together with an implementation for several types of data sources
- dojo.date: Parse, format, and i18n functions for date data
- dojo.dnd: DOM drag and drop
- dojo.fx: DOM effects
- dojo.i18n: Support for multiple locales; works in concert with dojo. cldr
- dojo.io: Functions for communicating with a server via script and/ or iFrame elements
- dojo.number: Parse, format, and i18n functions for number data
- dojo.parser: HTML parser
- dojo.regexp: Functions that help with building regular expressions
- dojo.rpc: Remote procedure call (RPC) framework
- dojo.string: A few common, otherwise-missing, string functions

We will be covering the module dojo thoroughly, and along the way, we're also going to cover many of the other modules found in Dojo Core.

Dijit Modules

The Dijit modules are contained in a separate source code tree and are defined from the root module dijit (*not* dojo.dijit). These modules implement Dojo's HTML widget system, which is fully described in Part III of the book.

Getting the Source

At the time of this writing, Dojo is available from four primary sources:

- You can find the current release at http://dojotoolkit.org/downloads where the Dojo Foundation publishes one gzipped tarball that includes the dojo/, dijit/, and dojox/ trees of the latest release. The dojo, dijit, and dijit-all modules are packaged in both compressed and uncompressed resources; all the remaining resources are not compressed. We'll discuss compressing and packaging in Chapter 11, *The Dojo Loader and Build System*, on page 283.

Sometimes this is referred to as the *binary build* because some resources are packaged and compressed. Except for a few images, no true binary (that is, something other than text) resources are included; every resource is a JavaScript, CSS, or HTML file. Distributions that don't contain any packaged or compressed resources are referred to as *source builds*.

- You can find current and previous, binary, and source builds, in zipped and gzipped tarball resources, together with MD5 checksums at http://download.dojotoolkit.org/.

- AOL serves binary builds from its content delivery network (CDN); see http://dev.aol.com/dojo.

- The source is also available for anonymous checkout from the SVN repository at http://svn.dojotoolkit.org/src/. The current development trunks are rooted at /dojo/trunk, /dijit/trunk, /dojox/trunk, and /util/trunk. Tagged releases are stored in /tags. There's also a set of svn:externals definitions at http://svn.dojotoolkit.org/src/view/anon/all/trunk/ that pulls in all four trunks in one anonymous checkout.

- Finally, the Trac bug-tracking database includes browser access to the SVN trees. All things Trac start at http://trac.dojotoolkit.org.

4.3 Loading Dojo

Now it's time to actually load the toolkit so we can start using it. dojo.js must be loaded before any other Dojo module or any of your own code that uses Dojo. Here is the absolute minimum statement required in your HTML document:

```
<script type="text/javascript" src="/dojoroot/dojo/dojo.js" /></script>
```

This line assumes that dojo.js is in the directory /dojoroot/dojo/.

A few runtime configuration switches can be set when loading dojo.js. Let's look at that next.

Alex Says...

Debugging Tools for Internet Explorer

The biggest debugging headaches always seem to occur on Internet Explorer 6 and 7. Since the full-blown Firebug isn't available there, we need to augment the arsenal. First, you'll need the Internet Explorer Developer Toolbar extension (available at http://www.microsoft.com/Downloads/details.aspx?familyid=E59C3964-672D-4511-BB3E-2D5E1DB91038). This is a marginally passable clone of the excellent Web Developer toolbar for Firefox. Despite its warts, the Internet Explorer Web Developer toolbar makes clearing the Internet Explorer cache much faster, and some of its DOM inspection facilities are useful in a pinch. Next, make sure you avoid the Microsoft Script Debugger (a toy) and instead use the Microsoft Script Editor (not a toy), which is found on the Office 2003 install discs. Microsoft pushes the full-blown Visual Studio and its Visual Web Developer variant for handling this kind of deep debugging, but I wouldn't touch them with a pole. The downloads are gigantic, the install interminable, and the benefit over MSE marginal (if that). That matters all the more when you're installing your debugging tools in a virtual machine. All of my Internet Explorer development and debugging is done in VMs, and I can't recommend that highly enough. Don't bother with things that pretend to let you run Internet Explorer 6 side by side with Internet Explorer 7 or Internet Explorer 8—they're not the same as having the "real thing" because of some fundamental features of Internet Explorer's design. Microsoft has recognized this flaw and makes prerolled virtual machine images available (available at http://www.microsoft.com/Downloads/details.aspx?familyid=21EABB90-958F-4B64-B5F1-73D0A413C8EF), although they're available only for Microsoft's Windows-only (albeit free) Virtual PC runtime. I personally use a mix of Parallels and VMware for my virtualization needs, but use whatever works best for you—just make sure you're testing!

Runtime Configuration

Back in the tutorial given in Chapter 2, *Powerful Web Forms Made Easy*, on page 13, we used the djConfig attribute in the script element that loaded dojo.js to specify the configuration switch parseOnLoad. Here is what that script element looked like:

```
Line 1    <script
    -        type="text/javascript"
    -        src="/dojoroot/dojo/dojo.js"
    -        djConfig="parseOnLoad: true">
    5     </script>
```

The same thing could be accomplished by explicitly setting the global variable djConfig. Since this must be set *before* dojo.js is loaded, the client program must create and initialize djConfig. This can be done in a single statement:

```
Line 1    <script type="text/javascript">
    -        djConfig= {parseOnLoad: true};
    -     </script>
    -
    5     <!-- now load dojo.js; note no djConfig attribute -->
    -     <script
    -        type="text/javascript"
    -        src="/dojoroot/dojo/dojo.js">
    -     </script>
```

Each of these methods accomplishes the same result. We prefer the djConfig attribute method since the configuration settings are encapsulated in the element that loads dojo.js. But if you are troubled by including nonstandard attributes, then use the other method (see the *Alex Says...*, on the next page if you really *are* troubled). If you happen to use both methods, any configuration switch set by the djConfig attribute will override any properties set in the djConfig global variable.

dojo.require

What if you need something that's not in the module dojo (that is, not loaded as a result of script including dojo.js)? For example, what if you need to do some remote scripting with dojo.io.script? How do you get this module loaded?

The answer is that everything else gets loaded with the function dojo. require.[6] It keeps track of the modules already loaded and ensures that

---

6. It can also load scripts that don't define modules. This is an advanced feature we'll discuss in Chapter 11, *The Dojo Loader and Build System*, on page 283.

Alex Says...

Using Nonstandard HTML Attributes

Dojo uses nonstandard HTML attributes to set configuration switches and configure Dijit widgets. This may raise some eyebrows, but in every case where it's allowed, we also provide ways to do equivalent things without nonstandard attributes.

We agree that, as a general principle, standards should be followed—so long as they don't get in the way of doing real work. After all, the very reason for standardizing is to make doing real work easier. But, when the cost of following them is greater than the cost of ignoring them, then they ought to be ignored. Dojo is above all (pardon the word) *pragmatic*. It exists solely to help build great applications. And anything that gets in the way of this goal is fungible, particularly when the default behavior of every browser on the planet is to allow the behavior in question. Nonstandard attributes are a "spirit of the law" type of technique, and we're happy to see that HTML 5 (currently in draft form) explicitly allows these so-called expando attributes, in effect legitimizing the approach Dojo has taken for years.

It is sad, though, that we even need to be having this discussion. Internet Explorer had HTCs for defining new element types and Mozilla implemented XBL, but they are not compatible with each other, so Dojo's widget system jumps into the breech to allow you to easily specify new "elements" in your document. It's our sincere hope that someday in the future all of this will be deprecated in favor of something like XBL2, but until then, pragmatism rules.

modules aren't loaded more than once (it simply returns immediately if the module already exists). It guarantees the requested module has loaded successfully before returning or throws an exception.

The sole required argument (a string) to dojo.require gives a module name. As discussed above in Section 4.1, *Modularizing JavaScript*, on page 65, these names map to the file system. For example, "dojo.a.b.c" maps to the script *dojo-module-path*/a/b/c.js, and loading the script is as simple as writing the following:

```
dojo.require("dojo.a.b.c");
```

There's actually a bit more to say about dojo.require, but since this additional material overlaps deployment issues, we're going to put the rest of the story on hold until Chapter 11, *The Dojo Loader and Build System*, on page 283.

Now that we have Dojo loaded and initialized, let's start using it. We'll begin with several little but useful extensions to core JavaScript. That's the subject of the next chapter.

Chapter 5

JavaScript Language Extensions

Dojo provides some functions that, loosely speaking, extend the core JavaScript library. These functions are not attached to a particular problem domain but rather are foundational to JavaScript programming. They are also at the very bottom of the dependency hierarchy.

The material in this chapter demonstrates some of JavaScript's true beauty and power. We'll see functions that write other little JavaScript functions on the fly, resulting in highly expressive, powerful, yet easy code. If you're already a JavaScript (or functional programming) guru, then you'll breeze through the material; if not, get set to use JavaScript for something more than glorified BASIC!

We'll begin by exploring dojo.hitch, a function that, directly or indirectly, is pervasive in Dojo. Next we'll look at Dojo's array functions—which actually *are* Mozilla JavaScript 1.6 core library functions. Unfortunately, not all browsers implement them yet. We'll conclude with a few utilities functions that test/manipulate an object's type/structure. All in all, the functions described will make your programs easier and more enjoyable to write.

5.1 Binding with dojo.hitch

Sometimes you need to pass a method of an object to another function as an argument. At one time or another, just about every programmer has tried to write something like someFunction(someObject.someMethod) to solve this problem...and failed. dojo.hitch solves this problem of binding context to a method.

Alex Says...

dojo.hitch Is Important

dojo.hitch is *very* important for two reasons. First, JavaScript functions are not bound to the scope in which they're defined. Languages such as Python have "implicit binding," which allows the assignment of function references to pseudomagically hold on to their "enclosing" object. JavaScript has no such implicit wrapping. Said another way, JavaScript functions are "promiscuous." They take easily to whatever scope you execute them in, and understanding how and why this is so provides deep insight into JavaScript as a language. Binding context and/or arguments is an idiom used frequently in functional programming (aka currying).*

Understanding JavaScript as a functional language can make you a much better JavaScript programmer. Second, many important Dojo functions take a context and a function as arguments, so getting used to the pattern will make many parts of Dojo feel more familiar. In each case, the semantics of these arguments are the same as with dojo.hitch.

---

*. Pure functional programs have no concept of state. In practical terms, this means they don't have an assignment operation or other side effects. If such a concept sounds exciting, check out (AS96), (Mac90), or my slides on aspect-oriented and functional programming in JavaScript (http://alex.dojotoolkit.org/wp-content/AOP_and_FP_in_JS.pdf).

Binding Context

Let's begin by exploring that naive attempt mentioned earlier to pass a method (m) of an object (o) as an argument to some function that will call o.m. Here's a simple object that accumulates a sum and returns the result. We'll use theAccumulator.getResult for o.m in our example:

```
Line 1   var theAccumulator= {
           total: 0,
           clear: function() {
             this.total= 0;
      5    },
           add: function(x) {
             this.total+= x;
           },
           getResult: function() {
     10      return this.total;
           }
         };
```

Next, we need a function that takes another function as an argument to demonstrate passing theAccumulator.getResult as a parameter. A function that prints the return value of calling its single argument will work:

```
Line 1   //display a message box with the result of calling f...
         function printResult(f) {
           alert("result= " + f());
         }
```

With this in place, let's use theAccumulator to add 100 to 200 and then print the total by calling printResult, passing theAccumulator.getResult as the argument. At one time or another, just about every programmer has tried something like this:

```
Line 1   theAccumulator.clear();
         theAccumulator.add(100);
         theAccumulator.add(200);

5        //this is wrong!
         printResult(theAccumulator.getResult);
```

We expect to see "result= 300" printed in the message box, but instead, the message box prints "result= undefined." Here's the problem: when theAccumulator.getResult is passed to printResult, the function isn't bound to any context. So, when the parameter f is invoked by printResult, this references the global object space and the global variable total is evaluated, *not* theAccumulator's total. The problem can be corrected by writing this:

```
printResult(function(){return theAccumulator.getResult();});
```

When the function function(){return theAccumulator.getResult();} is called by printResult, getResult is explicitly bound to theAccumulator, and "result= 300" is printed in the message box as expected.

The function dojo.hitch manufactures these little functions for us. For the moment, we'll limit the discussion to cases where dojo.hitch is given one or two arguments (it can take more, which we will discuss shortly). If two arguments are given, then the first argument (an object) gives the context in which the second argument (a function or string designating a function) should execute. dojo.hitch takes these arguments and returns a function that invokes the second argument in the context of the first. Here's how dojo.hitch works in code:

```
Line 1   dojo.hitch(o, o.f);
             //o an object, f a member function of o, returns...
             function() {return o.f.apply(o, arguments);}

5        dojo.hitch(o, "f");
             //o an object, f the name of a member function of o, returns...
             function() {return o["f"].apply(o, arguments);}
```

The only difference between the two forms is that the second argument is given as an identifier in the first example and a string in the second. When the second argument is a member function of the first argument as shown earlier (we'll see that this need not be the case in a moment), the second form saves some typing.

We can use dojo.hitch to write the function in the motivating example. This...

```
Line 1   printResult(function(){return theAccumulator.getResult();});
```

becomes the following:

```
printResult(dojo.hitch(theAccumulator, "getResult"));
```

Binding a member function to an object that defines that member is almost always what you want, but it is perfectly legal to bind an ordinary function or a function that's a member of another object. Here's how dojo.hitch works in both cases:

```
Line 1   dojo.hitch(o, f);
             //o an object, f a function, returns...
             function() {return f.apply(o, arguments);}

5        dojo.hitch(o, p.f);
             //o, p objects, o!=p, f a member function of p, returns...
             function() {return p.f.apply(o, arguments);}
```

By definition, this type of binding causes f, which is not a member of o to execute in the context of o. You can visualize this as a kind of dynamic, per-function mixing (as in mixin). This technique is actually a lot more useful than you might think; here's an example that demonstrates the use pattern.

Assume you have the function showData that gets a number from a data source and pushes it into a document element. The function might look something like this:

```
Line 1   function showData() {
             var x= this.getData();
             dojo.byId("showData").innerHTML= "The result= " + x;
         }
```

Notice that the data displayed by showData depends upon the value of this when showData is invoked. So, showData must be bound to a context that defines getData, and binding showData to different contexts will cause it to show different data.

Here are a couple of different data sources to exercise showData:

```
Line 1   //generates 1, 2, 3, ...
    -    var dataSrc1 = {
    -      value: 0,
    -      getData: function() {return this.value++;}
    5    };
    -
    -    //generates 5, 10, 15, ...
    -    var dataSrc2 = {
    -      value: 0,
    10     getData: function() {return (this.value+= 5);}
    -    };
```

Finally, here's an example of binding showData to these different data sources and hooking them to a click event.[1]

```
dojo.byId("f3").onclick= dojo.hitch(dataSrc1, showData);
dojo.byId("f4").onclick= dojo.hitch(dataSrc2, showData);
```

Clicking the "f3" element causes the first data source to be accessed, while clicking the "f4" element causes the second data source to be accessed.

If only one argument is given to dojo.hitch, then it is assumed that the context argument was omitted. Specifying null for the first argument has the same effect. Either way, the function is executed in the global object space. Here's how dojo.hitch works with these types of arguments:

```
line 1   //note: dojo.global holds a reference to the global object space
    -
    -    //first form
    -    dojo.hitch(null, f); //f a function, is the same as...
    5    dojo.hitch(f); //which returns...
    -      f
    -
    -    //second form
    -    dojo.hitch(null, "f"); //is the same as...
    10   dojo.hitch("f"); //which returns...
    -      function() {return dojo.global[f].apply(dojo.global, arguments);}
```

The first form selects f from the current scope, while the second form selects *global* f (that is, f in the global scope). In both cases, using dojo.hitch to bind a function with null isn't very useful—until we also bind arguments, the next topic in our discussion.

---

1. If we weren't trying to demonstrate hitch, we would actually bind showData to dataSrc1 and connect to the click event by writing dojo.connect(dojo.byId("f3"), "click", dataSrc1, show-Data); it's similar for binding dataSrc2. See Section 6.1, *Programming DOM Events with Dojo*, on page 95 for details about dojo.connect.

Binding Arguments

If you step back and think about it for a moment, you'll realize that the context in which a function is executed could be viewed as just another argument to the function. Since we just showed how dojo.hitch is used to bind context, you might ask, "Is it possible to bind other arguments?" As you probably guessed, the answer is "yes."

To motivate our discussion, consider a case where you want to pass additional arguments to an event handler and these arguments are determined when the handler is connected rather than when the handler is invoked. Heuristically, you'd like to do something like this:

```
//this won't work!
dojo.byId("someId").click= handler(someArg);
```

This won't work because the statement immediately calls handler and then passes the *result* as the handler—not a function that *invokes* handler(someArg). We can fix it by using a function literal:

```
dojo.byId("someId").click= function(){handler(someArg);};
```

Just like binding context, dojo.hitch can be used to build these little functions on the fly. If more than two arguments are provided to dojo.hitch, then a function object is manufactured that executes the passed function in the correct context *and* provides the extra arguments when the manufactured function object is executed. Here's what it looks like in pseudo-JavaScript:

```
Line 1   dojo.hitch(context, f, a1, ..., an); //returns...
           function(){return context.f.apply(
             context, [a1, ..., an].concat(arguments));};
```

[a1,..., an].concat(arguments) creates an array of arguments that's passed to context.f when it is invoked. The first *n* arguments are those that were provided when dojo.hitch was called; the remaining arguments (if any) are provided when the function object manufactured by dojo.hitch is invoked.

Since this can be a bit confusing, here's a quick example to drive it all home. First, define a function that takes three arguments and prints out the concatenated arguments to a message box:

```
function print3Args(a1, a2, a3) {
  alert(a1 + a2 + a3);
}
```

Next, use dojo.hitch to preset two of the arguments:

```
var printArg= dojo.hitch(null, print3Args, "this", " is ");
```

Finally, exercise printArg by invoking it with a *single* argument:

```
Line 1  printArg("easy.");  //...prints "this is easy"
   -       //effectively, print3Args("this", " is ", "easy.") was called.

   -     printArg("beautiful.");  //...prints "this is beautiful"
   5       //effectively, print3Args("this", " is ", "beautiful.") was called.

   -     printArg("not the key to life!");  //...prints "this is not the key to life!"
   -       //effectively, print3Args("this", " is ", "not the key to life!) was called.
```

In the previous code, dojo.hitch manufactured a function called print-Arg, which calls print3Args with the first and second arguments set to "this" and "is", respectively. Any arguments provided to printArg when *it* is invoked are passed along to print3Args subsequent to the first two arguments.

We also illustrated that *both* the context and the function must be specified when binding arguments. If the function is a method on another object, then there's nothing new here. But if the function is just an ordinary function defined in the current scope when passed to dojo.hitch, then null must be specified for context when binding arguments.

Recognizing that forcing null to be provided in these situations is a bit inconvenient, Dojo provides the function dojo.partial that *does not* accept a context argument. In effect, dojo.hitch(null, f,...) is equivalent to dojo.partial(f,...).

If we return to our motivating example, we wanted to bind arguments to an event handler when it was connected rather than when it is invoked. dojo.hitch allows us to solve the problem without explicitly writing out a function literal.

So the following...

```
dojo.byId("someId").click= function(){handler(someArg);};
```

becomes...

```
dojo.byId("someId").click= dojo.hitch(null, handler, someArg);
```

or, equivalently...

```
dojo.byId("someId").click= dojo.partial(handler, someArg);
```

Binding context and arguments to a function and returning another function is a cornerstone of functional programming. You will use dojo.hitch —directly or indirectly—all the time. You simply can't be a good Dojo programmer without understanding it well.

5.2 JavaScript 1.6 Array Methods

Ask yourself, how many times have you written something like for (var i= 0; i<someArray.length; i++)? Although the body of the loop is unique each time, the looping control statement is not, and this is an excellent time to employ the power of JavaScript to eliminate such rote code.

Indeed, JavaScript 1.6, as defined by Mozilla, includes several built-in array methods that help with these kinds of tasks.[2] Dojo provides the same functions for browsers that don't implement JavaScript 1.6 natively:

- dojo.indexOf: Returns the first index of a matching item in an array or -1 if not found
- dojo.lastIndexOf: Returns the last index of a matching item in an array or -1 if not found
- dojo.every: Tests whether all elements in an array cause a test function to return true
- dojo.some: Tests whether some elements in an array cause a test function to return true
- dojo.filter: Creates a new array composed of all elements in a array that pass through a filter function
- dojo.map: Creates a new array composed of the results of calling a function on every element in a array
- dojo.forEach: Passes each element in an array to a function

There are good reasons to use these Dojo functions. Certainly the code is cleaner and more expressive. Further, there is less opportunity to make many common coding mistakes since you don't have to hand-code a loop each time you need one of the algorithms.

Notice that dojo.every, dojo.some, dojo.filter, dojo.map, and dojo.forEach iterate through an array, applying a function (that we'll call the *callback* function) to each element in the array to achieve some result. Not surprisingly, these functions have the same signature: (a, f, context), where a is the array, f is the callback function, and context (optional) is the context in which to execute f. Effectively, given f and context, the callback function is given by dojo.hitch(context, f).

Similarly, a single signature is defined for the callback function: (item, index, array), where item and index are the current array element and index in the iteration and array is the array.

---

2. See http://developer.mozilla.org/en/docs/Core_JavaScript_1.5_Reference:Global_Objects:Array.

Let's work through a few quick examples here. A **for** loop that iterates through an array is probably the most frequently uttered code phrase of all time. Usually, it looks like this:

```
for (var i= 0, end= theArray.length; i<end; i++) {
  //do something interesting with theArray[i]
}
```

dojo.forEach is a drop-in replacement:

```
dojo.forEach(theArray, function(x){
  //called once for each array element
  //do something interesting with x which is theArray[i]
});
```

We specified a function literal for the callback function—a common idiom. Further, in our callback function, we didn't define the index and array arguments. This is perfectly legal and quite common. Of course, the arguments will be passed even if you don't use them.

There is one gotcha here. The JavaScript 1.6 array methods are defined by the built-in Array class, whereas the Dojo counterparts are just plain functions that must be given the target array as the first argument. Therefore, there is an extra argument required (the array) when the Dojo versions of these functions are used. Just for comparison, here is forEach in JavaScript 1.6:

```
theArray.forEach(function(x){
  //called once for each array element
  //do something interesting with x which is theArray[i]
});
```

Now that we've seen the basics, let's exercise each function in the API. We'll use the array src= [1, 2, 3, 4, 5] as input. Here's the code required to see whether all or some of the contents of src are odd numbers:

```
Line 1   var src= [1, 2, 3, 4, 5];
   -
   -     //see if every element is odd...
   -     var allOdd= dojo.every(src, function(x){
   5       return x%2;
   -     });
   -     //allOdd is now false
   -
   -     //see if some element is odd...
  10     var someOdd= dojo.some(src, function(x){
   -       return x%2;
   -     });
   -     //someOdd is now true
```

We can also make a new array that has just the odd numbers:

```
Line 1  //filter just the odd numbers out of src...
   -    var odds= dojo.filter(src, function(x){
   -      return x%2;
   -    });
   5    //odds is now [1, 3, 5]
   -    //src is STILL [1, 2, 3, 4, 5]
```

Next, let's make a new array by doubling each element in the src array:

```
Line 1  //make a new array by doubling each element in src...
   -    var multiplyBy2= dojo.map(src, function(x){
   -      return x*2;
   -    });
   5    //multiplyBy2 is now [2, 4, 6, 8, 10];
   -    //src is STILL [1, 2, 3, 4, 5]
```

None of this is particularly surprising or complicated. And that's *exactly* the point. It's much better than handwritten loops for all the reasons listed in the beginning of this section.

To demonstrate the context argument, let's calculate the sum of the contents of src. First, we need an accumulator object:

```
Line 1  var accumulator= {
   -      total: 0,
   -      add: function(x){this.total+= x;}
   -    };
```

Now we'll use dojo.forEach to pass each element in src to accumulator:

```
accumulator.total= 0;
dojo.forEach(src, accumulator.add, accumulator);
//accumulator.total is now 15
```

In the previous examples, notice that passing a function literal implies a fair amount of rote syntax:

```
Line 1  function(item [, index] [, array]) {
   -      //function-body
   -    }
```

The really interesting part is the function body. Recognizing this, these functions can accept the function body as a string. When this technique is used, a function is created on the fly with the parameter names item, index, and array. Here are all the examples rewritten in this alternate syntax:

```
Line 1  //see if every element is odd...
   -    var allOdd= dojo.every(src, "return item%2;");
   -    //allOdd is now false
   -
```

```
5   //see if some element is odd...
-   var someOdd= dojo.some(src, "return item%2;");
-   //someOdd is now true

-   //filter just the odd numbers out of src...
10  var odds= dojo.filter(src, "return item%2;");
-   //odds is now [1, 3, 5]
-   //src is STILL [1, 2, 3, 4, 5]

-
-   //make a new array by doubling each element in src...
15  var multiplyBy2= dojo.map(src, "return item*2;");
-   //multiplyBy2 is now [2, 4, 6, 8, 10];
-   //src is STILL [1, 2, 3, 4, 5]

-
-   var accumulator = {total: 0};
20  dojo.forEach(src, "this.total+= item;", accumulator);
-   //accumulator.total is now 15
```

The last example that accumulates a sum demonstrates a gotcha: the function is executed in the global scope unless a context argument is provided and is not closed on any local variables. For example, you can close on local variables when using the function literal syntax:

```
Line 1   var total= 0;
-        dojo.forEach(src, function(x){
-          total+= x;
-        });
5        //total is now 15
```

But something similar won't work using the function-body-as-a-string syntax:

```
Line 1   var total= 0;
-        try {
-          dojo.forEach(src, "total+= item;");
-        } catch (e) {
5          alert(e);
-        }
```

The previous code will throw an exception since total is not defined in the global scope.

This leaves us with the trivial dojo.indexOf and dojo.lastIndexOf. These functions search an array for the first/last occurrence of an object. Both have the signature (a, target, startIndex), where a is the array, target is the element to search for, and startIndex is the location in the array to begin the search. The JavaScript operator == is used to satisfy the search condition, and -1 is returned if a match is not found.

Here are a few examples:

```
Line 1   var src= [1, 2, 3, 3, 3, 4, 5];
    -    var result;
    -    result= dojo.indexOf(src, 3);            //result is now 2
    -    result= dojo.indexOf(src, 3, result+1); //result is now 3
    5    result= dojo.lastIndexOf(src, 3);        //result is now 4
    -    result= dojo.lastIndexOf(src, 3, result-1);  //result is now 3
```

Simple. Expressive. Too bad everything isn't so easy!

5.3 Support for Polymorphism

Polymorphism allows us to invoke a function and have the function do the right thing depending upon the types of the arguments provided. For example, invoking the method area on an instance of type Circle does something different than invoking area on an instance of type Rectangle. In both cases, the instance could be viewed as the first argument to the function area, which performs a computation depending upon the type of this first argument. In this sense, area is polymorphic.

It happens that most polymorphic functions resolve on a single type. It is easy enough to build such functions—just make them a method of each type that supports the function. However, sometimes this isn't practical for one or both of the following reasons:

- It is undesirable to include the method in the type definition (for example, the type's interface may be sprawling or closed, or the method may depend on several concepts independent of the type).

- The function's behavior depends on more than one argument's type.

In both cases we're left with branching to different execution paths based on the arguments' types. Most of the time, you'll be able to use JavaScript's instanceof operator to determine argument types. Occasionally instanceof doesn't work with the fundamental types. For example:

```
Line 1   function t1(theObject){
    -      return (theObject instanceof String);
    -    }
    -    function t2(theObject){
    5      return (typeof theObject == "string");
    -    }
    -
    -    var b;
```

```
      b= t1("test");        //b is false
10    b= t2("test");        //b is true
      s= new String("test");
      b= t1(s);        //b is true
      b= t2(s);        //b is false
```

Certain JavaScript interpreters included in various browsers also contain errors that further confound the problem with other types (for example, calculating whether an object is a function in Safari).

Dojo rescues us with a set of functions that abstract away all these problems:

- dojo.isString(test): Returns true if test is either a string literal or a string variable
- dojo.isArray(test): Returns true if test is an Array or derives from Array
- dojo.isFunction(test): Returns true if test is a function or derives from function
- dojo.isObject(test): Returns true if test is null, an object, an array, or a function
- dojo.isArrayLike(test): Returns true if test has a finite length property and is not a string, a function, or a DOM form node
- dojo.isAlien(test): Returns true if test is a built-in function that should report as a function but does not

Although JavaScript 1.*x* does not include the concept of function overloading, you can get the same effect by using these functions to branch code based on argument types. Essentially, this allows you to build functions that have semantics based upon not only their name but also upon the types of the arguments provided to the function at runtime. Here's an example of the use pattern:

```
Line 1    function someFunction(theValue){
            if (dojo.isString(theValue)) {
              _someFunction_string(theValue);
            } else if (dojo.isFunction(theValue)) {
5             _someFunction_func(theValue);
            } else {
              throw new Error("improper type for someFunction");
            }
          }
```

In the example, we dispatched to "private" functions based on the actual type of theValue.

This question arises: when should type calculations (that is, expressions that use types as operands) be used to alter the behavior of a single function compared to just defining multiple functions and instructing client code to call the correct version? There are two reasons to use type calculations to simulate function overloading:

- When the function is called by client code that may not know the argument types, factoring the type calculations into the function eliminates this code from being duplicated at every location that the function is called.

- To simplify the client API by providing fewer functions that work in more situations.

Clearly, a single function should always be used when conditions given by the first reason exist. On the other hand, the second reason is largely a matter of taste. But remember, if type calculations are used, then those calculations will be executed every time the function is executed, resulting in a performance hit. If the calculations are complicated and the function is invoked frequently, this performance hit may be noticeable. We generally use the following heuristic:

1. Always factor argument type calculations into the function when the calling clients do not know the types of the arguments.

2. Tend to factor argument type calculations into the function when the function call is written frequently (that is, written in the code) with a few, well-understood argument signatures.

3. Otherwise, tend to define a family of functions that requires different parameter signatures if any of the following conditions exist:

   - When the function is private

   - When the function is called frequently during execution

   - When the type calculations are complicated

5.4 Combining, Structuring, and Copying Objects

We're going to spend an entire chapter exploring how to use the function dojo.declare to build constructor functions that create classes of objects (see Chapter 9, *Defining Classes with dojo.declare*, on page 221). Sometimes dojo.declare is much more than you need. For example, copying the properties from one object into another object is a common

JavaScript programming pattern, and you shouldn't have to define a new class just to get this functionality. Dojo helps by defining several lightweight functions that accomplish per-object structure and content manipulations.

Mixing Objects

The function dojo.mixin(dest, src1, [src2, [...]]) copies all the properties from the object(s) src1, src2, ..., into dest. Copying is accomplished with the JavaScript assignment operator. So, numbers, booleans, and strings are copied by value, while all other types are copied by reference.

Let's look at a couple of common use patterns. Say you have an object myObject and you want to copy several properties into it. You could do it manually:

```
myObject.prop1= 123.456;
myObject.prop2= "hello, world";
myObject.someProp= yourObject;
```

Or, you could use dojo.mixin to accomplish the same thing:

```
dojo.mixin(myObject, {
    prop1: 123.456,
    prop2: "hello, world",
    someProp: yourObject});
```

Of course, this works with named objects...

```
myObject.prop1= yourObject.prop1;
myObject.prop2= yourObject.prop2;
myObject.someProp= yourObject.someProp;
```

which becomes the following:

```
dojo.mixin(myObject, yourObject);
```

dojo.mixin is slightly less verbose and adds a bit of modularity when compared to the manual method—both good things.

There are a few things to notice about dojo.mixin. First, if the destination object already has a property that is specified in a source object, then the original property *will be* overwritten. Further, when more than one source object is provided, the rightmost source wins. Here's an example that demonstrates this phenomenon:

```
myObject= {p: 1};
dojo.mixin(myObject, {p:2}, {p:3});
//myOjbect.p is now set to 3!
```

> ## What Is a Prototype?
>
> Every object in JavaScript contains a reference to another object termed its *prototype*. Since the prototype is another object itself, it also contains a reference to its prototype. This forms a chain of objects. The chain terminates with the prototype for the built-in Object type.
>
> When a property of an object is read, JavaScript looks for the property in the object. If not found, JavaScript then looks in the prototype object, the prototype of the prototype, and so on, up the prototype chain until the property is found or the chain is exhausted. Since a method is just a property that happens to be a function, this is how method dispatching occurs, and this system is called *prototypal inheritance*.

Second, with the exception of any property in Object's prototype, properties from the source object are fully enumerated. This means that any property that is defined in the prototype chain of each source object will be copied—up to but not including Object's prototype. If you need a quick refresher on prototypes, see the sidebar on the current page.

Finally, sometimes the name can be misleading. dojo.mixin does *not* create a mixin class (we'll talk about mixin classes in Chapter 9, *Defining Classes with dojo.declare*, on page 221). Instead, it is augmenting the source object by "mixing in" the properties from one or more other objects.

Copying Objects

Sometimes you need to copy a variable by value. This is easy if the variable is a number, boolean, or string since the semantics of the JavaScript assignment operator copy these types by value. But, if you need to copy any other type, the JavaScript assignment operator won't work (remember, it copies anything other than numbers, booleans, and strings by reference). Instead, you must traverse the entire object, including any nested objects, and *create* new instances at each node in the traversal. The function dojo.clone(src) accomplishes exactly this functionality.

To visualize the differences between assigning, mixing, and cloning, we'll create an object, exercise all three copy techniques, and then

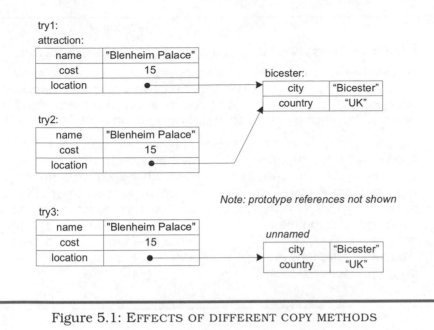

Figure 5.1: EFFECTS OF DIFFERENT COPY METHODS

draw out the resulting object space. The source object contains another object to fully demonstrate the differences. Here is the code:

```
//create an object with some properties
var bicester= {city: "Bicester", country: "UK"};
var attraction= {name: "Blenheim Palace", cost: 15, location: bicester};

var try1, try2, try3;
try1= attraction;
try2= dojo.mixin({}, attraction);
try3= dojo.clone(attraction);
```

In Figure 5.1, you can see the objects that are created by the code. Note how the JavaScript assignment operator (try1= attraction) just added another name to the source object (this is an example of a so-called shallow copy). At the other extreme, dojo.clone ensured that a completely new object space was created (a so-called deep copy).

Copying Array-like Objects

The last kind of copying that comes up occasionally involves turning array-like objects (for example, the built-in arguments object) into a real array. The function dojo._toArray(src, start) creates an array and fills it with src[start], src[start+1],..., src[src.length-1]. start is optional and, if missing, is assumed to be zero.

> ### Privacy in the Bedroom
>
> Remember when you were a kid playing and you tried to hide by jumping into a bed and pulling the covers over your head? You couldn't be seen, but everybody knew you were there because of the big breathing, laughing lump in the bed.
>
> We jokingly call variables with names that start with an underscore *bed lump* functions. They are supposed to be private, but everybody can see and use them. These kinds of private functions are every bit as robust as those found in the public interface. The only potential downside is that they are slightly (depending upon the function) more likely to change in future releases. As we explore the Dojo APIs, we'll describe a few bed lump functions that are particularly useful *and* unlikely to change in future releases.

Note the requirements for the source object: it must be an object and define the property length that returns an integer. In Dojo, functions that begin with an underscore are "kinda, sorta" private; see the sidebar on this page for details.

Chapter 6

Asynchronous Programming

If you want to program the browser to do anything dynamically—and we mean *anything*—you must hook up your code to a DOM event. Then you find out that there are two different event APIs. Not to be outdone, Internet Explorer provides a third API—complete with memory leaks for good measure. And a detailed study of these APIs reveals several browser-dependent inconsistencies and idiosyncrasies. Event programming quickly becomes a huge headache.

Fortunately for us, Dojo includes a complete event programming framework that fixes these problems. But Dojo doesn't stop with events. Event programming is an example of the asynchronous programming model, and Dojo includes several function families to build all kinds of interesting and powerful programs using this model.

This chapter is all about asynchronous programming with Dojo. We start by exploring Dojo's solution to the event programming mess created by the browser vendors. Then we look at how Dojo extends the event framework to handle user-defined events and further leverages user-defined events to provide a publish-subscribe framework—very cool stuff. We conclude the chapter with an in-depth example of Dojo's Deferred class, which manages complex interactions between asynchronous functions, their callbacks, and other interested processes.

6.1 Programming DOM Events with Dojo

Dojo provides a single DOM event framework that works identically across all supported browsers; Dojo even fixes the memory leaks that come for free with Internet Explorer. Dojo's DOM event framework functions mostly like the W3C DOM Level 2 event model (available from

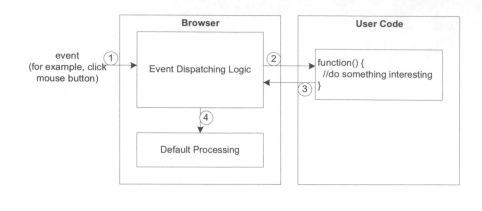

Figure 6.1: EVENT PROCESSING IN THE BROWSER

http://www.w3.org/TR/DOM-Level-2-Events/). In cases where the browser does this anyway, Dojo simply passes event handler connection/ disconnection requests to the DOM functions addEventListener/ removeEventListener. Where the browser model is grossly different from the W3C model, Dojo simulates the W3C model. Finally, where the W3C model leaves openings for implementation-defined behavior, Dojo defines this behavior.

Here's the event-driven programming model in a nutshell: when something happens (the *event*), a function is automatically invoked (the *handler*). The event, sometimes called a *signal*, may be a device event such as a mouse gesture or a software event such as submitting a form. The handler, also called a *listener* or *callback*, is a function that's passed a well-defined set of arguments and that executes in a well-defined context. In Figure 6.1, you can see a conceptual view of how event programming works in the browser.

Writing Event Handlers

We'll explore Dojo's DOM event framework by writing a simple event handler that prints out information about an event; later, we'll use Dojo to connect the handler to a click event. Along the way we will describe event propagation and default processing—both of which can be affected by an event handler. We'll also look at Dojo's extension to the W3C model for handling keyboard events.

The Handler Signature

Handlers are functions. The Dojo event framework provides a single argument termed the *event object* to handler functions; this object contains several properties/methods that describe/control the event as specified by the W3C event model—even when the browser happens to be Internet Explorer, which doesn't implement this model natively. If you're writing a handler that doesn't need the event object, just define a function with no parameters.[1] Since we'll use the event object to log information about the event, our handler function includes a parameter to receive the event object:

```
Line 1    function handleClick(eventObj){
   -        //TODO...print information about the event
   -      }
```

Three types of event objects form a single-inheritance chain: MouseEvent derives from UIEvent, which derives from Event. The complete event type space is shown in Figure 6.2, on the following page (the diagram also shows keyboard event objects, which we'll discuss in a moment). The diagram includes the read-only properties available with each event object type.

The actual type of event object passed to a handler function depends upon the type of event being processed. In Figure 6.3, on page 110, you can see the event catalog that gives the event object type provided with each event.

Since we're eventually going to hook up our handler to a click event, we'll receive an event object of type UIEvent. Our handler uses this object to print out information about the event to the debugging console:

```
Line 1    function handleClick(eventObj){
   -        console.log(
   -          "Event(" + eventObj.type +
   -          ") on DOM node " + eventObj.target.id +
   5          "; currentTarget= " + eventObj.currentTarget.id);
   -      }
```

Notice that our handler doesn't return a value. Handlers shouldn't return values, and anything returned will be ignored.

---

1. In JavaScript, it's perfectly legal to provide a function with more arguments than defined parameters. Dojo will provide an event object to the handler even if the handler doesn't define a parameter to receive it (that is, arguments[0] will *always* hold the event object).

class Event:

type *string*	the name of the event (e.g., "click")
target *DOM node*	The node on which the event occurred. This will never change as the event is bubbled. See Event.currentTarget; see xxx for a discussion of bubbling.
currentTarget *DOM node*	The node upon which the current handler was attached. This will change as the event is bubbled. See Event.target; see xxx for a discussion of bubbling.
eventPhase *number*	Says where the dispatcher is in the bubbling process. Either Event.AT_TARGET or Event.BUBBLING_PHASE . See xxx for a discussion of bubbling.
timestamp *Date*	The date-time that the event occurred.
bubbles *boolen*	True if this event bubbles; false otherwise. See xxx for a discussion of bubbling.
cancelable *boolen*	True if the default processing (i.e., the processing done by the web browser) associated with this event can be canceled; false otherwise. See xxx for a discussion of canceling.

class UIEvent:

view *object*	The Window object within which the event occurred.
detail *number*	Event-dependent additional information. See xxx.

class MouseEvent:

button *number*	0 => left; 1 => middle; 2 => right.
altKey *boolean*	True if alt key is pressed; false otherwise.
ctrlKey *boolean*	True if ctrl key is pressed; false otherwise.
metaKey *boolean*	True if meta key is pressed; false otherwise.
shiftKey *boolean*	True if shift key is pressed; false otherwise.
clientX,Y *number*	The viewport coordinates of the mouse pointer; scrolling is not taken into account.
screenX,Y *number*	The screen coordinates of the mouse pointer.
relatedTarget *DOM node*	The node the mouse just left for mouseover events; conversely for mouseout events.

properties added for
keyboard events

altKey *boolean*	True if alt key is pressed; false otherwise.
ctrlKey *boolean*	True if ctrl key is pressed; false otherwise.
shiftKey *boolean*	True if shift key is pressed; false otherwise.
keyCode *number*	The virtual key code of the key pressed/ released.
charCode *number*	The printable character implied by the keyCode after applying the shift state and keyboard locale.
keyChar *DOM node*	A string calculated on charCode as "charCode ? String.fromCharCode(charCode) : ''".

Diagram Legend

property-name *property-type*	*description*

note: only read-only properties shown;
event objects also contain several methods.

Figure 6.2: THE EVENT INTERFACES

Now that we have our event handler, the next step is to connect it to the event. We'll do that soon, but first, let's look at a few details of the Dojo DOM event framework.

Keyboard Event Objects

The Event, UIEvent, and MouseEvent types are standardized by the W3C DOM Level 2 event model. Unfortunately, W3C doesn't mention keyboard events (oops!). Dojo augments the model slightly by adding properties to the Event interface for key up/down/press events (also depicted in Figure 6.2, on the facing page).

When writing handlers that connect to keyboard events, beware that different browsers use different virtual key codes for the same key. For example, F10 is 121 in Firefox and Internet Explorer but 63245 in Safari. Dojo rescues us with dojo.keys, which provides a map from a special key name to a virtual key code. For example, we can write the following:

```
Line 1   function someKeyDownHandler(eventObj) {
  -        switch (eventObj.keyCode) {
  -          case dojo.keys.F10: //process F10 key....
  -            console.log("you just pressed the F10 key");
  5            break;
  -
  -          //etc...
  -
  -        }
 10      }
```

This code will work in any Dojo-supported browser. The following special keys are available as properties of dojo.keys:

- SHIFT, CTRL, ALT, CAPS_LOCK, NUM_LOCK, SCROLL_LOCK
- TAB, SPACE
- ENTER, ESCAPE, PAUSE
- SELECT, CLEAR
- PAGE_(UP|DOWN|LEFT|RIGHT), HOME, END, (LEFT|RIGHT)_ARROW,
- INSERT, BACKSPACE, DELETE
- NUMPAD_0..NUMPAD_9, NUMPAD_PLUS, NUMPAD_MINUS, NUMPAD_MULTIPLY, NUMPAD_DIVIDE, NUMPAD_ENTER, NUMPAD_PERIOD
- (LEFT|RIGHT)_WINDOW
- F1..F15
- HELP

Event Propagation

Depending upon the event, the browser may dispatch a single event to many DOM nodes; this process is called *event propagation*. Handlers can affect propagation, and it's important to understand propagation in order to construct optimal handler code.

Consider a click event: when a user clicks a DOM node, a click event is dispatched to the *target node* (the node upon which an event occurs is the target node) and then to its parent, grandparent, and so on, up to the top of the document tree. This dispatching process is called *bubbling*. Right or wrong, the W3C Event specification does not fully bubble some events, and Dojo does not change this behavior. In Figure 6.3, on page 110, you can see that events that bubble are marked with a *B*.

Bubbling allows us to consolidate code at parent nodes. For example, let's say we have a div node that contains 100 child subtrees that are all identical in structure and all require an identical handler for a click event. We could attach the same handler to the 100 subtrees, or we could attach a single handler to the parent div. The single handler can then inspect the target property of the event object to determine the actual subtree that was clicked. This is clearly a better way.

Often, you will want to stop bubbling. For example, if a node lower in the tree handles an event and that handler directly calls a handler higher in the tree, then we surely don't want to call the higher handler again as a consequence of bubbling. This is easily accomplished:

```
Line 1   function someHandler(eventObj) {
  -        //do something interesting...
  -
  -        //now, stop bubbling...
  5        eventObj.stopProgagation();
  -      }
```

Many browsers can execute *capturing* before the event is dispatched to the target node. Capturing works exactly the opposite of bubbling: the event dispatcher calls every click handler attached to every node that is an ancestor of the target node, starting with its most distant relative and ending with its parent.

So, the maximum event propagation path is given as follows:

1. Capturing phase: call handlers attached to ancestors of the target node, starting with the most distant and ending with the parent
2. Call handlers attached to the target node

3. Bubbling phase: call handlers attached to ancestors of the target node, starting with the parent and ending with the most distant

When a handler is attached to an event, it is attached to either the capturing phase or the bubbling phase; if you want to see the event during both phases, then two handlers must be attached (although both handlers could be the same function).

Propagation can be stopped by *any* handler *anywhere* along the process by calling stopPropagation on the event object.

It is also possible to skip the capturing phase without affecting the last two steps, and this is exactly how the Dojo event framework works. This is a Good Thing. When you think about it, capturing is usually wrong.[2] Capturing implies that more-general handlers are called before more-specific handlers. Why bother putting a handler lower in the DOM tree unless you want to "override" some handling higher in the tree? Of course, the higher-level handler can still be called directly from the lower-level handler if desired. This is much like calling a superclass method from within an overridden subclass method.

Let's enhance our click handler to prevent bubbling when Shift + click is pressed:

```
Line 1   function handleClick(eventObj){
           console.log(
             "Event(" + eventObj.type +
             ") on target " + eventObj.target.id +
      5      "; currentTarget= " + eventObj.currentTarget.id);

           //eventObj is of type MouseEvent
           if (eventObj.shiftKey) {
             //stop bubbling shift-click was pressed.
     10      eventObj.stopPropagation();
           }
         }
```

In a moment we'll hook this handler up to every node in a small DOM tree. The example will show bubbling in action (by pressing click), and bubbling stops immediately (by pressing Shift + click).

---

2. There is one case where handling an event during the capturing phase is required: capturing the mouse (that is, intercepting all mouse messages). Currently, Dojo does not expose a public interface to this functionality, and you must implement mouse capturing directly.

Default Processing

Each DOM event causes the browser to execute some default processing whether or not a handler is attached. For example, when the user clicks the submit button on a form, the browser sends the form data to the server. Event handlers can cancel the default processing for some kinds of events. For example, a submit event handler might prevent submitting a form to the server by canceling the default processing if errors are detected on the form.

Event handlers can cancel default processing by calling the preventDefault method on the event object like this:

```
Line 1   function someHandler(eventObj) {
  -        //do something interesting...
  -
  -        //now, prevent the default processing...
  5        eventObj.preventDefault();
  -      }
```

See Figure 6.3, on page 110, which shows a list of the events that are cancelable.

Finally, the convenience function dojo.stopEvent(event) calls both event. preventDefault() and event.stopPropagation().

```
Line 1   function someHandler(eventObj) {
  -        //do something interesting...
  -
  -        //the statement...
  5        dojo.stopEvent(eventObj);
  -
  -        //...is exactly equivalent to...
  -        eventObj.stopProgation();
  -        eventObj.preventDefault();
  10     }
```

That's all there is to writing handlers. Next, we'll solve the problem of connecting handlers to DOM events.

Connecting Handlers

Dojo provides the function dojo.connect for connecting handlers to DOM events (later, we'll see that dojo.connect can do more). It is the key to the Dojo event framework since it causes event handlers to work as we've described, independent of any particular browser. It has the following signature:

handle= dojo.connect(obj, event, context, handler)

Essentially, calling dojo.connect(obj, event, context, handler) connects a handler to a DOM node event as if the W3C DOM method obj.addEventListener(event, dojo.hitch(context, handler), false) had been called. And Dojo does this even if the current browser is an Internet Explorer version that does not directly support addEventLister.

The first two parameters, obj (a DOM node) and event (a string), define the event. In Figure 6.3, on page 110, you can see a list of available DOM events and their names. The second two parameters, context (optional, an object) and handler (a function or string), define the handler. The context parameter is syntactic sugar for designating a handler that requires binding a function to a context (for example, a method to an object) without calling dojo.hitch explicitly. We'll see this pattern used frequently in Dojo. If dojo.hitch is a little hazy, take a quick trip to Section 5.1, *Binding with dojo.hitch*, on page 77 for a refresher.

Armed with dojo.connect, we can connect the event handler on which we've been working. First, let's build a little document to exercise our handler:

```
asynchronous-programming/event.htm
```

```
Line 1   <body id="body">
    -      <div id="body-div">
    -        <p id="body-div-p">
    -          Now is the time to understand events!
    5        </p>
    -        <ol id="body-div-ol">
    -          <li id="body-div-ol-li-1">
    -            connect/disconnect handlers with dojo.connect/disconnect.
    -          </li><li id="body-div-ol-li-2">
    10           Handlers are always passed an event-object.
    -          </li><li id="body-div-ol-li-3">
    -            Don't use "this" to reference the current target.
    -          </li><li id="body-div-ol-li-4">
    -            Events that can bubble always bubble; events never propagate.
    15         </li><li id="body-div-ol-li-5">
    -            Keyboard events and associated event objects are fully defined.
    -          </li>
    -        </ol>
    -      </div>
    20   </body>
```

We'll connect the handler to each DOM node in the body subtree:

```
Line 1   function connectExercise() {
    -      dojo.connect(dojo.byId("body"), "click", handleClick);
    -      dojo.connect(dojo.byId("body-div"), "click", handleClick);
    -      dojo.connect(dojo.byId("body-div-p"), "click", handleClick);
```

```
5    dojo.connect(dojo.byId("body-div-ol"), "click", handleClick);
     dojo.connect(dojo.byId("body-div-ol-li-1"), "click", handleClick);
     dojo.connect(dojo.byId("body-div-ol-li-2"), "click", handleClick);
     dojo.connect(dojo.byId("body-div-ol-li-3"), "click", handleClick);
     dojo.connect(dojo.byId("body-div-ol-li-4"), "click", handleClick);
10   dojo.connect(dojo.byId("body-div-ol-li-5"), "click", handleClick);

     //Note!!
     //all the lines above can be replaced with
     //dojo.query("body *").connect("click", handleClick);
15   //see Chapter 7
   }
```

Since our handler does not require any particular context, we omitted the context argument.

It's important to keep in mind that we're building a demonstration of various event framework functionality—*not* optimal code to handle click events on all nodes of a DOM subtree. For example, although we've connected to every node to demonstrate bubbling, a "real" program would just connect the handler to the root of the subtree since the handler does the same thing no matter where it's connected. Also, we explicitly connected each node by finding the node by its id attribute. We'll see how this can be done in a single line when we explore dojo.query in Section 7.2, *Finding and Editing Nodes*, on page 140.

When the document is loaded and the second list item is clicked, the console will fill up with the following messages:

```
Line 1   Event(click) on target body-div-ol-li-2; currentTarget= body-div-ol-li-2
         Event(click) on target body-div-ol-li-2; currentTarget= body-div-ol
         Event(click) on target body-div-ol-li-2; currentTarget= body-div
         Event(click) on target body-div-ol-li-2; currentTarget= body
```

Notice how the first message shows that eventObj.currentTarget and eventObject.target are identical. As the event bubbles up, eventObject.target stays constant, but eventObject.currentTarget changes to reflect the handler's position in the subtree. Clicking the same list item with the Shift key pressed causes the handler to stop bubbling, resulting in a single message being sent to the debug console:

```
Line 1   Event(click) on DOM node body-div-ol-li-2; currentTarget= body-div-ol-li-2
```

Several different handlers can be connected to the same (node, event) using dojo.connect. In this case, the handlers may be called in any order. This is usually enough to suggest that it is a bad idea to connect multiple handlers. If you need to connect multiple handlers, it is almost always better to write a function that combines the handlers in a well-defined order. For example:

```
Line 1    function myClickHander1(event) {
    -         /* as required */
    -       }
    -       function myClickHander2(event) {
    5         /* as required */
    -       }
    -       dojo.connect(someDomNode, "click",
    -           function(event){ myHandler1(event); myHandler2(event); }
    -       );
```

The example uses a function literal to create a handler that calls two other handlers in a well-defined order. Also notice that we omitted the context argument. Remember, dojo.connect calculates the handler function by calling dojo.hitch(context, handler). Since context was not provided, the handler in the example is calculated as follows:

```
Line 1    dojo.hitch(
    -          function(event){ myHandler1(event); myHandler2(event); }
    -       );
```

This is exactly the effect we want. It also demonstrates a gotcha: the value of this *will not* reference the current target node when the handler is called. Although not specified by any standard, most native browser event APIs set this to reference the current target DOM node when the handler is invoked. But dojo.connect connects the result of dojo.hitch(context, handler) to the event, and the whole purpose of hitch is to call handler with this==context.[3]

Our advice: don't write code that assumes this references the current target in event handlers. Doing so will lead to brittle code that is not standards-compliant. Instead, use event.target or event.currentTarget, depending upon the semantics of the handler.

At this point, we can write handlers and connect them to events, but where do we put all the calls to dojo.connect? We'll answer that next.

Executing Initialization Code with dojo.addOnLoad

When we call dojo.connect to connect a handler to a DOM node, we'd better make sure that the DOM tree has been built by the browser

---

3. Of course you could force the context to be the node by writing something like dojo.connect(node, "click", node, f).

Alex Says...

The Good, the Bad, and Internet Explorer

The Dojo event system attempts to fill in the most common problems with browser event system implementations, but we wouldn't need to if all browsers implemented the W3C DOM Level 2 event model correctly. Internet Explorer 6 and 7 haven't even attempted to implement the W3C model, but that's the tip of the iceberg.

Internet Explorer has the potential to leak memory when event handlers contain circular references or when the handler references an object that points back to the DOM node to which the handler is attached. This happens all the time, sometimes by accident. When a circular reference chain is created between native browser objects and user JavaScript code, Internet Explorer isn't "smart" enough to decrement the reference counts to zero even though both objects are no longer referenced. The solution to this problem is to track all the connections and disconnect them manually before the page unloads, allowing the built-in garbage collector to fully flush its references. With Internet Explorer 7, Microsoft implemented a system to try to flush references more completely, but it also falls down when nodes are left "dangling" in the JavaScript object space but aren't attached to the visible document. The web community is still waiting on Microsoft to fix this decade-old problem definitively. Tracking connections by hand is long-winded and error prone, and Dojo handles it for you if you use dojo.connect.

Of course, for relatively simple web pages with a short lifetime, browser resource leaks are inconsequential. Your objects may not grow very large, and users may not spend enough time in the application for the cumulative leakage to slow things down noticeably. When writing more advanced applications—particularly single-page applications—resource leaks can cause huge performance hits to the point of making the application unusable. So long as you connect using Dojo's event API, you can ignore these types of browser errors completely.

and any other JavaScript that the handler references has been downloaded and evaluated. And what if our application requires other initialization work—maybe it creates some bookkeeping data structures or does some DOM manipulation? Here, again, we need to be sure that the JavaScript resources that we've dojo.required and/or the DOM tree are ready for use. All of these problems are solved by the function dojo.addOnLoad.

dojo.addOnLoad takes a reference to a function and guarantees that the provided function is executed immediately after the following three conditions are met:

- The DOM tree has been built by the browser and is available for use by client code. Note, this is different from saying that every resource (for example, images) has been loaded.

- All JavaScript resources demanded through the Dojo loader have been loaded.

- All Dojo widget parsing has been completed. As we saw in Chapter 2, *Powerful Web Forms Made Easy*, on page 13, Dojo lets you specify widgets directly in the HTML code. When you include Dojo widgets like this, Dojo must parse the HTML and replace each embedded widget with the actual HTML that implements the widget. If djConfig.parseOnLoad is true, then this is accomplished as soon as the DOM tree is loaded by the browser but *before* any function registered with dojo.addOnLoad is executed.

dojo.addOnLoad can be called any number of times, and each function given as an argument will be executed in the order it was provided. The argument can be either a reference to a function or a method name on an object. Here is an example of each usage:

```
Line 1   dojo.addOnLoad(f);                              //the function f
   -     dojo.addOnLoad(function(){/* statements */}); //a function literal
   -     dojo.addOnLoad(o, "f");                         //the function o["f"]
```

Let's cross the final "t" in the event example. Here's the completed code, including the call to dojo.addOnLoad:

asynchronous-programming/event.htm

```
Line 1   function handleClick(eventObj){
   -       console.log(
   -         "Event(" + eventObj.type +
   -         ") on DOM node " + eventObj.target.id +
   5         "; currentTarget= " + eventObj.currentTarget.id);
   -
```

```
       //eventObj is of type MouseEvent
       if (eventObj.shiftKey) {
         //stop bubbling shift-click was pressed.
10       eventObj.stopPropagation();
       }
     }

     function connectExercise() {
15     dojo.connect(dojo.byId("body"), "click", handleClick);
       dojo.connect(dojo.byId("body-div"), "click", handleClick);
       dojo.connect(dojo.byId("body-div-p"), "click", handleClick);
       dojo.connect(dojo.byId("body-div-ol"), "click", handleClick);
       dojo.connect(dojo.byId("body-div-ol-li-1"), "click", handleClick);
20     dojo.connect(dojo.byId("body-div-ol-li-2"), "click", handleClick);
       dojo.connect(dojo.byId("body-div-ol-li-3"), "click", handleClick);
       dojo.connect(dojo.byId("body-div-ol-li-4"), "click", handleClick);
       dojo.connect(dojo.byId("body-div-ol-li-5"), "click", handleClick);
     }
25
     dojo.addOnLoad(connectExercise);
```

That's all there is to the Dojo DOM event framework. From the programmer's point of view, the Dojo event framework couldn't be simpler:

- dojo.connect/disconnect connects/disconnects handlers.

- Handlers are always passed an event-dependent event object that gives details about the event.

- Use the target/currentTarget property of the event object instead of this to get to the target/current target DOM nodes.

- Events that can bubble always bubble; the capturing phase is always disabled.

- Keyboard events and associated event objects are defined (unlike the W3C specifications).

- Initialization functions that connect events should be called by registering them with dojo.addOnLoad.

And, most important, all of this is browser-independent.

We'll conclude this section with a handy table that includes everything you need to know about the catalog of DOM events.

Alex Says...

Use dojo.addOnLoad Rather Than DOM onload

Simple pages perform initialization by attaching to the onload event of the window object, but this won't scale. What if some other bit of code wants to listen to onload? If they register after you, will your code get called? How can you ensure that your onload handler isn't breaking someone else's handler? I've seen large development teams stopped in their tracks because someone checked in a stray window.onload = function(){.... Dojo's onload mechanism gives you a simple way to register multiple handlers, and using it can save you serious headaches.

Then there's the question of what we mean by "onload." The browser's default onload event is not fired until *all* external resources referenced on the page are loaded. This means we must wait for all images, objects, CSS files, and the rest to download. If the page contains many and/or large external resources and/or the connection is slow, the user is presented with a dysfunctional page (since the initialization code hasn't run)—perhaps for a significant period of time. We want our widgets and progressive enhancements to start rendering as soon as possible, and in an ideal world, the browsers would give us events for all of these steps in the page-building process ("oncssload," "onimgload," "ondomparsed," and so on). Instead, there is a patchwork of browser-specific hacks and workarounds that let us try to determine whether we can say that things are "loaded" well before all the images are fully resolved...but these may also not be what we want. If our code is counting on the layout being "stabilized" and then some extra bit of CSS gets loaded that changes the rules, our widgets may appear to be "broken." The semantic we'd really like to implement is something like "onlayoutstable," which is roughly the point at which all CSS rules are applied and all images have dimensions (if not actual content). There's no native event for this, but Dojo does its best to figure out when this happens, and *that* is when handlers registered through dojo.addOnLoad are called.

If you're using the cross-domain loader, say by loading Dojo from AOL's CDN, then some of the JavaScript resources that your page needs may not be available even when the native onload fires. dojo.addOnLoad is smart about this and won't fire until all the modules are available, no matter what package mode you're using.

Lastly, if you prefer using dojo.connect, you can connect to the dojo.loaded event instead of dojo.addOnLoad since all three methods are defined as soon as dojo.js is included.

Event	Event object type	Bubbles?	Cancelable?	Description
mousedown	MouseEvent	B	C	The pointing device was pressed.
mouseup	MouseEvent	B	C	The pointing device was released.
mousemove	MouseEvent	B		The pointing device was moved.
mouseover	MouseEvent	B	C	Generated when the pointing device moves onto an element.
mouseout	MouseEvent	B	C	Generated when the pointing device moves off of an element.
click	MouseEvent	B	C	Generated by mousedown immediately followed by mouseup (that is, no mousemove separate the mousedown and mouseup events).
keydown	kbEvent	B	C	A keyboard key was moved from the up position to the down position.
keyup	kbEvent	B	C	A keyboard key was moved from the down position to the up position.
keypress	kbEvent	B	C	A keyboard key was moved to the down position or has been held in the down position long enough to automatically repeat another keypress. One or more keypress events are always brackets by single keydown/keyup events.
load	Event			The browser has finished loading a document, frames within a frameset, or an object element.
unload	Event			The browser has finish removing a document from a window or frame.
abort	Event	B		The browser stopped loading an image.
error	Event	B		An image didn't load properly or an error occured during script execution.
select	Event	B		The user selected some text within a text.
change	Event	B		A control's value was changed and then lost focus
submit	Event	B	C	A form was submitted
reset	Event	B		A form was reset.
focus	Event			An element received the focus; applies only to form controls.
blur	Event			An element lost the focus; applies only to form controls.
resize	Event	B		The document view was resized.
scroll	Event	B		The document view was scrolled.
DOMFocusIn	UIEvent	B		An element received the focus; applies only to any control
DOMFocusOut	UIEvent	B		An element lost the focus; applies only to any control
DOMActivate	UIEvent	B	C	An element was activated.

Figure 6.3: THE EVENT CATALOG

DOM Event Catalog

The Dojo event framework works with the events shown in Figure 6.3.[4] The table lists each event name (this is the name you provide as the event argument to dojo.connect), a description of what causes the event to occur, and the following three attributes that apply to each event:

- The type of event object passed to handlers

- Whether the event bubbles (*B* means yes)

- Whether the default processing associated with the event is cancelable (*C* means yes)

---

4. Actually, almost all of these events are fired by the browser, and Dojo leverages this fact. Some keyboard events in some browsers *are* fired synthetically by Dojo.

Now that we've looked at DOM events, you might ask yourself whether the idea of events could be extended to your own objects. With Dojo, the answer is a resounding "yes!" Let's see how.

6.2 Connecting to User-Defined Events with Dojo

To understand user-defined events, let's think about what's happening behind the scenes when an event is fired. What, *exactly*, is the "thing" that causes a handler to be called? For example, you might respond, "a mouse click." But the browser is several layers of abstraction above a hardware device driver, so it's not the switch on the mouse that causes the event—at least not directly. And, semantic events certainly have nothing to do with hardware. Really, it's the execution of some function that causes handlers to be invoked. For example, in Windows, when a mouse button is pressed, a message is inserted into the message queue. The browser's message loop retrieves this message and calls a function that processes the message. The execution of this function (that we'll call the *trigger function*) is the "event" that causes the mouse click handlers to be invoked. Dojo takes this idea to the obvious extreme: dojo.connect can hook up handlers to *any* function—not just DOM events.

This functionality often eliminates the need for scaffolding machinery. For example, in a traditional application system, you might have a set of command objects (say, menus) and a set of command handlers. Then you would build some scaffolding to hook the two objects together. The command handlers "register" with the scaffolding, the command objects signal the scaffolding, and the scaffolding marshals signals from the command objects to the command handlers. All of this is unnecessary with dojo.connect. Just connect the command handler directly to the command object, and you're done.

Let's see how such a system might be implemented—it will help you to visualize what's going on behind the scenes if this concept is new.

Hooking JavaScript Functions

Say we have a function, f, and we want to augment f with a call to console.log("exiting f") after f completes. Here's one way to do it:

```
Line 1  var g= f;
   -    f= function() {
   -      var result= g.apply(this, arguments);
   -      console.log("exiting f");
   5      return result;
   -    };
```

A function is an object like any other object. Indeed, when we say the "function f," we are really saying the "function object that the variable f references." The previous code uses this fact to hold a reference to the *original* definition of f in the variable g. Then f is replaced by a new function that calls to the original f, saves the result, writes to the debug console, and finally returns the saved result.

Dojo uses this idea as follows: when the dojo.connect parameters obj and event specify a JavaScript function rather than a DOM node event, dojo.connect replaces that function with a new function that first calls the original function and then fires the handler given by the context and handler parameters. Let's try it by first defining a function that prints out "hello, world" and then hook an event to it:

```
function f() {
  console.log("hello, world");
}

function myHandler() {
  console.log("Hello from f's handler!");
}

var handle= dojo.connect("f", myHandler);
```

When f is invoked, you'll see two console messages: "hello, world" followed by "Hello from f's handler!"

Connecting User-Defined Events

dojo.connect is an overloaded function that connects a handler to either a DOM event or a trigger function based upon the obj argument:

- If obj is a DOM node, then event (a string) must specify a DOM event defined by that node. This type of event was the subject of Section 6.1, *Programming DOM Events with Dojo*, on page 95.

- If obj is an object but not a DOM node, then obj[event] (event, a string) must specify a function, and this function is used as the trigger function.

- If obj is null or missing, then dojo.global[event] (event, a string) must specify a function, and this function is used as the trigger function. Notice that event is always a string; this gives dojo.connect a way to determine whether obj was omitted.

Here are examples of the last two usages:

```
Line 1   //missing obj; event is a string:
    -    dojo.connect("functionName", context, handler);
    -    //is equivalent to explicitly specifying null for eventOwner
    -    dojo.connect(null, "functionName", context, handler);
    5    //in both cases, the triggering function is dojo.global["functionName"]
    -    //(recall that dojo.global references the global object space)
    -
    -    //with a non-null obj, an object, not a DOM node:
    -    dojo.connect(obj, "functionName", context, handler);
   10    //the triggering function is obj["functionName"]
```

When dojo.connect is used to connect a handler to a trigger function, the handler is automatically invoked after the trigger function completes and is passed the same arguments that were provided to the trigger function. Unlike connecting multiple handlers to a DOM event, when multiple handler functions are connected to a triggering function, they are fired in the order in which they were connected.

The rest of dojo.connect works just as we've already discussed. The handler is always calculated to be dojo.hitch(context, handler) (context, optional, an object; handler, a string or function), and the returned value can be used to dojo.disconnect the handler.

Let's drive these points home with a quick example. We'll define a function printArgs that simply prints out its arguments to the console. Then we'll hook up two handlers to printArgs that also print their arguments. So we can keep everything straight in the output, we'll have each function print it name. Here is the code:

```
Line 1   //print functionName (a string) and all of the elements of args (an array)
    -    //to the console
    -    function giveMessage(functionName, args) {
    -      var message= "In " + functionName + "; the arguments are: ";
    5      dojo.forEach(args, function(arg){message+= arg.toString() + " ";});
    -      console.log(message);
    -    }
    -
    -    //here is the function that we'll hook up to generate the event...
   10    function printArgs() {
    -      giveMessage("printArgs", arguments);
    -    }
    -
    -    //here is the first event handler...
   15    function firstHandler() {
    -      //this handler uses the arguments object to gain access to its arguments
    -      giveMessage("firstHandler", arguments);
    -    }
    -
```

```
20   //and the second event handler...
     function secondHandler(a1, a2) {
       //this handler explicitly declares what it expects for arguments
       giveMessage("secondHandler", [a1, a2]);
     }
25
     //connect the firstHandler to fire whenever printArgs is invoked...
     dojo.connect("printArgs", null, "firstHandler");

     //and likewise for secondHandler....
30   dojo.connect("printArgs", null, "secondHandler");

     //let's exercise our exercise...
     printArgs(1, 2);
```

When you run this code, you'll see the following console messages, in order:

1. "In printArgs; the arguments are: 1 2"

2. "In firstHandler; the arguments are: 1 2"

3. "In secondHandler; the arguments are: 1 2"

Notice that the handlers were called in the order that they were connected, and the arguments passed to the handlers were exactly those passed to the triggering function.

There is one small gotcha: in order to work its magic, Dojo replaces the original trigger function with a new function that orchestrates calling both the original trigger function and the handlers. If you come along later and replace the Dojo-provided trigger function with another function, the events will stop firing. So if you need to replace a triggering function, you must reconnect any handlers connected to that function. Disconnecting the old handlers is optional. So long as you don't hold on to a copy of the handles returned by dojo.connect, all objects created after the old connections will be garbage collected.

Dojo itself leverages dojo.connect to provide a publish-subscribe framework.

6.3 Publish-Subscribe

In Section 3.6, *Errors and Debugging*, on page 60, we used publish-subscribe to publish messages (XHR failure information) about xhrError. A Toaster widget that subscribed to the topic popped up on the screen and displayed the failure information when an XHR transaction failed. The cool thing about the whole design was that a single Toaster widget that subscribed to the xhrError topic just once could receive and process any number of messages from any number of sources; similarly, the XHR error functions didn't even know that a Toaster widget existed. We skipped a lot of detail when we gave the Toaster example; let's cover the whole story now.

In the publish-subscribe pattern, several functions register their interest in a "topic." Later, some process can publish something about the topic. Of course, in the context of a JavaScript program, the "something" published is just a set of arguments, and the action of "publishing" is accomplished by calling each subscriber with the given arguments. Dojo implements this pattern by providing three functions:

handle= dojo.subscribe(topic, context, handler)

> Causes the function given by dojo.hitch(context, handler) to be invoked when topic (a string) is published via dojo.publish. Returns handle that may be used to take down the connection by dojo. unsubscribe (see next).

dojo.unsubscribe(handle)

> Removes the connection previously made by dojo.subscribe. handle is the object returned by dojo.subscribe.

dojo.publish(topic, args)

> Publishes topic (a string) by calling all subscribers to the topic, passing the arguments given by args (an array) to each subscriber. The subscribing functions are called in the order in which they were subscribed.

Dojo leverages its own event machinery to implement publish-subscribe in about four lines of code. For all of us old C++ systems programmers, *that's* impressive! Take a look at connect.js in the Dojo source if you are interested.

Let's create a little example to demonstrate just how publish-subscribe works. Assume we have the topic "Numbers" that "publishes" numbers one at a time. Further assume that we are interested in accumulating the total of the numbers published as well as printing the current total after each publication. Here's one way to solve this problem with publish-subscribe:

1. Define an accumulator object that has a method that accumulates a running total; subscribe the method to the "Numbers" topic.
2. Define a function that prints the current total as given by the accumulator; subscribe this function to the "Numbers" topic.

Here is the code:

```
//a simple object that accumulates a sum of numbers...
var numberAccumulator = {
  total: 0,
  add: function(x){this.total+= x;}
};

//subscribe numberAccumulator.add to the topic "Numbers"
dojo.subscribe("Numbers", numberAccumulator, "add");

//prints numberAccumulator.total
function showTotal() {
  console.log("The total is: " + numberAccumulator.total);
}

//subscribe showTotal to the topic "Numbers"
dojo.subscribe("Numbers", showTotal);

//test it...
//NOTE: arguments passed as an array!
dojo.publish("Numbers", [1]);
dojo.publish("Numbers", [2]);
```

The program prints the following messages to the console in order:

1. "The total is 1"

2. "The total is 3"

dojo.publish("numbers", [1]) causes a call to numberAccumulator.add(1) followed by a call to showTotal(1). This demonstrates how dojo.publish *must* be provided an array for its second argument, but it deals the contents of the array out as individual arguments to all subscribed functions. Since showTotal doesn't care about the arguments, it just ignores them.

Also notice that the example demonstrates how to connect a handler that is a method on an object (line 8) as well as just a simple function (line 16).

Publish-subscribe is a very useful design pattern. The key to its power lies in its ability to separate concerns. The "publishing" process need not concern itself with the consequences of publishing but rather is concerned *only* with knowing when and what to publish. On the other hand, subscribers need concern themselves only with taking actions consequent to some publication. Indeed, publishers and subscribers don't even need to know about each other. Since each process (that is, each publisher and each subscriber) is independent, the complexity of each process is consequently decreased, which, in turn, increases the chances that each process will function as desired.

All things considered, both DOM and user-defined events are fairly easy to understand and use, particularly since Dojo works out browser incompatibilities for us. When we start working with more complicated asynchronous processes, this won't be true, and we'll want and need more capabilities. So, let's turn our attention to these more advanced models starting with Dojo's Deferred class.

6.4 Managing Callbacks with dojo.Deferred

Event programming is an example of a simple, loosely coupled asynchronous programming system. Communications between triggering functions and handlers are conceptually limited to a binary signal that says an event occurred. Yes, there is the event object, but the information contained within the object is very generic in nature. There is no provision for communicating more-elaborate results (for example, error conditions), and there isn't any process control (for example, canceling or chaining the handlers). Sometimes, more is needed.

In this section, we're going to explore dojo.Deferred—a Dojo class that manages more advanced interactions between an asynchronous function and one or more callback functions. Since some of the conceptual framework can be a bit abstract and theoretical, we'll work through a real-world example that illustrates how to use Deferreds effectively. Along the way, we'll see that building systems with Deferreds results in powerful, simple, and elegant solutions to otherwise-complicated asynchronous programming problems.

The Example: Building a High-Performance Display Engine

Let us consider the example of displaying a panel of data from a database. The process is governed by a display engine that makes a request to the server for both the metadata (background decoration, layout information, and user interaction logic) and the data (ultimately defined by some query). When the metadata arrives, the panel is created and initialized with various HTML controls, decorations, and event logic. Similarly, the data is stored in a cache when it arrives. Finally, after *both* the metadata and the data arrive, the data is pushed into the HTML controls on the panel, and the panel is released to the user.

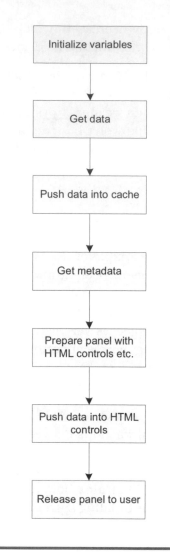

Figure 6.4: NAÏVE DISPLAY ENGINE DESIGN

A naïve implementation might use the algorithm given in Figure 6.4. The good thing about this design is that it is very simple and would surely work. Unfortunately, the browser may freeze for several seconds while the data and metadata are being retrieved. Further, the design retrieves and processes the metadata and data serially rather than concurrently as expressed by the process description. Our goal is to come up with an implementation that solves these problems while keeping the design simple.

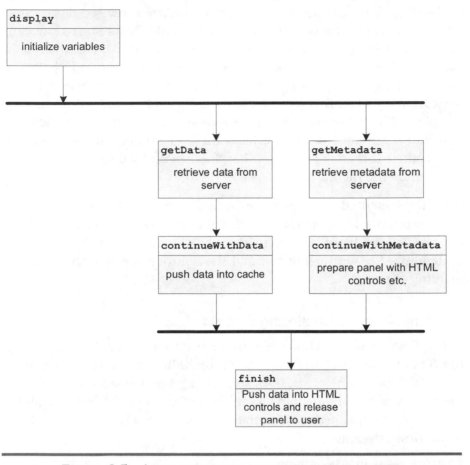

Figure 6.5: ASYNCHRONOUS DISPLAY ENGINE DESIGN

To achieve our goal, the metadata and data service requests are executed independently and asynchronously. This will keep the browser from freezing. Here are a few other reasons for this design:

- It is possible—even likely—that the metadata is already in a local browser cache. However, if we bundle the metadata with the data, then there is no chance that the metadata would ever be cached since the data is always changing.

- It's also possible that the metadata may be cached at an edge server, a physically different server than where the data resides. Clearly, two independent queries ought to be used in this scenario.

- After either the metadata or the data is received, there is some processing that takes place before both items are required to complete the overall task. Why not get this work done with the first arriving component while the other component is still transmitting?

In Figure 6.5, on the previous page, you can see a revised design that uses two asynchronous processes. The algorithm gets started by calling display, which sets up some infrastructure to coordinate the rest of the work, fires off two asynchronous functions (getData and getMetadata), and then returns. The asynchronous functions signal two callback functions (continueWithData and continueWithMetadata) when they complete. The callbacks take processing as far as possible along each fork and then call finish, which joins the two asynchronous processes into a single thread of execution that finishes up by displaying the data as given by the metadata.

If we implemented this system in terms of user-defined events, we'd have to build a fair amount of scaffolding that has nothing to do with the problem at hand. Fortunately, dojo.deferred already contains this scaffolding. So, we'll use it to build the solution. Let's start by implementing display.

Implementing the Controlling Process

Notice that the various functions are tightly coupled, as depicted in Figure 6.5, on the preceding page. Each function takes some information from the function before it, does something, and passes information to the next function. By defining all the functions within the display function, we can implement this coupling by sharing a local variable. Here is our first attempt:

```
Line 1  //implements a display engine:
        //display the data given by query in the panel given by panelId
        function display(panelId, query){

5         //displayInfo is a shared bookkeeping area
          var displayInfo = {
            panelId: panelId,
            query: query,
            processCompleteCount: 0
10        };

          //get an HTML div in which to place the panel
          //allocatePanel is provided by the pane management logic of our application
          displayInfo.div = allocatePanel(displayInfo);
15
          //TODO #1
          //make an asynchronous call to get the data
          //after the asynchronous call finishes,
          //continue by calling continueWithData
20
```

```
    //TODO #2
    //make an asynchronous call to get the metadata
    //after the asynchronous call finishes,
    //continue by calling continueWithMetadata

    //process the data as far as we can without the metadata
    function continueWithData(data){
      //put the data in an application-wide cache
      //for use with other requests
      //no need to wait for the metadata to do this!
      cacheData(data);

      //save quick access to the data
      displayInfo.data = data;

      finishDisplay();
    }

    //process the metadata as far as we can without the data
    function continueWithMetadata(metadata){
      //set up the HTML and other control structures
      //given by the metadata
      //no need to wait for the data to do this!
      preparePanel(metadata);

      //save quick access to the metadata
      displayInfo.metadata = metadata;

      finishDisplay();
    }

    //when continueWithData and continueWithMetadata have completed,
    //finish with the display process
    function finishDisplay(){
      //TODO #3
    }
  }
```

Try reading the code like a novel. Read each line, including comments, sequentially. We think this code is really elegant, and it's all because of the powerful programming paradigm that dojo.Deferred provides.

As for the TODOs, somehow we have to query the server for the data/ metadata asynchronously and then, upon completion of each of these functions, call continueWithData/continueWithMetaData, passing the received data/metadata. So, we need machinery to coordinate an asynchronous function call with a callback function. This is exactly what dojo.Deferred does.

Registering Callbacks with dojo.Deferred

dojo.Deferred is a constructor function that creates objects that manage the interaction between a single asynchronous function call, a chain of one or more callback functions, and other clients that are interested in the asynchronous operation.[5] The Deferred interface includes methods for the asynchronous function to signal normal or abnormal completion and return results as well as methods that let other clients:

- Specify a chain of functions to execute upon normal and/or abnormal completion of the asynchronous function (that is, a chain of callbacks).

- Check to see whether the asynchronous function completed and, if so, access any results returned.

- Cancel waiting for the asynchronous function.

Typically, the process making the asynchronous call creates a Deferred instance, shares it with the asynchronous function, adds one or more callbacks, and then forgets about it.

Getting back to our example, we have two independent callback functions, namely, continueWithData and continueWithMetadata, which continue after the asynchronous functions that get the data and metadata complete. We can use Deferreds to set this up:

```
Line 1   //TODO #1 partial implementation...
         displayInfo.dataDeferred= new dojo.Deferred();
         displayInfo.dataDeferred.addCallback(continueWithData);
         //still TODO:
     5   //somehow, get the data asynchronously and signal
         //displayInfo.dataDeferred when this completes

         //TODO #2 partial implementation...
         displayInfo.metadataDeferred= new dojo.Deferred();
    10   displayInfo.metadataDeferred.addCallback(continueWithMetadata);
         //still TODO:
         //somehow, get the metadata asynchronously and signal
         //displayInfo.metadataDeferred when this completes
```

The example shows that callback functions are registered by calling the Deferred method addCallback. We will discuss registering callback functions in detail in Section 6.4, *Specifying Callbacks and Errbacks*, on page 126.

---

5. Remember, any Dojo function that starts with a capital letter is a constructor function and consequently defines a class.

The asynchronous functions that retrieve the data and metadata could be some kind of remote scripting call (see Chapter 8, *Remote Scripting with XHR, script, and iframe*, on page 173) or a call to a Java applet, plug-in, or some other kind of browser extension. From the perspective of the display engine, it doesn't matter how the data/metadata is actually retrieved; all that matters is that when the data/metadata arrives, the Deferred objects are notified of the result.

We've implemented the asynchronous functions as mock services. They take a reference to the passed Deferred as well as the data query/metadata panelId. The completed example included in the code download displays a form with buttons to signal success or failure. If the success button is clicked, then the mock service calls the callback method of the associated Deferred, passing back the query/panelId. We'll talk about handling errors after we get the success case worked out. Here is how the asynchronous mock data service is implemented:

```
Line 1   var theDataRequest;   //holds the data query
    -    var theDataDeferred; //holds the Deferred that controls the data service
    -
    -    //the data service asynchronous function call...
    5    function makeAsynchronousServerDataCall(theDeferred, theRequest){
    -        theDataDeferred= theDeferred;
    -        theDataRequest= theRequest;
    -
    -        //the "real" asynchronous call would go here;
   10        //the mock server just displays the request in the form...
    -        dojo.byId("serverMockDataQuery").innerHTML= theRequest;
    -    }
    -
    -    //success and fail event handlers to simulate a service...
   15    function returnData(e){
    -        dojo.stopEvent(e);
    -        theDataDeferred.callback("result("+theDataRequest+")");
    -    }
    -    function failData(e){
   20        dojo.stopEvent(e);
    -        theDataDeferred.errback("failed");
    -    }
    -    //hook up the handlers to the form buttons...
    -    dojo.addOnLoad(function(){
   25        dojo.connect(dojo.byId("dataReturn"), "click", returnData);
    -        dojo.connect(dojo.byId("dataError"), "click", failData);
    -    });
```

Deferred.callback is always passed a single argument that holds the result of the asynchronous function computation (line 17). Since JavaScript is not capable of returning multiple results as some languages do, exactly one argument is expected. In the event you need to pass multiple results, simply wrap the results in either an array or an object. Here is the HTML form that makes the mock service go:

```
Line 1  <div>
   -      <h1>Server Mock</h1>
   -      <form class="request">
   -        <p>The data query is...</p>
   5        <p id= "serverMockDataQuery"></p>
   -        <p>
   -          <input id="dataReturn" type="submit" name="dataReturn" value="Send It!">
   -        </p>
   -        <p>
   10         <input id="dataError" type="submit" name="dataError" value="Signal Error">
   -        </p>
   -      </form>
   -    </div>
```

With this and similar code in place for the metadata service, we can complete TODO #1 and #2:

```
Line 1  //TODO #1 implementation...
   -    displayInfo.dataDeferred= new dojo.Deferred();
   -    displayInfo.dataDeferred.addCallback(continueWithData);
   -    makeAsynchronousServerDataCall(displayInfo.dataDeferred, query);
   5
   -    //TODO #2 implementation...
   -    displayInfo.metadataDeferred= new dojo.Deferred();
   -    displayInfo.metadataDeferred.addCallback(continueWithMetadata);
   -    makeAsynchronousServerMetadataCall(displayInfo.metadataDeferred, panelId);
```

Let's now turn to TODO #3, which joins the two asynchronous callback functions once they've both completed. The idea is to keep track of how many asynchronous processes have completed and, when they've all completed, continue with the process. Here is the JavaScript:

```
Line 1  //when continueWithData and continueWithMetadata have completed,
   -    //finish with the display process
   -    function finishDisplay() {
   -      //TODO #3 implementation...
   5      displayInfo.processCompleteCount++;
   -      if (displayInfo.processCompleteCount==2) {
   -        //both have completed...
   -        populatePanelWithData(displayInfo);
   -        releasePanelToUser(displayInfo);
   10     }
   -    }
```

The example also nicely demonstrates how to fork a single process into several processes (implemented as asynchronous function calls) and later join the processes back into a single process.

At this point, the basic display engine is complete and works perfectly so long as no abnormal conditions are encountered. If you step back for a moment, you'll notice a fairly complex algorithm was expressed in very clear and concise code. This was one of the promises we made at the beginning. Next we'll expand on the solution to include error handling.

Handling Errors

What should we do if either or both asynchronous calls fail? Perhaps the panel div was initialized with a message saying "Retrieving Data." If either asynchronous function fails, this message will stay forever, without any further notification to the user about the true status of the request. We must do better.

dojo.Deferred can register callback functions to execute if/when an error occurs. To avoid confusing "error path" callbacks with normal path callbacks, we'll call them *errbacks*. Naturally, they are registered with the dojo.Deferred method addErrback.

For our display engine, upon failure of either asynchronous function, we can use addErrback to hook up an errback that asks the user if he would like to retry the operation. If the user says "OK," then a new asynchronous function call is made; if the user says "cancel," then the div can be filled with a message saying the request failed.

Since the new design sets up the asynchronous function calls twice—the initial call and the call made by the retry—let's encapsulate this work in a couple of functions. Here's the code for getting the data (the code for getting the metadata looks similar):

```
Line 1  //important: this is put inside the function display()
        function getData() {
          displayInfo.dataDeferred= new dojo.Deferred();
          displayInfo.dataDeferred.addCallback(continueWithData);
      5   displayInfo.dataDeferred.addErrback(handleDataError);
          makeAsynchronousServerDataCall(displayInfo.dataDeferred, query);
        }
```

We've done two things here. First, we encapsulated TODO #1 in the function getData. getData must be defined within the body of the function display so that all the referenced functions and data are visible. Second, in addition to registering a callback function, we registered the errback function handleDataError (line 5).

Next, let's write handleDataError; it's trivial:

```
Line 1  //important: this is put inside the function display()

     -  //informs the user that an error occurred retrieving the data
     -  //gives the user the option to retry or cancel
     5  function handleDataError(){
     -    giveRetryCancelMessage(
     -      "The server failed to deliver the data.",
     -      getData,      //retry function
     -      function() { //cancel function
    10        doCancel(displayInfo.dataDeferred);
     -      }
     -    );
     -  }
```

The implementation of giveRetryCancelMessage isn't important to the discussion. It simply displays a dialog box that presents a message, asks the user whether she would like to retry or cancel, and provides OK/cancel push buttons. When the user clicks one of the buttons, giveRetryCancelMessage calls the appropriate function. Since getData is given as the retry function, another asynchronous call will be attempted if the user selects retry. Similarly, if the user clicks cancel, doCancel will be called. We'll say more about doCancel in a moment.

Our display engine is nearly complete. But before we do more, let's take a closer look at registering callbacks and errbacks.

Specifying Callbacks and Errbacks

The callback processing in the example is simple: if the asynchronous call succeeds, call one function (for example, continueWithData); otherwise, call another function (for example, handleDataError). Most of the time, this is all you'll need. For more-complex scenarios, Deferreds are capable of registering a list of callback and errback functions, and the functions will be executed in the order they were registered.

Deferreds maintain a queue that holds the functions waiting to execute. Callback/errbacks are always added to the queue in pairs—a callback paired with an errback. As the queue is traversed, one or the other functions is called depending upon whether the Deferred instance is in a normal or error state (we'll discuss these states in a moment).

There are four methods for appending continuation functions to the end of the queue:

addCallback(context, f)

> Add the (callback, errback) pair given by (dojo.hitch(context, f), null). When a null is encountered while traversing the queue, the entry is just ignored, and processing proceeds to the next entry.

addErrback(context, f)

> Add the (callback, errback) pair given by (null, dojo.hitch(context, f)); null is handled as described previously.

addBoth(context, f)

> Add the (callback, errback) pair given by (dojo.hitch(context, f), dojo.hitch(context, f)).

addCallbacks(callback, errback)

> Add the (callback, errback) pair given by (callback, errback).

Any of these methods can be called during the lifetime of the Deferred object. If the asynchronous call has already been completed and the queue is empty, then the newly registered callback/errback is executed immediately; otherwise, it goes to the back of the queue.

Each successive callback/errback is passed the result of the previous function in the queue. So, the first callback/errback is passed the result of the asynchronous function, the second callback/errback is passed the result of the first, and so on.

A Deferred enters an error state under any of the following conditions:

- The asynchronous function returns a result by calling the Deferred method errback.
- The asynchronous function or any subsequent callback/errback returns a result that is an instanceof Error.
- Any callback/errback throws an exception. If this occurs, then the Deferred instance will catch the exception, and the caught exception object becomes the next result.

On the other hand, a Deferred enters a nonerror state when the original asynchronous function or any subsequent callback/errback returns a result that is not an instanceof Error. This means that a Deferred object can enter into and out of an error state, and as the queue is traversed, either the callback or errback function is executed depending on the error state (that is, processing can switch back and forth between the callback and errback functions).

You can always query the current state of a Deferred object through its fired property:

- -1 indicates that the Deferred object is still waiting for the asynchronous function to finish computing.

- 0 indicates that the Deferred object has received results and is in a nonerror state.

- 1 indicates that the Deferred object has received results and is in a error state.

Given a Deferred instance d, the last results computed are also always available through d.results[d.fired].

Of course, there's no limitation on the type of single argument that is returned. This brings up the mind-boggling possibility that a callback/errback might return a Deferred. When this happens, any subsequent callback/errback function is not called until the returned Deferred has results.

Canceling Callback Processing

Let's get back to our example. So far, the panel starts life by telling the user that it is working on retrieving the data. If everything goes as planned, the data is displayed after both the data and the metadata arrive. On the other hand, if an error occurs, the user is given the option to retry or cancel the operation. So at this point, the user can cancel the request only if an error occurs.

There are other situations where the request should be cancelable. For example, the user may want to cancel the operation before it either completes or returns an error. Other processes may like to cancel asynchronous processing as well. Deferred provides a solution to just this problem.

When the Deferred method cancel is called on a Deferred instance that is still waiting on the asynchronous function, it stops waiting, sets its internal state to indicate an error (sets its fired property to 1), and begins traversing the callback queue. On the other hand, if the asynchronous function has already returned results and the queue has already been traversed, cancel has no effect except for one very odd circumstance: if the last callback/errback executed returned yet another Deferred instance as *its* result, then this other Deferred is canceled.

The default cancel processing can be a bit harsh since it just creates a JavaScript Error instance and starts down the error callback queue. Fortunately, there is a gentler way. The Deferred constructor takes an optional single argument—a function termed the *canceler*. If cancel is invoked on a Deferred instance that was created with a canceler, then the canceler is called with that Deferred instance passed as an argument. Armed with this information, we can make the final adjustments to the function display.

First we need to write a canceler function. It should cancel the other Deferred and clean up the panel. Here it is:

```
//Important: this function is put inside the function display().
function doCancel(theDeferred) {

  //execute this routine for the first Deferred canceled only...
  if (!displayInfo.dataDeferred) {
    return;
  }

  //figure out which Deferred was canceled and take
  //a reference to the other Deferred
  var temp= displayInfo.dataDeferred==theDeferred ?
    displayInfo.metadataDeferred : displayInfo.dataDeferred;

  //ensure this routine is executed only once
  displayInfo.dataDeferred= null;
  displayInfo.metadataDeferred= null;

  //cancel the other Deferred
  temp.cancel();

  //clean up the display
  destroyPanel(displayInfo);
}
```

Because the Deferred instance that is canceled first must cancel the other Deferred instance, a little care is required to avoid infinite recursion. The first Deferred instance canceled clobbers both displayInfo.metadataDeferred and displayInfo.dataDeferred so that the canceler will return immediately when the other Deferred instance is canceled.

The canceler should be hooked up to both Deferred instances when they are created, so the following line...

```
displayInfo.dataDeferred= new dojo.Deferred();
```

should be replaced with this line:

```
displayInfo.dataDeferred= new dojo.Deferred(doCancel);
```

And this must also be done for displayInfo.metadataDeferred. It is important to remember that when a Deferred instance is canceled, the error functions in the callback queue will be invoked. Since we don't want to give the user a "retry/cancel" message after she cancels, we'll modify the function handleDataError to give the message box only if the process has *not* been canceled. Here is the revised handleDataError (the errback for getMetadata looks similar):

```
Line 1    //informs the user that an error occurred retrieving the metadata
   -      //gives the user the option to retry or cancel
   -      function handleDataError(){
   -        if (displayInfo.dataDeferred) {
   5          giveRetryCancelMessage(
   -            "The server failed to deliver the data.",
   -            getData,      //retry function
   -            function() { //cancel function
   -              doCancel(displayInfo.dataDeferred);
  10            }
   -          );
   -        } else {
   -          //the process was canceled
   -        }
  15      }
```

Finally, a cancel button could be placed on the initial panel that currently says "Retrieving Data," and a click handler should be connected that executes displayInfo.dataDeferred.cancel().

That's it for our display example. We included the completed display function here so that you can read the finished code in a single, continuous presentation. A fully operational example, including mock data and metadata services, is available in the code download.

asynchronous-programming/deferred.htm

```
Line 1    function display(panelId, query) {
   -
   -        //displayInfo is a shared bookkeeping area
   -        var displayInfo= {
   5          panelId: panelId,
   -          query: query,
   -          processCompleteCount: 0};
   -
   -        //get an HTML div in which to place the panel
  10        displayInfo.div= allocatePanel(displayInfo);
   -
   -        getData();
```

```
  -     getMetadata();
  -
15      function getData() {
  -       displayInfo.dataDeferred= new dojo.Deferred(doCancel);
  -       displayInfo.dataDeferred.addCallback(continueWithData);
  -       displayInfo.dataDeferred.addErrback(handleDataError);
  -       makeAsynchronousServerDataCall(displayInfo.dataDeferred, query);
20      }
  -
  -     function getMetadata() {
  -       displayInfo.metadataDeferred= new dojo.Deferred(doCancel);
  -       displayInfo.metadataDeferred.addCallback(continueWithMetadata);
25        displayInfo.metadataDeferred.addErrback(handleMetadataError);
  -       makeAsynchronousServerMetadataCall(displayInfo.metadataDeferred, panelId);
  -     }
  -
  -     //process the data as far as we can without the metadata
30      function continueWithData(data){
  -       //put the data in an application-wide cache
  -       //for use with other requests...
  -       cacheData(data);
  -
35        //save quick access to the data
  -       displayInfo.data= data;
  -
  -       finishDisplay();
  -     }
40
  -     //process the metadata as far as we can without the data
  -     function continueWithMetadata(metadata) {
  -       //start to set up the HTML and other control structures
  -       //given by the metadata...
45        preparePanel(metadata);
  -
  -       //save quick access to the metadata
  -       displayInfo.metadata= metadata;
  -
50        finishDisplay();
  -     }
  -
  -     //when continueWithData and continueWithMetadata have completed,
  -     //finish with the display process
55      function finishDisplay() {
  -       displayInfo.processCompleteCount++;
  -       if (displayInfo.processCompleteCount==2) {
  -         //both have completed...
  -         populatePanelWithData(displayInfo);
60        releasePanelToUser(displayInfo);
  -       }
  -     }
  -
```

```
        function handleDataError(){
65        if (displayInfo.dataDeferred) {
            giveRetryCancelMessage(
              "The server failed to deliver the data.",
              getData,     //retry function
              function() { //cancel function
70              doCancel(displayInfo.dataDeferred);
              }
            );
          } else {
            //the process was canceled
75        }
        }


        function handleMetadataError(){
          if (displayInfo.metadataDeferred) {
80          giveRetryCancelMessage(
              "The server failed to deliver the metadata.",
              getMetadata, //retry function
              function() { //cancel function
                doCancel(displayInfo.metadataDeferred);
85            }
            );
          } else {
            //the process was canceled
          }
90      }


        function doCancel(theDeferred) {

          //execute this routine for the first Deferred canceled only...
95        if (!displayInfo.dataDeferred) {
            return;
          }

          //figure out which Deferred was canceled and take
100         //a reference to the other Deferred
          var temp= displayInfo.dataDeferred==theDeferred ?
            displayInfo.metadataDeferred : displayInfo.dataDeferred;

          //ensure this routine is executed only once
105         displayInfo.dataDeferred= null;
          displayInfo.metadataDeferred= null;

          //cancel the other Deferred
          temp.cancel();
110
          //clean up the display
          destroyPanel(displayInfo);
        }
      }
```

The example is fairly powerful. It has normal processing, has full error recovery, and is user cancelable. The code is easy to read and understand while also being very concise. We could have wired all this functionality together with events, but Dojo's Deferred did most of the work for us, so this was unnecessary.

If you find yourself having trouble with Deferreds, try not to worry too much about how they do things; instead, concentrate on what they do. Also, there's no need to bother with Deferreds unless the design includes problems like chaining callbacks and/or canceling. Deferreds shine in these situations, transforming an unmanageable mess of spaghetti into clean code.

Chapter 7

DOM Utilities

Document Object Model (DOM) programming seems almost trivial. The document is represented by a tree of nodes, and each node has a set of properties. You control the appearance of the document by inserting, deleting, and/or moving nodes and editing their properties. Too bad it's really not *that* easy.

As usual, the browser environment makes simple things difficult. Although the W3C-specified DOM API is fairly complete, it's frequently inconvenient.[1] Often, several lines of JavaScript are required to accomplish a trivial programming chore. And then there's the always-present browser incompatibilities.

Much of Dojo was built to solve this problem. We've already seen this at a high level of abstraction with Dijit widgets back in Chapter 2, *Powerful Web Forms Made Easy*, on page 13. But sometimes you need to be closer to the metal and manipulate raw DOM nodes directly. Dojo includes low-level functions that make this work easier, allowing you to do more in fewer lines than you thought possible. We'll show you how in this chapter as we explore Dojo functions that find, insert, delete, and move nodes as well as functions that get/set styles, classes, and other attributes.

7.1 Core Dojo DOM Utility Functions

We'll spend most of this chapter refining an ugly, static HTML document into an elegant, dynamic user interface; it'll even include a little animation. But, first we need to cover some basic Dojo DOM utility

---

1. The W3C DOM specifications begin at http://www.w3.org/DOM/DOMTR.

functions that you just can't live without. Knocking these out now will also keep us moving quickly through the rest of the material.

Perhaps the most basic DOM programming task is grabbing a Java-Script reference to a DOM node using the value of an id attribute. The W3C DOM API provides the function getElementById to do this. Unfortunately, Internet Explorer figured out how to implement it incorrectly.[2] Dojo includes the function dojo.byId that works across all browsers. dojo.byId takes a string argument that gives the value of the id attribute for a target DOM node and returns a reference to that node.[3] An optional second argument (a DOM Document object) may be provided to indicate the document to search. If missing, then dojo.doc—equivalent to window["document"] unless explicitly changed—is assumed.

Given a reference to a DOM node, setting/getting the node's class, style, and/or other attributes are chores you'll do again and again. The native APIs provided by the major browsers are all somewhat painful owing to the W3C specification, browser incompatibilities, or both. Dojo provides alternative functions:

- dojo.hasClass/dojo.addClass/dojo.removeClass/dojo.toggleClass: Tests for/adds/removes/toggles a class string within a node's class attribute. Since the class attribute can contain a list of several classes, these functions eliminate the tedious string work that is required when working with single class names within the list.
- dojo.style: Gets and sets the style for a node; normalizes for browser incompatibilities.
- dojo.attr/dojo.hasAttr/dojo.removeAttr: Gets and sets/tests/removes attribute values from a node.

The first argument to all of these functions is either a DOM node or a string that gives the id attribute value of a DOM node. If an id string is given, then the target node is always retrieved by calling dojo.byId. The operation of these functions is fairly trivial, but each function has a few subtleties that are easily missed by skimming the reference manual. So, we'll demonstrate each function, including the subtleties.

The class functions (hasClass, removeClass, toggleClass, and addClass) all take two arguments—a node and a class string. Usually, the class string contains a single class name, but this need not be the case.

---

2. getElementById will fail in Internet Explorer and Opera (fixed at v9.50a1) in some cases; see http://webbugtrack.blogspot.com/2007/08/bug-152-getelementbyid-returns.html for the story.
3. dojo.byId also accepts a DOM node for the first argument in which case it just returns the node. This can be useful for writing functions that take either a DOM node or an id attribute value—as do most of Dojo's DOM utility functions.

Here's a Firebug console session that shows some examples:

dom/core-dom-utils.js

```
Line 1   >>> //get a node to play with...
         >>> var node= dojo.byId("top");

         >>> //class names are added to the right side...
5        >>> dojo.addClass(node, "c1");
         >>> node.className;
         "c1"
         >>> dojo.addClass(node, "c2");
         >>> node.className;
10       "c1 c2"

         >>> //adding a class already there does nothing...
         >>> dojo.addClass(node, "c2");
         >>> node.className
15       "c1 c2"

         >>> //"c2 c1" NOT already there...
         >>> dojo.addClass(node, "c2 c1");
         >>> node.className;
20       "c1 c2 c2 c1"

         >>> //nothing surprising here...
         >>> dojo.hasClass(node, "c1");
         true
25       >>> dojo.hasClass(node, "c2");
         true
         >>> dojo.hasClass(node, "c1 c2 c2");
         true
         >>> dojo.hasClass(node, "c3");
30       false

         >>> //classes are removed from the left side...
         >>> dojo.removeClass(node, "c1");
         >>> node.className;
35       "c2 c2 c1"
         >>> dojo.removeClass(node, "c2 c2");
         >>> node.className;
         "c1"

40       >>> //nothing surprising here...
         >>> dojo.toggleClass(node, "c2");
         >>> node.className;
         "c1 c2"
         >>> dojo.toggleClass(node, "c2");
45       >>> node.className;
         "c1"
```

At line 18, adding the class string "c2 c1" to the className attribute with a current value of "c1 c2" demonstrates the biggest gotcha. dojo.addClass appends a *string value* (not necessarily a single class name) to a class-Name attribute value if that string value doesn't already exist in the current value. Since "c2 c1" does not exist in "c1 c2", it is appended, resulting in a new className attribute value of "c1 c2 c2 c1".

dojo.toggleClass can take a third argument (a boolean) that explicitly adds or removes the class string. This provides some syntactic sugar that can make some expressions more palatable:

`dom/core-dom-utils.js`

```
Line 1   //assume error is a boolean...
    -
    -    if (error) {
    -      dojo.addClass(someNode, "displayAsError");
    5    } else {
    -      dojo.removeClass(someNode, "displayAsError");
    -    }
    -
    -    //becomes...
    10
    -    dojo.toggleClass(someNode, "displayAsError", error);
```

Next, we'll look at dojo.style. This function can take one, two, or three arguments. As usual, the first argument is a DOM node or id string. If only one argument is given, then a W3C computed style object is returned. The second argument (a string) identifies a style to get or set. Finally, the third argument (a string) provides a style value to set. Here's more of the previous Firebug console session that demonstrates these functions:

`dom/core-dom-utils.js`

```
Line 1   >>> //single-argument variety => a getter
    -    >>> //returns a reference to a computed style object just
    -    >>> //like the DOM Window.getComputedStyle function
    -    >>> dojo.style(node);
    5    ComputedCSSStyleDeclaration borderLeftWidth=0px borderTopWidth=0px
    -
    -    >>> //three-argument variety => a setter
    -    >>> //styles values are just like in a style sheet
    -    >>> dojo.style(node, "border", "2px solid black");
    10   "2px solid black"
    -
    -    >>> //two-argument variety => a getter for a particular style
    -    >>> //NOTE: style names are CAMEL CASE!
    -    >>> dojo.style(node, "borderTopWidth");
    15   2
    -
    -    >>> //this WILL NOT WORK! (style names are camel case)
    -    >>> dojo.style(node, "border-top-width");
    -    0
```

Notice that style names are the same as those defined by the style property of a DOM node, not the names used in a style sheet (for example, borderTopWidth, *not* border-top-width).

Finally, the attribute functions take a DOM node or id string, an attribute name (a string), and optionally an attribute value (a string). The two-argument varieties test, get, or remove the attribute; the three-argument version sets the attribute:

dom/core-dom-utils.js

```
Line 1    >>> //3 arguments => setter
   -      >>> //sets the attribute "name" to "foo"
   -      >>> dojo.attr(node, "name", "foo");
   -
   5      >>> //2 arguments => getter
   -      >>> //returns "foo"
   -      >>> dojo.attr(node, "name");
   -      "foo"
   -
  10      >>> //no surprise here...
   -      >>> dojo.hasAttr(node, "name");
   -      true
   -
   -      >>> //this all works with user-defined attributes...
  15      >>> //add an attribute..
   -      >>> dojo.attr(node, "myAttrib", "myValue");
   -
   -      >>> //get its value...
   -      >>> dojo.attr(node, "myAttrib");
  20      "myValue"
   -
   -      >>> //check existence...
   -      >>> dojo.hasAttr(node, "myAttrib");
   -      true
  25
   -      >>> //remove it...
   -      >>> dojo.removeAttr(node, "myAttrib");
   -      >>> dojo.hasAttr(node, "myAttrib");
   -      false
```

There's also an alternative two-argument setter that takes a hash for the second argument that contains a set of (attribute-name, attribute-value) pairs to set. This is quite convenient when setting multiple attributes on the same node:

dom/core-dom-utils.js

```
Line 1    dojo.attr("nodeId", {
   -         tabIndex: "-1",
   -         customAttr: "custom value",
   -         title: "an awesome node"
   5      });
```

That's it for the necessary foundation. Let's move on to something more interesting.

7.2 Finding and Editing Nodes

We have a challenge. We've been given some trivial HTML that displays a list of questions:

dom/questions-book-frags.htm

```
Line 1   <body><div><form>
           <p>Programmer Interview Questions</p>
           <div class="questions">
             <p>
    5          <span><input type="radio" name="q1" value="yes">Yes</span>
               <span><input type="radio" name="q1" value="no">No</span>
               Are you a C programmer?
             </p><p>
               <span><input type="radio" name="q1-yes" value="yes">Yes</span>
   10          <span><input type="radio" name="q1-yes" value="no">No</span>
               <span><input type="radio" name="q1-yes" value="maybe">Don't know</span>
               Have you read Kernighan and Ritchie?
             </p><p>

   15          <!-- etc. -->

           </div>
         </form></div></body>
```

When rendered, it looks like Figure 7.1, on the facing page. Not too good. We need to fix it so that the questions are shown on alternating bands of light and dark gray, the options are lined up in columns, and the layout keeps looking good even when the user dynamically changes the viewport or text size. Also, notice how the second, fourth, sixth, and eighth questions are relevant only if the preceding question is answered "yes." We'll change the behavior of the form to animate an even question into view when its owning question is marked "yes" and out of view when marked "no."

But (there's always a but!), there are rules: we can't modify the source HTML (we can modify the contents of the head element); we *can* modify the DOM tree after the source is parsed by the browser; and, *no*, we can't cheat by replacing the whole thing with a JavaScript-generated table. We'll call this the "question-list challenge"; as we solve the puzzle, we'll demonstrate each major area covered by Dojo's DOM utility functions.

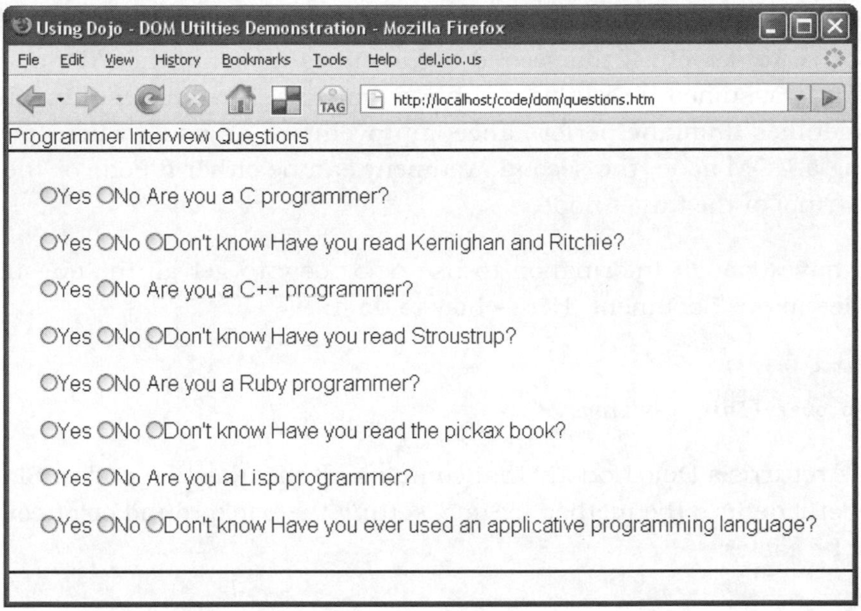

Figure 7.1: A POORLY FORMATTED SET OF QUESTIONS

dojo.query

As a first step, we'll color the background of the questions alternate shades of gray. To do this, we need to get the set of question nodes and then set the background color style as we traverse the list. Specifically, we need to get the set of p nodes that are descendents of the div node with the class questions. Hmmm...sounds like a CSS selector. But browsers don't give JavaScript access to their CSS query engines; fortunately, Dojo includes this functionality.[4]

The function dojo.query takes a CSS selector and returns an array of nodes that match the selector. The array of nodes is returned in a Dojo NodeList object, which behaves as if it were a subclass of Array. NodeLists include the Mozilla JavaScript 1.6 array extensions (discussed in Section 5.2, *JavaScript 1.6 Array Methods*, on page 84) as well as a few convenience functions for common node manipulation (we'll look at these in Section 7.2, *dojo.NodeList Capabilities*, on page 149).[5]

---

4. If you're not familiar with CSS selectors, [Mey06] is an excellent reference.
5. NodeList is not a subclass of Array but rather an Array object with several per-object

dojo.query also accepts an optional second argument that gives the subtree to search; if the second argument is missing, then the document is assumed. Providing a subtree limits the search, resulting in a sometimes-dramatic performance improvement. As usual when specifying a DOM node, the second argument can be either a node or the id (a string) of the target node.

We have enough information to use dojo.query to get all the question nodes in our document. Here's how to do it:

dom/frags.js

```
Line 1  dojo.query("div.questions p");
```

This returns a Dojo NodeList that contains all the question nodes. Since NodeList defines the method forEach, setting the background color could not be easier:

dom/questions1.htm

```
Line 1  dojo.query("div.questions p").forEach(function(node, i){
    -       dojo.addClass(node, (i % 2) ? "lightBand" : "darkBand");
    -     });
```

The code sets the class attribute on odd lines to lightBand and on even lines to darkBand.

The same technique can be used to fix up the form's title paragraph (the p element that contains the text "Programming Interview Questions"). We're after the first p element child of the form. The CSS selector form > p serves this up perfectly:

dom/questions1.htm

```
Line 1  dojo.addClass(dojo.query("form > p")[0], "formTitle");
```

There is a big gotcha here. dojo.query *always* returns a Dojo NodeList. It just doesn't matter that the particular CSS selector will find only a single element. So when you need to access a NodeList as if it were just a single element, you must specify this by selecting the first element with [0].[6]

---

methods added. Currently, it's impossible to derive from Array without undesirable side effects.

6. As we'll see in Section 7.2, *dojo.NodeList Capabilities*, on page 149, this line could also be written as dojo.query("form > p").addClass("formTitle");.

To make any of this work, we have to load dojo.js and a style sheet. Here's the head element:

```
dom/questions1.htm
```

```
Line 1   <head>
   -       <title>
   -        Mastering Dojo - DOM Utilities Demonstration - Question List Challenge Step 1
   -       </title>
   5
   -       <style type="text/css">
   -         @import "questions.css";
   -       </style>
   -
  10       <script
   -         type="text/javascript"
   -         src="/dojoroot/dojo/dojo.js"
   -         djConfig="isDebug: true">
   -       </script>
  15
   -       <script type="text/javascript">
   -         (function(){
   -           function layout1(){
   -             dojo.addClass(dojo.query("form > p")[0], "formTitle");
  20             dojo.query("div.questions p").forEach(function(node, i){
   -               dojo.addClass(node, (i % 2) ? "lightBand" : "darkBand");
   -             });
   -           }
   -
  25           dojo.addOnLoad(layout1);
   -         })();
   -       </script>
   -     </head>
```

See Section 6.1, *Executing Initialization Code with dojo.addOnLoad*, on page 105 if dojo.addOnLoad is hazy. Here is the style sheet:

```
dom/questions.css
```

```
Line 1   * {
   -       margin:0;
   -       border:0;
   -       padding:0;
   5       font-family:arial;
   -     }
   -
   -     body {
   -       background-color:#FCFCFC;
  10     }
   -
   -     .formTitle {
   -       padding: .5em;
```

```
          font-size:larger;
  15      font-weight:bold;
   -    }
   -
   -    div.question {
   -      overflow:hidden;
  20    }
   -
   -    .questions {
   -      border-top: 2px solid black;
   -      border-bottom: 2px solid black;
  25      padding: 1em;
   -    }
   -
   -    .questions p {
   -      padding: .5em;
  30    }
   -
   -    .lightBand {
   -      background-color:#EFEFEF;
   -    }
  35
   -    .darkBand {
   -      background-color:#E0E0E0;
   -    }
   -
  40    .choice {
   -      float:left;
   -      padding: .5em;
   -    }
```

At this point, the form looks like Figure 7.2, on the next page. We still have some work to do, but before we finish the challenge, let's take a moment to talk about dojo.query selectors and dojo.NodeList in detail.

dojo.query Selectors

dojo.query supports many (but not all) CSS 3 selectors, as specified at http://www.w3.org/TR/css3-selectors/#selectors. In Figure 7.3, on page 147, you can see the rows of the selector summary table, as it appears in the W3C standard, that are supported by dojo.query at the time of this writing [GÇH+05]. The second column gives an example of each query that can be used with the demonstration we'll develop in a moment.

dojo.query is likely to evolve and support more selectors as well as other types of query languages (for example, XPath). Currently, dojo.query is implemented in JavaScript since most browsers fail to give public access to their internal CSS query engines.

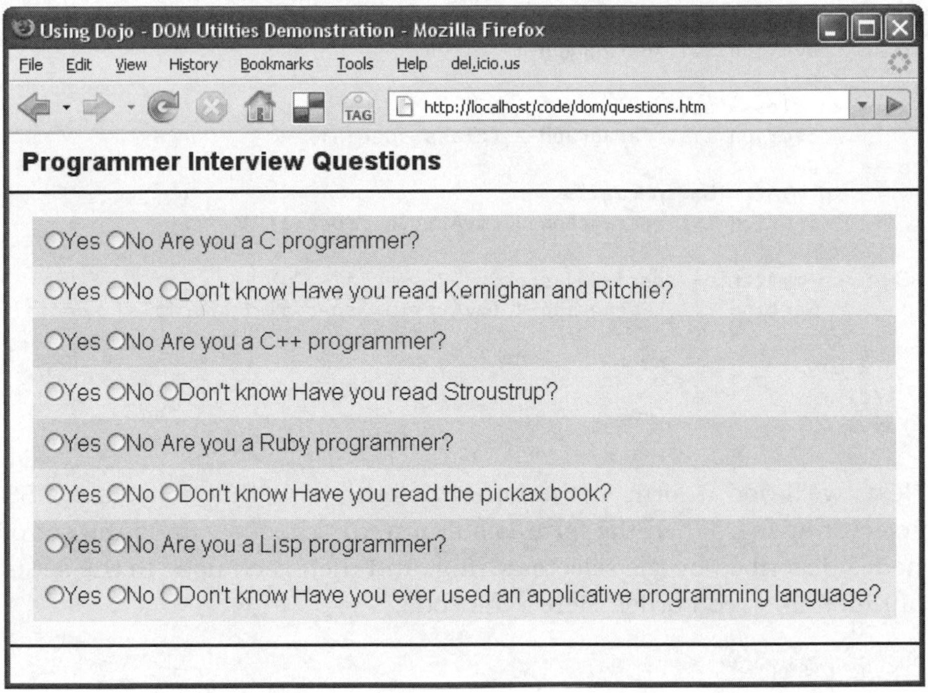

Figure 7.2: IMPROVEMENT

If/when browsers provide access, dojo.query will simply pass query requests through to the native CSS engine.

Let's build a demonstrator page that we can use to experiment with CSS selectors. First we need a little HTML document with enough elements, structure, classes, and attributes to demonstrate each selector in action:

`dom/query-demo.htm`

```
Line 1   <div id="fixture">
    -      <div class="section1">
    -        <h1>
    -          Section 1
    5        </h1>
    -        <p>
    -          Introduction Text
    -        </p>
    -        <div class="section1-1" >
    10         <h2>
    -            Section 1.1
    -          </h2>
```

```
-           <p>
-             Section 1.1, Paragraph-1
15          </p>
-           <p class="special">
-             Section 1.1, Paragraph-2 (class=special)
-           </p>
-           <p myAttrib="special">
20            Section 1.1, Paragraph-3 (myAttrib="special")
-           </p>
-           <p myAttrib="special-1 special-2 special-3">
-             Section 1.1, Paragraph-4 (myAttrib="special-1 special-2 special-3")
-           </p>
25        </div>
-       </div>
-     </div>
```

Next, we'll add a form to the bottom of the page that collects a CSS selector string. When the form is submitted, dojo.query finds the set of nodes described by the selector string, and then each node in the set is outlined in a red border. Here's the code:

`dom/query-demo.htm`

```
Line 1  <div class="queryTester" style="background-color:#DDDDDD; padding: 5px;">
-         <form id="qform">
-           Enter selector string; press &lt;enter&gt; to process:
-           <input id="query" type="text" name="querySelector" size="40">
5           <input type="submit">
-         </form>
-       </div>
-       <script type="text/javascript">
-         dojo.addOnLoad(function(){
10          dojo.connect(dojo.byId("qform"), "submit", function(e){
-             //stop default processing and propagation
-             //(we really don't want to submit the form)
-             dojo.stopEvent(e);

15            //erase any previous borders...
-             dojo.query("*", "fixture").style("border", "");

-             //set all elements found by the query to have a red border...
-             var query= dojo.byId("query").value;
20            dojo.query(query, "fixture").style("border", "2px solid red");
-           });
-         });
-       </script>
```

If we type ".special" into the input box and hit Enter, the second paragraph of section 1.1 will be outlined by a red border, as shown in Figure 7.4, on page 148.

Selector	Meaning example
*	any element *
E	an element of type E h1
E[foo]	an E element with a "foo" attribute p[myAttrib]
E[foo="bar"]	an E element whose "foo" attribute value is exactly equal to "bar" p[myAttrib="special"]
E[foo~="bar"]	an E element whose "foo" attribute value is a list of space-separated values, one of which is exactly equal to "bar" p[myAttrib~="special-2"]
E[foo^="bar"]	an E element whose "foo" attribute value begins exactly with the string "bar" p[myAttrib^="special-1"]
E[foo$="bar"]	an E element whose "foo" attribute value ends exactly with the string "bar" p[myAttrib$="special-3"]
E[foo*="bar"]	an E element whose "foo" attribute value contains the substring "bar" p[myAttrib*="spec"]
E:nth-child(n)	an E element, the n-th child of its parent div.section1-1 :nth-child(3)
E:nth-child(even)	an E element, the 2nd, 4th, ... children div.section1-1 :nth-child(even)
E:nth-child(odd)	an E element, the 1st, 3rd, ... children div.section1-1 :nth-child(odd)
E:first-child	an E element, first child of its parent div.section1-1 :first-child
E:last-child	an E element, last child of its parent div.section1-1 :last-child
E:not(s)	an E element that does not match simple selector s p:not(.special)
E:empty	an E element that has no children (including text nodes) div:empty
#myid	an element with ID equal to "myid" #fixture
E.myclass	An E element with class "myclass" p.special
E > F	an F element child of an E element div > p
E ~ F	an F element preceded by an E element h2 ~ p
E + F	an F element immediately preceded by an E element h2 + p
s1 s2	The set of elements returned by selector s2 that are decedents of the set of elements returned by s1 div p
s1, s2	The set of elements returned by selector s1 union the set of elements returned by selector s2 h1, h2

Figure 7.3: CSS 3 SELECTORS SUPPORTED BY DOJO.QUERY

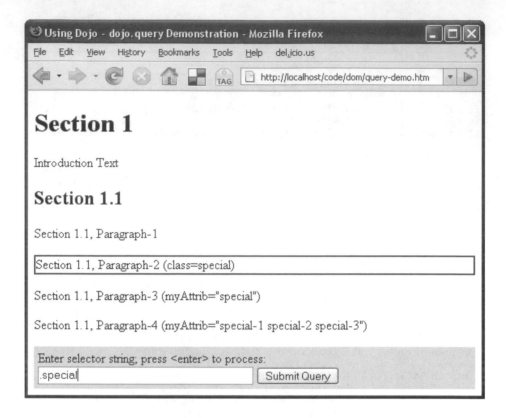

Figure 7.4: QUERY DEMONSTRATOR IN ACTION

The code also demonstrates the NodeList method style, which calls dojo.style for each item in the NodeList. So, the following...

dojo.query(selector).style(style, value);

is equivalent to this:

dojo.query(selector).forEach(function(n){dojo.style(n, style, value);});

You can use this technique in your own development work. When you're having trouble understanding the behavior of a CSS selector, you can add a form like the one we just developed to the bottom of your HTML document. Or, if you're using Firebug, forget about the form, and just type the dojo.query function call into the console to see what it returns.

Before we leave dojo.query, let's explore the NodeList objects it returns.

Alex Says...

dojo.query Today, querySelectorAll Tomorrow

Where it makes sense, Dojo is built to be compatible with upcoming standards. Eventually, these standards should be implemented by all browsers, and when they are, they'll be faster and easier to use than the scripted alternatives. dojo.query is a great example. The W3C Selectors API standard (http://www.w3.org/TR/selectors-api) describes an API for querying the DOM tree with CSS selectors and the Web API's working group has specified a programmatic variant, the function querySelectorAll, which returns an array of nodes just like dojo.query does. Dojo's CSS query engine has always been fast, and by keeping the query syntax to just what CSS provides, the design avoids getting into a situation where sending a scripted query engine down the wire will always be required. Instead, Dojo uses querySelectorAll on the browsers that support it sanely. Sooner or later, dojo.query will become nothing more than a call into querySelectorAll plus some syntactic sugar on the returned array. Best yet, the API won't change and you can get the speedup of having the query engine implemented in C++ on the browsers that support it now, knowing full well that things will only get faster and smaller in the future without backward-compatibility headaches. Investing in a toolkit that is paying attention to the evolution of the Web is already paying dividends for Dojo users.

dojo.NodeList Capabilities

NodeList objects are arrays with several additional per-object methods. They include all of the JavaScript core Array methods (concat, join, pop, and the rest).[7] These all work as expected. For example, given myNodeList (a NodeList), myNodeList.slice(2, 5) returns a new NodeList object that consists of the third through fifth elements of myNodeList.

We already mentioned that NodeList also includes the Mozilla JavaScript 1.6 array functions indexOf, lastIndexOf, every, some, map, and forEach. So, instead of writing this...

dojo.forEach(someNodelist, function(node){/*do something with node*/});

---

7. NodeList does not override join; consequently, join will return a result, but it usually isn't very useful.

you can write this:

```
someNodelist.forEach(function(node){/*do something with node*/});
```

Finally, NodeList includes a few methods that are syntactic sugar for applying common functions to each element. These methods are summarized here (myNodeList is a NodeList object):

- coords: Gets the top, left, height, and width of each node with dojo.coords (see Section 7.4, *Positioning with CSS and Dojo*, on page 156).

dom/frags.js

```
Line 1   result= myNodeList.coords();
   -     //is equivalent to...
   -     result= myNodeList.map(dojo.coords);
```

- attr: Gets or sets an HTML attribute of each node with dojo.attr. The get version returns an array of attribute values; the set version returns the source NodeList.

dom/frags.js

```
Line 1   //getter...
   -     result= myNodeList.attr(property);
   -     //is equivalent to...
   -     result= myNodeList.map(
   5        function(node){return dojo.attr(node, property);}
   -     );
   -     //result is an array of strings
   -
   -     //setter...
  10     result= myNodeList.attr(property, value);
   -     //is equivalent to...
   -     myNodeList.forEach(
   -        function(node){dojo.attr(node, property, value);}
   -     );
  15     result= myNodeList;
   -     //result is the original MyNodeList
```

- style: Works just like attr except for dojo.style.

- addClass: Adds a class string to each node with dojo.addClass; it returns the source NodeList.

dom/frags.js

```
Line 1   result= myNodeList.addClass(className);
   -     //is equivalent to...
   -     myNodeList.forEach(
   -        function(node){dojo.addClass(node, className);}
   5     );
```

```
-      result= myNodeList;
-      //result is the original MyNodeList
```

- removeClass: Works just like addClass except for dojo.removeClass.

- place: Places a node relative to a reference node with dojo.place (see Section 7.3, *Moving Nodes with dojo.place*, on page 155). The reference node can be given as either a DOM node or a query string.

`dom/frags.js`

```
Line 1  //referenceNode is a DOM node...
-       result= myNodeList.place(referenceNode, position);
-       //is equivalent to...
-       myNodeList.forEach(
5         function(node){dojo.place(node, referenceNode, position);}
-       );
-       result= myNodeList;
-       //result is the original MyNodeList
-
10      //referenceNode is a selector...
-       result= myNodeList.place(selector, position);
-       //is equivalent to...
-       myNodeList.forEach(
-         function(node){dojo.place(node, dojo.query(selector)[0], position);}
15      );
-       result= myNodeList;
-       //result is the original MyNodeList
```

- connect: Connects a handler to an event with dojo.connect.

`dom/frags.js`

```
Line 1  //no handler context provided
-       result= myNodeList.connect(event, handler);
-       //is equivalent to...
-       myNodeList.forEach(
5         function(node){dojo.connect(node, event, handler);}
-       );
-       result= myNodeList;
-       //result is the original MyNodeList
-
10      //with handler context
-       result= myNodeList.connect(event, context, handler);
-       //is equivalent to...
-       myNodeList.forEach(
-         function(node){dojo.connect(node, event, context, handler);}
15      );
-       result= myNodeList;
-       //result is the original MyNodeList
```

Alex Says...

Extending dojo.query

dojo.query is quite powerful out of the box. But, depending on your needs, you may find it convenient to add methods to the objects that dojo.query returns. For example, you might want to "yellow-fade" all the elements with the HTML class changed and then remove the class—that is, you'd like to write something like this:

dojo.query("#container .changed").fadeAndClear();

The key to extending dojo.query is understanding that it returns a dojo.NodeList instance. So to get the desired effect, you must add a property to the prototype object (see Section 9.2, *Prototypes and Prototypal Inheritance*, on page 222 for a discussion of prototypes) of the NodeList constructor function:

```
dojo.NodeList.prototype.fadeAndClear= function() {
  this.forEach(function(node){
    dojo.anim(node, {backgroundColor:yellow});
    dojo.removeClass(node, "changed"); }
  );
  return this;
};
```

Typically, you'll want to ensure that methods added to dojo.NodeList return the source instance so that several functions can be chained like this:

dojo.query("#container .changed").doThis().doThat().doTheOther();

- orphan: Removes nodes that are caught in a filter from their parent by the DOM function Node.removeChild; the nodes are also removed from the source NodeList. The filter must be a single-expression CSS selector (for example, .someClass); if the filter is missing, then all nodes in the NodeList are removed. It returns the removed nodes. Note that since the nodes are returned, they are *not* destroyed.

Notice how attr (setter version), style (setter version), addClass, removeClass, place, and connect all return the source NodeList. This allows several of these functions to be chained so that many operations can be accomplished in one statement.

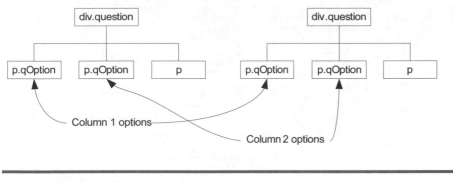

Figure 7.5: THE BASIC STRUCTURE FOR TWO QUESTIONS

For example, you can add the class "error" and remove the class "warning" to myNodeList in one statement by writing this:

myNodeList.addClass("error").removeClass("warning");

Now that we have a good handle on how to find DOM nodes and edit their properties, let's turn to the other side of DOM programming—manipulating the contents and structure of the DOM tree.

7.3 Inserting, Moving, and Deleting DOM Nodes

When we left the question-list challenge, the questions were colored with alternating shades of gray. As a second step, we'll get the options to line up in columns and make sure they stay lined up when the user changes the text size.

Example of DOM Tree Manipulation

To solve this part of the challenge, we'll change the structure of the document slightly. Each question will be contained in a div.question node (a div element with the class question). Each question option and the question text will be contained in p nodes that are children of the new div.question node with the classes qOption and qText, respectively. We'll finish the structure by decorating it with nodes from the original document. In Figure 7.5 you can see the basic structure for two questions.

The new structure makes it easy to position the options and question text in columns. The option paragraphs are floated left, and their widths are set to the maximum width of all options in the containing column. The question text is padded on the left enough to accommodate the sum

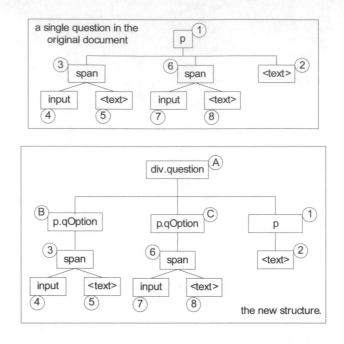

Figure 7.6: Original and new structure for a single question

of the widths of all the option columns. This design causes the options and the questions to line up.[8]

In Figure 7.6, you can see the before and after shots for a single question. Looking at the diagram, here's what needs to be done:

For each question...

1. Create a div.question node (A).

2. For each option in the current question (3 then 6)...

   a) Create a p.qOption node (B then C). Place this new node as the last child of the div.question node (A).

   b) Place the original span node (3 then 6) in the new p.qOption node.

---

8. Of course, there are many ways to solve the problem at hand (for example, it could be done without any node manipulation, relying solely on CSS styles). This is a teaching example constructed to demonstrate some Dojo functions.

3. At this point, the only thing left in the original question node (1) is the question text (2). Placing the original question node (1) as the last child of the div.question node (A) finishes the structure for a single question.

Moving Nodes with dojo.place

The function dojo.place inserts a node relative to another node. This one function is easier to use and replaces the W3C functions appendChild, replaceChild, and insertBefore. dojo.place takes a source node, a reference node, and a position ("before"; "after"; "first"; "last"; an integer; or missing, which implies "last") and inserts the node relative to the reference node as given by position:

- *before/after*: The node is placed before/after the reference node as a sibling.

- *first/last*: The node is placed as the first/last child of the reference node.

- *n*: The node is placed as the nth child of the reference node; zero implies the first child.

As usual, the node to be placed and/or the reference node can be specified by providing a DOM node or an id value for the target DOM node.

dojo.place and dojo.query make implementing the algorithm a snap:

dom/questions2.htm

```
Line 1    function restructure(){
   -        var questionGroup= dojo.query("div.questions")[0];//note [0]!
   -        dojo.query("p", questionGroup).forEach(function(node){
   -          var question= createNode("div", "question");
   5          dojo.place(question, questionGroup, "last");
   -          dojo.query("span", node).forEach(function(choiceNode){
   -            var choice= createNode("p", "choice");
   -            dojo.place(choice, question, "last");
   -            dojo.place(choiceNode, choice, "last");
   10         });
   -          dojo.place(node, question, "last");
   -        });
   -      }
```

restructure is hooked up to fire by dojo.addOnLoad. The function does not include the alternate shading accomplished earlier; this will be weaved back into the loop later. Finally, the function createNode is a little three-liner that creates a new DOM node and sets its class attribute.

```
dom/questions2.htm
```

```
Line 1    function createNode(tag, className){
    -         var newNode= document.createElement(tag);
    -         dojo.addClass(newNode, className);
    -         return newNode;
    5     }
```

There are a couple of other DOM structure functions that we should mention since they didn't make it into the example. First, there's dojo. isDescendant(node, ancestor), which returns true if node is a descendant of ancestor. And there's the bed lump function dojo._destroyElement(node) that destroys node and all of its children in a browser-independent manner that doesn't leak. The arguments in these functions can be either DOM nodes or ids.

Now that we have the structure set, we can move on to positioning elements.

7.4 Positioning DOM Nodes

Dojo provides several functions that take all the pain and mystery out of positioning DOM nodes. For example, to set the (top, left) position of a DOM node with CSS styles, you must write something like this:

dojo.style(myNode, "top", 20); dojo.style(myNode, "left", 30);

That's pretty verbose code for something as simple as setting a couple of coordinates. Dojo's positioning functions are more concise; they also clean up a few browser incompatibilities. After a quick review of CSS positioning, we'll describe Dojo's positioning functions, and then we'll use them to align the columns in the question-list challenge.

Positioning with CSS and Dojo

In addition to positioning a DOM element with the normal flow (position style static), CSS provides for positioning and sizing a block-level DOM element relative to the browser's viewport (fixed), relative to its containing parent node (absolute), or relative to its position in the normal flow (relative).[9] The various metrics defined by CSS are shown in Figure 7.7, on the next page.

---

9. Internet Explorer (at least up to version 7) does not support fixed positioning, and even Dojo cannot rectify this.

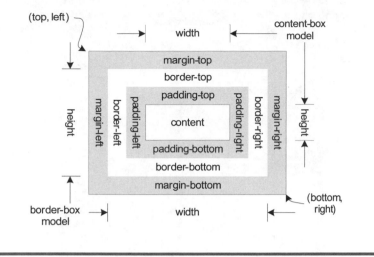

Figure 7.7: CSS POSITIONING METRICS

The diagram shows the two "box models" provided by CSS; these define the semantics of the width and height styles.

- "content-box" where the width/height style is equal to the content width/height. This is the default model.

- "border-box" where the width/height is equal to the width/height of the (left border + content width + right border)/(top border + content height + bottom border). This is available in browsers that support the CSS style box-sizing.[10]

The left, right, top, and bottom styles are the offset from the containing block's margin edge to the target block's margin edge (for example, see Figure 7.8, on the following page).

Consult [Mey06] for a detailed discussion of the arcana of CSS positioning if any of this is new to you.

Dojo defines positions and sizes by a JavaScript object with the properties l (left position or extent), t (top position or extent), w (width or left+right extent), h (height or top+bottom extent), x (horizontal scroll offset), and y (vertical scroll offset)—all in pixels. We'll term this object

---

10. Peter-Paul Koch has a nice write-up on this at http://www.quirksmode.org/css/box.html.

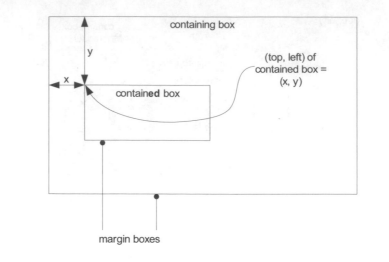

Figure 7.8: CSS POSITIONING METRICS

a Dojo *box object*, and it is used with most of the positioning functions. For example:

var box= dojo.marginBox(myNode);

box is a Dojo box object with the properties l, t, w, and h, which give the left, top, width, and height of the margin box of myNode.

The semantics of a box object property (whether the property is a position or an extent) depend upon the context in which the box object is used. For example, the function dojo.marginBox returns (top position, left position, width, height), whereas dojo._getMarginExtents returns (top extent, left extent, top+bottom extent, left+right extent) of the margins.

Dojo provides two public functions, dojo.marginBox(node, box) and dojo. borderBox(node, box), that can be used to get or set the position and/or size of the DOM node given by node. In both cases, box (optional) is a Dojo box object, without the x and y scroll offsets. If box is missing, then the functions get the current value of the appropriate box (the margin box or border box, depending upon which function you call). You can move and/or size a box by providing a box object.

For example:

```
dom/core-dom-utils.js
```

```
Line 1    //node is a DOM node

          //move node to 20 pixels right and 30 pixels down from the reference box
          //the box size is not changed.
     5    dojo.marginBox(node, {l:20, t:30});

          //size the box to 40 pixels wide by 50 pixels high
          //the box top-left corner is not moved
          dojo.marginBox(node, {h:40, w:50});
    10
          //do both of the operations above at once
          dojo.marginBox(node, {l:20, t:30, h:40, w:50});
```

Now that's easy! Dojo also includes quite a few bed lump functions that get/set various other box metrics:

- _getMarginExtents(node, computedStyle): Gets the height/width of the node's margins.
- _getPadExtents(node, computedStyle): Gets the height/width of the node's padding.
- _getBorderExtents(node, computedStyle): Gets the height/width of the node's borders.
- _getPadBorderExtents(node, computedStyle): Gets the height/width of the sum of the node's padding and border.
- _getMarginBox(node, computedStyle): Gets the left, top, width, height of the node's margin box.
- _getBorderBox(node, computedStyle): Gets the left, top, width, height of the node's border box.
- _getContentBox(node, computedStyle): Gets the left, top, width, height of the node's content box.
- _setBox(node, l, t, w, h, u): Sets the node's left, top, width, height. Pass NaN to *omit* setting any dimension. u (the metric units to use) is optional and defaults to pixels; specify a string (for example %) to override default behavior.
- _usesBorderBox(node): Returns dojo.boxModel=="border-box" || node.tagName=="TABLE" || node.tagName=="BUTTON" (browsers seem to treat table and button elements as the border box even if not explicitly set in the style sheet).
- _setContentSize(node, w, h, computedStyle): Sets the node's content box size.

- _setMarginBox(node, l, t, w, h, computedStyle): Sets the node's margin box; pass NaN to *omit* setting any dimension.
- coords(node, includeScroll): Gets the margin box and scroll offset for a node with absolute positioning. The scroll offset is given relative to the browser viewport when includeScroll is true and relative to the document otherwise.
- getComputedStyle(node): Returns the CSS computed style object for the node.

Finally, boxModel is a string ("content-box" or "border-box") that affects how box getters/setters compute space. It defaults to "content-box" unless Internet Explorer or Opera is in quirks mode but can be changed by user code.

Many of these functions take a computedStyle object that can be created by dojo.getComputedStyle. In all cases, this object is optional and will be automatically initialized if not passed (this design allows a small optimization when a get/set sequence is called on the same node).

The _get*Extents functions all return an object with the properties l, t, w, and h. In each case, l/t is the size of the left/top metric, and w/h is the size of the left+right/top+bottom metric. For example, assume the node myNode has left/top/right/bottom borders of 5/10/15/20. Then dojo._getBorderExtents will return the object {l: 5, t: 10, w: 20, h: 30}.

We have more than enough to solve the question-list positioning problem, so let's do that next.

Dynamic Positioning Nodes

To finish the question-list challenge layout, we need to calculate the widest option in each column; this value determines the width of each column. Then each option's margin box is set to the calculated width for the column in which it resides and floated left. The question text is padded by the total of all the column widths so that the questions always line up. Here's the code:

`dom/questions3.htm`

```
Line 1   //get the questions in a NodeList...
    -    var questions= dojo.query("div.question");
    -
    -    //find the maximum width of each column...
    5    var widths= [];
```

```
    -    questions.forEach(function(qNode){
    -      dojo.query("p.choice", qNode).forEach(function(choiceNode, i){
    -        var w= widths[i] || 0;
    -        widths[i]= Math.max(w, dojo.marginBox(choiceNode).w);
   10      });
    -    });

    -
    -    //set each option to the maximum width just calculated...
    -    questions.forEach(function(qNode){
   15      dojo.query("p.choice", qNode).forEach(function(choiceNode, i){
    -        dojo.marginBox(choiceNode, {w: widths[i]});
    -      });
    -    });

    -
   20   //calculate the total width of all the columns...
    -    var paddingLeft= 0;
    -    dojo.forEach(widths, function(w){paddingLeft+= w;});

    -
    -    //pad the question text by this width...
   25   dojo.query(".questionText").forEach(function(node){
    -      dojo.style(node, "paddingLeft", paddingLeft+10+"px");
    -    });
```

Since the algorithm iterates through the questions two times, the code takes a reference to the NodeList that holds the questions rather than issuing two identical queries (line 2). Although dojo.query is fast, this kind of small optimization is usually a good idea.

Next, the maximum width of each column is found by iterating through each option list for each question (lines 6 and 7); dojo.marginBox is used to get the width of each option. The calculations are applied by setting the margin box of each option with dojo.marginBox (line 16), computing the sum of the option column widths (line 21 and 22), and setting the padding-left style of the question text with the sum (line 26).

The question list now looks like Figure 7.9, on the next page.

Part of the challenge included ensuring the layout looks good when the user resizes the viewport or text size. For example, the layout must recalculate when the user presses Ctrl +.

Since there's no event that's fired when this happens, the code must monitor the text size. We did this by wiring the layout function to a timer that fires every two seconds.

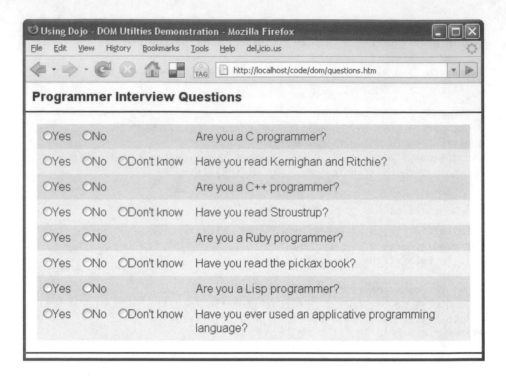

Figure 7.9: DONE

The layout function is augmented with a couple of lines that check to see whether the text size actually changed since the last time it was called:

`dom/questions3.htm`

```
Line 1    function layout3(){
    -       layout3.titleNode= layout3.titleNode || dojo.query("form > p")[0];
    -       var box= dojo.marginBox(layout3.titleNode);
    -       if (layout3.basis && box.w==layout3.basis.w && box.h==layout3.basis.h) {
    5         return;
    -       }
    -       layout3.basis= {w: box.w, h: box.h};
    -
    -       //the rest of the function omitted...
```

The code checks the size of the title paragraph and compares it to the last check. If it changes, then the text size must have changed, and the layout is recomputed. Both the title node and the last check are stored as properties of the layout function so that they persist between timer events.

The layout function is hooked to a timer:

`dom/questions3.htm`

```
window.setInterval(layout3, 2000);
```

7.5 Animation

Neither HTML nor the W3C DOM model includes any support for animation. However, animation can be implemented by setting a timer and drawing a new object on each timer event. Dojo includes a small but powerful set of functions to help you do this, which we'll explore next. We'll finish our discussion with an enhancement to the question-list challenge.

DHTML Animation Basics

Let's begin by briefly describing the underlying concept. Computer-based animation, whether in the browser or some other environment, works just like a movie or cartoon. A series of individual pictures (or frames) is rapidly displayed. So long as there is not too much time or difference between each picture, the human brain puts the pictures together so that they look like a smooth motion.

Here's a quick demonstration—we will refer to this example as the "bouncing-div"—that moves a div node across the browser viewport, bouncing off each side:

`dom/bouncing-div.htm`

```
Line 1    <html>
     -    <head>
     -      <title>
     -        Mastering Dojo - DOM Utilities - Bouncing DIV
     5      </title>
     -
     -      <style type="text/css">
     -        #ball {
     -          position: absolute;
    10          width: 20px;
     -          height: 20px;
     -          background-color: blue;
     -        }
     -      </style>
    15
     -      <script
     -        type="text/javascript"
     -        src="/dojoroot/dojo/dojo.js"
     -        djConfig="isDebug: true">
    20      </script>
     -
```

```
       <script type="text/javascript">
         var currentPosition= 0;
         var leftToRight= true;
25
       function moveNode(){
         //get the ball node
         var ball= dojo.byId("ball");

30       //move it
         (leftToRight ? currentPosition++ : currentPosition--);
         dojo.marginBox(ball, {l: currentPosition});

         ///twiddle leftToRight if about to go off the end
35       var containerBox= dojo.marginBox("frame");
         var ballBox= dojo.marginBox(ball);
         if (leftToRight) {
           if (currentPosition+ballBox.w-1 > containerBox.l+containerBox.w) {
               leftToRight= false;
40           }
         } else {
           if (currentPosition < containerBox.l) {
               leftToRight= true;
           }
45       }
       }

         dojo.addOnLoad(function(){
           window.setInterval(moveNode, 20);
50       });
       </script>
     </head>
     <body>
       <div id="frame">
55         <p id="ball"></p>
       </div>
     </body>
     </html>
```

The timer is set to call moveNode every 20ms (line 50). moveNode (line 27) moves the div.ball node 1 pixel to the right until it hits the end of the containing box, then reverses course, and so on, forever. If you try the demo on your own computer, you'll see the limits of DOM-based animation—particularly as you crank the timer interval down toward zero.[11] Although there is a little jerkiness, it's good enough for most uses. And, it's the only way to do animation without a plug-in.

---

11. You can try setting the timer to 1ms and see that the browser will fail to execute a timeout this fast. Currently, the shortest interval the browser will fire is between 10ms and 20ms.

Animating with dojo.animateProperty

The function dojo.animateProperty returns a dojo._Animation object that can be used to animate a set of style properties on a DOM node. It takes a hash that includes a node, a set of styles to animate on the node, and optionally, several other properties. The animation is then executed by calling the play method on the returned object. So, the bouncing-div could be moved from one side to the other with dojo.animateProperty like this:

```
dom/animation-examples.htm
var ball= dojo.marginBox("ball");
var containerBox= dojo.marginBox("frame");
dojo.animateProperty({
  node: dojo.byId("ball"),
  properties: {
    left: {
      start: containerBox.l,
      end: containerBox.l+containerBox.w-ball.w
    }
  }
}).play();
```

Not all styles can be animated. For example, animating the style overflow (which takes on the values visible, hidden, and scroll) is meaningless. Animating works only for styles that can take on continuous numeric values (like left in the previous example). And, as we'll see in a minute, this includes colors—even when specified as words. For example, it *is* legal to animate between red and blue.

As shown in the example, the properties to animate are themselves given in a hash. The manner in which each property is animated is controlled by the values of start, end, and units, which give the starting and ending values of the style. The units suffix "px" is assumed.

If the desired animation needs something else (for example "%"), then set units explicitly; otherwise, omit it as we did. start *or* end can be omitted in which case the value of the style immediately before the animation is played is used for missing specification. So if you specify backgroundColor: {start: yellow} and the current background color is white when the animation is played, then the animation will play backgroundColor: {start: "yellow", end: "white"}. And, yes, this is the so-called yellow-fade animation.

Here's the complete function call:

`dom/animation-examples.htm`

```
Line 1    dojo.animateProperty({
    -       node: someNode,
    -       properties: {
    -          backgroundColor: {
    5             start: "yellow"
    -          }
    -       }
    -    }).play();
```

The previous examples invoked play immediately without saving the returned object to a local variable. However, taking a reference to the returned object and manipulating it directly is perfectly legal. Arguments can be set/reset, and methods can be called. For example, here are two calls that look quite different but accomplish the same thing:

`dom/animation-examples.htm`

```
Line 1    dojo.animateProperty({
    -       node: someNode,
    -       properties: {
    -         backgroundColor: {
    5            start: "yellow"
    -         }
    -       }
    -    }).play();
    -
    10   //can also be stated like...
    -
    -    var myAnimation1= dojo.animateProperty({});
    -    myAnimation1.node= someNode;
    -    myAnimation1.properties= {backgroundColor: {start: "yellow"}};
    15   myAnimation1.play();
```

Specifically, you can call the same animation object several times:

`dom/animation-examples.htm`

```
Line 1    //take a reference to the returned object...
    -    var myAnimation= dojo.animateProperty({
    -       node: someNode,
    -       properties: {
    5         backgroundColor: {
    -            start: "red", end: "blue"
    -         }
    -       }
    -    });
    10
    -    //play it...
    -    myAnimation.play();
```

```
      -   //play it again, sam...after waiting 3s
      -   myAnimation.play(3000);
```

The example illustrates an important point: the method play returns immediately; the animation plays in the background consequent to timer interrupts. So, writing myAnimation.play(); myAnimation.play() would cause the animation to immediately restart. You would *not* see two distinct animations. The example used a timer to play the animation the second time well after the first animation completed.[12]

As implied by the function signature, you can animate several properties at once. Here's the div moving across the screen and changing its color:

dom/animation-examples.htm

```
Line 1   var ball= dojo.marginBox("ball");
     -   var containerBox= dojo.marginBox("frame");
     -   var animation= dojo.animateProperty({
     -     node: dojo.byId("ball"),
     5     properties: {
     -       left: {
     -         start: containerBox.l,
     -         end: containerBox.l+containerBox.w-ball.w
     -       },
    10       backgroundColor: {end: "red"}
     -     }
     -   }).play();
```

_Animation objects include several properties that can be set either by the argument to dojo.animateProperty or on the object itself:

- duration: The length of the animation in milliseconds; defaults to 1000
- repeat: The number of times to repeat the animation; defaults to 0
- rate: Frequency of timer in milliseconds for animation; defaults to 10
- delay: The number of milliseconds to delay the animation after play is called; defaults to 0

_Animation objects are controlled through the following methods:

- play: Plays the animation
- pause: Pauses the animation; animation can be restarted from the paused position by calling play

---

12. There is a better way to do this: dojo.fx.chain(myAnimation, myAnimation). We'll talk about dojo.fx at the end of this section.

- stop: Stops the animation; calling play will restart from the beginning
- gotoPercent: Goes to a certain point in the animation
- status: One of paused, playing, stopped

As their descriptions indicate, the operation of these methods is quite straightforward. Finally, there are several events defined on _Animation objects:

- onBegin: Fired after play returns during first timer event
- onAnimate: Fired before each timer event
- onEnd: Fired after the last timer event
- onPlay: Fired every time play is invoked
- onPause: Fired if/when the animation is paused
- onStop: Fired if/when the animation is stopped

Client code must connect to these events by dojo.connect (or equivalent). Here's an example that connects the bounding-div animation to the onBegin, onAnimate, onEnd, and onPlay events:

dom/animation-examples.htm

```
Line 1    var ball= dojo.marginBox("ball");
    -     var containerBox= dojo.marginBox("frame");
    -     var animation= dojo.animateProperty({
    -       node: dojo.byId("ball"),
    5       properties: {
    -         left: {
    -           start: containerBox.l,
    -           end: containerBox.l+containerBox.w-ball.w
    -         }
   10       }
    -     });
    -
    -     var feedbackNode= dojo.byId("target2");
    -     feedbackNode.innerHTML= "";
   15     function append(text) {
    -         feedbackNode.innerHTML= feedbackNode.innerHTML + " " + text;
    -     }
    -
    -     dojo.connect(animation, "onBegin", dojo.partial(append, "onBegin"));
   20     dojo.connect(animation, "onAnimate", dojo.partial(append, "."));
    -     dojo.connect(animation, "onEnd", dojo.partial(append, "onEnd"));
    -     dojo.connect(animation, "onPlay", dojo.partial(append, "onPlay"));
    -
    -     animation.play();
```

Each handler prints out its feedback by adding text to the target paragraph node.

Animating with dojo.anim

Although dojo.animateProperty is very powerful, it's also a bit cumbersome to use for many common animation tasks. The function dojo.anim solves this problem by wrapping dojo.animateProperty with a more convenient, if somewhat less powerful, interface. The easiest way to understand dojo.anim is to simply look at its implementation:

`dom/animation-examples.htm`

```
Line 1   dojo.anim = function(node, properties, duration, easing, onEnd, delay){
  -        return dojo.animateProperty({
  -          node:       node,
  -          duration:   duration || dojo._Animation.prototype.duration,
  5          properties: properties,
  -          easing:     easing,
  -          onEnd:      onEnd
  -        }).play(delay||0);
  -      };
```

For example, this makes the yellow-fade task a one-liner:

`dom/animation-examples.htm`

```
Line 1   dojo.anim(someNode, {backgroundColor: {start: "yellow"}});
```

In practice, you should use dojo.anim anywhere you don't need to control any of the dojo.animateProperty features that dojo.anim doesn't recognize (for example, any of the events other than onEnd) and want the animation to unconditionally play (perhaps after a delay).

Let's get back to the question-list challenge and bring it to life with dojo.animateProperties.

Animating the Question-List Challenge

Remember how the second, fourth, sixth, and eighth questions are relevant only if the preceding question is answered "yes" (see Figure 7.9, on page 162)? Now, we'll change the behavior of the form to animate an even question into view when its owning question is marked "yes" and out of view when marked "no."

We'll call the odd questions "pQuestions" for primary questions and the event questions "sQuestions" for secondary questions. Here's the plan:

1. Connect a click event to one of each of the pQuestions' option nodes; this gets fired if any of the option nodes change value. The handler will animate the sQuestion into view if the pQuestion was marked "yes" and out of view if marked "no."

2. Change the color banding to color a pQuestion/sQuestion pair the same color. This signals that an sQuestion is part of a pQuestion when it is shown and makes the interface look good when it's not.

3. Calculate the height of each sQuestion; record the value as the custom attribute qHeight of the sQuestion node.

4. Initialize the height of an sQuestion to zero if the owning pQuestion is not answered "yes."

The changes to the restructure function are quite minor:

dom/questions4.htm

```
Line 1  function restructure(){

          dojo.query("form > p").addClass("formTitle");

     5    var questionsDiv= dojo.query("div.questions")[0];
          dojo.query("p", questionsDiv).forEach(function(node, questionNumber){
            var pQuestion= !(questionNumber % 2);

  ▶         var band= (questionNumber % 4)<2 ? "lightBand" : "darkBand";
    10
            var className= "question " + band;
            var question= createElement("div", className);
            dojo.place(question, questionsDiv, "last");
            dojo.query("span", node).forEach(function(choiceNode){
    15        var choice= createElement("p", "choice");
              dojo.place(choiceNode, choice, "last");
              dojo.place(choice, question, "last");

  ▶           if (pQuestion && choiceNode.firstChild.value=="yes") {
  2▶            dojo.connect(question, "click",
  ▶               dojo.partial(checkSQuestion, question, choiceNode.firstChild));
  ▶           }

            });
    25      dojo.addClass(node, "questionText");
            dojo.place(node, question, "last");
          });
        }
```

Deciding how to color a question (line 8) involves trivial arithmetic: the color changes every two questions instead of every other question.

We used dojo.partial to construct the handler (line 20). This way, when the handler is called, the required nodes are passed into the handler already initialized and ready to go—no need to query or navigate from the event object. Here is the event handler that's fired when the pQuestion option is changed:

```
dom/questions4.htm
Line 1   function checkSQuestion(pQuestion, choiceNode){

           var sQuestion= pQuestion.nextSibling;

    5      //assume we're showing the sQuestion...
           var start= 0, end= dojo.attr(sQuestion, "qHeight");

           //if hiding, then reverse start and end...
           if (!choiceNode.checked) {
   10        start= end; end= 0;
           }

           dojo.anim(sQuestion, {
               backgroundColor: {start: "yellow"},
   15          height: {start: start, end: end}
           }).play();
         }
```

The routine animates the height to end at the value that the layout routine (see the next code snippet) saves in the custom attribute qHeight if the pQuestion is marked "yes" or to end at zero otherwise. Leveraging dojo.anim makes this routine trivial! When a pQuestion is changed to "yes," the question list after that pQuestion slides down, revealing the sQuestion. The opposite occurs when a pQuestion is marked "no."

Finally, here is the changed main loop in the layout routine:

```
dom/questions4.htm
Line 1   //find the maximum width of each column and
    -    //calculate height and show/hide the sQuestions...
    -    var widths= [];
    -    questions.forEach(function(qNode, questionNumber){
    5      dojo.query("p.choice", qNode).forEach(function(choiceNode, i){
    -        var w= widths[i] || 0;
    -        widths[i]= Math.max(w, dojo.marginBox(choiceNode).w);
    -      });

   1▶      //calculate the height of the sQuestions;
    ▶      //hide if the primary is NOT "yes"
    ▶      if (questionNumber % 2) {
    ▶        //let the browser layout engine calculate the height...
    ▶        dojo.style(qNode, "height", "");
   1▶        var height= dojo.style(qNode, "height");
    ▶
    ▶        //stuff the height into a custom attribute for use by the event handler...
```

```
    ▶        dojo.attr(qNode, "qHeight", height);
    ▶
 2  ▶        //hide the question if the pQuestion isn't yes...
    ▶        if (!dojo.query("input[value='yes']", qNode.previousSibling)[0].checked) {
    ▶          dojo.style(qNode, "height", 0);
    ▶        }
    ▶      }
 25 });
```

Remember, this routine may get called anytime the user does something that changes the layout (for example, resizes the viewport or changes the text size). So before we get the height of the sQuestion (line 15), the height style is set to empty (line 4), which lets the browser calculate the height as if it were shown. After we record this value in the qHeight attribute, the sQuestion height is set back to zero if the owning pQuestion is *not* marked "yes."

The technique of sliding in a box like we did here is so common in modern browser user interface design that Dojo includes the functions dojo.wipeIn and dojo.wipeOut that wrap this functionality. Each function takes a hash with semantics just like dojo.animateProperty and returns a dojo._Animate object that will wipe in/out the node given in the args hash. Here is the event handler implemented with dojo.wipeIn/Out:

dom/questions4.htm

```
Line 1  function checkSQuestion(pQuestion, choiceNode){
    -     var f= dojo.fx[choiceNode.checked ? "wipeIn" : "wipeOut"];
    -     f({node:pQuestion.nextSibling}).play();
    -   }
```

dojo.wipeIn/Out are part of the module dojo.fx, which is not included in Dojo base, so you must dojo.require("dojo.fx") for this to work. dojo.fx includes a few other useful functions:

- slideTo: Slides a node from its current position to a position given by the top, left styles of properties

- chain: Chains an array of separate _Animate objects into a single new _Animate object that runs each of the provided objects one after the other

- combine: Chains an array of separate _Animate objects into a single new _Animate object that runs all the provided objects concurrently

Chapter 8

Remote Scripting with XHR, script, and iframe

Remote scripting is the process of communicating with a server from a client-side script without requiring a page reload. Several techniques have evolved that implement remote scripting using only the browser's native capabilities.[1] These are some of the most important advances in browser-based programming since they eliminate the page-at-a-time paradigm and allow the browser to behave like any other modern client in a client-server system. Remote scripting is also the basis for a wide range of UI techniques. Controls that change behavior based on partial user input (for example, displaying a list of words after a few characters are typed), forms that validate on the server *without* reloading when an error is detected, and single-page web applications are all examples of UIs that require remote scripting.

8.1 Native Remote Scripting

There are three well-known methods to implement native remote scripting:

- Using an XMLHttpRequest (XHR) object
- Dynamically loading an iframe element
- Dynamically loading a script element

---

1. Although this is one of the cornerstones of Ajax, these techniques were known well before 2005 when the term *Ajax* was coined; Ajax implies much more than just remote scripting.

Each method has advantages and disadvantages. Although XHR began life as a Microsoft-only technology, it is now available in all modern browsers. It allows for full control of the HTTP transaction (URL, headers, content), can use any HTTP method (GET, POST, PUT, DELETE, HEAD), and can be executed both synchronously and asynchronously. On the other hand, because of the same-origin policy, an XHR object cannot communicate with a server that resides at a different origin than the document that contains the script making the service request.[2] Finally, the XHR API cannot send files to the server like a normal form POST.

Dynamic iframes *are* still subject to the same-origin policy, but they solve the problem of POSTing a file without reloading the page. On the other hand, the script technique is free from the same-origin policy and can address any URL.

iframes expect an HTML response message, while dynamic script elements expect a script for the response message. In either case, receiving content types other than those expected (for example, XML or JSON) is problematic. In such cases, machinery is required to wrap the response message appropriately at the server and unwrap it at the client.

Both iframe and script techniques offer very limited HTTP method support: POST and GET are possible with iframe; script supports only GET.

In the final analysis, you need all three techniques:

- When you need to send a file to the server asynchronously, use the iframe technique.
- When you need to get around the same-origin restriction, use the script technique (typically JSONP).
- Use XHR for everything else.

Unfortunately, each of the three methods are implemented quite differently. And then there's the usual browser mess of incompatibilities and memory leaks to deal with. It shouldn't be this hard to make a quick server request and receive a response. But, unless and until the browser venders agree on a unified API, this is what we're left with. Dojo rescues us by providing a simple, consistent, and powerful set of functions that execute an HTTP transaction through any of the three methods on all supported browsers. These functions are the main subject of this chapter. We'll finish up by showing one application of remote

---

2. Origin is given by protocol, domain name, and port number. The same-origin policy is a security feature.

scripting (web services) and solving a problem that comes with remote scripting (making the browser's Back button work).

8.2 Using the Dojo XHR Framework

Much has been written about native XHR objects elsewhere, so rehashing this information is beyond the scope of this book.[3] We do want to mention that not all browsers create XHR objects in the same way. Nor do the objects they create all work the same way. And finally, there are sequences of asynchronous and synchronous calls that can be made on some browsers that will lock the browser. Of course, Dojo fixes all of these problems behind the scenes, so you don't need to give them another thought.

But even if none of these problems existed, native XHRs would still lack several important features required for the construction of modern web applications:

- Support functions to encode URL parameters and HTML form elements
- Functions for processing common types of response text (for example, JSON)
- The ability to time out a request
- The ability to cancel a request
- Robust and easy-to-use error recovery

Dojo's remote scripting functions include all of these features. The core functions are dojo.xhrGet, dojo.xhrPost, dojo.rawXhrPost, dojo.xhrPut, dojo.rawXhrPut, and dojo.xhrDelete, which correspond to the HTTP methods GET, POST (two variants), PUT (two variants), and DELETE.[4] We'll refer to these functions collectively as the Dojo dojo.xhr* functions.

Calling dojo.xhr*

Each of the dojo.xhr* functions takes a single argument hash named args that fully describes the request. The properties defined by args are the same for all six functions, and default values are defined for many of these properties. The dojo.xhr* functions are quite powerful, and args

---

3. Chapter 20 in [Fla06] provides a nice description about native XHR programming.
4. As of Dojo version 1.1, there's also the function dojo.xhr that takes the XHR verb (GET, POST, and so on) as the first argument.

controls this power. We'll start with a simple proof-of-concept example, and then we'll build and use a web page to demonstrate each args property.

We've made every attempt to avoid discussing server-side issues, but remote scripting involves making a request to and receiving a response from a server. The code download includes a very simple Ruby WEBrick server that implements all of the server-side functionality included in this chapter.

Let's start with a simple dojo.xhrGet function call. Here's how to HTTP GET from the URL demo/id1 (a relative URL) and display the contents of the response in an alert box:

remote-scripting/remote-scripting.js

```
Line 1    function example1(){
   -        dojo.xhrGet({
   -          url: "demo/id1",
   -          load: function(response){alert(response);},
   5          error: function(error){alert(error.message);}
   -        });
   -      }
```

In this example, the server returns a response that includes the text "hello, world" when the resource demo/id1 is requested.

In the example, args specified three items:

- url (a string): Typically, the URL does not include the user or password components (if necessary at all) or any component after the path (the parameter or query components). We'll see how these are specified in a moment. Because of the same-origin policy, the URL is almost always a relative URL.
- load: The function to call on successful completion of the request.
- error: The function to call upon failure of the request.

And we relied upon default values for these items:

- handleAs (a string): How to preprocess the response; defaults to handle as "text", which implies no preprocessing is executed on the response
- sync (a boolean): Sends the XHR synchronously or not; defaults to send asynchronously
- preventCache (a boolean): Prevents cached resources from being returned; defaults to false

We'll discuss each of these items in more detail later in this section.

The example sends the response to an alert box if the XHR was successful; if the XHR fails, then the message given by the Error instance created as a result of the failure is sent to the alert box.

The result of a dojo.xhr* call is passed as the first argument to the load (upon success) or error (upon failure) functions. If the call succeeded, then the result is the content that was retrieved by the XHR call after it's passed through a content handler. The default content handler just passes the content as received from the server; we'll discuss other content handlers shortly. If the call failed, then the result is a JavaScript Error object that describes the error.

It is also possible to specify one function to handle both success and failure conditions by providing a function for the args property handle. For example:

`remote-scripting/remote-scripting.js`

```
Line 1    function example2(){
    -       dojo.xhrGet({
    -         url: "demo/id1",
    -         handle: function(response){
    5           if (response instanceof Error) {
    -             //failed...
    -             alert("failed: " + response.message);
    -           }
    -           else {
    10            //success...
    -             alert('succeeded: "' + response + '"');
    -           }
    -         }
    -       });
    15    }
```

args, ioArgs, and Handler Functions

When the dojo.xhr* functions orchestrate the XHR call, they synthesize the full set of arguments required to make the call and place the result in a hash named ioArgs. The synthesized arguments come from three places:

- Directly from args (for example, the URL in the previous example)
- Indirectly from args (for example, a parameter string may be calculated from a HTML form node given in args)
- Default values (for example, sync in the previous example)

ioArgs is always passed as the second argument to the load, error, and handle functions (from now on, we'll refer to the load/error/handle functions collectively as the *handler functions*). Finally, the handler functions are called in the context of args—that is, when these functions are executed, this references args.

Before we go further, let's set up an example framework that we'll use to demonstrate Dojo's remote scripting functions. Here's a web page that can select and trigger an example. It also contains a pre element to hold the response and a div element to hold object dumps.

remote-scripting/remote-scripting.htm

```
Line 1  <html>
   -    <head>
   -      <title>
   -        Mastering Dojo - Remote Scripting
   5      </title>
   -
   -      <style type="text/css">
   -        @import "/dojoroot/dojo/resources/dojo.css";
   -        @import "remote-scripting.css";
  10      </style>
   -
   -      <script
   -        type="text/javascript"
   -        src="/dojoroot/dojo/dojo.js"
  15        djConfig="isDebug: true"></script>
   -
   -      <!--
   -        this script contains code to call an example
   -        function and dump the results
  20      -->
   -      <script
   -        type="text/javascript"
   -        src="remote-scripting-lib.js"></script>
   -
  25      <!--
   -        this script contains all the example functions
   -      -->
   -      <script
   -        type="text/javascript"
  30        src="remote-scripting.js"></script>
   -    </head>
   -    <body>
   -      <div>
   -        <h1>Remote Scripting Exercises</h1>
  35        <form><p>
   -          Example Identifier:
   -          <input id="exId" type="text" size="2" maxLength="2" name="exId">
```

```
 -          <input id="exTrigger" type="submit" name="exTrigger" value="Go!">
 -        </p></form>
40     </div>
 -     <div>
 -       <h1>Result:</h1>
 -       <pre id="result"></pre>
 -     </div>
45     <div>
 -       <h1>Object Dumps:</h1>
 -       <div id="objects"></div>
 -     </div>
 -   </body>
50 </html>
```

Next, the input text field (input#exId) and button (input#exTrigger) are
wired to fire an example function:

remote-scripting/remote-scripting-lib.js

```
Line 1  function doExample(e){
 -        //prevent submitting the form...
 -        dojo.stopEvent(e);

 5        var exampleId= Number(dojo.byId("exId").value);
 -        if (window["example"+exampleId]) {
 -          //clear out the last results...
 -          var resultNode= dojo.byId("result");
 -          resultNode.innerHTML= ""
10          dojo.toggleClass(resultNode, "error", false);
 -          dojo.byId("objects").innerHTML= "";

 -          //run the example...
 -          window["example"+exampleId]();
15        } else {
 -          alert("Invalid example identifier provided.  Try again.");
 -        }
 -      }

20      dojo.addOnLoad(function(){
 -        dojo.connect(dojo.byId("exTrigger"), "click", doExample);
 -      })
```

When the button is pressed, the value is retrieved from the text field.
If it is a valid example function, then the function is executed; otherwise, a warning is given. For example, entering "1" and clicking the
button results in executing the function example1. The event is stopped
because we don't want to submit the form. Now we can go about writing
several example functions to demonstrate the dojo.xhr* functions.

To begin, let's improve the "hello, world" example by writing a handler
function that dynamically fills the pre element with the response and
dumps the contents of this and ioArgs.

Here's that code:

remote-scripting/remote-scripting.js

```
function handler1(response, ioArgs){
  var error= response instanceof Error;
  var responseText= error ? response.message : response;
  var resultNode= dojo.byId("result");
  resultNode.innerHTML= responseText.replace(/</g, "&lt;");
  dojo.toggleClass(resultNode, "error", error);
  dojo.byId("objects").innerHTML=
    dumpObject({"this": this, ioArgs: ioArgs});
}

function example3(){
  dojo.xhrGet({
    url: "demo/id1",
    handle: handler1
  });
}
```

The handler function is trivial. If the call was successful, it pushes the response into the pre element; otherwise, it pushes the text of the Error object into the element. Any left-angle brackets in the response are escaped so that we can see the contents of the response rather than the rendering in case the response is HTML. Finally, handler1 uses the function dumpObject to format an object into a set of nested tables.[5] Executing exercise3 results in the output given in Figure 8.1, on the next page in Firefox.[6]

There you can see that both this and ioArgs.args reference the args hash that was passed to dojo.xhrGet. The second argument passed to handler1 is the ioArgs hash that was constructed by dojo.xhrGet. Within ioArgs, you can see the following:

- ioArgs.url (a string) gives the URL for the call; in this case, it's equivalent to args.url, but we'll see that the URL can also be read from a form attribute.
- ioArgs.query (a string) gives any URL query parameters.
- ioArgs.handleAs (a string) says how to preprocess the response before passing to the handler functions.

---

5. dumpObject doesn't do anything that a Firebug console dump couldn't accomplish other than make the screen shots for this dead-tree book easier to read. The full text of dumpObject is included in the code download.
6. Executing this example in different browsers shows how native XHR objects are structured quite differently across different vendors.

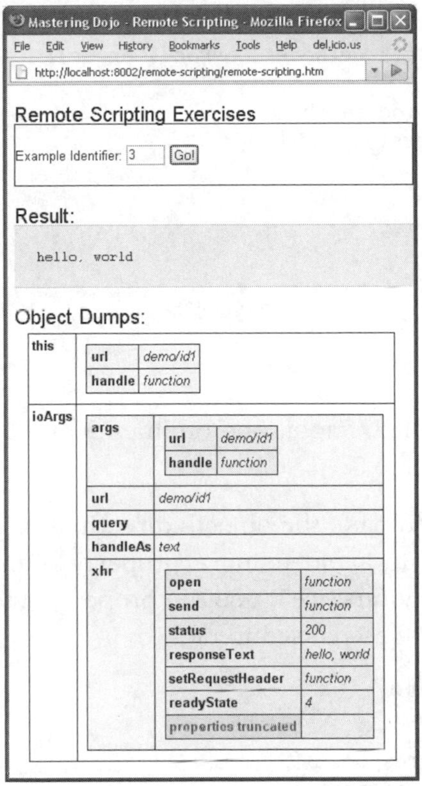

Figure 8.1: OBJECTS RETURNED BY DOJO.XHR

- ioArgs.xhr (a native XHR object) is the actual XHR object used to execute the XHR call.

If you need to access objects in the handler functions that are determined when the XHR call is made, then two techniques are available. (Of course, you can also use a global variable, but that's a bit sloppy.) First, the handler function can be closed on the objects like this:

`remote-scripting/remote-scripting.js`

```
Line 1   function example4(){
           //get some variables that we'll use in the handler function...
           var targetNode= dojo.byId("result");

      5    //make a handler closed on the variables we made...
           function handler2(response){
             var error= response instanceof Error;
             var responseText= error ? response.message : response;
```

```
 10        targetNode.innerHTML= responseText.replace(/</g, "&lt;");
           dojo.toggleClass(targetNode, "error", error);

           //note: NOT dumping anything...
           dojo.byId("objects").innerHTML= "";
         }
 15
       //make the XHR call...
       dojo.xhrGet({
         url: "demo/id1",
         handle: handler2
 20    });
     }
```

When handler2 is called, targetNode on lines 9 and 10 will still hold the value calculated at line 3.

Second, you can also pass the objects directly in the args hash. A little caution is required to avoid using a property name that's already in use by the Dojo functions; we'll use the property _user. Here's the same example with targetNode passed in args:

`remote-scripting/remote-scripting.js`

```
Line 1 function example5(){
         function handler3(response){
           var error= response instanceof Error;
           var responseText= error ? response.message : response;
 5         this._user.targetNode.innerHTML= responseText.replace(/</g, "&lt;");
           dojo.toggleClass(this._user.targetNode, "error", error);

           //note: ONLY dumping this...
           dojo.byId("objects").innerHTML=
 10          dumpObject({"this": this});
         }

       //make the XHR call...
       dojo.xhrGet({
 15      url: "demo/id1",
         handle: handler3,
         _user: {targetNode: dojo.byId("result")}
       });
     }
```

Since this references args when handler3 is called and also since args._user.targetNode was initialized prior to the XHR call, it will be there waiting for us in the handler. Passing objects around in this manner is slightly more efficient than creating a closure, but in most cases the speed differences are inconsequential, and you should look to other factors such as clarity of expression to decide which technique to employ.

Alex Says...

JSON Vulnerabilities

Given the obvious security issues surrounding cross-domain scripts and data, it might then surprise you to learn that the dynamic nature of JavaScript also places regular JSON data at risk via an attack inartfully named *cross-site request forgery* (aka CSRF) and *JavaScript hijacking*. Briefly, CSRF uses your session cookies against you. Say you're logged into FooBlog and it uses cookies to authenticate users. Part of the FooBlog application hands back a list of private comments that users have left for the moderators, not to be seen by other users; furthermore, let's assume that FooBlog hands this data back as a JSON document. Seems pretty straightforward.

Now, during your daily FooBlog moderation work, you see a message that is interesting, but you haven't heard of the commenter, so you click the link to go to the website. Upon visiting the site (Evil.com), the page at Evil.com tries to make a cross-site script request to include the moderation feed JSON into the document. Because JSON is just JavaScript and will be evaluated as such and because your browser is already authenticated on FooBlog, this request will succeed. But remember that this is all happening inside your browser, not on Evil.com's servers. How could your data be at risk here? Well, it turns out that the dynamic nature of JavaScript allows you to reprogram the constructor function for even the most fundamental classes like Object. Since the included JSON file will execute as a script and the anonymous objects inside it will be instantiated via the Object constructor, this gives a script on the Evil.com page an in. Using this language loophole, it's possible to use CSRF to attack sensitive JSON data living at stable or predictable URLs.

Content Handlers

When the response is successfully received, it is passed through the content handler specified by the handleAs property (a string) of args. Six content handlers are available:

- "text" (the default handler): No processing takes place; the response text is returned without any transformation.
- "json": The response is processed as JSON by the function dojo. fromJson, and the resulting object is returned. dojo.fromJson takes a single argument string, evaluates it, and returns the result.
- "json-comment-filtered": The text within a /*... */ comment is processed as JSON by dojo.fromJson, and the resulting object is then returned. See the *Alex Says...*, on page 190 to learn about comment-filtered JSON.
- "json-comment-optional": If the response contains a /*... */ comment, then the text within the comment is processed as JSON by dojo. fromJson, and the resulting object is returned; otherwise, the entire response is processed as JSON by dojo.fromJson.
- "javascript": The response is processed as JavaScript by dojo.eval; and the result is returned; dojo.eval evaluates the response in the global scope.
- "xml": The result of the XHR method responseXML is returned.

In the examples so far, we did not specify a value for args.handleAs; therefore, the response was handled as "text", and no transformation took place before the response was passed to the handler functions. To exercise each of the content handlers, assume the server returns the following responses when sent these URLs (note that the responses are strings of characters, not JavaScript objects):

demo/id2
```
{"firstName": "George", "lastName": "Bush", "address": {"street": "1600 Penn-
sylvania Avenue NW", "city": "Washington", "state": "DC", "zip": "20500"}}
```

demo/id3
```
/*{"firstName": "George", "lastName": "Bush", "address": {"street": "1600 Penn-
sylvania Avenue NW", "city": "Washington", "state": "DC", "zip": "20500"}}*/
```

demo/id4
```
Number(dojo.byId("exId").value) * 10
```

demo/id5

<contact><firstName>George</firstName><lastName>Bush</lastName>
<address street="1600 Pennsylvania Avenue NW" city="Washington"
state="DC" zip="20500" /></contact>

Now we can demonstrate retrieving JSON by setting args.handleAs to
"json":

remote-scripting/remote-scripting.js

```
function handler4(response, ioArgs){
  var error= response instanceof Error;
  var responseText= error ? response.message : ioArgs.xhr.responseText;
  var resultNode= dojo.byId("result");
  resultNode.innerHTML= responseText.replace(/</g, "&lt;");
  dojo.toggleClass(resultNode, "error", error);
  dojo.byId("objects").innerHTML=
    dumpObject({response: response});
}

function example6(){
  dojo.xhrGet({
    url: "demo/id2",
    handleAs: "json",
    handle: handler4
  });
}
```

The example constructs a new handler (handler4) that displays both the
raw response and the final result after applying the content handler to
the raw response. Usually, you won't be interested in the raw response,
but it is available at ioArgs.xhr.responseText (line 3). Notice that the processed response is *not* text but, rather, is a full-fledged JavaScript
object. In Figure 8.2, on the next page, you can see the result of running
example 6.

If you run the example with the debug console open, you will see a
warning appear something like "Consider using mimetype:text/json-
comment-filtered to avoid potential security issues with JSON endpoints (use djConfig.usePlainJson=true to turn off this message)."

There are two solutions to eliminating this message. First, you can
follow the instructions and set djConfig.usePlainJson to true when loading dojo.js (see Section 4.3, *Loading Dojo*, on page 72). Otherwise, you
can change the server to send comment-filtered JSON and specify "json-
comment-filtered" for args.handleAs.

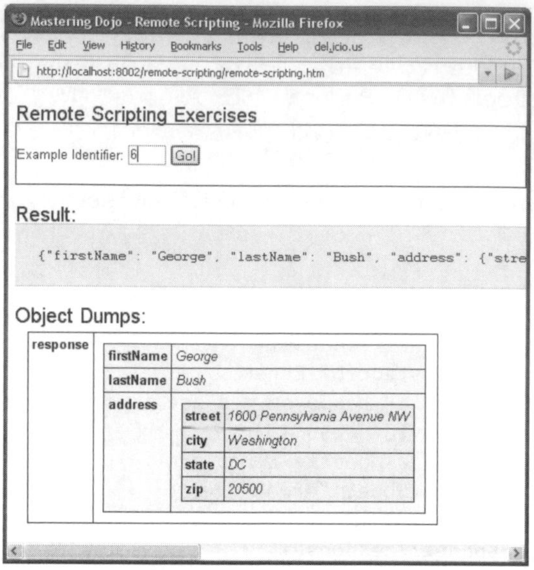

Figure 8.2: RETRIEVING JSON

Here's what that looks like:

`remote-scripting/remote-scripting.js`

```
Line 1   function example7(){
    -      dojo.xhrGet({
    -        url: "demo/id3",
    -        handleAs: "json-comment-filtered",
    5        handle: handler4
    -      });
    -    }
```

The resulting output is given in Figure 8.3, on the next page.

Notice that the "json" handler *prohibits* comment-filtered JSON, while "json-comment-filtered" *requires* it. The handler "json-comment-optional" solves this problem by treating the response as "json-comment-filtered" and falling back to "json" if this fails. The code download includes examples 8 and 9 that demonstrate the "json-comment-optional" handler.

Specifying "javascript" for args.handleAs causes the response text to be evaluated in the global scope by dojo.eval. Our test server has concocted a little calculation based on the value of the input#exId element when the URL demo/id4 is requested.

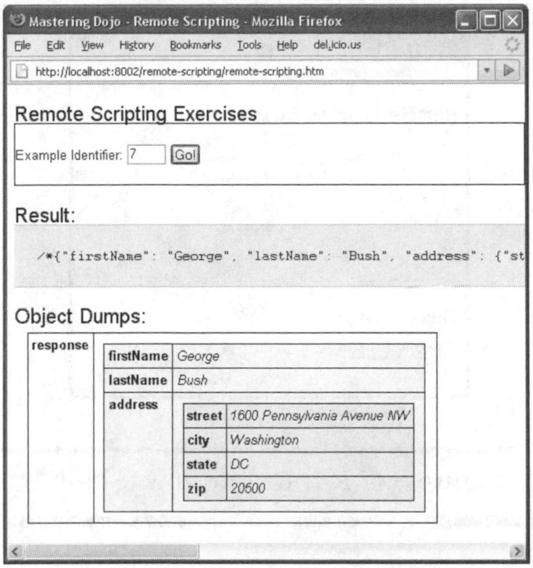

Figure 8.3: RETRIEVING COMMA-FILTERED JSON

Here's the example:

```
remote-scripting/remote-scripting.js
```

```
Line 1  function example10(){
   -      dojo.xhrGet({
   -        url: "demo/id4",
   -        handleAs: "javascript",
   5        handle: handler4
   -      });
   -      //returns "Number(dojo.byId("cxId").value) * 10"
   -    }
```

The resulting output is given in Figure 8.4, on the following page.

Finally, specifying "xml" for args.handleAs causes the XHR responseXML property to be returned as the result. Some help is given in certain cases where Internet Explorer fails to properly parse a good document.

Figure 8.4: RETRIEVING JAVASCRIPT

Here's the example to get an XML document:

```
remote-scripting/remote-scripting.js
Line 1  function example11(){
          function handler5(response, ioArgs){
            var error= response instanceof Error;
            var responseText= error ? response.message : ioArgs.xhr.responseText;
     5      var resultNode= dojo.byId("result");
            resultNode.innerHTML= responseText.replace(/</g, "&lt;");
            dojo.toggleClass(resultNode, "error", error);
            dojo.byId("objects").innerHTML=
              dumpObject({response: response});
    10      }

          dojo.xhrGet({
            url: "demo/id5",
            handleAs: "xml",
    15      handle: handler5
          });
        }
```

The resulting output is given in Figure 8.5, on the next page.

Controlling the HTTP Transaction

At its heart, an XHR simply executes an HTTP transaction. So far, we've
seen only how to specify the URL. Let's look at other aspects of the HTTP
transaction that can be configured.

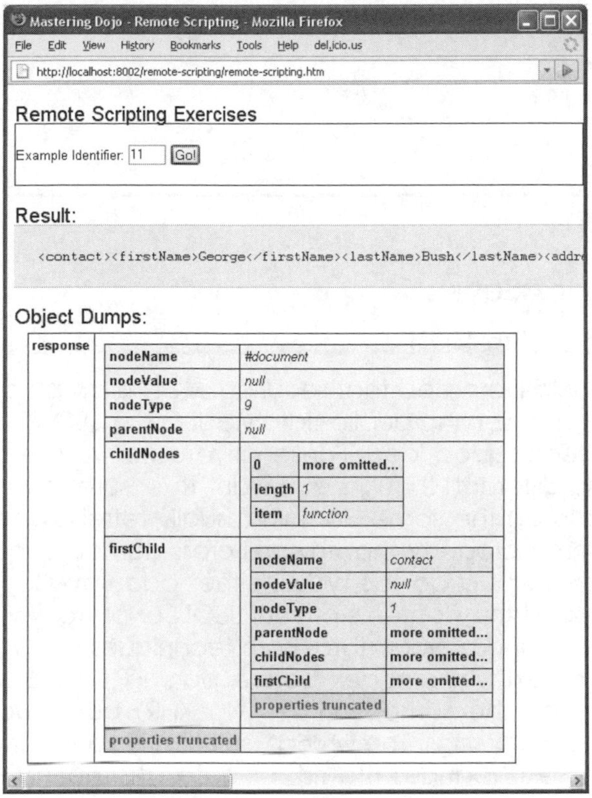

Figure 8.5: RETRIEVING XML

First, the XHR open method can accept optional user and password values for servers that require authentication. These values can be set by the args properties user and password, respectively. Setting args. preventCache to true causes the parameter "dojo.preventCache=*current-timestamp*" to be appended to the URL. Since the current time will change with each XHR execution, the URL will change, and any cache should be defeated.

A hash of headers to be sent with the transaction can be given at args.headers. The Content-Type header can be specified in either args. contentType or args.headers["content-type"]. At most, one of these locations should be used; if completely missing, then Content-Type defaults to "application/x-www-form-urlencoded". If you make a mistake and specify the content type in both places, the value of args.contentType wins.

Alex Says. . .

Securing JSON

First, it should be noted that securing JSON is an issue only for sensitive data. Serving public data via JSON or JSONP at stable URLs is often a good idea. For sensitive data, you need to do something different, though. You want to ensure that your use of the data on the same domain (usually retrieved with XHR) exhibits some property that thwarts cross-domain requests via a *<script>* tag. To do this, you'll either add JavaScript comments around the contents of your JSON or put a while(1); line at the beginning of your data. Both techniques allow processing of the text via a regex before parsing the JSON when requested on the same domain (via XHR) but thwart inclusion via *<script>* tags. The while(1); solution is considered superior because it reduces the risk of data attempting to inject escape sequences, although Dojo today uses json-comment-filtered (JSON with comments around it) as a default and warns if JSON data is requested via XHR without this kind of protection.

In any case, the strongest solutions to these problems are on the server side: sensitive data should not be served at predictable URLs, and some security token other than cookies should be used to validate a request. One good solution is to force the requesting system to include the contents of one of the cookies in the body of the request, which is something a script on the same domain can easily do but Evil.com's script can't. Regardless, assertions that JavaScript toolkits need to "do something" about CSRF and JavaScript hijacking are largely bogus. Dojo goes as far as it can to help developers do the right thing, but real solutions to CSRF all require server-side code to be fixed.

Setting args.sync to hold the identity true causes the XHR to be executed synchronously. Note carefully that args.sync must be set to the boolean value true (that is, sync===true must evaluate to true) in order for to send the XHR synchronously. So, for example, sync:1 would not do the trick; you must say something like sync:true or sync:(!!callSynchronously). You should avoid making synchronous XHR calls since the browser will be locked until the call returns.

Finally, URL query parameters can be specified by providing them in the args.content hash directly.

Let's put all of this together and execute an XHR transaction that exercises these properties. Here's an example:

remote-scripting/remote-scripting.js

```
Line 1   dojo.xhrGet({
  -        url: "demo/id6",
  -        user: "john",
  -        password: "open-sesame",
  5        content: {
  -          param1: "someParamValue",
  -          param2: 2.7183
  -        },
  -        contentType: "text/plain",
  10       headers: {
  -          myKey: "someValue",
  -          anotherKey: 3.1416
  -        },
  -        synch: true,
  15       preventCache: true,
  -        handleAs: "json-comment-filtered",
  -        handle: handler12
  -      });
  -    }
```

When you run the example in Firefox with Firebug, you'll see the actual URL used is http://john:open-sesame@localhost:8002/remote-scripting/demo/id6?param1 = someParamValue&param2 = 2.7183&dojo.preventCache= 1209234790968. Notice the URL includes the user ID/password fragment john:open-sesame@. The parameter fragment ?param1=someParamValue& param2=2.7183&dojo.preventCache=1209234790968. param1 and param2 were set by args.content, while dojo.preventCache was set since args. preventCache was true (1203402063531 was the current time the XHR was executed).

The args property timeout can be used to set the time in milliseconds to wait for the XHR to complete. Of course, timeout is meaningful only when the XHR is executed asynchronously. If the XHR has not completed within the allotted time period, then it will be aborted, and the error and/or handle function will be called. If timeout is omitted, the XHR will time out as provided by the browser.

Using Forms

Often a form is used to collect information that is passed to the server through an XHR transaction. Unlike native XHR objects that provide no help in bundling the information contained in the form, the dojo.xhr* functions do most of this work for you. Let's look at an example; first we need a form:

remote-scripting/remote-scripting2.htm

```
Line 1   <form id="exForm" method="post" action="demo/id7" enctype="text/plain">
   -        <p>Name:<br>
   -        <input type="text" name="name" size="40"></p>
   -        <p>Sex:<br>
   5        <input type="radio" name="sex" value="m"> Male<br>
   -        <input type="radio" name="sex" value="f"> Female</p>
   -     </form>
```

The contents of the form can be transacted with the server by specifying the form node or id attribute of the form node in the args.form property. The URL is taken from the form's action attribute. Here's the code:

remote-scripting/remote-scripting.js

```
Line 1   function example13(){
   -        dojo.xhrGet({
   -          form: "exForm",
   -          handleAs: "json-comment-filtered",
   5          handle: handler4
   -        });
   -     }
```

Assuming the user supplied "Jane Doe" for the name and clicked the female radio button, then an HTTP GET transaction is executed with the relative URL demo/id7&name=Jane%20Doe&sex=f. What could be simpler?

There are two places where certain XHR parameters can be "overdetermined." For example, the URL can be specified both in args.url and in the form's action attribute. Similarly, both the contents of the form and the value of args.contents are destined to the parameters portion of the URL (or, as we'll see in a moment, the POST body content). In each case, when there is a clash, the values in args win. For example, writing this...

remote-scripting/remote-scripting.js

```
Line 1   function example14(){
    -      dojo.xhrGet({
    -        form: "exForm",
    -        content: {sex: "m", anotherParam: 3.1416},
    5        handleAs: "json-comment-filtered",
    -        handle: handler4
    -      });
    -    }
```

results in the parameter string demo/id7?name=Jane%20Doe&sex=m& anotherParam=3.1416. Notice how "sex=f" from the form was overwritten by "sex=m" as specified by content. Sorry, Jane.

Posting and Other HTTP Methods

dojo.xhrPost works just like dojo.xhrGet except that an HTTP POST transaction is executed and parameters given by args.content and args.form are sent in the HTTP request body rather than as a query string encoded in the URL.

dojo.rawXhrPost also executes an HTTP POST transaction, but it completely ignores args.content and args.form. Instead, the string value of the args.postData property is sent verbatim in the request body.

dojo.xhrPut and dojo.rawXhrPut work like dojo.xhrPost and dojo.rawXhrPost except that an HTTP PUT transaction is executed. In similar fashion, dojo.xhrDelete works like dojo.xhrGet.

It's easy to get confused about all of this; here's a summary of how parameters are specified:

- The request parameters for dojo.xhrGet, dojo.xhrDelete, dojo.xhrPost, and dojo.xhrPut are specified by args.content and args.form (both properties are optional). When there is a clash and both args. content and args.form try to specify a value for the same property, args.content wins.

- The request parameters for dojo.rawXhrPost and dojo.rawXhrPut are specified, verbatim, by the postData and putData properties of args, respectively; the parameters in args.content and args.form are ignored.

And here's a summary of how parameters are sent in the request:

- The request parameters for dojo.xhrGet and dojo.xhrDelete are encoded as a parameter string and appended to the URL.
- The request parameters for dojo.xhrPost, dojo.xhrPut, dojo.rawXhrPost, and dojo.rawXhrPut are sent in the request body.

The Rest of the Story

In most cases, XHR calls should be made asynchronously (this is easily accomplished by leaving args.sync uninitialized). When the native XHR object returns a response, the dojo.xhr* functions first call the content handler and then pass the results of this call to the load/error/handler function specified in args. This pattern of a chain of functions executing after an asynchronous function completes should sound familiar since it is precisely the pattern dojo.Deferred manages that we discussed in Section 6.4, *Managing Callbacks with dojo.Deferred*, on page 117. So, it's no surprise that the dojo.xhr* functions use dojo.Deferred instances to manage the XHR call.

Each of the dojo.xhr* functions constructs a dojo.Deferred object that manages the XHR process, and the dojo.xhr* function calls the Deferred's callback with the result of the content handler. This starts processing down the Deferred callback queue. Usually, there is only one callback function waiting—the function specified by args.load or args.handle. If an error occurred (for example, the XHR fails or times out), then the dojo.xhr* function calls the Deferred's errback, passing the Error object. Again, this usually results in executing the function specified by args. error or args.handle.

In most cases, you won't care about all this gory detail—you'll just specify a handler function. But some designs can be expressed quite elegantly in terms of the callback queue implemented by dojo.Deferred. Since the dojo.xhr* functions return the dojo.Deferred object that controls the XHR process, you can add functions to the callback/errback queues as well as cancel the XHR.

8.3 Remote Scripting with script

When you need to dynamically load a JavaScript resource from a server that resides at a different origin than the document, XHR won't work because of the same-origin policy. Instead, inserting a script element into the document is the method of choice. The idea is simple: create a script element, set its source attribute to reference the resource, and then attach the element to the document. Here's the code:

```
Line 1   var element = dojo.doc.createElement("script");
         element.type = "text/javascript";
         element.src = url;
         dojo.doc.getElementsByTagName("head")[0].appendChild(element);
```

The resource identified by the URL given at line 3 will be downloaded and evaluated. And since there is no restriction on the src attribute of a script element, any resource on any server can be referenced. This gets around the same-origin restriction.[7] There is still one problem to solve: how do you know when the script has arrived and been evaluated?

Detecting Dynamically Loaded Scripts

This problem has two common solutions. First, assuming the client-side code downloading the script has knowledge of some variable defined by the script, then the client-side code could set a timer and watch for this variable to become defined. Finding the variable exists indicates that the script has been downloaded and evaluated. Here is a complete example that implements this idea:

```
Line 1   function example15(){
           function loadScript(url, checkString){
             var element = dojo.doc.createElement("script");
             element.type = "text/javascript";
5            element.src = url;
             dojo.doc.getElementsByTagName("head")[0].appendChild(element);
             var intervalId= setInterval(check, 50);

             function check(){
10             if (eval("typeof(" + checkString + ") != 'undefined'")) {
                 clearInterval(intervalId);
                 o = dojo.getObject(checkString);
                 dojo.byId("result").innerHTML = o.result.replace(/</g, "&lt;");
               }
15           }
           }

           loadScript("demo/id8", "id8Object")
         }
```

---

7. While dynamic script technique solves the same-origin restriction, it still has the limitation that only JavaScript content can be transferred. If you need to retrieve something else (for example, text, HTML, or XML), then that something else must be wrapped in a JSON object.

Alex Says...

Cross-Domain Scripts and Security

Browsers are naive. For as much commerce is done online and for as much effort is put into web application security, browsers today enforce more or less the same set of rules about where code and data comes from as they did a decade ago. The same-origin policy (see http://en.wikipedia.org/wiki/Same_origin_policy) that browsers enforce isn't part of any W3C specification, and for the most part, it has served to keep private data private when implemented robustly enough. The theory has been that if you can keep bad things from getting into the page, then there's no problem. All data and code that live on the same page therefore have unfettered access to each other.

But things are changing, and as mashups become ever more common, it has become accepted practice to pull in data and scripts from multiple domains. In many cases, this is actually desirable for performance reasons, and browsers make no attempt to stop this unless a page is served in "SSL mode." Because browsers are designed to trust things that somehow got into the page, scripts loaded from other servers can provide both code and data to applications. In fact, the Web critically depends on this feature: without it, most ad services would fail because they use cross-domain script loading to hand pages customized, targeted ads for each visitor. The JSONP style of data loading takes advantage of this feature, but as you can imagine, there are some security risks involved. What if the script that you're pulling in is compromised? Or what if the data isn't correctly escaped? These are serious issues that need server-side solutions for now and browser-based solutions soon (Google Gears' cross-domain thread worker is a promising option). Today, it's best to pull in cross-domain scripts from places that you can trust and avoid it otherwise.

For this to work, the server must send back some JavaScript that actually defines the watched variable. Our test server sends back the following code for the URL demo/id8:

```
id8Object= {};
id8Object.result= "exercise15--hello, world";
```

When this code is evaluated, the function dojo.setObject causes the object exercise15.myObject to be defined. The next timer interrupt will find eval("typeof(exercise15.myObject) != 'undefined'") to evaluate to true, stop the timer, and push the result into the web page.

This method isn't ideal since it requires all scripts downloaded in this manner to maintain at least one object name that is unique to each script. This is to say, scripts that may have no knowledge of each other must somehow construct identifiers that are unique—which requires some knowledge of each other![8]

The second method to determine when the script has been downloaded requires some coordination between the browser and the server. When the browser makes a request for a script, it informs the server of a callback function name through the URL query string. The server then delivers a script that calls the designated function with the result of the script. Exercise 16 demonstrates this technique:

```
Line 1   function example16(){
  -        function loadScript(url, callback){
  -          dojo.setObject(callback, function(o){
  -            dojo.byId("result").innerHTML = o.result.replace(/</g, "&lt;");
  5        })

  -        var element = dojo.doc.createElement("script");
  -        element.type = "text/javascript";
  -        element.src = url + "?callbackName=" + callback;
  10       dojo.doc.getElementsByTagName("head")[0].appendChild(element);
  -      }

  -      loadScript("demo/id9", "exercise16.myCallback")
  -    }
```

---

8. In practice, there are techniques for choosing names (for example, the Microsoft Guid-Gen program) that virtually assure clashes will not occur.

Our test server sends back the following code for the URL demo/id9:

remote-scripting/remote-scripting.js

```
exercise16.myCallback({"result": "hello, world"});
```

When the previous code is downloaded and evaluated by the dynamic script element, exercise16.myCallback is executed, and result is pushed into the web page. Notice that the example effectively delivers a JSON object to the callback function. This technique is called JSONP because it prepends JSON with a function call. JSONP is becoming increasingly common and used by several large information suppliers.

Dojo Support for Dynamic Script Elements

While these techniques are implemented quite differently when compared to orchestrating an XHR call, functionally they are very similar: a URL is specified, and a response is received. Dojo leverages this fact and provides the function dojo.io.script.get that works much like dojo.xhrGet.

dojo.io.script.get takes a single argument hash called args, which has semantics mostly the same as the args used with the dojo.xhr* functions (we'll term the args hash used with dojo.io.script.get "script args" to avoid confusion). The script args properties content, headers, query, timeout, and preventCache have the same semantics as the dojo.xhr* functions. Since the response is always JavaScript and usually JSON (JSON could be used to encode any other type—HTML, XML, or others), there is no need to specify a content handler, and args.handleAs is ignored. There are also a couple of additional properties that orchestrate the two dynamic scripting techniques we just discussed.

To make a dynamic script call that signals completion by defining a variable, set args.checkString to the variable name. Here is example 15 reimplemented using dojo.io.script.get:

remote-scripting/remote-scripting.js

```
Line 1  dojo.require("dojo.io.script");
     -  function example17(){
     -
     -    function handler17(response, ioArgs){
     5      var error= response instanceof Error;
     -      var responseText= error ? response.message : id8Object.result;
     -      var resultNode= dojo.byId("result");
     -      resultNode.innerHTML= responseText.replace(/</g, "&lt;");
     -      dojo.toggleClass(resultNode, "error", error);
    10      dojo.byId("objects").innerHTML=
     -        dumpObject({response: response, ioArgs: ioArgs});
     -    }
     -
```

```
      dojo.io.script.get({
 15     url:"demo/id8",
        checkString:"id8Object",
        handle:handler17
      });
   }
```

dojo.io.script is not included in dojo.js, so it must be dojo.required explicitly. This is done at line 1. The resulting output is given in Figure 8.6, on the next page. Note that, upon success, the result passed to the handler function is ioArgs, *not* the response. In fact, it is impossible to gain access to the verbatim text that is sent to fill the script element. Presumably, the client side knows which objects to expect from the script, so the result of the dynamic script can be accessed directly, as we've done at line 6 in the example. In keeping with the idea that dojo.io.script.get works like dojo.xhr*, ioArgs is also passed as the second argument. Similarly, an Error object and ioArgs are passed to error/handle functions if an error occurs (for example, if a timeout as specified by args.timeout occurs).

dojo.io.script.get also implements the JSONP protocol. The parameter name in which to stuff the callback function name is specified by args. callbackParamName. Here is example 18 reimplemented using dojo.io. script.get:

remote-scripting/remote-scripting.js

```
Line 1  function example18(){
          dojo.require("dojo.io.script");

          function handler18(response, ioArgs){
 5          var error= response instanceof Error;
            var responseText= error ? response.message : response.result;
            var resultNode= dojo.byId("result");
            resultNode.innerHTML= responseText.replace(/</g, "&lt;");
            dojo.toggleClass(resultNode, "error", error);
 10         dojo.byId("objects").innerHTML=
              dumpObject({"response": response, ioArgs: ioArgs});
          }

          dojo.io.script.get({
 15         url:"demo/id9",
            callbackParamName:"callbackName",
            handle:handler18
          });
        }
```

The resulting output is given in Figure 8.7, on page 201. Notice that Dojo constructed the URL demo/id9?callbackName=dojo.io.script.jsonp_dojoIoScript1._jsonpCallback. The query parameter was "callbackName" as

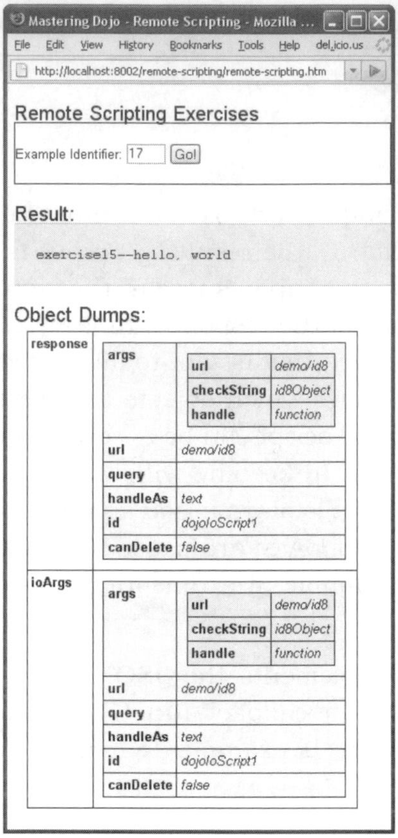

Figure 8.6: EXECUTING DOJO.IO.SCRIPT.GET

specified in args.callbackParamName, and dojo.io.script.get created a callback function named dojo.io.script.jsonp_dojoloScript1._jsonpCallback. It was up to the server to return a script that calls this function, passing a single argument according to the semantics of the delivered script. The callback function implemented by dojo.io.script.get is simply a function that receives a single argument, and whatever is passed for this argument is forwarded to the load/handle functions. Usually the single argument is a JavaScript object, in which case the call is just a simple JSONP transaction, but there is nothing preventing the server from sending a script that passes something other than an object (for example, a number or string) to the callback function.

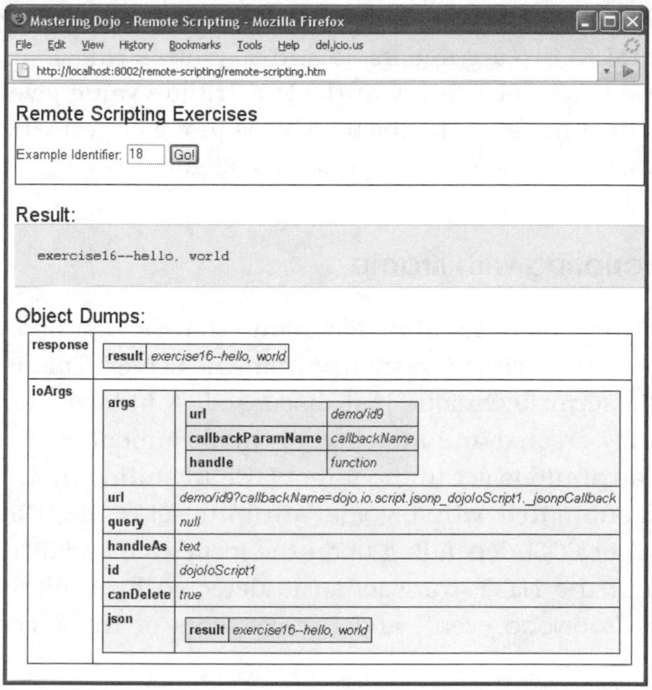

Figure 8.7: DOJO.IO.SCRIPT.GET WITH A CALLBACK

The single argument sent to the callback function is passed on as the first argument to the load/handle functions; the second argument is ioArgs. Errors are handled as usual.

As with the dojo.xhr* functions, dojo.io.script.get returns a dojo.Deferred instance that manages the process. ioArgs contains two additional public properties:

- id: The HTML id attribute for the dynamically created script element
- json: The argument passed to the callback function (applicable only when args.callbackParamName is specified)

If JSONP is used (by providing args.callbackParamName), then the dynamically created script element will be automatically destroyed some time after the callback function has executed. On the other hand, if args.checkString is given, then it is left to the client code to manage the lifetime of the script element. You can destroy this element by calling the function dojo.io.script.remove(ioArgs.id).

Finally, Dojo's script machinery includes the function dojo.io.script. attach that takes two arguments, id and url (both strings), and dynamically creates a script element with the id attribute value given by the id and the src attribute given by the url. This is just a convenience function when you need to dynamically add a script element.

8.4 Remote Scripting with iframe

The last native remote scripting technique that Dojo supports uses an iframe element to retrieve a response from the server. This is similar to the dynamic script technique just discussed. A hidden iframe element is dynamically created and attached to the document. Then either the iframe's src attribute is set to the target URL (resulting in an HTTP GET) or a form is submitted with its target attribute set to the URL (resulting in either GET or POST depending upon the form's method attribute). The completion of the HTTP transaction is detected by hooking an event to the iframe's onload event, and the contents of the iframe hold the response.

The server response must be an HTML document since this is the only content that an iframe can legally contain. If the URL is actually delivering some other content type (for example, JSON), then the server-side and client-side code must agree on a method to wrap and unwrap the content in HTML. Finally, the iframe technique is subject to the same-origin policy. So if the source URL references a different origin than the main document, it is *impossible* to share data between the two documents. Given all this pain, why would you ever want to use the iframe technique?

Historically, some browsers didn't implement the XHR API. In this case, the iframe technique was essentially equivalent to the script technique when retrieving from the same origin as the main document (retrieving HTML is slightly easier with iframes; retrieving JavaScript is slightly easier with script elements). Now that XHR is universally available, XHR should be favored over iframes since iframes are a hack. But there is still one place where iframes are required: XHRs can't post a file; iframes can. So if you want to post a file asynchronously without a plug-in, the iframe technique is your only choice.

Dojo Support for Scripting with iframes

The function dojo.io.iframe.send implements scripting with iframes and has semantics almost identical to the dojo.xhrGet and dojo.xhrPost functions. It takes a single argument, args, that defines the same properties as dojo.xhr* args (we'll term the args hash used with dojo.io.iframe.send "iframe args" to avoid confusion). iframe args also defines the additional property method (a string) that designates which HTTP method (GET or POST) to use for the transaction.

Let's look at an example; first we need a form with a file input element:

remote-scripting/remote-scripting3.htm

```
Line 1  <div>
          <form id="exForm" method="post" action="demo/id11"
            enctype="multipart/form-data">
            <p>Name:<br>
5           <input type="text" name="name" size="40"></p>
            <p>Sex:<br>
            <input type="radio" name="sex" value="m"> Male<br>
            <input type="radio" name="sex" value="f"> Female</p>
            <p>About me:<br>
10          <input type="file"  name="aboutMe" size="40" maxlength="255"></p>
          </form>
        </div>
```

And here's how to use dojo.io.frame.send to HTTP POST the contents of the form asynchronously:

remote-scripting/remote-scripting.js

```
Line 1  dojo.require("dojo.io.iframe");
        function handler20(response, ioArgs){
          if (!(response instanceof Error)) {
            dojo.byId("objects").innerHTML=
5             dumpObject({response: response, ioArgs: ioArgs});
          } else {
            var resultNode= dojo.byId("result");
            resultNode.innerHTML= response.message;
            dojo.toggleClass(resultNode, "error", true);
10          dojo.byId("objects").innerHTML=
              dumpObject({response: response, ioArgs: ioArgs});
          }
        }

15      function example20(){
          dojo.io.iframe.send({
            form: "exForm",
            url: "demo/id11",
            method: "post",
20          handleAs: "json",
            handle: handler20
          });
        }
```

dojo.io.iframe is not included in dojo.js, so it must be dojo.required explicitly. This is done at line 1. The iframe args argument should look familiar. The example explicitly set args.url and args.method, but these two properties could have been omitted in which case they would have been taken implicitly from the form's action and method attributes, respectively. If you specify these properties in both places, args wins. Finally, dojo.io.iframe.send returns the dojo.Deferred object that controls the process just like dojo.xhr*.

The example gave "json" for args.handleAs. dojo.io.iframe.send also allows "html", "text", and "javascript", but it does not support "xml". When "html" is given, the document object that is contained by the iframe is returned. Other response types require more work since the result is embedded in the HTML document that is contained by the iframe. dojo.io.iframe.send makes the assumption that the response will contain a single HTML textarea element that holds the result. For the example, the server returned the following HTML:

`remote-scripting/remote-scripting.js`

```
Line 1   <html>
   -       <body>
   -          <textarea>{result: "OK"}</textarea>
   -       </body>
   5     </html>
```

textarea elements are fairly easy to work with, but certain kinds of content will cause problems. For example, if the JSON {"nasty": "</textarea>"} were embedded in a textarea element, the browser would fail to parse the document correctly, and the transaction would fail. These problems can be avoided by using HTML character entities to encode ampersand and left-angle bracket characters.

Following this advice, the nasty example looks like <textarea>{nasty: "</textarea>"}</textarea>, which parses successfully. This is a server-side issue and can largely be avoided by minimizing the use of iframes for anything other than posting a file; if you need to retrieve complicated content, use dojo.xhr*.

There is one small gotcha in dojo.io.iframe. When dojo.io.iframe.send is called the first time, it dynamically creates an iframe element and appends it to the main document. When this element is created, the src attribute is set to *dojo-module-path*/resources/blank.html (remember, *dojo-module-path* gives the path to the dojo module). So long as you are serving Dojo from your own server, everything will work perfectly. However, if you're retrieving Dojo from another server (for example, from a CDN server) or you are executing HTTPS GET transactions through dojo.io.iframe.send after loading dojo.js with the HTTP scheme, then the transaction will fail since the src of an iframe can't change the origin.

The djConfig property dojoBlankHtmlUrl can be used to specify the src attribute when the iframe is created. So, for example, if the main document resides at https://www.someCompany.com/main.htm and you are using the cross-domain version of Dojo sourced from the AOL CDN server, you must specify dojoBlankHtmlUrl like this:

`remote-scripting/remote-scripting.js`

```
Line 1  <script
          type="text/javascript"
          src="http://o.aolcdn.com/dojo/1.1.0/dojo/dojo.xd.js"
          djConfig=
     5      "dojoBlankHtmlUrl: 'http://www.someCompany.com/dojo/resources/blank.html'">
        </script>
```

If you forget to set dojoBlankHtmlUrl under these circumstances, you will get a console warning message, and dojo.io.iframe.send will fail as described earlier.

iframe Utility Functions

dojo.io.iframe includes three utility functions that are useful if you are building machinery that uses iframes. The function dojo.io.iframe.create creates a new iframe and appends it to the document. It takes the name, onload, and src attribute values (all strings) as arguments. The onload and src arguments are optional; if the src argument is missing, then the value of dojo.config["dojoBlankHtmlUrl"] || dojo.moduleUrl("dojo", "resources/blank.html") is used. To create the iframe element <iframe name="myIframe" onload="loadMyIframe();" src="demo/id11"></iframe>, write the following:

dojo.io.iframe.create("myIframe", "loadMyIframe();", "demo/id11");

Once you have an iframe, you can force a new document to dynamically load with the function dojo.io.iframe.setSrc. This function takes an iframe name that's been previously created and a URL and reloads the iframe. A third parameter (a boolean) instructs the function to use the DOM function location.replace, instead assigning to the location property when specifying the new URL. This results in keeping the navigation out of the browser history.

So, to change the content of the iframe we created earlier to some other content (say "other/content"), write the following:

dojo.io.iframe.setSrc("myIframe", "other/content", true);

Finally, dojo.io.iframe.doc takes a DOM node that references an iframe element and returns the document contained by that element.

8.5 Leveraging Remote Scripting to Access Web Services

The three native remote scripting techniques we've been discussing are fairly primitive: send a request; get a response. The formulation and semantics of both the request and the response are left to the programmer. It is possible to build higher levels of abstraction. What's even better is that we can use these higher abstractions to interface with several commercial web service providers (for example, Yahoo Search Services, http://developer.yahoo.com/search).

Broadly speaking, a web service is a set of information products that are accessible by executing an HTTP transaction. For example, concoct a magical URL, and you'll get back a JSON object that describes the result of a web search from Yahoo. While not required, many web services publish a description of the service in a computer-readable language. This presents an opportunity to build abstractions by using these service descriptions to *automatically* produce code that interfaces with the described services. Dojo's remote procedure call machinery implements this idea.

Remote Procedure Calls Defined

Loosely speaking, a remote procedure call (RPC) is a mechanism for one process to execute a function in another process and receive the result as if the function call were local. Although it's true that any interprocess communication (IPC) ultimately executes a function in another process, the bit about "as if the function were local" is what differentiates RPC from generic IPC.

All RPC systems have similar design. A package is constructed by the calling process that contains the identification of the function to call as well as the argument values to pass to that function. The package is sent to the executing process, which executes the function, creates a package that contains the result, and sends the result package back to the calling process. For example, say an HTTP server publishes the function add at the URL http://calculator.com and uses JSON to package the request and results. We could calculate "1 + 2" by sending the server {proc: "add", op1: 1, op2: 2}; the server should return {"result": 3}. The full call might look like this:

```
remote-scripting/remote-scripting.js
Line 1   function example21(){

           function add(x, y) {
             var result;
    5        dojo.xhrPut({
               url: "http://calculator.com",
               content: {proc: "add", op1: x, op2: y},
               synch: true,
               handle: function(result_) {
    10             result= result_;
               }
             });
             return result;
           }
    15
           var one_plus_two= add(1, 2);

           alert("add(1, 2)= " + one_plus_two);

    20   }
```

The call add(1, 2) at line 16 looks just like a local function call, yet the function is actually executed on a remote server.

Most RPC systems include a description language that is used to describe the functions published by the remote server. Descriptions are fed into machinery that generates proxies to the remote functions. In the previous example, the function add starting at line 3 is a proxy.

There are two popular ways to package the RPC request and response over HTTP: JSON-RPC[9] and XML-RPC.[10] In our view, JSON is lighter and easier to use than XML (at least in the web app arena) without losing any significant functionality.

The service description language for JSON-RPC is the Simple Method Description (SMD) language. At the time of this writing, there is no official, approved standard for SMD. However, the Dojo developers responsible for Dojo's RPC machinery (Dustin Machi and Kris Zyp) are work-

---

9. See http://json-rpc.org/wd/JSON-RPC-1-1-WD-20060807.html.
10. See http://www.xmlrpc.com/.

ing hard within the JSON-RPC community[11] to finalize a standard. It is likely that SMD will eventually look like the example given at http://dojotoolkit.org/~dmachi/rpc/V2example-3.smd.

As of version 1.1, Dojo provides some support for JSON-RPC in both Dojo and Dojox. Since neither JSON-RPC nor SMD is an approved standard, this part of Dojo is likely to experience some evolution in the near future. Still, the architecture is stable, and it is unlikely that new functionality will break existing functionality. Most important, the current RPC system is worth knowing about since it can be used to build and deploy elegant and useful services.

Executing RPCs with dojo.rpc

Dojo's RPC machinery takes an SMD description and produces an object that can be used to make remote procedure calls. Here's an example SMD description for a service that publishes the functions add and subtract:

remote-scripting/remote-scripting.js

```
Line 1   var arithmeticService = {
  -        serviceURL: "demo/id7",
  -        methods: [{
  -          name: "add",
  5          parameters: [{
  -            name: "op1",
  -            type: "number"
  -          }, {
  -            name: "op2",
  10           type: "number"
  -          }]
  -        }, {
  -          name: "subtract",
  -          parameters: [{
  15           name: "op1",
  -            type: "number"
  -          }, {
  -            name: "op2",
  -            type: "number"
  20         }]
  -        }]
  -      };
```

Assuming the server at demo/id7 accepts requests and delivers responses in JSON, the function dojo.rpc.JsonService will take this description

---

11. http://groups.google.com/group/json-rpc

and return an object that can be used to make the function calls.[12] dojo.
rpc.JsonService expects a single argument that specifies the SMD description in one of three ways:

- As a URL (a string) that delivers a JSON-comment-optional response that contains the SMD description; an HTTP GET transaction is used.
- As an SMD description object in the form of a JSON string. The
  string must be provided in an object at the property smdStr so the
  constructor can differentiate it from a URL string.
- As an SMD object (an object).

Assuming the SMD description of arithmeticService given earlier, here is
an example of passing the SMD as an object:

`remote-scripting/remote-scripting.js`

```
//don't forget the keyword new!
var calculator = new dojo.rpc.JsonService(arithmeticService);
```

We'll term the objects created by dojo.rpc.JsonService *RPC dispatchers*.
They include a method for each item in the methods array of the SMD
description; we'll term these *RPC dispatcher methods*. RPC dispatcher
methods should be called with arguments described by the associated params array in the SMD description and return a dojo.Deferred
object that executes the remote procedure call (we'll term this the *call-
controlling Deferred*). You access the results by providing callback functions to call-controlling Deferred. For example, we could use arithmetic-
Service to calculate 3 + 4 and send the result to an alert like this:

`remote-scripting/remote-scripting.js`

```
Line 1  calculator.add(3, 4).addCallback(function(result){
   -      alert("3 + 4= " + result);
   -    });
```

calculator is the RPC dispatcher, add is an RPC dispatcher method, and
calculator.add(3, 4) returns a call-controlling Deferred that controls the
remote procedure call to add.

RPC dispatcher methods execute a dojo.xhrPost to make the remote procedure call. The contents of the post is a JSON object with the properties method (a string, the method name), params (an array, the arguments provided), and id (an integer, starting at 1 and incremented

---

12. Notice that JsonService is capitalized, indicating that the function is a constructor that
returns new objects of the class dojo.rpc.JsonService.

with each remote procedure call made on a particular RPC dispatcher object). The example will post the following:

remote-scripting/remote-scripting.js

```
{"params":[3,4],"method":"add","id":1}
```

The response from the server must be a JSON object; this object is passed to the call-controlling Deferred's errback or callback methods as follows:

```
Line 1   //resultObject is the JSON object returned...
    -    if (resultObject.error!=null) {
    -      call_controlling_deferred.errback(parseError(resultObject));
    -    } else {
    5      call_controlling_deferred.callback(owning_rpc_dispatcher.parseResults(obj));
    -    }
```

If an error is indicated, then the call-controlling Deferred's errback method is called, as shown earlier (line 3). Otherwise, the call is assumed to have completed successfully, and the result object is transformed by the owning RPC dispatcher method parseResults and then passed to the call-controlling Deferred's callback method (line 5). dojo.rpc.JsonService provides the following default parseResults method:

```
Line 1   //resultObject is the JSON object returned...
    -    function parseResults(resultObject) {
    -      if (dojo.isObject(resultObject)) {
    -        if ("result" in resultObject) {
    5          return resultObject.result;
    -        }
    -        if ("Result" in resultObject) {
    -          return resultObject.Result;
    -        }
    10         if ("ResultSet" in resultObject) {
    -          return resultObject.ResultSet;
    -        }
    -      }
    -      return resultObject;
    15   }
```

For our example, the server returns {"result": "7"}, which achieves the desired effect with the default implementation of parseResults. parseResults can be replaced if the semantics of the server require something else. For example, assuming arithmeticService returns JSON objects like {"arithmeticServiceResult": "7"}, a customized parseResults could be used like this:

```
var calculator = new dojo.rpc.JsonService(arithmeticService);
calculator.parseResults= function(resultObject){
  return resultObject.arithmeticServiceResult;
}
```

A server can indicate an error by returning an object that includes the properties error and id. The property error may be an object, string, or number. If an object, then it must contain the properties message (a string), code (no type requirements), and error (no type requirements). RPC dispatcher methods extract information out of the response object when an error is indicated as follows:

```
Line 1   //resultObject is the JSON object returned...
    -    function parseError(resultObject) {
    -      var error;
    -      if (typeof resultObject.error == 'object') {
    5        error = new Error(resultObject.error.message);
    -        error.code = resultObject.error.code;
    -        error.error = resultObject.error.error;
    -      } else {
    -        error = new Error(resultObject.error);
   10      }
    -      error.id = resultObject.id;
    -      error.errorObject = resultObject;
    -      return error;
    -    }
```

Dojo also includes the function dojo.rpc.JsonpService that works with servers that return JSONP instead of JSON. dojo.rpc.JsonpService leverages dojo.io.script to execute the JSONP transaction. The script args callbackParamName property defaults to "callback" but can explicitly be set by specifying a value for the property callbackParamName in the RPC dispatcher returned by dojo.rpc.JsonpService. For example, assume that arithmeticService returns JSONP and expects that callback parameter name to be specified in the URL parameter "arithmeticService-callback-name". Here's how to do it:

```
var calculator = new dojo.rpc.JsonpService(arithmeticService);
calculator.callbackParamName = "arithmeticService-callback-name";
```

Now, we can use calculator very much as with the dojo.io.JsonService:

```
remote-scripting/remote-scripting.js
```
```
calculator.add({op1: 3, op2: 4}).addCallback(function(result){
  alert("3 + 4= " + result);
});
```

Notice that the parameters must be passed in a hash with their names ("{op1: 3, op2: 4}"). Since JSONP uses the dynamic script remote scripting technique, the parameters have to be passed in the URL, and consequently, they need names. The calculator.add resulted in the URL demo/id7?op1=3&op2=4&dojo.preventCache=1203893657656&arithmeticSer\
vice-callback-name=dojo.io.script.jsonp_dojoIoScript1._jsonpCallback.

Using Dojo RPC with Yahoo

Yahoo offers a number of free services that are easy to use with dojo.rpc. We'll demonstrate how to use the web search service (http://developer. yahoo.com/search/web/V1/webSearch.html). To actually use this example, you'll have to navigate to Yahoo developer services and register to get your own appid—a key that gives you access to the services (we didn't publish our real appid in the book).

The first thing we need is some SMD that describes the service. Lucky for us, this is already done: the file tests/resources/yahoo_smd_v1.smd in the dojo/ directory of the source release includes a JSON object that describes many of the Yahoo services. We simply cut out the web search service used for this example. Here's what that looks like:

remote-scripting/rpc-demo.htm

```
Line 1  var smd= {
          "SMDVersion":".1",
          "objectName":"yahoo",
          "serviceType":"JSON-P",
     5    "required": {
            "appid": "dojotoolkit",
            "output": "json"
          },
          "methods":[
    10      //
            // WEB SEARCH
            //
            {
              // http://developer.yahoo.com/search/web/V1/webSearch.html
    15        "name":"webSearch",
              "serviceURL": "http://api.search.yahoo.com/WebSearchService/V1/webSearch",
              "parameters":[
                { "name":"query", "type":"STRING" },
                { "name":"type", "type":"STRING" },
    20          { "name":"region", "type":"STRING" },
                { "name":"results", "type":"INTEGER" },
                { "name":"start", "type":"INTEGER" },
                { "name":"format", "type":"STRING" },
                { "name":"adult_ok", "type":"INTEGER" },
    25          { "name":"similar_ok", "type":"INTEGER" },
                { "name":"language", "type":"STRING" },
                { "name":"country", "type":"STRING" },
                { "name":"site", "type":"STRING" },
                { "name":"subscription", "type":"STRING" },
    30          { "name":"license", "type":"STRING" }
              ]
            }
          ]
        }
```

Next we need to use this SMD to create an RPC dispatcher. Since Yahoo is at a different origin than the main document, dojo.rpc.JsonpService must be used:

remote-scripting/rpc-demo.htm

```
Line 1  dojo.require("dojo.rpc.JsonpService");
    -   dojo.addOnLoad(function() {
    -     var service= new dojo.rpc.JsonpService(
    -       smd, {appid: "your-appid-goes-here"});
    5   });
```

Notice that the call to create the RPC dispatcher is made by a function registered to dojo.addOnLoad. This ensures that dojo.rpc.JsonpService will be loaded before any attempt is made to access objects defined by dojo.rpc.JsonpService.

Finally, the service is called through the RPC dispatcher method web-Search. In the following example, the query asks for web pages that contain "mastering dojo" located on the pragprog.com site. webSearch returns a dojo.Deferred.

remote-scripting/rpc-demo.htm

```
Line 1  dojo.require("dojo.rpc.JsonpService");
    -   dojo.addOnLoad(function() {
    -     var service= new dojo.rpc.JsonpService(
    -       smd, {appid: "your-appid-goes-here"});
    5     var theResult= service.webSearch(
    -       {query:'"mastering dojo"', site:"pragprog.com"});
    -     theResult.addCallback(function(result){
    -       console.dir(result);
    -     });
    10  });
```

The example dumps the result to the debug console. In a real application, the result would be traversed, and HTML would be built that displayed the results.

8.6 Bookmarking and the Back Button Without Navigating

None of the remote scripting techniques we've been discussing changes the DOM window.location property. As a result, it is impossible to bookmark a remote scripting operation, and therefore the state of the web page cannot be moved backward and forward through the browser's Back and Forward buttons. In many cases, it doesn't matter. For example, displaying an error message shouldn't be bookmarked. But, if you are building a web site that displays significant static content without

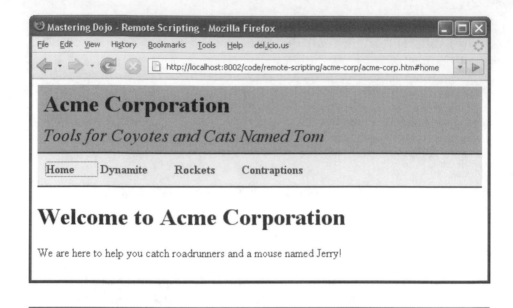

Figure 8.8: ACMECORP SINGLE WEB PAGE

changing the page URL, the Back/Forward buttons and bookmarking are important. Dojo includes machinery to fix this problem.

A Simple Single-Page Web App

Let's build a web site that sells products to Wile E. Coyote and Tom the Cat. It has four pages: Home, Dynamite, Rockets, and Contraptions. Each of these pages has identical title banners and menus; only the content is different. In Figure 8.8, you can see the Home page.

The web site is implemented by a single HTML file that dynamically loads the content portion of the page through an XHR call when a menu item is clicked. Here's the file:

remote-scripting/acme-corp/acme-corp0.htm

```
Line 1   <html><head>
    -      <title>
    -        Mastering Dojo - Remote Scripting
    -      </title>
    5
    -      <style type="text/css">
    -        @import "acme-corp.css";
    -      </style>
    -
```

```
10   <script
  -     type="text/javascript"
  -     src="/dojoroot/dojo/dojo.js"
  -     djConfig="isDebug: true"></script>

15   <script
  -     type="text/javascript"
  -     src="acme-corp0.js"></script>
  -   </head><body>
  -     <div class="titleBanner">
20       <h1>Acme Corporation</h1>
  -       <p class="tagline">Tools for Coyotes and Cats Named Tom</p>
  -     </div>
  -     <div id="menu">
  -       <p>
25         <a href="#home">Home</a>
  -         <a href="#dynamite">Dynamite</a>
  -         <a href="#rockets">Rockets</a>
  -         <a href="#contraptions">Contraptions</a>
  -       </p>
30     </div>
  -     <div id="content">
  -     </div>
  -   </body></html>
```

The menu is implemented by the set of anchors within div#menu. When
an anchor is clicked, a handler executes a dojo.xhrGet to retrieve the
content and then push it into div#content:

remote-scripting/acme corp/acme-corp0.js

```
Line 1   function loadContent(fragment){
  -        dojo.xhrGet({
  -          url:  fragment + ".htm",
  -          handleAs: "text",
5            handle: function(response){
  -            dojo.byId("content").innerHTML = response;
  -          }
  -        });
  -      }
10
  -      function doMainMenu(e){
  -        dojo.stopEvent(e);
  -        var fragment= e.target.getAttribute("href").split("#")[1]
  -        loadContent(fragment);
15     }

  -      dojo.addOnLoad(function(){
  -        dojo.connect(dojo.byId("menu"), "click", doMainMenu);
  -        loadContent("home");
20     })
```

As usual, initialization is accomplished by a function that is fired by dojo.addOnLoad. The anchor click events are handled by the div#menu handler; the event object target property will hold the actual anchor that was clicked. Since acme-corp.htm doesn't actually contain any content, the Home page content is also loaded as part of initialization.

The design assumes that the content is included in the resources home. html, dynamite.html, and the rest. Here's what dynamite.htm looks like:

remote-scripting/acme-corp/dynamite.htm

```
<h1>Dynamite to Blow Things Up</h1>
<p>Try these great products that go boom!</p>
```

Running the page at this stage demonstrates the problem: the URL in the navigation bar never changes even though the user can navigate to four seemingly distinct web pages. Further, the browser history is never changed, so the Back and Forward buttons don't work, and the only page that can be bookmarked is the Home page. Clearly, these deficiencies are unacceptable for a commercial web site.

Navigation Single-Page Web Apps with dojo.back

The Dojo module dojo.back includes machinery to fix these problems. The idea is to manually change the DOM property window.location when content changes by setting the window.location.hash property. Editing this property has the effect of changing the URL in the address bar and adding an item to the browser history but does not reload the page since only the fragment identifier (that's the part of the path URL after the # character) is changed. With the browser history filled with distinct URLs, the Back and Forward buttons will cause navigation to these URLs by changing window.location. dojo.back watches window.location and fires an event when it changes. Your code can connect to this event to load content as indicated by the changed fragment identifier.

Although dojo.back does all the heavy lifting, your code is responsible for signaling a navigation by sending a "state" object to dojo.back. dojo.back will extract the fragment identifier from the state object and use it to change window.location.hash as well as store the state object for later use when navigating with the Back/Forward buttons. When dojo.back detects back/forward navigation, it retrieves the state object associated with this and fires functions that are included in that object to signal that a back or forward navigation was demanded. To get all of this to work, we need to build a state object class, initialize dojo.back, and pass state objects to dojo.back at each content navigation.

The state object must include the property changeUrl, which holds the fragment identifier associated with a particular state. Optionally, the state object can include the functions back and/or forward. dojo.back fires these when Back-button or Forward-button navigation occurs. State object classes can be complex or simple depending upon what meaning your application attaches to clicking the Back and Forward buttons. For example, if an application treats the Back/Forward buttons as undo/redo buttons, then the state objects will hold undo/redo data. Our example uses the buttons to signal a URL change, so the state objects don't need anything other than the required changeUrl property.

Here is the revised code that implements the state object class and then uses it to make the Back/Forward buttons work properly:

`remote-scripting/acme-corp/acme-corp.js`

```
Line 1  dojo.require("dojo.back");
     -  (function() {
     -
     -    function getFragment(){
     5      var parts= window.location.href.split("#");
     -      if (parts.length==2) {
     -        return parts[1];
     -      } else {
     -        return "home";
    10      }
     -    }
     -
     -    var State = function(fragment){
     -      this.changeUrl = fragment;
    15    }
     -
     -    dojo.extend(State, {
     -      back: function() {
     -        loadContent(this.changeUrl);
    20      },
     -      forward: function(){
     -        loadContent(this.changeUrl);
     -      }
     -    });
    25
     -    function loadContent(fragment){
     -      dojo.xhrGet({
     -        url:  fragment + ".htm",
     -        handleAs: "text",
    30        handle: function(response){
     -          dojo.byId("content").innerHTML = response;
     -        }
     -      });
     -    }
    35
```

```
      function doMainMenu(e){
        dojo.stopEvent(e);
        var fragment= e.target.getAttribute("href").split("#")[1]
        loadContent(fragment);
40      dojo.back.addToHistory(new State(fragment));
      }

    dojo.addOnLoad(function(){
      dojo.connect(dojo.byId("menu"), "click", doMainMenu);
45    var initialFragment= getFragment();
      loadContent(initialFragment);
      dojo.back.setInitialState(new State(initialFragment));
    })

50 })();
```

dojo.back is not included in dojo.js, so it must be loaded with dojo.require (line 1). The rest of the code is wrapped in a function literal that's immediately executed to avoid polluting the global namespace (lines 2 and 50). Our state object class is defined at lines 13 through 24; dojo.extend adds functions to the prototype object of a constructor function. The Back and Forward functions simply load the content indicated by the given state.

In addition to hooking up the event handler (line 44), the initialization function calculates the fragment identifier of the page and loads the initial content implied by this identifier (lines 45 and 46). This technique allows the page to be bookmarked. For example, if the page is loaded from <...>/acme-corp.htm#dynamite, then the dynamite content will be loaded. getFragment (line 4) handles calculating the fragment identifier; it returns "home" if the URL doesn't include one. dojo.back.setInitialState must be called with a state object that represents the first page (line 47). Notice that a call to dojo.back.addToHistory was added to doMainMenu (line 40) whenever a content navigation occurs; dojo.back.addToHistory takes a state object that represents the state of that particular history item. This causes dojo.back to edit window.location.hash as well as push a new state object on its own history stack. loadContent didn't change from its original version.

Finally, to make Internet Explorer work correctly, dojo.back.init must be called from a script element in the body of the main page.

remote-scripting/acme-corp/acme-corp.htm

```
<script type="text/javascript">
  dojo.back.init();
</script>
```

Loading the page and navigating by clicking the menu items results in the proper content being loaded without a page reload just like before, but now the fragment identifier of the URL changes with each click. After making a few menu selections, you can use the Back and Forward buttons to trace backward and forward over the sequence of content you selected. Each time a Back/Forward button is clicked, the back/forward function is called in the context of the state object associated with that particular history item. This object holds the fragment identifier that is used to reload the content.

Notice that the pages can also be bookmarked. And, since the initialization code looks for a fragment identifier, the bookmarks will load the correct content.

Chapter 9

Defining Classes with dojo.declare

JavaScript doesn't explicitly include the concept of classes, yet the core language can be used to build object systems that work similarly to those found in languages that include native support for object-oriented programming (Java, Ruby, C++, and the rest). Of course, building a class definition system is a lot of work. Fortunately, Dojo does this for you. dojo.declare, the subject of this entire chapter, defines class definition machinery, complete with single-inheritance, mixins, two-phase construction, and several other features.

Since JavaScript is a dynamic language, it can generate code on the fly that can be consumed immediately (we first talked about this idea in Section 5.1, *Binding Context*, on page 78). Dojo leverages this capability with the function dojo.declare, which takes the definition of a class as input and produces a constructor function that creates instances of that class. This function is so powerful that it is possible to map its arguments to most of the class definition syntax found in other languages, and visa versa.

9.1 Why Use Object-Oriented Programming in JavaScript?

At this point, you might ask the question, why do I care about doing object-oriented programming in JavaScript? There are a couple of ways to answer this question. The first reason for learning dojo.declare is that it is pervasive in Dojo. Every Dijit widget is defined by a dojo.declare function call. If you ever want to define a new widget or specialize an existing one, understanding dojo.declare is a prerequisite. dojo.data, Dojo's powerful session data framework, uses dojo.declare. As of version 1.1, there are nearly 400 classes defined by Dojo, Dijit, and Dojox in terms of dojo.declare.

The second reason for learning dojo.declare is that object-oriented programming allows you to write programs at a higher level of abstraction (your code is closer to the problem) in a manner that is more robust (your code is modular, orthogonal, minimal, reusable, and all those other good things). Although it's true you don't need something as heavy as object-oriented programming to hang a little function off a click event, with Dojo you can write browser-based JavaScript programs that do big things. For example, it is possible to move the entire view component of a Model-View-Controller to the browser. Real view components are complex; dojo.declare gives you the power to conquer this complexity with object-oriented techniques. And this isn't theoretical hand waving; in Part IV of the book, we'll use dojo.declare extensively to build just such a view component.

dojo.declare is one of the most misunderstood, even mysterious, functions defined by Dojo. It's the subject of many forum questions, and its misuse/abuse is the root cause of many failed attempts to modify some existing class. Because of this, we're going to use a classic teaching example to demonstrate dojo.declare exhaustively. This keeps the "what" we are building out of the way of "how" we are building it. The example may not be very exciting, but trust us, the investment in understanding this material will pay huge dividends.

9.2 Defining a Simple Class

A good understanding of core JavaScript language concepts is required to use Dojo's class definition machinery effectively. Just to make sure we are all "singing from the same sheet of music," let's review a few concepts.

Prototypes and Prototypal Inheritance

Every object in JavaScript includes a reference to another object termed the first object's *prototype*. Since the prototype is another object itself, it also contains a reference to *its* prototype. This forms a chain of objects. The chain terminates with the prototype for the built-in Object type. Although you can't access an object's prototype directly as if it were an ordinary property, we'll show an object's prototype as the property __PROTO__ when we draw diagrams.

When a property of an object is read, JavaScript looks for the property in the object. If not found, JavaScript then looks in the object's prototype, the prototype's prototype, and so on, up the prototype chain until the property is found or the chain is exhausted. Since a method is just a property that happens to be a function, this is how method dispatching occurs, and this system is called *prototypal inheritance*.

This explanation does *not* apply when a property is written. When a property is written to an object, it is automatically created if it does not already exist. Notice that *looking up* a method is a read-only operation even if *executing* the method found results in changing the contents of the object.

An object's prototype reference is set when it is created, and there is no way to change this reference for the lifetime of the object. Since there are two ways to create objects in JavaScript, there are two ways to set an object's prototype reference. First, every object created by an object literal has its prototype reference set to the prototype of the built-in type Object:[1]

```
Line 1    var o1= {};
     -    var o2= {};
     -    var o3= new Object();
     -    //o1, o2, and o3 all have the same prototype object
```

Second, every object created by the keyword new combined with a constructor function has its prototype reference set to the prototype property of the constructor function:

```
Line 1    var p1= {};
     -    function SomeConstructor(){}
     -    SomeConstructor.prototype= p1;
     -    SomeConstructor.prototype.constructor= SomeConstructor;
     5
     -    var o1= new SomeConstructor();
     -    var o2= new SomeConstructor();
     -    //o1, and o2 have the same prototype object, p1
```

Here's the punch line:

- Class hierarchies are simulated in JavaScript by building prototype chains.
- Class instances are created by constructor functions that hold references to these prototype chains in their prototype properties.

---

1. An object literal is an object defined inline by enclosing zero or more properties with curly braces. For example, in the statement var x= {name: "dojo", version: 1.1}, the curly braces and everything in between are the object literal.

And dojo.declare builds these prototype chains and constructor functions for us. Finally, here are a few key terms:

object
> An instance of the JavaScript type Object (note the capital O), which is an area of memory that holds values for a set of properties.

instance
> Synonym for an object.

property
> A named storage location contained by an object.

method
> A property that references a function.

class
> An abstract notion of a set of objects that contain the same properties and define the same semantics for each contained property.

type
> Synonym for a class.

object space
> A set of objects that was created as a result of executing some code.

The Shape Class Hierarchy

The shape hierarchy is used so often when teaching object-oriented programming techniques that you're probably already familiar with it. It may be a little artificial, but it eliminates many distracting debates about "is a" versus "has a" relationships, behaviors versus data, and other issues. The shape hierarchy we'll use is given in Figure 9.1, on the next page. It has the following characteristics:

- A shape has a color; that's all we can say about a shape.
- A circle is a shape that has a radius and can calculate its area.
- A rectangle is a shape that has a length and a width and can calculate its area.
- A position is a point on an x-y plane and can be moved.
- A positioned shape is a shape and is a position. This class is not drawn in the diagram because dojo.declare does implement multiple inheritance. We'll see how to solve the problem of a positioned shape in Section 9.4, *Mixins and Multiple Inheritance*, on page 235.

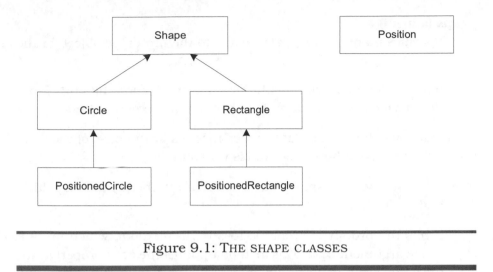

Figure 9.1: THE SHAPE CLASSES

With the preliminaries out of the way, let's build the class hierarchy with Dojo.

Defining a Simple Class with dojo.declare

In JavaScript-speak, "defining a class" means defining a constructor function that will create objects with the properties (data and methods) that the class contains. This is exactly what dojo.declare does. It takes three arguments:

className **(a string)**

The name of the constructor function that is created; in idiomatic JavaScript, the name of a constructor function also serves as a class name.

This name is created in the global object space. Since creating variables in the global object space is usually a bad thing, you can use a dot-separated name to store the new constructor in another object space. For example, if "myNamespace.Shape" was given, then the constructor function will be created as the property Shape in the object myNamespace, and the object myNamespace will be created as a property of the global object if it didn't already exist.

superclass **(null, a function, or array of functions)**

Describes the superclass (optional) and additional classes that are mixed in (also optional). We'll describe this fully in the next two sections.

props **(a hash)**

Specifies (name, value) pairs to add to the prototype object for the class being defined.

If a function is provided with the name constructor, then this function, termed the *initializer*, is used to initialize new objects.

We'll start by defining the class Shape since it's at the base of the hierarchy, doesn't use inheritance, and is very simple:

- It has the per-instance property color (a number), which is initialized to black (zero).

- It has the prototype property, setColor (a method), which takes a single argument color. This method updates the color property with the value given by its argument.[2]

Here's how to use dojo.declare to create the class Shape with these properties:

```
Line 1   dojo.declare(
    -       //the name of the constructor function (class) created...
    -       "Shape",

    5       //this is where the superclass (if any) goes...
    -       null,

    -       //this object contains everything to add to the new class's prototype...
    -       {
   10         //default property values can go in prototype...
    -         color: 0,

    -         //here is the single prototype method...
    -         setColor: function(color){
   15           this.color= color;
    -         }
    -       }
    -   );
```

The three arguments are given at lines 3, 6, and 9. The props argument (line 9) is usually provided as an object literal as shown in the example. props also includes the default value for the color property (line 11) and the single method setColor (line 14).

---

2. For now, the method setColor doesn't do anything that couldn't be done by just accessing the property color directly. But it's easy to imagine that setColor may include side effects (like setting an HTML element's style) in a real application.

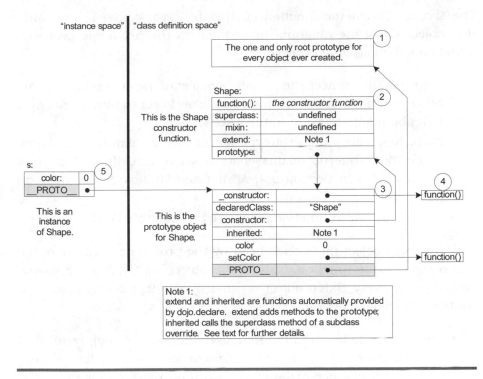

Figure 9.2: THE SHAPE OBJECT SPACE

Now that Shape is defined, we can use it:

```
Line 1    //create a new Shape instance...
          var s= new Shape();

          //exercise it...
5         var check1= s.color;   //check1 is 0
          s.setColor(0x0000FF); //shape.color is now red
          var check2= s.color;   //check2 is red
```

In particular, notice that the keyword new is required to create new instances just like any other constructor function (dojo.declare does *not* create an object factory).

The Objects Created by dojo.declare

In Figure 9.2, you can see what dojo.declare creates for our Shape example. The diagram also includes the single instance of Shape we created with the statement var s= new Shape(). The object space constructed has many capabilities.

The Shape constructor function created by dojo.declare is the function object (2) in the diagram; in addition to the prototype property, it includes the following properties:

- superclass: References the prototype object of the superclass, if any. Since Shape has no superclass, superclass is set to undefined. We'll talk about superclasses in the next section.
- mixin: References the prototype object of the mixin class, if any. Since Shape has no mixins, mixin is set to undefined. We'll talk about mixins in Section 9.4, *Mixins and Multiple Inheritance*, on page 235.
- extend: Advanced functionality; we'll discuss this later.

The unnamed object (3) is referenced by the prototype property of the Shape constructor function. This is the object that will serve as the prototype for every Shape object created by the Shape constructor. It contains the following properties:

- _constructor: References the initializer function (if any); recall that the initializer is passed in props.constructor. The initializer should accomplish any per-instance initialization required for the class. You should never call this function directly (notice that it's marked private by the leading underscore); the constructor function manufactured by dojo.declare will automatically call it when a new object is created.
- declaredClass: The value of the first argument given to dojo.declare. This can be useful for debugging.
- constructor: References the Shape constructor function. This implements the standard JavaScript idiom where, given a constructor function ctor, ctor.prototype.constructor references ctor.
- inherited: References a function used to call superclass methods; we'll discuss this in a later section.
- Each of the properties contained in the props hash is assigned by the JavaScript assignment operator (=) to an identically named property in the prototype. In the example, there were two properties, color and setColor (a function). Owing to the definition of the assignment operator, some properties may be copied by value, while others are copied by reference.
- Since Shape did not designate a superclass, the prototype of the prototype references the one and only root prototype for every object created (1).

The Elegance of JavaScript

Take another look at Figure 9.2, on page 227. We put a vertical line on the diagram to separate the objects that are instances of the class from objects that define the class. Do you see the elegance of the system as a whole? *Everything* is an object. The constructor function is an object. The prototype inheritance chain is made of objects. This is the reason JavaScript doesn't need the extensive "class-definition" syntax that is present in so many "object-oriented" languages. Yet, JavaScript can be used to describe class systems with all of the power of these other languages. In a way, JavaScript gives you a free lunch—the ability to define class systems without the need for a special syntax to do it. Now *that's* elegant!

Finally, we created one Shape instance referenced by the variable s (5).

Standard Use Patterns

dojo.declare follows standard JavaScript idioms when it creates constructor functions. One implication is that the JavaScript instanceof operator works as expected. For example:

```
var s= new Shape();
var check1= s instanceof Shape;  //check1 is true
var check2= s instanceof Object; //check2 is true
```

Sometimes you need to know the *exact* type of an object. In this case, you can't use the JavaScript instanceof operator because it will tell you only whether the target type is somewhere in the prototype chain. Instead, you need to know the constructor function that created the object—this reveals the exact type of the object. As mentioned earlier, dojo.declare includes a reference to the constructor function in the constructor property of the prototype object. For example, you can get to the constructor of s by writing this:

```
s.constructor
```

According to the semantics of JavaScript, access to the constructor function for an object implies access to the prototype of that object. The prototype of s is given by the following:

```
s.constructor.prototype
```

9.3 Defining a Subclass with Single Inheritance

In the shape hierarchy, circles and rectangles are also shapes. This is to say that circles and rectangles have all the properties that shapes have, plus a few others to make them behave as circles and rectangles. If we were to define circles and rectangles in isolation, we would lose an important piece of information: any operation valid on shapes is also valid on circles and rectangles. To capture this information, we don't define circles and rectangles in isolation but rather define them as refinements of shape. In object-oriented parlance, we say that Circle and Rectangle are derived from Shape and inherit from Shape, that Shape is the superclass to Circle and Rectangle, and that Circle and Rectangle are subclasses of Shape.

In the previous section we created a class that had no user-defined ancestors. (We say "user-defined" because *all* objects in JavaScript ultimately inherit from Object; this is built in to the language and can't be changed.) Now let's turn our attention to defining the subclasses Circle and Rectangle. Recall from Section 9.2, *The Shape Class Hierarchy*, on page 224 that Circle has the per-instance property radius, Rectangle has the per-instance properties length and width, and both Circle and Rectangle have the prototype property area (a method).

To derive from a superclass, you need to specify the superclass as an argument to dojo.declare. Prototype properties and the optional initializer for the new subclass are specified in the props hash as usual. dojo.declare sets up the object space for you and creates a constructor that ensures the superclass constructor chain is called properly when creating new objects. Assuming Shape is already defined, here's the code to define the Circle and Rectangle classes:

```
Line 1  dojo.declare(
   -      "Circle", //classname...
   -
   -      Shape, //superclass: Circle inherits from Shape...
   5
   -      //props hash...
   -      {
   -        //default value for radius...
   -        radius: 0,
  10
   -        //the property named "constructor" is used to initialize new instances...
   -        constructor: function(radius) {
   -          this.radius= radius || this.radius;
   -        },
  15
```

```
         //these go in the prototype for Circle...
         setRadius: function(radius) {
           this.radius= radius;
         },
20
         area: function() {
           return Math.PI * this.radius * this.radius;
         }
       }
25   );

     dojo.declare(
       "Rectangle", //classname...
       Shape, //superclass: Rectangle inherits from Shape...
30
       //props hash...
       {
         //default values for l, w...
         length: 0,
35       width: 0,

         constructor: function(l, w) {
           this.length= l || this.length;
           this.width= w || this.width;
40       },

         //these go in the prototype for Rectangle...
         setLength: function(l) {
           this.length= l;
45       },

         setWidth: function(w) {
           this.width= w;
         },
50
         area: function() {
           return this.length * this.width;
         }
       }
55   );

     //create a Circle and exercise it...
     var c= new Circle(5);
     var test= c.area();
60
     //Circles are also shapes...
     c.setColor(0x0000FF);
```

From the previous code, we can see that in order to inherit a superclass,
we simply state the superclass's constructor as the second argument
to dojo.declare.

This has two effects:

- dojo.declare will set up the new class's prototype object to refer-ence the superclass's prototype object.

- The constructor function that dojo.declare manufactures will call the superclass's constructor before calling the subclass's initial-izer function.

This last point is worth repeating in code. The following gets executed when a new Circle object is created:

```
Line 1    //creating a new circle...
   -      var c= new Circle(5);
   -
   -      //...results in the Circle constructor executing the following...
   5      Shape.apply(this, arguments);
   -      Circle._constructor.apply(this, arguments);
```

This ensures proper per-instance initialization all the way up the inher-itance hierarchy. The previous example also demonstrates that initial-izer functions can take arguments. We'll have an extended discussion about initializer function arguments in Section 9.5, *Preprocessing Con-structor Arguments*, on page 244.

The Circle Object Space

In Figure 9.3, on the facing page, you can see the object space for Circle. If we had drawn it, Rectangle would be similar. Although not drawn, Circle and Rectangle constructors reference *the same* Shape con-structor; similarly, the Circle and Rectangle prototype objects reference the same Shape prototype object. This works since there are no ref-erences pointing down and out of the Shape part of the object space into classes derived from Shape. Otherwise, Circle, and its associated prototype property, looks and works just like Shape and its associated prototype property.

Calling Superclass Methods

Frequently a subclass will override a function defined by a superclass, and further, the overridden function will call the superclass's version of that function. dojo.declare automatically includes the function inherited in every prototype object. When this.inherited is called from any subclass method, it invokes the same method in the superclass.

To make this idea crystal clear, let's have Circle override Shape's set-Color method as follows: if the sum of the red-green-blue components

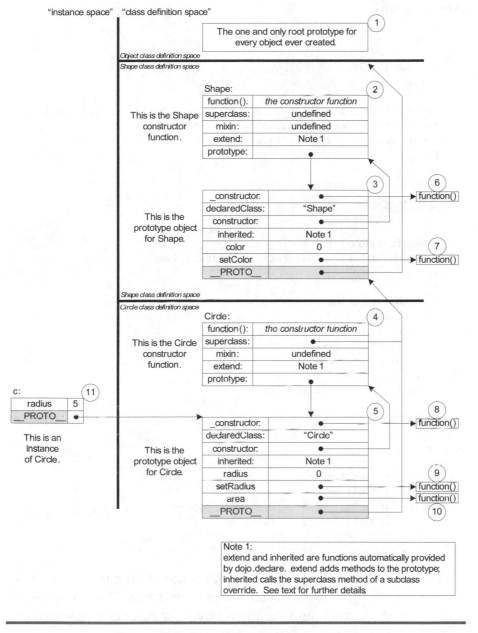

"instance space"   "class definition space"

The one and only root prototype for every object ever created.

Object class definition space

Shape class definition space

This is the Shape constructor function.

Shape:

function().	*the constructor function*
superclass:	undefined
mixin:	undefined
extend:	Note 1
prototype:	●

This is the prototype object for Shape.

_constructor:	●
declaredClass:	"Shape"
constructor:	●
inherited:	Note 1
color	0
setColor	●
__PROTO__	●

function()

function()

Shape class definition space

Circle class definition space

This is the Circle constructor function.

Circle:

function():	*the constructor function*
superclass:	●
mixin:	undefined
extend:	Note 1
prototype:	●

c:

| radius | 5 |
| __PROTO__ | ● |

This is an Instance of Circle.

This is the prototype object for Circle.

_constructor:	●
declaredClass:	"Circle"
constructor:	●
inherited:	Note 1
radius	0
setRadius	●
area	●
__PROTO__	●

function()

function()
function()

Note 1:
extend and inherited are functions automatically provided by dojo.declare. extend adds methods to the prototype; inherited calls the superclass method of a subclass override. See text for further details.

Figure 9.3: THE CIRCLE OBJECT SPACE

is greater than 350, accept the change; otherwise, ignore the change. Here is how such an override could be done:

```
dojo.declare(
  "Circle",
  Shape,
  {
    //default value for radius...
    radius: 0,

    //the property named "constructor" is used to initialize new instances...
    constructor: function(radius) {
      this.radius= radius || this.radius;
    },

    setRadius: function(radius) {
      this.radius= radius;
    },

    area: function() {
      return Math.PI * this.radius * this.radius;
    },

    setColor: function (color) {
      var total=
        ((color & 0xFF0000) >> 16) +
        ((color & 0x00FF00) >> 8) +
        (color & 0x00FF);
      if (total>350) {
        this.inherited(arguments);
      }
    }
  }
);

//exercise the new functionality...
var c= new Circle();
c.setColor(0x010203);  //should result in no-op
var test1= c.color;    //yup, test1 is 0
c.setColor(0x808080);  //should set the color
var test2= c.color;    //test2 is 0x808080
```

This example is admittedly artificial, but it does illustrate the ability to get to a specific function in the inheritance hierarchy. Eventually, you'll probably have to reach into the hierarchy. Now you know how to do it.

Manually Adding Superclass Methods

In rare circumstances, you come across the need to add or change a method in a class defined by dojo.declare, but you don't want to derive a subclass or change the current class definition (maybe such an action would break other code somehow). This is easily accomplished by adding/changing a property in the class prototype. For example, we could add the property setBorderStyle to Shape by writing the following:

```
Shape.prototype.setBorderStyle= function(style) {
  this.borderStyle= style;
};
```

Dojo even includes the helper function dojo.extend that takes a constructor function and a hash of properties and copies the contents of the hash into the constructor's prototype property. setBorderStyle could be added to Shape with dojo.extend like this:

```
Line 1   dojo.extend(Shape, {
   -       setBorderStyle: function(style) {
   -         this.borderStyle= style;
   -       }
   5     });
```

There is one gotcha here: adding methods to prototypes of classes defined with dojo.declare breaks the inherited method we just discussed. To fix this problem, each constructor function returned by dojo.declare includes the method extend that takes a hash of properties to copy to the class's prototype. Here's the correct way to add setBorderStyle to Shape:

```
Line 1   Shape.extend({
   -       setBorderStyle: function(style) {
   -         this.borderStyle= style;
   -       }
   5     });
```

To add properties to the prototype property of any constructor function defined with dojo.declare, always use the dojo.declare-provided extend. For constructor functions *not* defined by dojo.declare, you should use dojo.extend to add properties to the prototype.

9.4 Mixins and Multiple Inheritance

So far, we've explored deriving one class from another *single* class. Naturally, this technique is called *single inheritance*. Single inheritance says "subclass is a superclass" but with some more specialized functionality added. For example, Circle "is a" Shape, but with a radius and the ability to calculate its area. But how do you model a situation where a new subclass is more than one thing?

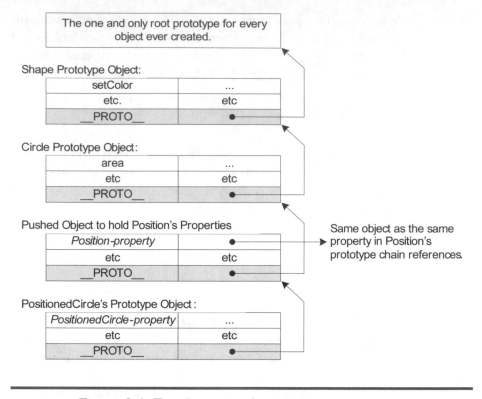

Figure 9.4: THE POSITIONEDCIRCLE PROTOTYPE CHAIN

In our little Shape hierarchy depicted Figure 9.1, how should we model the notion of a Shape positioned in an HTML document? Surely it's reasonable that a positioned object "is-a" position.[3]

Since the abstract idea of a shape is independent of a position, it would be wrong to derive Shape from Position, or visa versa. What we'd like to do is include *both* Shape and Position as superclasses of Circle and Rectangle. This is to say that Circle would inherit both Shape and Position. Naturally, this technique is called *multiple inheritance*. Unfortunately, it's not supported by the prototypal inheritance model that JavaScript provides. Although there is nothing that Dojo can do to fix this, dojo.declare does include the ability to define classes with most of the effects of multiple inheritance.

---

3. For some of the object-oriented lawyers out there, we hear you objecting that a positioned object "has-a" position; it "is-NOT-a" position. We'll take your objection under consideration, but note that we might like to move shapes, which implies that modeling them as positions is reasonable. In any event, this argument is not germane to teaching how Dojo implements mixins.

The idea is simple. If you have a class (the mixin class) with functionality that you'd like to include in a new class but have already spent your one inheritance ticket, then just push another empty object onto the prototype chain and "mix in" (copy) all of the properties from the mixin class. In Figure 9.4, on the preceding page, you can see how this idea works when creating a PositionedCircle—a Circle that has all the functionality of a Position. An extra prototype object is pushed on top of PositionedCircle's prototype chain, and this object holds references to all the properties in Position. It's important to notice that this extra object fully enumerates Position's prototype object, which means it will hold *all* properties that exist anywhere in Position's prototype chain. The rest of PositionedCircle's prototype chain looks just like Circle's prototype chain: Circle's prototype references Shape's prototype, which references Object's prototype. You can view this as a sort of deep aggregation. Rather than aggregating an instance of another class as a property, you aggregate the definition (that is, the contents of the prototype chain) of another class.

Deriving Classes with Mixins

With the theory out of the way, let's use dojo.declare to define the class PositionedCircle. First we need to define the class Position, which models a point on an x-y plane that can be moved:

```
Line 1   dojo.declare(
  -        "Position",
  -        null,
  -        {
  5          x: 0,
  -          y: 0,

  -          constructor: function(x, y){
  -            this.x= x || this.x;
  10           this.y= y || this.y;
  -          },

  -          setPosition: function (x, y) {
  -            this.x= x;
  15           this.y= y;
  -          },

  -          move: function (deltaX, deltaY) {
  -            this.x+= deltaX;
  20           this.y+= deltaY;
  -          }
  -        }
  -      );
```

Alex Says...

Class Design in JavaScript

If you're coming from a community with lots of rules imposed either by the language or by convention, you may be surprised by some of the idioms you'll see in JavaScript. For example, in JavaScript, it's convenient to include default values for various properties in the prototype object. This technique has three nice side effects. First, it eliminates a set of assignment statements in the initializer that would be executed each time a new object is created. This is incredibly important in keeping code terse, which is a primary goal of JavaScript development because of the nature of how scripts are sent to browsers. Second, it allows a default value to be easily changed at runtime; you would have to create a subclass to change default values set in the initializer. Third, it encapsulates the properties a particular class defines in an object (the prototype) rather than in lines of code (the initializer), which would need to be executed for every object initialization.

You'll also notice that positional constructor arguments were used in the examples presented in this chapter; this was intentional to highlight various initialization issues that come with subclassing. However, it's often better to define initializers that take a single hash argument that's used to initialize new objects. Dojo uses this convention heavily and extends it with a second optional positional argument, which may be a reference to a DOM node that the constructed instance should act on. Using a terse convention like this makes it easy to understand how to construct a broad variety of object types without having to know the specifics of each class's constructor. Remembering the order of many positional arguments can also be painful (although code-completing editors help a lot). Also, if various combinations of arguments are optional, then you'll either have to specify null for the optional arguments or build some really tricky logic in the initializer to figure out what the client intended (and "really tricky" usually translates to buggy followed by impossible). Finally, there's the problem of argument juggling when subclassing, as discussed in this chapter. Having your classes follow the "property object plus optional node" convention makes it simple to integrate with others, makes it easy to subclass, and leans on a convention that all Dojo developers already know.

There is nothing new here. Position is a simple base class that doesn't inherit from any other user-defined class.

Now, we'll use dojo.declare, Position, and Circle to create the new constructor function PositionedCircle that creates objects that have all of the power of both Circles and Positions. Here is the code:

```
Line 1    dojo.declare(
   -        "PositionedCircle",
   -
   -        //inherits from Circle and mixes in Position
   5        [Circle, Position],
   -
   -        {
   -          constructor: function(radius, x, y){
   -            this.setPosition(x, y);
  10          }
   -        }
   -    );
```

Notice that the superclass argument to dojo.declare is an array. When an array is given, the first element in the array is interpreted as the superclass, and any subsequent elements are interpreted as mixin classes. In Figure 9.5, on the following page, you can see the object space that is built (it includes the Position constructor and prototype but does not include the Circle and Shape constructors and prototypes).

As a consequence of copying properties from the mixin Position, the prototype chain of PositionedCircle contains the properties setPosition and move (9). These properties reference the same function objects as the setPosition and move properties in Position's prototype object.

Note that when dojo.declare copies a property from the mixin class, a regular JavaScript assignment expression is used, which results in copying references unless the property held is a boolean, integer, string, or null value, in which case the property is copied by value. This isn't a problem since the prototype chain should contain read-only properties; it's probably a design mistake to include updateable data in prototype objects.[4]

Per-instance Initialization

The constructor functions manufactured by dojo.declare call all the mixin constructors just like they call the superclass constructor chain,

---

4. Per-class updateable data should be made a property of the constructor function.

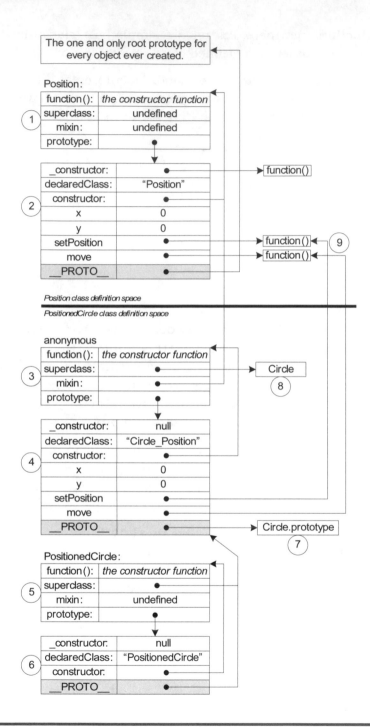

Figure 9.5: THE POSITIONEDCIRCLE OBJECT SPACE

as we discussed earlier. In code, the following gets executed when a new PositionedCircle object is created:

```
Line 1    //creating a new PositionedCircle...
   -      var pc = new PositionedCircle(5, 1, 2);
   -
   -      //...results in the function PositionedCircle executing the following...
   5      Circle.apply(this, arguments);
   -      //...which results in...
   -      Shape.apply(this, arguments);
   -
   -      //...then the mixin constructor is executed...
  10      Position.apply(this, arguments);
   -
   -      //...finally the init function is executed...
   -      PositionedCircle._constructor.apply(this, arguments);
```

This code reveals the algorithm used for the constructors that dojo.declare makes:

1. Call the superclass constructor function (line 5). This step is executed (line 7) all the way up the inheritance chain to the root class.
2. Call all mixin constructor functions (line 10), in the order they are given in the superclass array.
3. Call the initializer function (line 13).

Let's step back for a minute and see whether we've accomplished our mission of making a class that behaves as both a Circle and a Position. If we exercise an instance of PositionedCircle, all of the Position methods work just as if the object were a Position and all of the Circle methods as if the object were a Circle:

```
Line 1    var pc= new PositionedCircle(5, 1, 2);
   -
   -      //try the Shape functionality...
   -      var color1= pc.color;  //color1 is black
   5      pc.setColor(0x0000FF);
   -      var color2= pc.color;  //color2 is now red
   -
   -      //try the Circle functionality...
   -      var radius1= pc.radius; //radius1 is 5
  10      var area1= pc.area();    //area1 is 78.54
   -      pc.setRadius(10);
   -      var radius2= pc.radius; //radius2 is 10
   -      var area2= pc.area();    //area2 is 314.16
   -
  15      //try the Position functionality...
   -      var position1= [pc.x, pc.y]; //position1 is [1, 2];
   -      pc.move(3, 5);
   -      var position2= [pc.x, pc.y]; //position2 is [4, 7];
```

Alex Says...
Caveats for Object-Oriented Experts

Notice that the prototype chain (depicted in Figure 9.4, on page 236) puts the mixin under the new subclass being defined. So, for example, if one of Position's methods calls this.inherited(arguments), properties defined in PositionedCircle's prototype are never considered. This is contrary to one view of the role of a mixin that says a mixin is an incomplete class that is put on top of some other class that contains methods required to complete the mixin class. A classic example is the idea of an enumerator with methods such as find, map, and sort that are plopped on top of various container classes like vector, list, and tree. The enumerator implements certain algorithms (for example, map), assuming certain other functions are provided by the hosting class (for example, first, next, end). Depending on the algorithm, the mixin class may call this.inherited(arguments), and the design given would fail. (BC90) provides a detailed discussion on the theory of mixins.

Also notice that the mixin properties hide any properties of the same name lower in the prototype chain. We'll discuss this in detail in a later section. But, clearly, dojo.declare does not implement a model that is equivalent to multiple inheritance, and we are not making this claim.

The reason Dojo is not working too hard to expose a more classical OO model inside JavaScript is that it would be both brittle and slow. dojo.declare is designed so that you can compose classes not defined by dojo.declare with those that are, and systems that try to do more rigorous, class-based OO often find that it's harder to mix and match code developed inside the assumptions their system with code developed elsewhere. dojo.declare isn't perfect, but it helps you "play well with others" and is a prime example of where Dojo's strong emphasis on going as far as the language will let you—and no further—pays off in both speed and stability. By respecting the principle of least astonishment, we give good JavaScript hackers a natural path to writing classes more tersely and give novice users an abstraction that's good-enough to let them be productive quickly and discover the power of the language progressively.

So, on this level, we can say that we've succeeded. Still, there is one material difference.

Type Testing with Mixins

To see one difference between the mixin pattern and true multiple inheritance, notice that a class that is defined by mixing in another class has all the capabilities of the mixed-in class but is *not* an instance of the mixed-in class. Contrast this to deriving a subclass from a super-class: the subclass *is* an instance of the superclass. Most of the time this distinction doesn't matter. As long as an object provides the behavior of some class, then we can use it as if it were an instance of that class. Of course, this is the concept of "duck typing" (that is, if it walks like a duck and quacks like a duck, then it's a duck). Still, this is a key difference between using mixins and multiple inheritance.

And, this difference has a practical implication. Looking at Figure 9.5, on page 240, notice that our new class, PositionedCircle, has the pro-totype object chain given by the objects (6)–>(4)–>(7)–>Shape.prototype–>Object.prototype. Position is *not* in the chain. Consequently, an instance of PositionedCircle is an instance of PositionedCircle, Circle, Shape, and Object but *is not* as instance of Position. Here are the consequences in code; notice that line 8 shows pc is not a position:

```
Line 1   var pc= new PositionedCircle(5, 1, 2);

         var test;
         test= pc instanceof PositionedCircle; //test is true
      5  test= pc instanceof Circle;           //test is true
         test= pc instanceof Shape;            //test is true
         test= pc instanceof Object;           //test is true
         test= pc instanceof Position;         //test is false!
```

When testing whether an object is a class that may be included as a mixin, you can't use the JavaScript instanceof operator. Instead, you must test the object for the existence of a set of properties that indicate the type you are looking for (that is, a *property signature*).[5]

That's it for mixins basics.

---

5. You may have noticed that dojo.declare fills the declaredClass property of the synthetic prototype objects used to hold mixin properties with a synthetic name. Although you could inspect this name to determine what's been mixed in, the algorithm used to create the synthetic name may change. Indeed, it is possible that the synthetic name may be removed from future versions of dojo.declare.

This leaves us with three details to discuss regarding inheritance and mixins:

- How to handle constructor argument signatures that are different between the subclass, the superclass, and any mixins
- How to handle property name clashes when deriving and mixing
- How to implement two-phase construction

Let's turn our attention to the first issue, sorting out constructor argument signatures when we use derivation and/or mixins.

9.5 Preprocessing Constructor Arguments

Consider the problem of creating and initializing a new PositionedCircle object. Shapes don't take any constructor arguments, Circles take a radius argument, and Positions take x and y arguments. Clearly, we have three constructor signatures: (), (radius), and (x, y). On the other hand, the constructor of PositionedCircle should define the signature (radius, x, y). Then, we can create and initialize a new PositionedCircle object by writing the following:

```
//radius=5, x=1, y=2
var pc= new PositionedCircle(5, 1, 2);
```

The constructor function that dojo.declare creates must somehow deal out any arguments to the superclass and the mixins. By default, arguments passed to the constructor are just blindly passed first to the superclass's constructor, then to each mixin's constructor, and finally to the subclass's initializer. In code, this looks like this following:

```
Line 1   //writing...
    -    var pc = new PositionedCircle(5, 1, 2);
    -
    -    //results in the following being executed...
    5    Circle.apply(this, [5, 1, 2]);
    -    //call Circle's superclass...
    -    Shape.apply(this, [5, 1, 2]);
    -    //call PositionedCircle's mixin...
    -    Position.apply(this, [5, 1, 2]);
   10
    -    //call PositionedCircle's initializer--if there is one...
    -    if (PositionedCircle.prototype._constructor) {
    -      PositionedCircle.prototype._constructor.apply(this, [5, 1, 2]);
    -    }
```

Circle will be initialized correctly because it expects a single argument—the radius. Since the radius is the first argument in the PositionedCircle constructor signature, Circle will use the argument correctly and ignore the last two arguments.

Similarly, Shape will just ignore all of the arguments. Unfortunately, Position fails to initialize properly. It expects two arguments, (x, y), but gets three arguments, (radius, x, y). So, it will interpret radius as x and x as y and will ignore the last argument.

If you look at our definition of PositionedCircle, you'll see that we provided an initializer that explicitly initializes the Position mixin. Here is the initializer again:

```
function(radius, x, y){
  setPosition(x, y);
}
```

The initializer we provided correctly accepts three arguments: radius, x, and y. Consequently, it reinitializes the Position instance variables with the correct values of x and y. But, before setPosition is called in this initializer, the Position instance properties x and y will be initialized with the values intended for radius and x (recall the constructors of the superclass and all mixins are called before the initializer).

Using this technique to fix up all the initialization mistakes, although a bit sloppy, will work in many cases. But sometimes this is not good enough since some initializers will cause bad side effects (for example, throw an exception) if they are passed improper arguments. We will use PositionedCircle to illustrate how we can massage constructor arguments.

Having Your Way with Constructor Arguments

dojo.declare accepts a preprocessor that reformats constructor arguments before passing them on to the superclass and mixin(s) class constructors. The preprocessor is specified by providing a function for the property preamble in the props hash argument of dojo.declare. If specified, the function is passed the set of arguments provided to the subclass constructor (that is, the constructor created by dojo.declare) and returns an array of arguments that are passed to the superclass and mixin(s) constructors.

So, let's assume that a preamble was provided to PositionedCircle; then, when a new PositionedCircle is created, the PositionedCircle constructor calls the superclass and mixin constructors by executing the following:

```
Line 1   //writing...
         var o = new PositionedCircle(radius, x, y);

         //results in calling the superclass and mixin constructors like this...
    5    var superArgs = PositionedCircle.prototype.preamble.apply(this, [radius, x, y]);
         PositionedCircle.prototype.superclass.apply(this, superArgs);
         PositionedCircle.prototype.mixin.apply(this, superArgs);
```

Notice that the preamble takes a set of arguments and returns an array. Although there is no restriction on what processing is accomplished by a preamble, typically a preamble is used to reformat arguments from a format expected by the subclass to a format expected by the superclass *and* any mixins. And this algorithm works all the way up the single-inheritance chain. For example, another preamble could be specified for Circle, which would fix up arguments for the Shape constructor.

Preambles solve argument-reformatting problems when there is no mix-in or when both the superclass and all mixins expect the same arguments. Unfortunately, the design fails when there is both a superclass *and* one or more mixins that expect different argument signatures. The PositionedCircle class is an example of such a failure since Circle (the superclass) and Position (a mixin) take different argument signatures.

To solve the problem, you need to create a class, sometimes termed a *shim class*, that derives from the mixin class and provides a preamble that picks and orders constructor arguments. Here is the shim class we need with Position:

```
Line 1   dojo.declare("PositionedCircleShim", Position,
            {
              preamble: function(radius, x, y){
                return [x || null, y || null];
    5         }
            }
         );
```

Note carefully that preamble is provided with the arguments that were passed to the owning constructor and returns an array; this is a little obtuse the first time you write a preamble.

PositionedCircleShim works just like Position except that it initializes its superclass Position correctly when it is provided the signature (radius, x, y)—which is precisely the signature that PositionedCircle is going to give it. With this in place, we can define PositionedCircle to mix in Positioned-CircleShim (no preamble is given for PositionedCircle):

```
Line 1   dojo.declare(
   -       "PositionedCircle",
   ▶       [Circle, PositionedCircleShim],
   -       {}
   5     );
```

Notice that the new PositionedCircle does not need an initializer function since Position will be initialized correctly now. Here is what actually happens when a new PositionedCircle object is created:

```
Line 1   //creating a new PositionedCircle...
   -     var pc = new PositionedCircle(5, 1, 2);
   -     //...results in the function PositionedCircle executing the following...
   -
   5     //call the single inheritance chain...
   -     //the superclass of PositionedCircle...
   -     Circle.apply(this, [5, 1, 2]);
   -       //which calls Shape, the superclass of Circle...
   -       Shape.apply(this, [5, 1, 2]);
   10
   -     //call the mixin class...
   -     PositionedCircleShim.apply(this, [5, 1, 2]);
   -       //...which results in executing...
   -       Position.apply(this,
   15        PositionedCircleShim.prototype.preamble.apply(this, [5, 1, 2]));
   -       //...which reduces to Position.apply(this, [1, 2]);
   -
   -     //lastly, call PositionedCircle's initializer--if there is one...
   -     if (PositionedCircle.prototype._constructor) {
   20      PositionedCircle.prototype._constructor.apply(this, [5, 1, 2]);
   -     }
```

Circle is still passed three arguments even though it uses only one. However, since the first argument passed is correct, there is no need to shim Circle.

Using Hashes to Specify Arguments

Often the problem of constructor argument signature incompatibilities can be eliminated by using a single hash as a constructor argument to pass initialization values.[6]

---

6. Of course, hashes can have name clashes just as positional arguments have position clashes, but these are less likely.

For example:

```
Line 1   var shape = new PositionedCircle({
    -        x: 1,
    -        y: 2,
    -        radius: 5
    5    });
```

This is a popular JavaScript idiom. If each class uses this idiom, then initializers can simply pick out the properties they need.

Often initialization does not require any specific processing other than copying the values out of the hash into the new instance object. In these cases, dojo.mixin can be used to quickly accomplish this task. For example, Shape's initializer could be written as follows:

```
Line 1   constructor: function(args){
    -        //args is a hash of initial property values
    -        dojo.mixin(this, args);
    -    }
```

Notice how this initializer correctly initializes Circle and Position when a new PositionedCircle is given the hash {x: 1, y: 2, radius: 5} as previously! In case there are some classes (either superclasses or mixins) lower in the hierarchy that rely on positional arguments, preambles can be used, as we discussed earlier, to pick the appropriate argument signature out of the hash.

Generally speaking, if a constructor takes more than three or four arguments, then it's probably a good candidate to use the single-argument hash technique. This technique is also less susceptible to typing the parameters in the wrong order when expressing code.[7]

9.6 Resolving Property Name Clashes

There's another potential problem when we use dojo.declare to create a new class that's derived from a superclass and mixes in a mixin class. Since the mixin's prototype properties are mixed into a new class's prototype chain above the superclass, a mixin's property will be found before a superclass's property if the properties have the same name. This is almost certainly what you *don't* want. The new class is derived from the superclass, so instances of the new class are also instances of the superclass; they are *not* instances of the mixin.

---

7. Of course, you can still express hashes that include properties with misspelled names quite easily.

Alex Says...

Make the 80% Case Easy

The main argument against defining initializers that take single-argument hashes is parsimony. If you have a class that has a very common construction pattern that requires only a few values, then specifying this...

```
var x= new MyClass({
  thisProperty: 1,
  thatProperty:2,
  theOtherProperty:3
});
```

is a royal pain. But there's an easy solution—define a quick helper:

```
function makeMyClass(thisProperty, thatProperty, theOtherProperty){
  return new MyClass({
    thisProperty: thisProperty,
    thatProperty: thatProperty,
    theOtherProperty: theOtherProperty
  });
}
```

Now you can write var x= makeMyClass(1, 2, 3). Ahhh, that's better. And, you'll never forget to type new! By the way, this is exactly what Dojo does all the time. For an example, compare dojo.animateProperty to dojo.anim.

Now you can write var x = makeMyClass(1, 2, 3). With the wrapper function, you can also avoid typing new. Inside of Dojo, we use this wrapper style all the time to first expose powerful APIs and then provide easy-to-use versions for the 80% case.

Yet accessing the property resolves to the mixin property. The object behaves like something it's not. Let's drive this point home with our PositionedCircle example.

If you examine the set method names of the Shape, Circle, and Position classes, you see setColor, setRadius, and setPosition, respectively. But, in Shapes, the only thing to set is a color; likewise, Circles set only radii, and Positions set only—you guessed it—positions. So, why the long method names? Let's rename all these methods to set. With this modification, which is very possible if you didn't have control of the whole hierarchy, the set method for PositionedCircles calls Position.set, and it's difficult to get to the other set methods. Here's code that illustrates the problem:

```
Line 1   //assume that Shape, Circle, and Position all define
    -    //"set" rather than "set(Color|Radius|Position)"...
    -    var pc = new PositionedCircle(); //radius=0, x=0, y=0
    -    pc.set(5); //oops! calls Position.Set instead of Circle.Set...
    5    var test;
    -    test = pc.radius; //radius is still 0, but...
    -    test = pc.x; //x was set to 5
    -    //it can be done...painfully...
    -    Circle.prototype.set.apply(pc, [5]);
   10    //but at least it worked; test is 5
    -    test = pc.radius;
```

First we need to stop the mixin from stepping on our superclass's method. The idea here is to rename the mixin's property to something that doesn't clash. How about setPosition? This can be done immediately after the class definition like this:

```
Line 1   dojo.declare(
    -      "PositionedCircle",
    -      [Circle, PositionedCircleShim],
    -      {}
    5    );
    -    PositionedCircle.extend({
    -      setPosition: Position.prototype.set
    -    });
    -    delete PositionedCircle.superclass.set;
```

Since we deleted set from PositionedCircle's superclass prototype (the synthetic prototype object that holds all of Position's prototype properties), a call to set on a PositionedCircle object will find Circle.set. So, let's try it:

```
var pc= new PositionedCircle(5, 1, 2); //radius=5, x=1, y=2
pc.setPosition(3, 4); //call Position.Set...
pc.set(6); //call Circle.Set...
```

This is looking a lot better. There is a gotcha here: renaming has the undesirable side effect of breaking the built-in inherited function: calling this.inherited(arguments) will not work from a function that has been renamed. In practice, this problem rarely occurs. Nevertheless, it is a limitation of the current dojo.declare implementation.

Next let's turn our attention to disambiguating Shape.set and Circle.set. This is simply a design error. When Circle was defined, it defined the method set that was also defined in the superclass Shape, but Circle.prototype.set was not an override to Shape.prototype.set. Indeed, Circle.prototype.set has completely different semantics to Shape.prototype.set; therefore, it should be a different name. The original design was more correct; we made the original change only as a teaching example.

So far, the discussion has been limited to properties that end up in the prototype object. It is also possible for per-instance property names to clash. Resolving this problem requires a great deal of care since renaming these properties has broad implications: prototype methods that manipulate per-instance properties do not know about name changes that the subclass may make. Frankly, these types of clashes need to be avoided to begin with by employing good coding techniques that have nothing to do with dojo.declare.

9.7 Two-Phase Construction

Occasionally, you'll want to define a superclass that accomplishes some processing in its initializer that requires the instance to be fully initialized. This causes a problem when a subclass is derived from the superclass because the superclass's initializer is executed before the subclass's; therefore, the processing that required the object to be fully initialized is executed before the subclasses initializer runs. Since this is a bit obtuse in words, let's look at an example.

Say the class Base includes the statement doSomething(this) in its initializer, and further assume that doSomething requires that the instance referenced by this must be fully initialized. The Base initializer might look something like this:

```
Line 1  dojo.declare("Base", null, {
          constructor: function() {
            //initialize the instance as required...

    5       //now that the instance is initialized, call
            doSomething(this);
          }
        });
```

This works fine. But next, the class Subclass is derived from Base. Since Subclass's constructor calls Base's initializer before Subclass's initializer, the Subclass instance passed to doSomething will not be fully initialized. This design requires a constructor algorithm that first initializes the object all the way up the inheritance chain and then does one more thing (so-called two-phase construction).

Two-phase construction is specified by providing a function for the property postscript in the props hash argument of dojo.declare. After a new object has been fully initialized (the superclass and mixin constructors and the subclass initializer have been called), the method postscript is called in the context of the new instance and is passed the arguments provided at construction. Unlike preambles that are called all the way up the inheritance chain, postscript, if provided, is called only from the most-derived class's constructor. Of course, if a postscript is provided in a superclass and not overridden in a subclass, the superclass postscript will be called. Similarly, a superclass's postscript method can be called from a subclass's overridden postscript method by writing this.inherited(arguments) as inside the overridden method.

Let's work through a quick example. We'll build a toy hierarchy that requires two-phase construction, demonstrate the problem, and then fix it by defining a postscript. Every initializer in the hierarchy pushes the arguments it receives into the instance variable args. The second phase of construction formats args into a JSON string and dumps the string to the console. Here is a base class that fits the bill and works as far as it goes:

```
Line 1   dojo.declare("Base", null, {
    -      constructor: function() {
    -        this.args = {base_args: dojo._toArray(arguments)};
    -        console.log(dojo.toJson(this.args, true));
    5      }
    -    });
    -    var x= new Base(1, 2, 3);
```

Next, we'll derive a subclass from Base. We'll include a preamble to pass only the first three arguments to Base:

```
Line 1   dojo.declare("Subclass", Base, {
    -      constructor: function() {
    -        this.args.subclass_args= dojo._toArray(arguments);
    -      },
    5      preamble: function(args) {
    -        //the superclass (Base) only gets the first three arguments...
    -        return dojo._toArray(arguments).slice(0, 3);
    -      }
    -    });
```

```
10    var x= new Subclass(1, 2, 3, 4, 5, 6);
```

This causes the second phase to stop working. When Base's initializer dumps the contents of args, it misses Subclass's arguments.

The problem can be fixed by adding a postscript to Base and moving the dump to the postscipt:

```
Line 1   dojo.declare("Base", null, {
   -       constructor: function() {
   -         this.args = {base_args: dojo._toArray(arguments)};
   -       },
   5       postscript: function(){
   -         console.log(dojo.toJson(this.args, true));
   -       }
   -     });
```

When the Subclass instance is created, both Base's and Subclass's initializers are called before postscipt is called. Subclass can override Base's postscript by defining its own. Overridden postscripts almost always call the superclass method, as demonstrated here:

```
Line 1   dojo.declare("Subclass", Base, {
   -       constructor: function() {
   -         this.args.subclass_args= dojo._toArray(arguments);
   -       },
   5       preamble: function(args) {
   -         //the superclass (Base) only gets the first three arguments...
   -         return dojo._toArray(arguments).slice(0, 3);
   -       },
   -       postscript: function(){
   10        console.log("In Subclass's postscript.");
   -         this.inherited(arguments);
   -       }
   -     })
```

9.8 Creating Custom Objects Without Constructors

Usually, the prototype object is connected to an object implicitly via the constructor function that created the object. But, sometimes it is useful to create a single new object and exercise direct control over the prototype object—without going to the bother of creating a new constructor function. dojo.delegate(obj, props) creates and returns a new object with the prototype reference pointing to obj. The optional props argument is mixed into the new object by dojo.mixin.

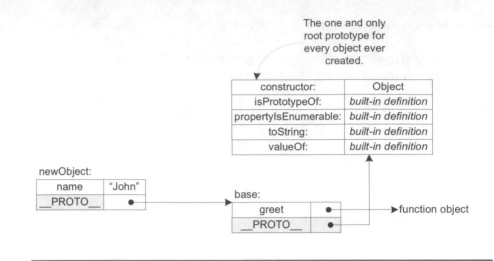

Figure 9.6: DELEGATE IN ACTION

To see dojo.delegate in action, we'll exercise it and then draw out the resulting object space:

```
Line 1    //create an object with some properties
    -     var base= {
    -       greet: function(){
    -         return "hello, my name is " + this.name;}
    5     }
    -     var newObject= dojo.delegate(base, {name: "John"});
```

In Figure 9.6, you can see the objects that are created by the code. Notice how the prototype of newObject was set to base. This is the whole point. By the way, newObject.greet() returns "hello, my name is John."

Given the power of dojo.declare, dojo.delegate is rarely needed. However, if you are building some kind of specialized class definitional machinery (akin to dojo.declare) or if you need to create a single object with a specific superclass, dojo.delegate will come in handy.

If nothing else, this chapter has shown off some really powerful Java-Script.[8] The function dojo.declare is very capable and can be used to build class hierarchies that model complex real-world things. Certainly, the Dojo toolkit employs dojo.declare extensively.

---

8. In fact, all the capabilities of dojo.declare are expressed in about sixty-five lines of code, lending even more evidence that JavaScript is quite a powerful language.

We've also pointed out some edge cases that you may run against if you are doing something outside of dojo.declare's design bounds. Look for some of these cases to be fixed with minor enhancements to dojo.declare. However, one of the key requirements of dojo.declare is to keep it light. And, since so much of Dojo uses dojo.declare, an incompatible signature change just isn't going to happen (nor should it)! So, there are some things that dojo.declare might never do (for example, more complete multiple inheritance renaming support). Look for more-advanced object systems in Dojox to solve these kinds of problems. But, even when available, such a system should probably be used only if required. In almost all cases, dojo.declare will solve your object modeling problems.

Chapter 10

dojo.data

Some web pages crave data. Data providers send it in all different for-mats: JSON, XML, comma-separated, and so on. Data consumers refor-mat the data in all kinds of ways: in tabular or hierarchical display, in drop-down boxes, and so on. The result is a veritable Tower of Babel. A drop-down widget must learn how to speak JSON and XML. So must a Grid widget. So must a tree widget. On the other end, data providers may need to speak different dialects of JSON: one for drop-downs, one for grids, and one for trees.

To straighten up this mess, the Dojo programmers invented a single API specification called dojo.data. The spec maps out four standard sets of methods called *features*: one each for reading, writing, identifying, and notifying. A *driver* class implements some or all of the dojo.data features. Bundled with Dojo are drivers for JSON, XML, CSV, and other data formats but also drivers for web services such as Flickr and Picasa. In other words, dojo.data abstracts not just the data format but the source as well.

The data might be an in-memory data structure, a stream of JSON or XML, a distributed database on another machine, or a web service from across the Internet. Now a widget need speak only one language— dojo.data—to get data from a provider, no matter what the source.

The main JavaScript object you'll use is a *data store*, which is an instance of the driver. Each data store connects to one and only one set of data. In your application, one driver class may have many data store objects spawned from it.

Working with dojo.data involves the following steps:

1. Choose the widget, or determine what you'll need to do with the data store in JavaScript.
2. Choose a dojo.data driver that fits your needed data format, data source, and features. Often the widget will determine which features you need. If the bundled drivers don't fit your needs, you may subclass a bundled driver or write your own.
3. Create your data store object declaratively or programmatically.
4. Hook the data store to your widget, or interact with the data store in your own JavaScript code.

In this chapter, we'll hit each of these steps. In the process you'll learn about Dijit's data-enabled incremental search widgets FilteringSelect and ComboBox.

10.1 The Big Picture

In Figure 10.1, on the facing page, you can see the relationships among the driver, the dojo.data specs, the data, and your code. dojo.data is actually four specifications called *features*, each of which packages a set of related methods. A driver may choose to implement some or all of these features. The driver ItemFileReadStore implements the methods in features dojo.data.Read and dojo.data.Identity. dojo.data.Read specifies, among other methods, a fetch method. The widget calls fetch, which gets JSON data from the server or its cache, massages it, and makes it available through getValue and other Read methods.

Bundled Drivers

Dojo comes complete with the following dojo.data drivers:

- dojo.data.ItemFileReadStore, dojo.data.ItemFileWriteStore, and dojox.data.QueryReadStore for JSON
- dojox.data.XmlStore for XML
- dojox.data.CsvStore for comma-separated variables
- Drivers for various photo-sharing web services: dojox.data.PicasaStore, dojox.data.FlickrStore, and dojox.data.SnapLogicStore
- Interesting experimental drivers like dojox.data.KeyValueStore for Java-style property files

Of these, ItemFileReadStore, ItemFileWriteStore, and QueryReadStore are the ones we'll use in this book.

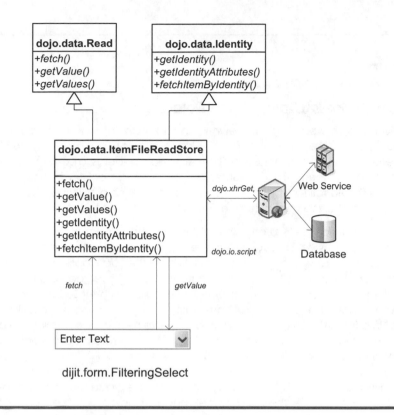

Figure 10.1: DOJO.DATA ARCHITECTURE

Data Stores Are Not Databases

Choosing a driver also involves knowing what features you need. But before doing that, it's essential to get a proper fundamental grounding.

Relational database technology is pervasive in web applications, so you probably already know its terminology: databases, tables, rows, and columns, and so on. But dojo.data drivers talk to more than just databases, so the dojo.data documentation uses different, wider, and more inclusive terms. For example, what you would traditionally call a "column" in a database, a "property" in JSON, or a "tag name" in XML becomes a *property* in dojo.data land.

It's important to know these terms since they're used in many dojo.data method names. You won't find a getRows method in the documentation, for example, but you will find getItems. That trips up many folks using dojo.data for the first time.

Alex Says. . .
Session Data != Model Data

Most major web app frameworks include an interface to a relational database. I'm not a fan of relational databases for many web-development tasks. Although the relational model is clearly a good method for storing large volumes of inter-related persistent data (OK, that's Rawld talking, but he's not wrong), it's just as clearly not the preferred method to manipulate session data (that is, data the UI is using).

The reason for this is pretty simple. One of the relational model's primary strengths is that it can return the answers to interesting questions—questions that weren't considered when the database was constructed. It does this by storing all data in a set of predicates and providing a language (unfortunately, SQL) to reason with those predicates. But, we don't need any of this complexity when we're displaying a data set in a form. When we're wiring up a UI, we're nearly always talking to a service that can answer a particular question. The return data is often a simple document, either a flat list of answers or possibly a nested group of properties and their values! Further, since we're concerned with other things in the UI—such as changing an item in one place results in changing it every place—the data model used to back a UI needs features the relational model may not handle well, particularly when it comes to enforcing security constraints or other business logic. Additional code is needed, and it's best not to replicate that on both sides of the wire.

That's one of the key ideas behind dojo.data: constructing a simple session and service-oriented data model that includes functionality needed to develop robust UIs. The abstractions in dojo.data are designed to allow widgets to interface with disparate data sources though a unified API without taking on responsibilities that the browser can't handle well anyway. For instance, it's the UI's job to provide user feedback when an operation might take a little while, so many of the dojo.data abstractions are explicitly asynchronous to make sure that the UI code has a chance to communicate effectively about the state of the app. Conversely, dojo.data makes no explicit gaurantees about data's relationships to other bits of data, allowing data stores to be implemented on top of existing services and without forcing data store authors to think about tasks that the browser can't do efficiently anyway. By making things that should be the browser's job easy and things that should usually happen on the server harder, dojo.data helps keep applications out of the gutter in terms of performance.

dojo.data is there to make building UIs easy. Nothing more, nothing less.

data store

A JavaScript object that makes available the data from a *data source*. A data store is always an instance of a dojo.data driver class. The terminology is a bit jarring at first, but you can think of a data store as a "mini-driver": one that handles the operations of one particular data source.

A *data store* connects to exactly one data source, which is in turn backed by a URL or a JavaScript string. You can have more than one data store defined for a particular data source—for example, you can provide read-only access through one data store and read-write access through another.

data source

The URL or JavaScript string variable where the raw data comes from. If you use the URL method, which is more common, the data may be fed from a static file, a server program hooked to a database, or some other form of web service. The dojo.data driver doesn't care where the data comes from or how it's generated. It cares only what format the data is in. The data may be nested, which separates it from a pure relational table. This is analogous to *table or nested tables*.

attribute

A field name, for example "Street Address." This is sometimes called a *property*. This is analogous to *column*.

value

The contents of an *attribute*, for example, "1127 North Spring Ave."

multivalue

One to many values belonging to the same attribute. This is analogous to storing an array in a database column (which some databases let you do; others don't).

item

An object in the data store containing attributes and values. Items in the same data store aren't required to have the same attributes; for example, one item may have an addressLineFive attribute, and another may not. But they usually have *some* attributes in common, or else items would be impossible to display and compare. This is analogous to *row*.

To make things interestingly recursive, an attribute's value may itself be an item. You can have nested items, items with more than one parent, and even circularly related items.

identity

A value used to uniquely identify an item within a single data store. When a data store has an identity, each item in that store must provide an identity value. Some drivers force you to provide the identity in an attribute, but some drivers generate it for you. If you're providing the identity, *it is very important to ensure identity values are unique*—most dojo.data drivers will alert you if they find a violation. This is analogous to *primary key*.

label

An attribute functioning as the human-readable equivalent of an identity. For example, an item may have the identity customerNumber:999135 and the label customerName:"Jane Public". Data-enabled widgets such as Tree use the label as an item's visible symbol. Unlike identity values, label values do not need to be unique.

query

A request for some subset of data store *items*. A query is a hash whose property name-value pairs are matched against items. This is analogous to the WHERE clause of a SQL select.

internal data representation

The private data structures that a *data store* uses to cache data in local memory (for example XML DOM nodes, JavaScript hashes, or arrays of arrays).

request

The parameters that are used to limit and sort a set of items. This includes the query, sorting attributes, upper and lower limits, and handlers.

fetch

The operation that takes a request and returns items matching that request. This may trigger a server request via XHR, or it may not (for example, if the data is cached).

Features

Now that we're working with a standard terminology, we can talk about driver features. Here, we're using the word *feature* in the precise way dojo.data defines it, that is, as a group of related methods. dojo.data methods are grouped into features named Read, Write, Identity, and Notification. A driver may implement some or all of these features. So, for example, ItemFileReadStore and ItemFileWriteStore use the same JSON-based data format, but only the latter has the Write and Notification features. Still, the Read methods are the same no matter what driver you use, and that's the beauty of the dojo.data specification.

A driver's features are usually listed in its documentation, but you may also call the method data store.getFeatures(), which returns a hash with properties named after the dojo.data features. For example, if ifrs is of type dojo.data.ItemFileReadStore, then ifrs.getFeatures() returns { dojo.data.Read: true, dojo.data.Identity: true }. The latter technique is useful for writing generalized data-enabled widgets, where you have no idea which driver is on the other side.

Here are the features and their methods' general responsibilities:

dojo.data.Read

A driver is fairly useless without this feature, because its methods enable fetching items and reading the attributes inside. Not surprisingly, all bundled dojo.data drivers implement this. The Read feature contains methods to load items, view their attributes, compare an item value, handle multivalued attributes, paginate, sort, and filter the items.

dojo.data.Write

This feature enables writing to the items as well. These methods change the in-memory copy of the data, but they can also save data back to a server. Some drivers like ItemFileWriteStore allow a custom save handler to precisely control client-to-server writing. We will look at an example in Chapter 13, *Tree*, on page 339.

dojo.data.Identity

Closely aligned with Read, Identity methods perform quick unambiguous random-access lookups. To use these methods, each data store item must have a unique identity value. The Dijit components ComboBox, FilteringSelect, and Tree require the Identity feature.

dojo.data.Notification

This feature allows you to hook into data store events. You provide an appropriately named handler to the driver, and the driver then calls it whenever that event occurs. For example, if you provide an onDelete handler to a Notification-enabled data store, that handler is called whenever an item is deleted. This is particularly useful for posting new, updated, or deleted records back to the server.

The bundled drivers implement these features:

- The dojo.data.ItemFileReadStore, dojox.data.QueryReadStore, and dojox.data.CsvStore drivers implement the dojo.data.Read and dojo.data.Identity features.
- The dojo.data.ItemFileWriteStore driver implements dojo.data.Read, dojo.data.Identity, dojo.data.Write, and dojo.data.Notification.
- The dojox.data.XmlStore driver implements the dojo.data.Read and dojo.data.Write features.
- The dojox.data.PicasaStore, dojox.data.FlickrStore, and dojox.data.SnapLogicStore drivers implement the dojo.data.Read feature.

An Example Using dojo.data.ItemFileReadStore

Let's look at a concrete example of a data store using ItemFileReadStore to see where all these terms apply. We have some JSON-formatted experimental data in code/data/datasources/genetox.json.[1] Each item describes a genetic experiment: apply a foreign agent to a live subject, and see whether it causes genetic damage. So, for example, the first experiment describes subjecting vivo mammalian somatic cells to irradiated potato extract. The results, under the result attribute, are "no conclusion." (Moral: Stay away from the irradiated potato extract aisle of your supermarket, just in case.)

JSON data handled by the ItemFileReadStore must follow this structure:

```
{
    identifier: «identifierAttribute»,
    [ label: «labelAttribute», ]
    items: [
        {
            «identifierAttribute»: «idValue»,
            [«labelAttribute»: «labelValue»,]
            «attribute1»: «value1»,
            «attribute2»: «value2»,
            ...
        },
        ...
    ]
}
```

---

1. The sample data comes from GENETOX, a U.S. government database of toxic genetic effects on organisms. This is just one of the free, fun databases available at http://www.nlm.nih.gov.

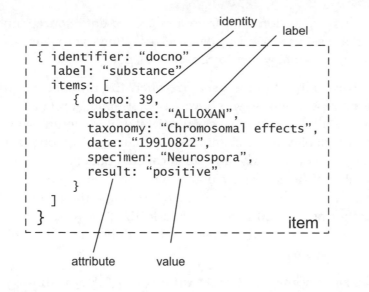

identity   label

```
{ identifier: "docno"
  label: "substance"
  items: [
    { docno: 39,
      substance: "ALLOXAN",
      taxonomy: "Chromosomal effects",
      date: "19910822",
      specimen: "Neurospora",
      result: "positive"
    }
  ]
}                                    item
```

attribute   value

Figure 10.2: A DOJO.DATA.ITEMFILEREADSTORE DATA SOURCE

The identifier property points to the identifier attribute in items. The optional label property points to the label attribute. Finally, the data itself comes in items, always an array of JSON hashes even if there are 0 or 1 of them.

Our test data, whose first few lines are shown in Figure 10.2, fits that structure. Each item has the identifier attribute, in this case docno, and the label attribute, in this case substance.

So, that's an ItemFileReadStore-based data store in a nutshell. For this chapter, we'll concentrate on this driver and its cousin QueryReadStore. Another popular driver, ItemFileWriteStore, will show up in Chapter 13, *Tree*, on page 339. The important thing here is that an item is an item is an item, no matter what dojo.data driver you use.

With a sure grounding in the fundamentals, we can start shoveling data into widgets.

10.2 dojo.data and Incremental Search

A popular Ajax user interface pattern is the *incremental search box*, sometimes known as a suggestion widget. Dijit implements incremental search in two widgets: dojo.form.FilteringSelect and dojo.form.ComboBox.

Each gets its suggestion data from a dojo.data data source, and each resembles a <select> tag. But FilteringSelect limits your choices to the provided suggestions, while ComboBox does not.

These widgets outperform a <select> when the number of options is high. Here's how: suppose you have 1,000 options. A regular <select> would create all 1,000 <option> tags. Dijit's incremental search widgets instead display a small number of matching options after each keystroke. Each of these option sets is called a *page*, and the *page size* is the number of items displayed at one time. If the page size is 30, the first keystroke will generate one page of 30 items, the second will generate another page of 30 items, and so forth. This technique is called *lazy rendering*, because the widget creates option markup only when absolutely necessary.

In the next few sections, we'll set up a FilteringSelect with suggestions from the experiment data store. The customization options are similar in ComboBox, and we'll show a few unique features of each.

Creating a Data Store Object

To begin the widget, you must first instantiate the data store object. As with most things in Dojo, you can create the data store object declaratively or programmatically. Here's the declarative style:

data/genetox_def.html

```
<div dojoType="dojo.data.ItemFileReadStore"
    url="datasources/genetox.json"
    jsId="genetoxStoreDeclarative" />
```

The declaration requires a driver class name, specified in dojoType=. jsId= declares a JavaScript variable holding the data store handle. You'll use that variable to connect the data store to the widget.

Different drivers require different sets of attributes. With ItemFileReadStore, you may specify either the url= attribute or the data= attribute, but not both. URL-backed data stores get data from a server. The data= property, on the other hand, specifies a JavaScript string holding the data. This method is rarer but occasionally useful for small, client-generated data stores. The programmatic version is similar:

data/genetox_def.html

```
genetoxStoreProgrammatic =
  new dojo.data.ItemFileReadStore({
    url: "datasources/genetox.json"
  });
```

Once you have the data store handle in a JavaScript variable, you can pass it to the incremental search widget like this:

`data/genetox_def.html`

```
<div dojoType="dijit.form.FilteringSelect"
          store="genetoxStoreProgrammatic"
          labelAttr="substance"
          searchAttr="docno"
          name="substance"/>
```

So, you have a pipe carrying data from the data store to the widget. Now you just need to control the flow a bit.

Pulling Suggestion Values

In our example, throwing the entire data store of experiments at the widget is way too much. So, you must tell the widget the suggestions are values in the substance attribute like this:

`data/genetox_def.html`

```
<div dojoType="dijit.form.FilteringSelect"
          store="genetoxStoreProgrammatic"
          labelAttr="substance"
          searchAttr="docno"
          name="substance"/>
```

Here, the labelAttr= property points to the human-readable label attribute, and searchAttr= points to the server-consumable value. You can think of it like an *<option>* tag with labelAttr= containing the option body and searchAttr= containing the option's value attribute.

When you type some letters in the FilteringSelect, the attribute specified in labelAttr= is matched against it. FilteringSelect, in the background, copies the corresponding value in searchAttr= into a hidden field. When the form is submitted, this is the value sent. (We'll see how this mechanism works in Chapter 15, *Form Controls*, on page 393.) It's just like a *<select>* in that respect.

AutoComplete

FilteringSelect takes a lot of the guesswork out of typing a value, but not all of it. Suppose the user types PZ, which matches no values, and tries to press Tab. In that case, the value is considered illegal, and the Tab is ignored. And what about the opposite problem? Perhaps they type PH, which matches many documents. What happens if the user tries to tab out then?

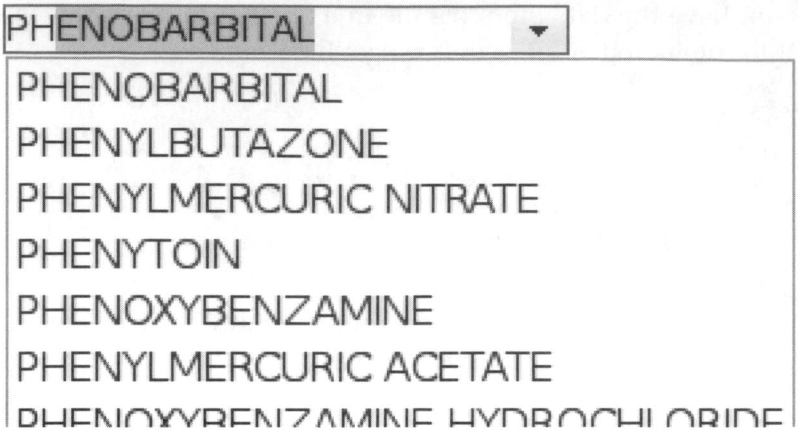

PHENOBARBITAL ▼

PHENOBARBITAL
PHENYLBUTAZONE
PHENYLMERCURIC NITRATE
PHENYTOIN
PHENOXYBENZAMINE
PHENYLMERCURIC ACETATE
PHENOXYBENZAMINE HYDROCHLORIDE

Figure 10.3: AUTOCOMPLETE HELPS A USER SELECT THE APPROPRIATE VALUE.

Here, FilteringSelect's autoComplete= attribute can help. Set to **true**, the first document matching PH will automatically display in the field, and the user can simply tab out to set it. This is illustrated in Figure 10.3. Set to **false**, the user must either type the entire document name or select it by arrowing down the drop-down list and pressing Enter.

ComboBox, which accepts values not in the data store, does not have to deal with this stuff. Like a regular textbox, it passes the displayed text to the server as name. So, ComboBox has only a searchAttr= attribute.

Queries

Sometimes you may not want all the values available for suggestions, just a subset of them. For instance, you may want to display substances with experiments performed in 2001. Queries can help you here.

Many of Dojo's bundled drivers like ItemFileReadStore and XmlStore support a "semistandard" query language that you can tap into. It's not a full regular expression or SQL-like query language: there are no ORs, NOTs, set operations, numerical comparison operators, or joins. The standard format is as follows:

```
{ «attribute1»: "«expression1»"
  [, «attribute2»: "«expression2»"]
  , ...
}
```

The commas are implied ANDs, so query="{ date:'2001*', result:'positive'}" matches 2,001 documents with a positive result. In the expressions, the wildcard * matches any sequence of characters (including the empty string), and ? matches one character. You use the * operator like this:

data/genetox_init_query.html

```
<div dojoType="dijit.form.FilteringSelect"
        store="genetoxStoreDeclarative"
        searchAttr="docno"
        labelAttr="substance"
        name="subname"
        query="{ date: '1995*' }"
        />
```

This query language also supports two query modifiers, which you pass as a hash literal to queryOptions=:

ignoreCase

Setting ignoreCase to true initiates a case-insensitive search.

deep

When the driver supports nested items, setting deep="true" will cause these nested items to be searched as well. Nesting is a subject we'll cover in Chapter 13, *Tree*, on page 339.

dojo.data does not require all drivers to support this query language. The example that ends this chapter—Section 10.5, *A Yahoo Search Driver*, on page 277—does not support wildcards, mainly because the backing Yahoo Search web service doesn't allow them. But since all bundled dojo.data-enabled widgets assume the same query language, it's a good idea to support it as far as possible.

10.3 Partitioning with QueryReadStore

FilteringSelect *lazy renders* data by constructing one page of items at a time from browser memory. That speeds up a drop-down list of 1,000 items. Now suppose you have 100,000 options. Many Dojo users try to feed a FilteringSelect a data store of this magnitude, only to find the performance drop substantially. How could that be? After all, you are still rendering a page of items at a time, right?

Why You May Need Partitioning

The bottleneck is in ItemFileReadStore. The driver creates an XHR request from the URL you provide. When the first fetch occurs from FilteringSelect (that is, the first keystroke), ItemFileReadStore dutifully loads everything that /path/to/myjson.json returns—*all 100,000 items*. XHR requests cannot say, "Give me the data from /path/to/mydata.json, but only items 300–330." It's all or nothing.

To its credit, ItemFileReadStore makes the XHR request only once and caches all the items in browser memory. So when the second keystroke into a FilteringSelect generates the second fetch to ItemFileReadStore, it simply hands over the page of items from the cache.

Still, at 100,000 items, it's the initial load that kills performance. The driver must take all the data and pull out a page worth of items to match the query FilteringSelect constructs from the keystrokes. When faced with a job this big, you really need a different design. Hmmmmm.

The server is not doing much work. If it could do the sorting and selecting job and then send down just the page of data needed, the browser could be free to do the rendering. You'd use less network bandwidth and less client processing. This technique is called *partitioning*: you split a large job between a client partition and a server partition.

Fortunately, Dojo comes bundled with a partitioning JSON driver called dojox.data.QueryReadStore. It implements the same dojo.data APIs that dojo.data.ItemFileReadStore does and reads the same data format. But it delegates the sorting and selection to the server. The server portion is not magic—you must program it in your server-side language. That part is beyond the scope of this book. Still, programmers find this natural when they already have a server-side program converting data (say, from a database) to JSON for Dojo's use.

Translating dojo.data Queries to Server URLs

It'd be nice to simply replace dojoType="dojo.data.ItemFileReadStore" with dojoType="dojox.data.QueryReadStore" and leave it at that. In fact, you *can* try it, but the search box will perform even worse than ItemFileReadStore. It all stems from fetching philosophies. ItemFileReadStore is absolutely conservative—it will issue only one XHR request no matter how many times one calls fetch. QueryReadStore is absolutely liberal—it will issue an XHR request for every fetch. If your URL passes back 100,000 items and you use it unchanged in QueryReadStore, it will keep fetching the same 100,000 items over and over again. Uggggh. That's not the direction we want to go!

The server needs more information. It needs to know what records to look for, how many to return, and how to sort them. That sounds a lot like a dojo.data request. And in fact, if your server program could parse and understand a request like this...

`data/datasources/simple_request.js`

```
{
    query: {name: "A*"},
    queryOptions: {ignoreCase: true},
    sort: [{attribute:"name", descending:false}],
    start: 100,
    count: 10
}
```

then everything would be hunky-dory. But different server-side programs require different forms of URLs. For example:

```
mystore.php?query=A\%&page=1&itemsperpage=10&sort=name
```

Rather than be dictatorial, QueryReadStore allows you to plug in code to rewrite the dojo.data request as a URL. You do this by writing a subclass of QueryReadStore and using *that* for your driver instead.

Fortunately, the subclass you must write will be quite simple. You only need to override the fetch method, which will rewrite the request hash into server parameters. You'll place the parameters in a hash literal and assign it to the QueryReadStore property serverQuery, which resembles the content hash of dojo.xhr*.

In our example, there are a couple of transformations. First, QueryReadStore's wildcard character * must be replaced with the server program's wildcard character %. Second, the count parameter is copied to the server parameter itemsperpage= and the query parameter to q=. Finally, a starting row, 100, must be transformed into a page number, 10. Here's the complete driver you need:

`data/datasources/sample_rewriter.js`

```
dojo.provide("dojobook.data.datasources.sample_rewriter");

dojo.require("dojox.data.QueryReadStore");

dojo.declare(
    "dojobook.data.datasources.sample_rewriter",
    dojox.data.QueryReadStore, {

    fetch:function(request) {
        request.serverQuery = {
            q: request.query.substance.replace("*", "%"),
```

```
            itemsperpage: request.count,
            page: Math.floor(request.start / 10)
        };

        // Call superclasses' fetch
        return this.inherited(arguments);
    }
});
```

QueryReadStore sends both the request.query and the request.serverQuery properties combined. In the previous example, mystore.php?q=A&page=10&itemsperpage=10&query=A*&start=1&count=10 gets sent. As long as the extra parameters do not interfere with the server program, you needn't worry about it. If they do, you can simply null out request.query.field in the QueryReadStore subclass.

10.4 Calling Read Methods from JavaScript

Up until now, we've let the widgets call the various driver methods. Now we'll call them ourselves from JavaScript. This extends the range of what you can do with data stores. For example, you can loop through a data store's values to find the maximum. You can rig a Button widget to add an item to the data store. Or you can duplicate-check a newly entered value against existing data store values. Of course, you can use JavaScript to write your own data-enabled widget as well. Ah, the possibilities!

You'll use Read more than any other feature in your own code. In Chapter 13, *Tree*, on page 339, we'll cover the important methods of Write, Notification, and Identity.

As with widgets, to use a data store you must first create a data store object as we detailed in Section 10.2, *Creating a Data Store Object*, on page 266. That gives you a JavaScript variable with the data store object in it. Then you call methods on it.

fetch and Pagination

Let's start with fetch. Functioning much like SQL's SELECT verb, fetch takes a query, a sorting hash, and parameters for the page location (start, count), then grabs the appropriate items from the data source. It's a fairly complex function call, but it's usually the first method you call on a data store. Once you learn it, the rest of the dojo.data methods make sense.

fetch takes only one parameter: the request hash whose properties are as follows:

```
{
  query: /* String or hash */
  queryOptions: /* hash */
  sort: /* Array of hashes */
  start: /* Number */
  count: /* Number */
  // Handlers
  scope: /* Object */
  onBegin: /* function */
  onItem: /* function */
  onComplete: /* function */
  onError: /* function */
} → dojo.data.Request
```

Most requests need only a subset of these properties. You've seen some of them before: in particular, query and queryOptions for selecting. Some of the properties are ignored in some drivers; for example, a driver that does not support sorting will not recognize the sort parameter.

Some drivers support pagination, and like querying, it can be done on the client or server. ItemFileReadStore paginates solely on the client, meaning it gets all the data from the server at once but can hand over a page of results at a time. QueryReadStore can paginate on the client or the server; with server pagination, the server program must recognize parameters identifying the page. For example, in the previous section, our PHP program needed the parameters page and itemsperpage.

The properties start, which is the item number you want fetched first, and count, which is the number of items you want returned, define the scope. You usually initialize these to 0 and your desired page size, respectively. fetch adds the count to the start property and hands the request object back on return. To get the next page, you just re-pass this request object to fetch.

Sorting

Many bundled dojo.data drivers (ItemFileReadStore and XmlStore among them) support client-side sorting as well. You simply pass the sort property an array of hash literals. Each hash corresponds to one attribute of a compound key. The classic example is "last name, first name" in which there are two attributes—last name and first name—scrunched into one compound key.

Each sort array hash has the following attributes:

attribute

> This is the data store attribute whose values you want to sort.

descending

> By default, values sort in ascending order. Set this attribute to **true** to sort descending instead. **null** is considered higher than any other value, so they sort to the bottom for ascending order and the top for descending.

The order of the attributes goes from most significant to least. So, the compound key [{attribute: "date"}, {attribute:"substance"}] sorts first by date and then, for two documents with the same date, by substance.

fetch Handlers

The scope property value becomes **this** in the handlers onBegin, onItem, onComplete, and onError. It is similar to the context parameter in dojo. hitch.

These handlers are similar to those used in remote scripting methods like dojo.xhr*. fetch itself does not return items. Instead, it kicks off an asynchronous request and returns control to your program immediately. The fetch continues in the background, first waiting for the data from the XHR request and then assembling the data into items. The handlers you provide in the onBegin, onItem, onComplete, and onError properties execute at key points during the process. These handlers, listed here in the order they're called, are as follows:

```
onBegin(Number itemCount)
```

The onBegin handler is called before the first item returns. If the dojo. data driver can determine the number of items beforehand, it is passed in itemCount; otherwise, it's set to -1. A popular use of this handler is to initialize a dijit.ProgressBar widget with the total number of items and then use the onItem handler to update the progress.

```
onItem(dojo.data.Item item)
```

onItem is called when an item is available for processing. You can use the item to, for example, keep a running sum of values. When the onItem handler returns, the fetching continues.

```
onError(Error errorData)
```

If a transmission error occurs, the driver calls your onError handler. Like the error handler in dojo.xhr*, this reports only errors getting the data, not errors reported from the server, such as "no data found."

Also like dojo.xhr*, the error data is passed back in the first parameter.

```
onComplete(dojo.data.Item[] items)
```

Finally, the onComplete handler is called after all the items are fetched. If there's no onItem handler, the first argument will be an array of all the items. If there is an onItem handler, this parameter will be null. Essentially, this means you can process the items one-by-one through onItem or all at once with onComplete, but not both.

More Read Methods

Once you've fetched items, you can read them:

```
datastore.hasAttribute(dojo.data.Item item, String attr) → Boolean
datastore.getLabel(dojo.data.Item item) → Object
datastore.getValue(dojo.data.Item item, string attr) → Object
```

One common mistake is trying to call methods on an item. You always call dojo.data methods on a data store object. If you're calling per-item methods, item is always the first parameter, not the object.

hasAttribute returns **true** if an item has a particular attribute. This may look strange if you're used to relational tables, where all rows have the same set of columns. Data store items, on the other hand, may or may not have a particular specified attribute, which is the reason for the test. getLabel and getValue return the value for the label attribute or an arbitrary attribute, respectively.

The following example shows a fetch in action and illustrates some of the other Read methods. This code will list all the specimen values in a bulleted list with duplicates removed.

data/genetox_api_demo.html

```
Line 1  var genetox =
   -        new dojo.data.ItemFileReadStore({
   -            url: "http://localhost/dojobook/data/datasources/genetox.json"
   -        });
   5
   -    // Organisms will be placed in a dictionary
   -    var organismList = new dojox.collections.SortedList();
   -
   -    // Fetch all the values once the page has loaded
  10    dojo.addOnLoad(function() {
   -        genetox.fetch({
   -
   -            onBegin: function() {
   -                console.debug("Begun");
  15            },
   -
```

```
            onError: function(errData, request) {
                console.debug("Error Occurred");
                console.dir(errData);
20          },

            onItem: function(item) {
                if (! genetox.hasAttribute(item, "endOfFile")) {
                    console.debug("Loaded "+genetox.getLabel(item));
25                  var spec = genetox.getValue( item, "specimen");
                    organismList.add(spec, spec);
                }
            },

30          // When everything's done, list them in the page
            onComplete: function(items, request) {
                listNode = dojo.byId("resultUl");
                organismList.forEach(function (org) {
                    var listItem = document.createElement("li");
35                  listItem.innerHTML = org;
                    listNode.appendChild(listItem);
                });
            }
        });
40  });
```

The onItem handler at lines 22 to 28 executes once for each item fetched. The last item in the data store is a sentinel record { endOfFile: true } for which the hasAttribute call at line 23 tests.

The getLabel call gets the label of an item, where the label attribute is in the data store (in our data store, that's substance). Finally, the getValuecall at line 25 simply gets the value for the named attribute in the given item.

The code saves all specimens in a dojox.collections.SortedList collection, which simultaneously sorts the values and ignores all duplicates. The onComplete handler from lines 31 to 38 simply reads the set back out, writing it to a bulleted list. onComplete doesn't touch the data store at all. That makes sense because when an onItem handler is provided, onComplete gets nothing passed to it.

The fetch operation does a lot of work. But the Read feature has many more useful methods as well, and rather than list them all, we'll actually *build* a driver implementing Read and Identity. It's not as difficult as you'd think!

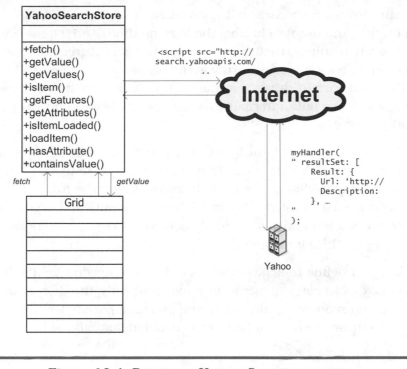

Figure 10.4: PLAN FOR YAHOO SEARCH DRIVER

10.5 A Yahoo Search Driver

dojo.data drivers traditionally connect to web services that you control. But there's nothing limiting you to your own network or data formats. With a little work, you can build a dojo.data driver connecting to web services beyond your network. Really! The driver we'll build will call Yahoo Search with terms like "ben and jerrys" and feed the results into a grid, much like the cigar example in Chapter 3, *Connecting to Outside Services*, on page 31. But the resulting code is easier and reusable.

In Figure 10.4, you can see the strategy. You send the Yahoo Search service some terms, and Yahoo sends back a page of results in JSON format. It's not appropriate for ItemFileReadStore for two reasons. First the web service is out of the browser's domain, and ItemFileReadStore, being based on dojo.xhrGet, must follow the same-domain rule. Second, the web service results are not in ItemFileReadStore format.

But our driver won't care. It'll use JSONP to get around the same-domain rule and use it right from the fetch method. And it'll use Yahoo's own search results structure as its internal structure. For example, Yahoo sends back its results array in the property Results.Result. Remember that a dojo.data driver is a black box. It doesn't matter how the driver stores the data internally, as long as the dojo.data methods respond properly.

It is customary and helpful to link each item to its store through an added property _S. We need this to properly enforce methods like isItem. If someone were to hand off an item to isItem, it could be from a different data store even if the attributes and values are identical to a given item. To prevent such mixups, you simply compare the _S property with the data store (in the **this** variable).

So, first you define the class itself. A data store needn't be a subclass of any dojo.data class; it needs to implement only the dojo.data APIs. Each search request requires only one dynamic parameter, the search terms, so those are defined first in the constructor call.

data/datasources/YahooSearchStore.js

```
dojo.declare("dojobook.data.datasources.YahooSearchStore", null, {
    searchTerms: "",

    constructor: function(args){
        if (args && args.searchTerms) {
            this.searchTerms = args.searchTerms;
        }
    },
```

Now we'll implement the Read API methods, one by one. First, getFeatures returns the APIs the driver implements. getAttributes defines attributes so that driver users can iterate through them with getValue. Fortunately, you don't need attributes for every data element Yahoo returns—just ones the driver users will find interesting.

data/datasources/YahooSearchStore.js

```
_searchUrl: "http://search.yahooapis.com/WebSearchService/V1/webSearch",

// A reference to the store is kept in every item in the _S attribute. That
// way, we catch errors with items being passed to us from different stores.
_storeRef: "_S",

getFeatures: function(){
    return {
        'dojo.data.api.Read': true
    };
},
```

```
getAttributes: function(item){
    // These are all the interesting properties coming back
    // from Yahoo
    return ["Url", "Title", "Summary"];
},
```

fetch is the heart of the driver and often is the most difficult to write.
But if you can get all the data store elements in one remote scripting
call and store them in a JavaScript array, dojo.data provides a shortcut.
The dojo.data.util.simpleFetch class implements a fetch that handles pagination, sorting, and simple events for you. You mix its methods into
your own drivers like this:

data/datasources/YahooSearchStore.js

```
// End of the dojo.declare for YahooSearchStore
});

dojo.extend(
    dojobook.data.datasources.YahooSearchStore,
    dojo.data.util.simpleFetch
);
```

Note the dojo.extend statement comes after the entire dojo.declare statement. Then all you must do is implement a handler for simpleFetch's
_fetchItems extension point, which looks like this:

```
_fetchItems(
    /* dojo.data.request */ request,
    /* function */ fetchHandler,
    /* function */ errorHandler
)
```

_fetchItems takes in a dojo.data request and assembles an array of items.
But since most drivers act asynchronously and ours is no exception,
you can't just say return items;. Instead, simpleFetch passes in a handler
through the fetchHandler parameter. Your code then calls fetchHandler
when it's done retrieving items. If you've used dojo.xhr* at all, this technique should look familiar.

YahooSearchStore's _fetchItems bears a striking resemblance to the Yahoo
Search example earlier in Chapter 3, *Connecting to Outside Services*, on
page 31. The actual processing of the list gets delegated to the private
method _processSearchData.

data/datasources/YahooSearchStore.js

```
_fetchItems: function(request, fetchHandler, errorHandler){
    if(!request.query){
        request.query={};
    }

    //Build up the content to send the request for.
    var content = {
        appid: "DEMO",
        query: this.searchTerms,
        output: "json"
    };

    // self is pulled into handler by closures.
    var self = this;

    var deferred = dojo.io.script.get({
        url: this._searchUrl,
        content: content,
        callbackParamName: 'callback',
        handle: function(data){
                // Process the items.  fetchHandler is a reference to
                // a function that simpleFetch passes here
                fetchHandler(self._processSearchData(data), request);
        }
    });

    deferred.addErrback(function(error){
        errorHandler(error, request);
    });
},

// HTTP requests don't need closing
close: function(request){ },
```

_processSearchData takes the array of items and adds an _S property to point to the outlying store:

data/datasources/YahooSearchStore.js

```
_processSearchData: function(data){
    // Default to empty store
    var items = [];
    if(data.ResultSet){
        // The ResultSet field comes back as an array of Result objects
        items = data.ResultSet.Result;
        //Add on the store ref so that isItem can work.
        var storeObject = this;
        dojo.forEach(items, function(item) {
            item[storeObject._storeRef] = storeObject;
        });
    }
    return items;
},
```

Checking an item for containment in our data store is fairly easy. A few auxiliary procedures, mandatory in dojo.data.Read, do the job:

data/datasources/YahooSearchStore.js

```
isItem: function(item){
    return item && item[this._storeRef] === this;
},

// The following two functions are used for lazy-loading
// data stores who fetch only the identifiers up front, then
// fill in the rest as they're accessed.  YahooSearchStore does not
// lazy-load, so these are trivial.

isItemLoaded: function(item){
    return this.isItem(item);
},

// loadItem
loadItem: function(keywordArgs){ },
```

The getValues may look strange—why pass back an array when clearly each property has one value? Hierarchical data stores, which we'll meet in Chapter 13, *Tree*, on page 339, can have more than one value per property. We include it here for completeness:

data/datasources/YahooSearchStore.js

```
getValues: function(item, attribute){
    //  summary:
    //      See dojo.data.api.Read.getValue()

    if(!this.isItem(item)){
        throw new Error("YahooSearchStore: invalid item");
    }
    if(typeof attribute !== "string"){
        throw new Error("YahooSearchStore: invalid attribute");
    }

    try {
        return [ item[attribute] ];
    } catch (e) {
        return [];
    }
},

getValue: function(item, attribute){
    // Basic read out of the items array
    var values = this.getValues(item, attribute);
    return values.length == 0 ? undefined : values[0];
},
```

```
hasAttribute: function(item, attribute){
    // We simply look up the attribute
    return this.getValues(item,attribute) > 0;
},

containsValue: function(item, attribute, value){
    var values = this.getValues(item,attribute);
    return dojo.some(values, function(thisValue) {
        return thisValue == value;
    });
}
```

With that, our driver is complete. Using it with widgets is no more difficult than using a bundled driver, as you can see in this demo:

`data/yahoo_search_store.html`

```
<div dojoType="dojobook.data.datasources.YahooSearchStore"
    jsId="searchStore" searchTerms="ben and jerry ice cream">
</div>

<table id="grid" dojoType="dojox.grid.Grid" store="searchStore"
            clientSort="true"
            style="width: 35em; height: 15em;">
    <thead>
        <tr>
            <th field="Title">Title</th>
            <th field="Url" >Url</th>
        </tr>
        <tr>
            <th field="Summary" colSpan="2" >Summary</th>
        </tr>
    </thead>
</div>
```

The driver could stand some extensions. It gets only the first page of data. Since Yahoo Search itself contains start and count parameters, you can extend the YahooSearchStore to pass these parameters on. SimpleFetch, however, will not work in this case since you obtain results incrementally. You would need to write your own fetch method. But overall, this class is useful and provides a blueprint for other web service calls.

dojo.data drivers are to data processing what widgets are to UI processing: they package the details in neat, reusable boxes. You can plop these store definitions into any page with a couple of lines of markup and use it to feed dojo.data-enabled widgets.

Here we covered dojo.data and the data-enabled widgets FilteringSelect and ComboBox. In Part III, we'll look at two very sophisticated and useful widgets: Tree and Grid, which do more sophisticated kinds of display.

The Dojo Loader and Build System

One of the best ways to simplify a big, complex project is to divide it up into a bunch of small, simple projects. So when you're implementing the next killer app, you'll want to build a well-organized collection of smallish JavaScript source files rather than a few huge monoliths. Unfortunately, many small source files have a cost: if each of these resources required an independent, sequential round-trip to the server, the load times could be sluggish.

Together, the Dojo loader and build system let you modularize a large project into any number of independent source files (which controls complexity) yet package that same project into only a few, highly compressed files (which optimizes download times). Currently, Dojo is the only pure-JavaScript toolkit that has this capability.[1] This chapter describes how to use these systems.

Before we dive in, a caveat is in order: you are not *required* to use these systems for your own code. If your web app is small, then just throw your code in a JavaScript source file, reference it from a script element, and you're done.

---

1. Some toolkits include processes that package the toolkit but not generic machinery that you can use to package your own code. There are also server-side tools and/or client-side tools that require plug-ins that implement various kinds of packaging; naturally the footprint of these tools is much larger.

11.1 The Big Picture

The Dojo loader and build system are both powerful and flexible. Because of this, covering every possible use case isn't practical. However, the background provided in this section together with the examples in the remainder of the chapter will arm you with the knowledge and tools required to organize and deploy your own projects optimally.

How the Loader and Build System Play Together

In Chapter 4, we described how Dojo was divided into three source trees: dojo/, dijit/, and dojox/. Each of these trees defines a hierarchy of modules. The function dojo.require maps a module name to a URL, downloads, and then evals that resource. The Dojo machinery that collectively implements dojo.require is termed the *loader*.

The idea of mapping a hierarchy of modules into URLs is termed the *Dojo module system*. The Dojo module system allows a large code base to be progressively divided into branches of independent functionality with manageable size. When you are building applications large enough to warrant this kind of organization, you can use the Dojo module system for your own code.

Once the application is ready to deploy, the *Dojo build system* fixes latency problems that result from downloading many small files.[2] The idea is to concatenate several source files together into one file. For example, if module x dojo.requires modules y and z, then a single file could be constructed by replacing the dojo.require statements in x.js (the source file that implements module x) with the contents of y.js and z.js (the source files that implement modules y and z). This single file is then mapped to a module name (either x or some new module name). When the new module is dojo.required, retrieving the single resource results in all three modules being loaded. The concept of combining several resources into a single resource is termed *packaging*.

Once the number of resources is controlled, the size of the resources becomes important to minimizing download times. Since typical JavaScript source files include lots of extra junk—comments, whitespace, descriptive variable names—that doesn't affect how the interpreter executes the code, deleting and compacting this junk can result in dramatic space savings; compression rates of 75% are common.

---

2. Latency is the overhead cost to make a round-trip to the server. Latency is often much more expensive than bandwidth for small resources.

The Dojo build system packages and compresses sets of modules. Note that the build system must understand how the loader works so it can scan source files looking for dojo.require function calls and construct packages of code that behave as if those function calls already occurred—in the proper order.

The Cross-Domain Loader

Dojo includes two loaders:

- The *standard loader*: Able to load resources from the same origin as the main document—*only*[3]

- The *cross-domain loader*: Able to load resources from any origin

The cross-domain loader can affect the way your code executes. Coding and deployment mistakes can cause failures that are frustrating to diagnose. This need not be so. The cross-domain loader is easy to understand and, once understood, is powerful and easy to use. We'll sketch out its operation so you can develop some intuition.

The standard loader retrieves resources by executing a synchronous XHR call. However, if any URL resolved by dojo.require references a different origin other than the main document, then the cross-domain loader *must be* employed. The cross-domain loader also retrieves any resources with the same origin as the main document with a synchronous XHR. However, since XHR does not work when addressing a different origin than the main document, the cross-domain loader employs a dynamic script technique similar to JSONP (as we discussed in Section 8.3, *Remote Scripting with script*, on page 194) to solve this problem.

Using a dynamic script element to load a script has an important consequence: once dojo.require sets up the new script element, it returns—*before the resource is loaded*. Similarly, if the resource itself contains dojo.require function calls that load other JavaScript resources located at a different origin than the main document, these function calls will also return immediately. *This breaks the promise* that any dojo.required resource will be evaluated before dojo.require returns.

---

3. Two URLs reference the same origin when their scheme, host, and port are identical. In http://www.acmecorp.com/index.htm, http is the scheme, www.acmecorp.com is the host, and since the port is not provided explicitly, port 80 is implied by the scheme http. Therefore, http://www.acmecorp.com/contact.htm references the same origin, but https://www.acmecorp.com/account does not.

To address this problem, the build system and loader work together to guarantee that *nested* dojo.require calls are executed in order. When the build system is used to create a cross-domain build, it determines the dependencies for each JavaScript resource referenced in the build. Then it constructs a function call back into the cross-domain loader, passing dependency information together with the source code contained by the resource. This function call is written to the original resource name plus the suffix .xd.js. For example, given a.js...

```
Line 1   dojo.provide("acmecorp.a");
   -     dojo.require("acmecorp.b");
   -
   -     acmecorp.a.f= function() {
   5       //do something interesting...
   -     }
```

the build system would write something like the following to a.js.xd.js:[4]

```
Line 1   dojo._xdResourceLoaded({
   -       depends: [
   -         ["require", "acmecorp.b"]
   -         ["provide", "acmecorp.a"]
   5       ],
   -       defineResource: function(){
   -         acmecorp.a.f= function() {
   -           //do something interesting...
   -         }
   10      }
   -     });
```

The code calls back into the cross-domain loader (line 1), passing an object that contains two properties. The first property, depends (line 2), is an array of pairs listing any module dependencies (in this case, acmecorp.b) and the module this resource implements (acmecorp.a). The second property, defineResource (line 6), defines a function that contains the source for the module. Executing the function yields the same result as evaluating the original source.

When the cross-domain loader loads a different-origin JavaScript resource through a dynamic script element, it appends .xd.js to the src URL (for example, /acmeCorp/lib/a.js becomes /acmeCorp/lib/a.xd.js). Upon downloading the resource, the script will execute, causing the function written by the build system (line 1) to call the cross-domain loader with the dependency information and the resource source code. The cross-

---

4. This is not exactly what the build system would produce, but it's similar enough to sketch out how the system works.

domain loader loads any dependencies if they're not already loaded before executing the source code, thereby guaranteeing any nested dojo. required resources are present before the script is executed.

Notice that there is nothing the cross-domain loader can do to ensure non-nested dojo.require calls that load different-origin resources complete before returning. Indeed, such calls will *never* complete before returning. This has some coding implications we will discuss in Section 11.2, *Coding for the Cross-Domain Loader*, on page 293.

You can employ the cross-domain loader by loading dojo.xd.js in place of dojo.js.[5] This might seem a bit odd since the system could have been built to automatically switch from the standard loader to the cross-domain loader when/if required. The design choice was made to minimize the dojo.js download size. Since you will know whether a particular web app references cross-domain resources, explicitly making the choice of which loader to employ is not a big burden.

The bottom line is this: if you are going to dojo.require scripts from a different origin than the main document, then

- You must use the cross-domain loader.

- You must prepare those scripts with the build system.

- However, you don't need to prepare scripts that reside at the same origin as the main document, no matter which loader you use.

If you are serving Dojo and all dojo.required resources from the same origin as the main document, then you can ignore the cross-domain loader. We'll work through complete examples in Section 11.3, *Optimizing Deployment with the Dojo Build System*, on page 296.

That's it for the big picture. The rest of the chapter explores the loader and the build system in detail; we'll start with the loader.

11.2 The Dojo Loader

So far, we've used only dojo.require to load modules defined by Dojo or Dijit. This section describes how to construct your own modules.

---

5. This is a slight exaggeration. Technically, you could switch from the standard loader to the cross-domain loader after dojo.js is loaded or, with more effort, back the other way. But the current implementation wasn't designed to make this on-the-fly loader switch, and any attempt to execute such a switch would depend upon loader internals that may change in future releases. Therefore, don't do it!

dojo.require

Although we've always used dojo.require with only one argument, it actually accepts two:

moduleName (a string)

> Designates the module to be loaded. Module names map to URLs. For example, "dojo.a.b.c" maps to *dojo-module-path*/a/b/c.js, where *dojo-module-path* gives the URL path that was used to load dojo.js. We'll use the term *implied resource* to designate the URL implied by a module name. We'll have more to say about this in a moment.

omitModuleCheck (optional, a boolean)

> If false or missing, dojo.require checks that the JavaScript object given by moduleName has been defined after the implied resource has been loaded and throws an exception if not; if true, then this check is not executed.

dojo.require keeps track of the resources already loaded and ensures they aren't loaded more than once—it simply returns immediately if the module already exists *or* if the implied resource has already been loaded. Typically, the second argument is omitted.

Sometimes it's convenient to divide a particular module into several files where some of the files do *not* define a child module. For example, a largish module might rely on a couple of independent sets of utility functions. In this case, it is reasonable to divide these two sets into separate "utility" scripts, resulting in a structure like this:

```
myApp/
    myModule/
        utilsA.js  //does NOT define a module
        utilsB.js  //does NOT define a module
    myModule.js

    //other stuff...
```

Assuming myApp.myModule depends upon the functions defined in myApp.myModule.utilsA and myApp.myModule.utilsB, it will dojo.require these modules. However, since the utility modules do not define module objects, the second argument to dojo.require must be provided with a value of true to avoid the normal module check like this:

```
//inside myApp.myModule.js...
dojo.require("myApp.myModule.utilsA", true);
dojo.require("myApp.myModule.utilsB", true);
```

These two lines load the utility modules as usual but won't insist that the variables myApp.myModule.utilsA and myApp.myModule.utilsB are defined. Notice that most of the functionality of dojo.require is still there: the module name is converted to a URL, and a check is made before loading the URL to prevent loading the same URL more than once.

Module Paths

A module path is nothing more than a *runtime configurable* map from a module name to a relative or absolute URL.[6] Module paths let you root different module "family trees" at different URLs. For example, you could place different versions of a module hierarchy at different URLs and then choose which version to load at runtime.

dojo.require maps a module name to a URL as follows:

1. The most specific parent module with a module path is replaced with that path (for example, myApp.myModule is more specific than myApp). If no module path is found, then the relative path ../ is prepended to the module name; this will have the net effect (after step 3) of causing the parent module to look like a sibling to the module dojo.

2. Any remaining dots are replaced by slashes.

3. .js is appended as a suffix. If the URL is still relative, then the path given by dojo.baseUrl is prepended. If the URL (now guaranteed to be absolute) references a different domain than the main document, then .xd.js is appended as a suffix.

dojo.baseUrl is the URL path to the dojo module. It can be set by the configuration option baseUrl (a string). As with all configuration options, baseUrl can be specified with the djConfig attribute or the djConfig object. If baseUrl is not explicitly set, then it is automatically set to the absolute URL path from which dojo.js was loaded. Since every web page that uses Dojo includes a script element that looks something like this...

```
<script
  type="text/javascript"
  src="/dojoroot/dojo/dojo.js"></script>
```

---

6. Warning: Currently, the cross-domain loader has a slightly odd behavior in that it won't handle an absolute path for a same-origin resource correctly. In practice, this should never be an issue since a same-origin script should always have a relative path.

dojo-module-path can be calculated when the script is loaded by search-ing the DOM tree for a script element with an href that ends in dojo.js. For example, assume that the previous script element is contained in a web page that resides here:

```
http://www.acmecorp.com/public/apps/email/index.htm
```

Then, *dojo-root* would be as follows:

```
http://www.acmecorp.com/dojoroot/dojo/dojo.js
```

Unless you've renamed dojo.js, you should let Dojo autodetect baseUrl.

Setting Module Paths

The function dojo.registerModulePath adds module paths. It takes two arguments, moduleName and path (both strings), that give the map from a module name to an absolute or relative URL. As mentioned earlier, if a relative URL is provided, then the path is relative to dojo.baseUrl; if an absolute URL is given, then the path is relative to the root of the server that served the document; finally, a complete URL can be given by including the scheme and server. Here's an example.

Assume you've created the following directory structure accessible from the root of the server http://www.acmecorp.com:

```
public-libs/
  dojo/
    dojo/
      dojo.js
      ...
    dijit/
      dijit.js
      ...
myApp/
  a.js
  b.js
  mySubsystem.js
  mySubsystem/
    c.js
  lib/
    version-1/
      x.js
    version-2/
      x.js
```

The only module path that is automatically registered by Dojo is dojo => /public-libs/dojo/dojo. So, in order to load the resources a.js and b.js with dojo.require, the module path for myApp must be registered:

```
dojo.registerModulePath("myApp", "../../../myApp");
```

Now you can load the scripts as usual with dojo.require:

```
dojo.require("myApp.a");
  //loads /public-libs/dojo/dojo/../../../myApp/a.js

dojo.require("myApp.b");
  //loads /public-libs/dojo/dojo/../../../myApp/b.js
```

You could accomplish the same thing by giving an absolute path:

```
dojo.registerModulePath("myApp", "/myApp");
```

The require statements look the same and end up loading the same resources, but the actual resolved URLs are slightly different:

```
dojo.require("myApp.a"); //loads /myApp/a.js
dojo.require("myApp.b"); //loads /myApp/b.js
```

Using Module Paths to Control Version Publication

dojo.registerModulePath can be used to break the "direct" mapping from module name to filename for good purpose. For example, you can map the module name lib to the path /lib/version-1:

```
dojo.registerModulePath("lib", "../../../myApp/lib/version-1");
```

Now, in order to load /lib/version-1/x.js, write the following:

```
dojo.require("lib.x"); //loads lib/version-1/x.js
```

When a new release of the library is ready for publication, the location of the library module—and all scripts that are children of this module – can be set to /lib/version-2 by simply changing the dojo.registerModulePath call. Even better, the argument to dojo.registerModulePath could be set by some runtime function.

```
dojo.registerModulePath("lib", getLibVersion());
```

Module paths can also be set by the configuration option modulePaths (a hash). For example, you could set the myApp module path through the djConfig attribute like this:

```
<script
  type="text/javascript"
  src="../../dojo/dojo.js"
  djConfig="modulePaths: {myApp: '../../../myApp'}">
</script>
```

dojo.provide

All objects defined by a module are created as properties of the module object. The function dojo.provide takes a single argument, a module name (a string), and creates the module object given by that name.

When dojo.provide creates a module object, any undefined parent module objects are simply created as empty objects. For example, if the script /myApp/mySubsystem/c.js from the previous directory tree defines the module myApp.mySubsystem.c, then c.js should include a call to dojo. provide like this:

```
dojo.provide("myApp.mySubsystem.c");
```

And this causes the following to be evaluated:

```
Line 1  //note: dojo.global references the global object space
        if (typeof dojo.global.myApp=="undefined") {
          dojo.global.myApp= {};
        }
   5    if (typeof dojo.global.myApp.mySubsystem=="undefined") {
          dojo.global.myApp.mySubsystem= {};
        }
        if (typeof dojo.global.myApp.mySubsystem.c=="undefined") {
          dojo.global.myApp.mySubsystem.c= {};
  10    }

        //other stuff...

        return dojo.global.myApp.mySubsystem.c;
```

Notice that dojo.provide simply guarantees that the required hierarchy of objects exists. It is up to the script that defines the module to populate the module object with interesting properties. In particular, notice that although dojo.provide("myApp.myModule.c") may cause the objects myApp and myApp.myModule to be created, it does not load the modules myApp and myApp.myModule.

On the surface, it doesn't look like dojo.provide does much, but it's required to make the build system work correctly. So unless you're doing something special, you should always dojo.provide a module name inside the script that defines the given module. Typically, this is done in the first statement of a module.

The Module Pattern

dojo.require, dojo.provide, and the so-called module pattern are often used together when authoring modules. We will demonstrate this by showing the skeleton for the script c.js with the following attributes:

- It depends on the myApp.a, myApp.b, and myApp.mySubsystem modules (lines 8, 9, and 10).
- It defines the module myApp.mySubsystem.c (line 5).

- It defines the functions awesome and reallyAwesome, which are members of the module myApp.mySubsystem.c (lines 22 and 26).
- It defines the helper functions helper and anotherHelper (lines 13 and 17), which are used internally by the module but are not accessible outside the module (they are private to the module).

Here's c.js:

```
Line 1  //enclose all source in a function literal
    -   //to avoid polluting the global namespace...
    -   (function(){
    -     //define myApp.mySubsystem.c and take a reference...
    5     var thisModule= dojo.provide("myApp.mySubsystem.c");
    -
    -     //all modules used by myApp.mySubsystem.c go here...
    -     dojo.require("myApp.a");
    -     dojo.require("myApp.b");
    10    dojo.require("myApp.mySubsystem");
    -
    -     //private functions go here...
    -     function helper(){
    -       //...
    15    }
    -
    -     function anotherHelper(){
    -       //...
    -     }
    20
    -     //public functions go here...
    -     thisModule.awesome= function() {
    -       //...
    -     }
    25
    -     thisModule.reallyAwesome= function() {
    -       //...
    -     }
    -
    30  //execute the function literal...
    -   })();
```

By enclosing the entire contents of c.js in a function literal (line 3) that is immediately executed (line 31), c.js can define local objects without polluting the global namespace.

Coding for the Cross-Domain Loader

The differences between the standard loader and the cross-domain loader arise from the fact that dojo.require returns immediately if the requested module exists at a different origin than the main document (termed a *cross-domain resource*). We already discussed how the cross-domain loader fixes this problem for nested dojo.require calls. However, when you dojo.require a cross-domain resource in code contained by a script element, it's not nested, and there's nothing dojo.require can do to help the situation—*it returns immediately before the script has been downloaded and evaluated!* If you invoke a function that is defined in the dojo.required script before that script has been loaded, JavaScript will throw an exception. This point is bit subtle but critical, so let's look at an example.

Suppose you have the module myApp.a that defines the single function sayHello:

```
dojo.provide("myApp.a");

myApp.a.sayHello= function() {
  alert("hello, world");
}
```

Then you write some JavaScript within a script element that uses myApp.a.sayHello twice: first in another function definition (line 5) and second by invoking it directly within the script (line 9):

```
Line 1   <script type="text/javascript">
    -        dojo.require("myApp.a");
    -
    -        sayHelloAndGoodbye= function() {
    5            myApp.a.sayHello();
    -            alert("goodbye");
    -          }
    -
    -        myApp.a.sayHello();
   10    </script>
```

If myApp.a references a cross-domain resource, then line 2 will return before myApp.a has been loaded. Since JavaScript does not require that all symbols be defined when translating a definition, line 5 doesn't cause a problem; however, myApp.a.sayHello *must* be defined prior to its use in line 9. Since it's not, line 9 will result in an error.

There are a couple of ways to solve this problem. First, you could wire the myApp.a.sayHello call to the onLoad event as follows:

```
Line 1   <script type="text/javascript">
    -        dojo.require("myApp.a");
    -
    -        sayHelloAndGoodbye= function() {
    5          myApp.a.sayHello();
    -          alert("goodbye");
    -        }
    -
```

```
►    dojo.addOnLoad(function(){
1►      myApp.a.sayHello();
►    });
-  </script>
```

Dojo fires all functions registered with dojo.addOnLoad when all scripts that are "in flight" have landed and been evaluated. So, the little function literal passed to dojo.addOnLoad won't be executed until myApp.a has been loaded.

The second way to solve the problem leverages the fact that the cross-domain loader guarantees that nested dojo.require function calls will be executed completely before they return. With this in mind, you can avoid the problem of attempting to reference an object before it has been defined by following these two coding rules:

1. After loading dojo.js, load JavaScript source files exclusively via dojo.require; never use the src attribute of a script element to explicitly load a module.[7] Instead, divide all code out into separate modules and load them with dojo.require.

2. Do not assume that anything other than dojo.js has been fully loaded when writing code directly in a script element.

None of this is a burden since it's a good practice anyway. So, we could fix the example by copying all the code that's contained in the script element into another module, say myApp.b:

```
Line 1  dojo.provide("myApp.b");
    -   dojo.require("myApp.a");
    -
    -   sayHelloAndGoodbye= function() {
    5     myApp.a.sayHello();
    -     alert("goodbye");
    -   }
    -
    -   myApp.a.sayHello();
```

Then, replace the contents of the script element with a single statement that dojo.requires "myApp.b":

```
<script type="text/javascript">
  dojo.require("myApp.b");
</script>
```

---

7. "Never" is a pretty obnoxious word. If you can't live with it, then use the dojo.addOnLoad technique discussed earlier.

Alex Says...

More Dojo Debugging Options

When you load Dojo, there are a couple of djConfig properties that can help. First, setting the property isDebug (a boolean) to true causes Dojo to write more verbose warning and error messages to the debug console. On browsers that don't have Firebug installed, turning isDebug on also causes Dojo to pull in Firebug Lite, which will give you a lightweight console in your page. It's a good idea to develop with isDebug set to true; you'll see this in many of the examples in the book.

Second, some debuggers have trouble working with JavaScript code that's loaded by the eval function. Setting the property debugAtAllCosts (a boolean) to true forces Dojo to load all code by appending a script element to the head element. It's important to realize that enabling debugAtAllCosts causes the loader to behave differently, more like the cross-domain loader than the regular synchronous system. As a result, any code using Dojo modules *must* be run from a function registered with dojo.addOnLoad. You should avoid using debugAtAllCosts unless your debugger is choking on an evaled script. Another option to debugAtAllCosts is to make a cross-domain build of your project and use the cross-domain loader, which can efficiently use script tag injection because the build step preprocesses the dependency graph.

If myApp.a is a cross-domain resource, then the cross-domain loader will guarantee that it has been loaded before line 9 is executed. This fixes the problem.

11.3 Optimizing Deployment with the Dojo Build System

The Dojo build system includes two basic functions. First, it can package several JavaScript resources into a single resource; this *eliminates* any penalty for modularizing an application! Second, the build system can compress JavaScript resources; this minimizes download times— even when developing advanced JavaScript applications that contain lots of code.

The build system includes a customized version of Rhino, Mozilla's Java-based JavaScript interpreter. We'll call the customized interpreter

Dojo-Rhino; it is a full version of Rhino with a bit of extra functionality that compresses JavaScript code. Since Dojo-Rhino is a Java program, you will also need a Java runtime environment, version 1.4.2 or greater (available at http://www.java.com). The build system also includes build, a JavaScript program that packages sets of JavaScript resources. build must be run inside Dojo-Rhino. Both of these tools are located in the util/ tree of the source distribution of Dojo: Dojo-Rhino is located at util/shrinksafe/custom_rhino.jar, and build is located at util/buildscripts/build.js.[8]

You have several options when preparing a web app for deployment. You can package and/or compress the JavaScript resources. You can deploy using either the standard loader or the cross-domain loader. And, of course, you can do nothing at all.

Obviously, doing nothing is easiest. And, this may be perfectly reasonable. If a web app includes a small amount of JavaScript compared to other resources (for example, images), then squeezing every last ounce of download performance out of the JavaScript resources may result in no detectable difference in application performance. If this is the case, your time is better spent doing other things. The remainder of this section describes how to use the build system to prepare an application for deployment.

Packaging a Release with build

build includes several functions that automate publishing a release of a Dojo-based application:[9]

- It creates a release directory where all output is written.
- It copies a specified set of source trees to the release directory.
- It combines sets of source files into single source files (recall that this is termed *packaging*).
- It prepares JavaScript source files for use with the cross-domain loader.
- It compresses JavaScript source files.

All but the first two functions are optional, and each option has several tuning features. Since we've already covered the design of the system,

---

8. Some Dojo documentation refers to the usage of Dojo-Rhino for compression as *shrinksafe*.
9. Another name for a release is a *build*.

let's dive in and demonstrate how everything works by progressively optimizing an example.

Acmecorp's Magi-Browse

We'll demonstrate build by releasing Magi-Browse, Acmecorp's revolutionary web-based data browser. The development directory for Magi-Browse is shown below. The basic structure should look familiar. It has a document root, public/, which contains directories that hold CSS style sheets (css/), HTML documents (doc/), images (images/), and JavaScript scripts (js/). The js/ directory contains subdirectories that hold code used by multiple Acmecorp applications (acmecorp/), code specific to Magi-Browse (magiBrowse/), and the Dojo source distribution (dojo/).[10] Notice all directories under magi-browse/public/js/ are valid JavaScript identifiers. This makes it easy to map from filename to module name. If this were not the case, then a module path would have to be set to map the directory name to a module name. Here's the directory tree:

```
magi-browse/ ---------------->magi-browse is a web app
  dev-tools/
    build-scripts/ ---------->we'll put dojo build scripts here
  public/ ------------------->document root for the web server
    index.htm --------------->the entry page for magi-browse
    css/
    docs/
    image/
    js/ -------------------->all JavaScript goes here
      acmecorp/ ------------->classes/modules used by multiple apps
        acmeDigit/ ---------->acmecorp dijit-based widgets
          Navitgator.js ----->the "acmeDigit.Navigator" widget
        acmeLib/ ------------>the acmecorp library
          nav.js ------------>the "acmeDigit.nav" module
      dojo/ ----------------->the dojo source release
        dojo/
        dijit/
        dojox/
        util/
      magiBrowse/ ----------->classes and modules specific to magiBrowse
        main.js ------------->the module magiBrowse.main
        MainController.js --->the class magiBrowse.MainController
        sessionData.js ------>the module magiBrowse.sessionData
        sessionView.js ------>the module magiBrowse.sessionView
        sessionView/ -------->children of magiBrowse.sessionView go here
          DijitContainer.js ->the class magiBrowse.sessionView.DijitContainer
          util.js ----------->the module magiBrowse.sessionView.util
```

---

10. Since acmecorp/ and dojo/ are used by several projects, these are likely symbolic links to a single directory tree that's used by many projects.

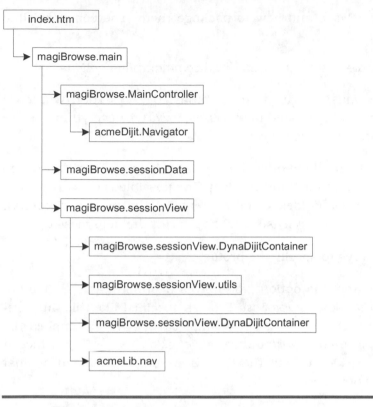

Figure 11.1: MAGI-BROWSE MODULE DEPENDENCY TREE

Magi-Browse defines the class magiBrowse.MainController as well as the modules magiBrowse.main, magiBrowse.sessionData, and magiBrowse. sessionView; magiBrowse.sessionView defines the class magiBrowse. sessionView.DijItContainer and the module magiBrowse.sessionView.util. Also, Acmecorp has built the Dijit-based widget acmeDijit.Navigator and the utility library acmeLib.nav; both of these components are used in several of the company's products (that's why these components are under the /acmecorp tree). The dependency tree for all of these components is shown in Figure 11.1. Of course, a real application would likely contain tens of files. But this is enough to demonstrate how build works.

Step 1: Defaults for Everything

For the first step, we will rely on defaults as much as possible. The build program is controlled by command-line arguments and a control file termed a *profile* that specifies the set of JavaScript source files to include in the release and how to package them. The command line looks like this:

java -jar ../shrinksafe/custom_rhino.jar build.js *command-line-options*

Currently, this *must* be run from util/buildscripts/. build.bat (Windows) and build.sh (*nix), also located in util/buildscripts/, type everything before the command-line options for you.

To get build to do anything other than print a help message, an action command-line option must be specified. The possible values are release (build a release), clean (delete the contents of the release directory), clean,release (clean then release), and help (print the help message).

There are two ways to specify the profile:

- The command-line option profile gives a profile name that must exist in util/buildscripts/profiles/. Profiles specified like this must include the suffix .profile.js. For example, profile=myApp implies the profile is located at util/buildscripts/profiles/myApp.profile.js. Since it isn't a good idea to edit the Dojo trees, we recommend against using this option.

- The command-line option profileFile gives the filename of the profile. If a relative name is given, it must be relative to util/buildscripts/.

Looking back at the Magi-Browse directory tree, profiles are stored at magi-browse/dev-tools/build-scripts/. The first profile we'll use is profile-1.js. So, the command-line argument for the profile should be profileFile=../../ ../../../dev-tools/build-scripts/profile1.js. We'll describe what's in this file in a moment.

When build writes a release, it creates a directory tree rooted at *release-directory* concatenated with *project-name*. By default, *release-directory* is set to dojo/../release/, and *project-name* is set to dojo. This is almost certainly not what you want. The command-line options releaseDir and releaseName can be used to set *release-directory* and *project-name*. build just blindly concatenates these two options, so if you want *project-name* to be a subdirectory of *release-directory* (or not), make sure the *release-directory* ends with / (or not). We will use the values releaseDir=../../../ release/ and releaseName=magi-browse to put the release at /magi-browse/ public/js/release/magiBrowse.

That's all we need for the command line; here it is:

java -jar ../shrinksafe/custom_rhino.jar build.js action=release profileFile=../../../
../../dev-tools/build-scripts/profile1.js releaseDir = ../../../release/ releaseName =
"magiBrowse"

Next we need to construct a profile. A profile is simply a JavaScript script that defines the variable dependencies (an object) that describes how to package the release.[11] dependencies.layers specifies how to combine modules into packages; we'll delay talking about layers until step 2. dependencies.prefixes is an array of pairs (given by a two-element array), with each pair giving a map from module name to module path—just like dojo.setModulePath. Path names are relative to dojo/. Any directory specified in the prefix array is assumed to be part of the release and is copied to the release directory; the build system automatically includes the pair ["dojo", "."]. So, for our first attempt at a release, we'll just get the development tree into a release directory. Here's what that profile looks like:

```
build_system/magi-browse/dev-tools/build-scripts/profile1.js
```

```
Line 1   dependencies = {
             prefixes: [
                 ["acmeDijit", "../../acmecorp/acmeDijit"],
                 ["acmeLib", "../../acmecorp/acmeLib"],
      5          ["magiBrowse", "../../magiBrowse"]
             ]
         }
```

Before we execute the command line, there are four painful gotchas that are important to keep in mind. First, mistyping a command-line option (particularly character cases—command-line options are case-sensitive) will result in the option being *silently* ignored! Similarly, typos or outright mistakes in the profile file are also often silently ignored. Incorrect paths are particularly common. build writes several progress messages to the console that can help track down mistakes. Third, build expects dojo/ and util/ to be siblings and have contents as released. Finally, relative paths for items on the command line are relative to util/buildscripts/, while relative paths for items in the profile file are relative to dojo/.

---

11. build simply evaluates the profile file with eval. So, you can define any number of variables and even write executable code in the file. Such advanced usages are beyond the scope of this book.

So, after carefully typing the command line, you hit Return, and lots of messages go whizzing by. Hopefully, you'll see something like "Build time: 12.203 seconds" for the last message. Success!

build published a release to magi-browse/public/js/release/magi-browse/. Here's what that directory tree looks like:

```
magi-browse/public/js/release/magiBrowse/
  acmeDijit/  -->from magi-browse/public/js/acmecorp/acmeDijit
  acmeLib/    -->from magi-browse/public/js/acmecorp/acmeLib
  dojo/       -->from magi-browse/public/js/dojo/dojo
  magiBrowse/ -->from magi-browse/public/js/magiBrowse
  util/       -->create and filled by build
```

It includes directories acmeDigit/, acmeLib/, and magiBrowse/, sourced from magi-browse/public/js/acmecorp/acmeDijit/, magi-browse/public/js/acmecorp/acmeLib/, and magi-browse/public/js/magiBrowse/ as specified in the prefixes array of the profile. build automatically copied the entire dojo tree to the dojo/ directory and constructed both a compressed and an uncompressed packaged dojo.js just like the binary release of Dojo. Finally, build copied the Dojo Object Handler (doh) unit test framework to util/doh/ (doh is beyond the scope of this book).

Notice that the directory trees were "flattened"—the release directories are all at the same level, while the source directories are not. This causes several module paths to change. The development version has these module paths:

```
acmeDijit   --> "js/acmecorp/acmeDijit",
acmeLib     --> "js/acmecorp/acmeLib",
magiBrowse  --> "js/magiBrowse"
dojo        --> "js/dojo/dojo"
```

And the release version has these module paths:

```
acmeDijit   --> "js/acmeDijit",
acmeLib     --> "js/acmeLib",
magiBrowse  --> "js/magiBrowse"
dojo        --> "js/dojo"
```

As you probably recall from Section 11.2, *Module Paths*, on page 289, the algorithm used by dojo.require to resolve a module name into a URL assumes root modules without specific module paths are siblings of the module dojo. So, this flattened structure has the side effect of eliminating the need for module paths (all root modules are siblings of dojo). In any event, unless a web app is developed with all root modules as siblings of dojo (not the case in our example), the module paths for the development directory tree and the release tree will be different. There are several ways to handle this problem:

- Construct different versions of any static HTML files that load dojo and/or set module paths. This works fine for single-page web apps but quickly becomes unworkable when many pages are affected.

- Add server-side functionality to generate the correct paths for dojo and other modules for any dynamic HTML files.

- Configure the web server to alias the paths differently depending upon the directory tree the server is publishing. This is likely the best option.

This completes step 1. You can copy the contents of magi-browse/public/js/release/magi-browse/ to magi-browse/public/js on the production server (or alias magi-browse/public/js on your development server), and you've just deployed your first web app.

Step 2: Packaging

So far, we haven't done any packaging—JavaScript resources are just as fragmented in the release as they are in the development environment. To prove this, we can hijack dojo.require after loading dojo.js to log entering and exiting dojo.require to the Firebug console. Here's what the hijack looks like:

`build_system/build-system.js`

```
Line 1  <script
   -        type="text/javascript"
   -        djConfig="isDebug: true"
   -        src="js/release/magiBrowse/dojo/dojo.js" ></script>
5
   -    <script type="text/javascript" >
   -      console.log("Finished script-include dojo.js");
   -
   -      //hijack dojo.require to log message before and after it's called...
10      var realDojoRequire= dojo.require;
   -      var id= 0;
   -      dojo.require= function(moduleName) {
   -        var thisId= ++id;
   -        console.log('Start(' + thisId + ') dojo.require("' + moduleName + '")');
15        realDojoRequire.apply(dojo, arguments);
   -        console.log('Finished(' + thisId + ') dojo.require("' + moduleName + '")');
   -      }
   -
   -      dojo.require("magiBrowse.main");
20    </script>
```

The code takes a reference to dojo.require (line 10) and then replaces dojo.require (line 12) with a function that calls console.log before and after (lines 14 and 16) calling the original dojo.require (line 15). After navigating to Magi-Browse's top page (index.htm), the Firebug console shows that all the dojo.require calls contained in the various modules essentially trace the dependency tree shown in Figure 11.1, on page 299:

```
Line 1   Finished script-include dojo.js
    -    Start(1) dojo.require("magiBrowse.main")
    -    GET http://localhost:8002/js/release/magiBrowse/magiBrowse/main.js
    -    evaluating magiBrowse.main
    5    Start(2) dojo.require("magiBrowse.MainController")
    -    GET http://localhost:8002/js/release/magiBrowse/magiBrowse/MainController.js
    -    evaluating magiBrowse.MainController
    -    Start(3) dojo.require("acmeLib.nav")
    -    GET http://localhost:8002/js/release/magiBrowse/acmeLib/nav.js
    10   evaluating acmelib.nav
    -    Finished(3) dojo.require("acmeLib.nav")
    -    Finished(2) dojo.require("magiBrowse.MainController")
    -    Start(4) dojo.require("magiBrowse.sessionData")
    -    GET http://localhost:8002/js/release/magiBrowse/magiBrowse/sessionData.js
    15   evaluating magiBrowse.sessionData
    -    Finished(4) dojo.require("magiBrowse.sessionData")
    -    Start(5) dojo.require("magiBrowse.sessionView")
    -    GET http://localhost:8002/js/release/magiBrowse/magiBrowse/sessionView.js
    -    evaluating magiBrowse.sessionView
    20   Start(6) dojo.require("magiBrowse.sessionView.DynaDijitContainer")
    -    GET http://localhost:8002/js/release/magiBrowse/magiBrowse/sessionView...
    -    evaluating magiBrowse.sessionView.DynaDijitContainer
    -    Finished(6) dojo.require("magiBrowse.sessionView.DynaDijitContainer")
    -    Start(7) dojo.require("magiBrowse.sessionView.utils")
    25   GET http://localhost:8002/js/release/magiBrowse/magiBrowse/sessionView...
    -    evaluating magiBrowse.sessionView.utils
    -    Finished(7) dojo.require("magiBrowse.sessionView.utils")
    -    Start(8) dojo.require("acmeDijit.Navigator")
    -    GET http://localhost:8002/js/release/magiBrowse/acmeDijit/navigator.js
    30   evaluating acmeDijit.Navigator
    -    Finished(8) dojo.require("acmeDijit.Navigator")
    -    Finished(5) dojo.require("magiBrowse.sessionView")
    -    Finished(1) dojo.require("magiBrowse.main")
```

The call to dojo.require("magiBrowse.main") (line 2) doesn't return until line 33; all the other calls are nested inside this call since magiBrowse.main is the root of the dependency tree. Notice that each call to dojo.require results in a separate transaction with the server. That's bad because each round-trip incurs a latency cost, no matter how big or small the resource. Let's fix it.

The dependencies variable in the profile defines the property layers (an array of objects), with each object specifying how to combine several JavaScript resources into one resource. Each element in the layers array defines three properties:

- name (a string) gives the filename of the packaged resource, relative to the dojo/ directory.

- dependencies (an array of strings) gives the module names to include in the packaged resource.

- layerDependencies (an array of strings) gives the packages upon which this layer depends.

The build system constructs a JavaScript resource for each layer object. The resource is written to name and includes all modules specified in the dependencies array, plus any modules that these modules directly or indirectly dojo.require, minus any modules contained in any other layers mentioned in the layerDependencies array.

The main page of the Magi-Browse web app dojo.requires the module magiBrowse.main. It turns out that the dependency tree of this module includes all other modules in the magiBrowse/, acmeDijit/, and acmeLib/ trees. So, by building a layer that includes magiBrowse.main, the build system creates a package (a single JavaScript resource) that includes all these modules. Then, when magiBrowse.main is dojo.required, all of these modules will be loaded in a single server transaction. Here's what the new profile looks like:

```
build_system/magi-browse/dev-tools/build-scripts/profile2.js
```

```
Line 1  dependencies = {
   -      layers: [
   -        {
   -          name: "../magiBrowse/main.js",
   5          layerDependencies: [],
   -          dependencies: ["magiBrowse.main"]
   -        }
   -      ],
   -      prefixes: [
   10         ["acmeDijit", "../../acmecorp/acmeDijit"],
   -          ["acmeLib", "../../acmecorp/acmeLib"],
   -          ["magiBrowse", "../../magiBrowse"]
   -      ]
   -    }
```

After running build with this profile, the release looks the same, except that /public/js/release/magiBrowse/magiBrowse/main.js now includes all the modules as given by the dependency tree of /public/js/magiBrowse/main.js. If this dependency tree were, say, fifty scripts, then the unpackaged version would require fifty server round-trips, but the packaged version requires only one round-trip! That's the whole point.

This brings the design full circle—the build system automatically re-assembles many small scripts (that were great for development) into a single script (that is great for deployment). After reloading Magi-Browse's top page with the new release, the Firebug console looks like this:

```
Line 1   Finished script-include dojo.js
    -    Start(1) dojo.require("magiBrowse.main")
    -    GET http://localhost:8002/js/release/magiBrowse/magiBrowse/main.js
    -    evaluating acmelib.nav
    5    evaluating magiBrowse.MainController
    -    evaluating magiBrowse.sessionData
    -    evaluating magiBrowse.sessionView.DynaDijitContainer
    -    evaluating magiBrowse.sessionView.utils
    -    evaluating acmeDijit.Navigator
   10    evaluating magiBrowse.sessionView
    -    evaluating magiBrowse.main
    -    Finished(1) dojo.require("magiBrowse.main")
```

Since magiBrowse.main includes all the modules in its dependency tree, only one round-trip to the service is required.

By default, packages are written as compressed and uncompressed resources. The uncompressed resource has the suffix .uncompressed.js. So, in the previous example, build wrote main.js (compressed) and main.js. uncompressed.js (uncompressed). As usual, the uncompressed version is useful for debugging packages.

Step 3: Layering Packages

It may be suboptimal to put all resources into a single package when releasing a large, real-world web app. For example, several pages may use the same subset of resources, or a single-page application may load resources as they are needed.

In these cases, it's better to create several different packages. When you do this, one package will often depend upon another, and the web app will load one package "on top" of another (this is the origin of the property name layer). The layerDependencies property in a layer object is used to specify these dependencies.

For example, Acmecorp may decide to package all its company-wide Dijit-based widgets and utility libraries into one package. Then every individual web app developed by Acmecorp could reference these resources identically. First, a new module must be created that holds the resources that are going to be packaged. That looks like this:

```
build_system/magi-browse/public/js/magiBrowse/acmeBase.js
```

```
Line 1   //for demonstration purposes...
    -    console.log("evaluating magiBrowse.acmeBase");
    -
    -    dojo.provide("magiBrowse.acmeBase");
    5    dojo.require("acmeDijit.Navigator");
    -    dojo.require("acmeLib.nav");
```

Next, create a profile that defines the new package (line 3) and the dependency between magiBrowse.main and magiBrowse.acmeBase (line 9):

```
build_system/magi-browse/dev-tools/build-scripts/profile3.js
```

```
Line 1   dependencies = {
    -      layers: [
    -        {
    -          name: "../magiBrowse/acmeBase.js",
    5          layerDependencies: [],
    -          dependencies: ["magiBrowse.acmeBase"]
    -        },{
    -          name: "../magiBrowse/main.js",
    -          layerDependencies: ["../magiBrowse/acmeBase.js"],
    10          dependencies: ["magiBrowse.main"]
    -        }
    -      ],
    -      prefixes: [
    -        ["acmeDijit", "../../acmecorp/acmeDijit"],
    15         ["acmeLib", "../../acmecorp/acmeLib"],
    -        ["magiBrowse", "../../magiBrowse"]
    -      ]
    -    }
```

Since this profile says that the package magiBrowse.main depends on the package magiBrowse.acmeBase, magiBrowse.acmeBase must be dojo. required before *and independently* of magiBrowse.main (that is, you cannot dojo.require magiBrowse.acmeBase from within magiBrowse.main). This is a subtle point; let's restate it: you cannot dojo.require a layer inside another layer that depends on the first layer.

We'll solve the problem by creating a new index2.htm that dojo.requires magiBrowse.acmeBase before magiBrowse.main.

After running build with the new profile and loading index2.htm, the Firebug console looks like this:

```
Line 1   Finished script-include dojo.js
   -     Start(1) dojo.require("magiBrowse.acmeBase")
   -     GET http://localhost:8002/js/release/magiBrowse/magiBrowse/acmeBase.js
   -     evaluating acmeDijit.Navigator
   5     evaluating acmelib.nav
   -     evaluating magiBrowse.acmeBase
   -     Finished(1) dojo.require("magiBrowse.acmeBase")
   -     Start(2) dojo.require("magiBrowse.main")
   -     GET http://localhost:8002/js/release/magiBrowse/magiBrowse/main.js
   10    evaluating magiBrowse.MainController
   -     evaluating magiBrowse.sessionData
   -     evaluating magiBrowse.sessionView.DynaDijitContainer
   -     evaluating magiBrowse.sessionView.utils
   -     evaluating magiBrowse.sessionView
   15    evaluating magiBrowse.main
   -     Start(3) dojo.require("magiBrowse.acmeBase")
   -     Finished(3) dojo.require("magiBrowse.acmeBase")
   -     Finished(2) dojo.require("magiBrowse.main")
```

Two packages are loaded as expected (lines 3 and 9).

Step 4: Using the Cross-Domain Loader

By default, build packages all resources for use with the standard loader and includes the standard loader in dojo.js. Preparing a release for use with the cross-domain loader is as simple as specifying the command-line option loader=xdomain. When this option is given, build compiles a release that includes both standard and cross-domain versions of all resources. For example, the standard version of the module magiBrowse.MainController is written to magiBrowse/MainController.js, and the cross-domain version is written to magiBrowse/MainController.xd.js. You can choose which loader to use by selecting either dojo.js (the standard loader) or dojo.xd.js (the cross-domain loader).

So if we reference dojo.xd.js inside a script element, we should see the cross-domain loader in action. After making that change to index2.htm and reloading, you'll see the same Firebug output as before. Why didn't it work?

Recall that the cross-domain loader will use XHR if the resource resides at the same origin as the main document. So, in order to see the cross-domain loader in action, the resources must be loaded from a different origin.

We can trick the loader into thinking the resources are at a different origin by specifying module paths with schemes like this:

```
Line 1    djConfig= {};
    -     djConfig.modulePaths = {
    -       acmeDijit: "http://localhost:8002/js/release/magiBrowse/acmecorp/acmeDijit",
    -       acmeLib: "http://localhost:8002/js/release/magiBrowse/acmecorp/acmeLib",
    5       magiBrowse: "http://localhost:8002/js/release/magiBrowse/magiBrowse"
    -     };
```

Loading index-xd.htm (a version of index2.htm script-including dojo.xd.js and includes these module paths) results in Firebug output that looks like this:

```
Line 1    Finished script-include dojo.js
    -     Start(1) dojo.require("magiBrowse.acmeBase")
    -     Finished(1) dojo.require("magiBrowse.acmeBase")
    -     Start(2) dojo.require("magiBrowse.main")
    5     Finished(2) dojo.require("magiBrowse.main")
    -     evaluating acmeDijit.Navigator
    -     evaluating acmelib.nav
    -     evaluating magiBrowse.acmeBase
    -     evaluating magiBrowse.MainController
    10    evaluating magiBrowse.sessionData
    -     evaluating magiBrowse.sessionView.DynaDijitContainer
    -     evaluating magiBrowse.sessionView.utils
    -     evaluating magiBrowse.sessionView
    -     evaluating magiBrowse.main
```

Notice that there is *not one single XHR transaction!* If you inspect the document tree through the Firebug HTML tab, you will see that two scripts have been added:

```
Line 1    <script
    -       type="text/javascript"
    -       src="http://localhost:8002/js/release/magiBrowse/magiBrowse/acmeBase.xd.js">
    -     </script>
    5     <script
    -       type="text/javascript"
    -       src="http://localhost:8002/js/release/magiBrowse/magiBrowse/main.xd.js">
    -     </script>
```

These are the packaged modules magiBrowse.acmeBase and magiBrowse.main. They were inserted by the cross-domain loader and caused the cross-domain loader to effectively download and evaluate the modules, as we described earlier in Section 11.1, *The Cross-Domain Loader*, on page 285.

Notice also that the cross-domain loader loads a cross-domain module asynchronously. You can see this back in lines 2–5 in the earlier console output—dojo.require returns immediately, *before the resource is actually loaded*. On the other hand, when either loader loads a module that resides at the same origin as the main document, a synchronous XHR is employed. This means that the browser will "lock" for whatever period it takes to complete the XHR. Usually, this isn't a problem. However, so long as you follow the advice about coding for the cross-domain loader, using the cross-domain loader can result in a better user experience.

Step 5: Compression

By default, build compresses any packaged resources and does not compress any other resources. Both of these behaviors can be controlled by the command-line options layerOptimize (for packaged resources) and optimize (for all other resources). The possible values for these options are as follows:

- "": Don't compress.
- shrinksafe: Use Dojo-Rhino to delete whitespace and comments and shorten variable names.
- shrinksafe.keeplines: Same as shrinksafe, but keep newlines.
- packer: Use the Dean Edwards packer; see (http://dean.edwards. name/packer/).

Whenever build compresses a resource, it writes both an uncompressed version to *module-name*.js.uncompressed.js and a compressed version to *module-name*.js.

Dojo-Rhino can also compress JavaScript resources independent of build. We'll discuss compression in more detail in the next section.

11.4 Compressing JavaScript Resources with Dojo-Rhino

Dojo-Rhino walks a Rhino-generated parse tree and dumps compressed JavaScript code. The compression function can be called from the command line to compress an individual file. This technique for compressing JavaScript is both powerful and safe. Since the routines that execute the compression are working off the parse tree, the compression is based on semantic algorithms rather than pattern matching. Consequently, obscure transformation errors are unlikely; this is not always the case when the script is compressed by applying pattern matching algorithms.

The compression algorithms remove whitespace and comments and shorten variables names. This means that the output is still valid Java-

Script source code; specifically, there is no decompressor required to unpack the source. The compression rate will vary greatly depending upon the input. If the input source is well-commented, well-formatted JavaScript with good, human-readable variable names, then compression rates of 50% to 75% are common. On the other hand, if the code is already compressed by bad coding practices, then the compression rate may be less than 10%. Manually compressed code (so-called write-only code, because once it's written, nobody can read it) is almost never smaller than well-written code submitted to the Dojo compressor. So, *write good code and let the tool take care of compression.*

Let's run a file through the compressor. Here's a JavaScript file with comments and nice formatting and variable names:

build_system/uncompressed.js

```
Line 1  /**
        * Mastering Dojo - JavaScript and Ajax Tools for Great Web Experiences
        *
        * This is a sample module that shows off Dojo JavaScript compression.
     5  *
        */
        (function(){
          dojo.provide("myApp.uncompressed");

    10    //
          // someFunction: a private function to this module
          //
          function someFunction(
            parameter1, //(type) this is the documentation for parameter1
    15      parameter2, //(type) this is the documentation for parameter2
            parameter3  //(type) this is the documentation for parameter3
          ){
            var aWellNamedVariable= parameter1 + parameter2;
            return aWellNamedVariable*parameter3;
    20    }


          //
          // publicFunction: a function published by this module
          //
    25    myApp.uncompressed.publicFunction= function(
            parameter1, //(type) this is the documentation for parameter1
            parameter2, //(type) this is the documentation for parameter2
            parameter3  //(type) this is the documentation for parameter3
          ){
    30      return someFunction(parameter1, parameter2, parameter3);
          }

        })();
```

Dojo-Rhino will compress a single JavaScript source file by issuing the command line:

java -jar custom_rhino.jar -c *source-to-compress* > *destination-of-output* 2>&1

custom_rhino.jar is Dojo-Rhino located at util/shrinksafe/; if you're running the command from another directory, you'll need to include the complete path. *source-to-compress* and *destination-of-output* are the filenames of the uncompressed and compressed files. The cryptic 2>&1 redirects the error output stream to the standard output stream. This command line is fairly painful to use when you want to compress many files spread throughout a directory tree; it's best to write a little shell script or Window's batch file to make such tasks more palatable.

uncompressed.js is 1,014 bytes long; after compressing, the file is a mere 209 bytes long—a compression rate of 79%. Here is what the compressed file looks like:

```
build_system/compressed.js
```

```
Line 1    (function(){
   -      dojo.provide("myApp.uncompressed");
   -      function someFunction(_1,_2,_3){
   -      var _4=_1+_2;
   5      return _4*_3;
   -      };
   -      myApp.uncompressed.publicFunction=function(_5,_6,_7){
   -      return someFunction(_5,_6,_7);
   -      };
  10      })();
```

There are a few coding techniques that can squeeze a few more bytes out of the compression process without sacrificing readability.

First, rather than define functions with the syntax function someFunction(/* ... */), use the syntax var someFunction= function(/* ... */) (call this rule 1). This lets the compressor compress the function name. The same economy can be realized by defining a locale variable to hold the module name. For example, rather than writing myApp.mySubsystem.f= for each property defined by myApp.mySubsystem, instead write thisModule= dojo.provide("myApp.mySubsystem); followed by thisModule.f= for each property (call this rule 2). The compressor cannot compress the variable myApp.mySubsystem but can compress thisModule. Lastly, rather than writing this...

```
Line 1    var myVariable1= expression;
   -      var myVariable2= expression;
```

```
   -    var myFunction1= function(/*...*/){
   5      /*...*/
   -    }
   -
   -    var myFunction2= function(/*...*/){
   -      /*...*/
  10    }
```

write this:

```
Line 1  var
   -      myVariable1= expression, //note comma
   -      myVariable2= expression, //note comma
   -
   5      myFunction1= function(/*...*/){
   -        /*...*/
   -      }, //note comma
   -
   -      myFunction2= function(/*...*/){
  10        /*...*/
   -      }; //note semicolon
```

These are equivalent, yet with many definitions, the second form is
more economical. Call this rule 3. Here is uncompress.js after applying
the three rules; we've marked the edits with the rules used:

build_system/uncompressed2.js

```
Line 1  /**
   -     * Mastering Dojo - JavaScript and Ajax Tools for Great Web Experiences
   -     *
   -     * This is a sample module that shows off Dojo JavaScript compression.
   5     *
   -     */
   -    (function(){
  ▶     var //Rule 3; begin a list of definition
  ▶
 1▶     thisModule= dojo.provide("myApp.uncompressed"), //Rule2, Rule3
   -
   -      //
   -      // someFunction: a private function to this module
   -      //
 1▶     someFunction= function( //Rule1, Rule3
   -        parameter1, //(type) this is the documentation for parameter1
   -        parameter2, //(type) this is the documentation for parameter2
   -        parameter3  //(type) this is the documentation for parameter3
   -      ){
  20      var aWellNamedVariable= parameter1 + parameter2;
   -        return aWellNamedVariable*parameter3;
   -      }
   -
  ▶     ;//Rule 3; end a list of definitions
  25
```

```
        //
        // publicFunction: a function published by this module
        //
 ▶      thisModule.publicFunction= function( //Rule 2
30        parameter1, //(type) this is the documentation for parameter1
          parameter2, //(type) this is the documentation for parameter2
          parameter3  //(type) this is the documentation for parameter3
        ){
          return someFunction(parameter1, parameter2, parameter3);
35      }

    })();
```

After compression, compressed2.js looks like this:

`build_system/compressed2.js`

```
Line 1  (function(){
        var _1=dojo.provide("myApp.uncompressed"),_2=function(_3,_4,_5){
        var _6=_3+_4;
        return _6*_5;
5       };
        _1.publicFunction=function(_7,_8,_9){
        return _2(_7,_8,_9);
        };
        })();
```

The new version of uncompressed.js takes a mere 179 bytes after compression—an additional 10% better than the first compressed file. Although these rules may look like squeezing blood from a turnip, they don't cost anything, and the savings really do become noticeable in large applications.

Compression can save substantially on bandwidth (the number of bytes pushed down the pipe). If you have a few large JavaScript files that are slowing the load time of your application, then compression will likely improve performance significantly. Also, don't forget to set up your HTTP server to gzip resources. However, if you have many files, then latency (the overhead for each round-trip) is usually a much bigger factor; use build as previously discussed to solve that problem.

Part III

Advanced Dijit

Scripting Widgets

In the past few chapters, we've seen how Dojo streamlines browser applications—from the click to the event to the server request and response to the DOM node restructuring. Now let's relate this back to Dijit.

In Part I, we used Dijit components to build better forms. The Dijit components were very useful, but they just. . . well. . . sat there. Now we're going to push them further. Using JavaScript, we will create Dijit widgets, move them, repopulate them, recolor them, and destroy them. From the code point of view, this involves locating widget objects, initializing their properties, calling their methods, and adding little bits of custom behavior. We'll tour all of these and pull them together into Ajax user interface patterns in the last section of this chapter.

12.1 What Exactly Is a Widget?

Dijit components are handy encapsulations of user interface functionality. That's what made Visual Basic's component-based technology so appealing twenty years ago. You started with components on a palette, dragged them onto a canvas, and then wrote some code to manipulate them. We've lost this power in the Internet age. If you've been yearning for that easy, componentized development, you'll find this method of programming familiar and appealing.

Widgets are components in the abstract sense, but what are they from a coding standpoint?

So far we have a vague idea, at least for the declarative case, that a widget is a snippet of HTML with a dojoType, like this:

widgets/declarative_vs_programmatic.html

```
<div dojoType="dijit.layout.ContentPane"
     href="http://localhost/too/many/slashes.html" ></div>
```

The story goes deeper than that. dijit.layout.ContentPane is really a Dojo class. Its methods dispatch Dojo API calls to handle communication with the browser, the DOM tree, and the server. And you can write JavaScript to call these methods.

For a solid foundation, let's clarify the terms:

widget class

A widget class is any class descended from dijit._Widget. It may be a direct subclass of dijit._Widget or a subclass of another widget.

widget

A widget is a JavaScript object, an instance of a widget class. So if your page has twelve validation textboxes, it has twelve widgets, all of them instances of the widget class dijit.form.ValidationTextBox.

attribute

In Chapter 9, *Defining Classes with dojo.declare*, on page 221, you saw how to create properties of classes using dojo.declare. An attribute is a just a property in the widget class. We call it an attribute in deference to HTML lingo.

An attribute is initialized at widget creation time but cannot be manipulated directly afterward. In other words, you cannot say myWidget.disabled = true; to disable a widget. Instead, you'd use a method call like myWidget.disable().

extension point

An extension point is a method meant to be overridden by the programmer. For example, you can override the isValid extension point of dijit.form.ValidationTextBox with a function of your own. That function can apply to one widget, using techniques we'll see in this chapter, or an entire widget class, as we'll see in Chapter 17, *Creating and Extending Widget Classes*, on page 455.

As far as JavaScript is concerned, both methods and extension points are just widget class methods. The difference is semantic. Generally, methods have a full implementation, and extension point methods have a very skimpy or empty implementation.

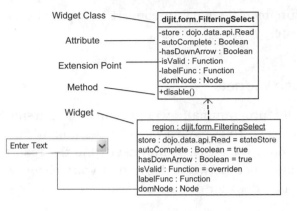

Figure 12.1: RELATIONSHIPS BETWEEN WIDGET ELEMENTS

Some extension points are named after events like onClick or onChange. These extension points pass more specific parameters than just a big DOM Level 2 event object, as a corresponding event would.

In Figure 12.1, you can see the widget region and its associated widget class in UML notation.

Declarative Widgets

So far in the book, all we have seen are declarative widgets—widgets created with HTML markup and a dojoType= attribute. We'll go over programmatic widgets in a minute. But note that declarative and programmatic widgets *differ only in the way they are created.* Once the setup is done, there's no difference between the two. Every widget class can create widgets either declaratively or programmatically.

The Dojo parser turns declarative widgets into JavaScript objects. It does this by scanning the entire HTML source, picking up any tags with a dojoType= attribute, and creating a widget object with that type.

It's tempting to call the HTML tag with a dojoType= attribute a widget. That's not technically correct. Though there is a one-to-one correspondence between the tags and declarative widgets, the tag is a JavaScript DOM object. The DOM node has a style property, but the widget does not. Widgets have widget class methods like setLabel, but DOM nodes do not. Fortunately, it's easy to convert between the two, which we'll see in a minute.

Programmatic Widgets

Fundamentally, programmatic widgets omit the parsing step used for declarative widgets. You create a widget programmatically by calling the **new** operator on a widget class and assigning the result to a variable. There's no difference between doing this yourself or letting the Dojo parser do it, as it does for declarative widgets.

Programmatic widgets are best when you need an indeterminate number of widgets or you don't know their placement ahead of time. Also, programmatic widgets can use JavaScript expressions to initialize the attributes, where declarative widgets cannot. We'll see how this works in Section 12.3, *Creating Instances Programmatically*, on page 325

12.2 Finding and Manipulating Declarative Widgets

Normally when you use JavaScript objects, it's in the context of a program: you create an object with a constructor, put it in a variable, and then call methods on that variable. Simple enough. But in the case of declarative widgets, you didn't create the widget objects—dojo.parser did that. (See the sidebar on page 17 for details.) So, on which variable do you invoke the method? Where do you find the object?

There are a few ways to do so. To illustrate, we'll write an application called Unusual Pet Store, or UPS. UPS's job is to aggregate content from the Internet into an Accordion layout widget like Figure 12.2, on the facing page. The web pages are loaded in the background, and you can slide the pane into view by clicking its title bar.

Because these portal pages are loaded by XHR, they are subject to the same-origin rule. Therefore, as we saw in Chapter 3, *Connecting to Outside Services*, on page 31, we need to use a proxy server component. Here's a PHP proxy script that does the job very minimally, not even parsing HTTP parameters. We do just a bit of parsing on the URL before allowing the request to go through. (A wide open proxy is a security hazard, since anyone can pass an arbitrary URL to it and wreak all kinds of havoc.)

Figure 12.2: UPS (NO RELATION)

widgets/services/pure_proxy.php

```php
<?php
// To prevent this from being a security hazard (and because this is
// just a demo), limit the URLs that can be served

$urlToServe = $_GET["url"];
if (preg_match('/^entomology.unl.edu/',$urlToServe) ||
    preg_match('/^animals.nationalgeographic.com/',$urlToServe) ||
    preg_match('/^www.hermitcrabassociation.com/',$urlToServe)) {

    // This proxy service doesn't do query strings, but it works
    // for static stuff
    readfile("http://" . $_GET["url"]);
} else {
?>
  Access denied
<? } ?>
```

The HTML file declarative_portal.html uses dijit.layout.AccordionPane to call
this proxy service and grab content:

```
widgets/declarative_portal.html
<!DOCTYPE HTML PUBLIC "-//W3C//DTD HTML 4.01//EN"
            "http://www.w3.org/TR/html4/strict.dtd">
<html>
<head>
<title>Unusual Pet Store Application</title>
    <style type="text/css">
        @import "/dojoroot/dijit/themes/tundra/tundra.css";
        @import "/dojoroot/dojo/resources/dojo.css"
    </style>
    <script type="text/javascript" src="/dojoroot/dojo/dojo.js"
            djConfig="parseOnLoad: true"></script>
    <script type="text/javascript">
      dojo.require("dojo.parser");
      dojo.require("dijit.layout.AccordionContainer");
    </script>
</head>
<body class="tundra">

<div dojoType="dijit.layout.AccordionContainer" id="ups"
    style="width:500px;height:500px">

<div dojoType="dijit.layout.AccordionPane"
    title="Madagascar Hissing Cockroach"
    href=
"services/pure_proxy.php?url=\
  entomology.unl.edu/k12/Croach/roachinfo/roachpage.html"
></div>
<div dojoType="dijit.layout.AccordionPane" title="Wallaby"
    href=
"services/pure_proxy.php?url=\
  animals.nationalgeographic.com/animals/mammals/wallaby.html"
></div>
<div dojoType="dijit.layout.AccordionPane" title="Hermit Crab"
    href=
"services/pure_proxy.php?url=www.hermitcrabassociation.com/phpBB/index.php"
></div>

</div>
</body></html>
```

In our first crack at this program, we're giving the user some default
pets to review. On the slight chance that the user is not enamored
with our defaults, we'll give them the option to change the URL of the
currently selected pane.

> ### dojo.byId vs. dijit.byId
>
> You might ask, "Why do I need to call dijit.byId(id)? Can't I just call dojo.byId(id)?" It depends on what you want. dojo.byId returns a plain-vanilla DOM node, while dijit.byId returns a widget object. Since there's exactly one DOM node with a dojoType, it's easy to get them confused. The main difference is this: you can call standard JavaScript methods on DOM nodes, but to call widget methods you must use the widget object.
>
> You can actually convert between the two easily. dijit.byId("id") == dijit.byNode(dojo.byId("id")), and dojo.byId("id") == dijit.byId("id").domNode. We will see more of the domNode= attribute in Chapter 17, *Creating and Extending Widget Classes*, on page 455.

There are five main ways to get a widget reference:

- You can set the jsId= attribute in the tag, which creates a global JavaScript variable with that name.

- You can use dijit.byId(id). This is useful if you had set the id= attribute on your widget.

- You can use dijit.byNode(nodeVariable) when you don't have the id attribute but you have the DOM node itself.

  What? You don't even have the DOM node? You can usually get it with dojo.query, detailed in Chapter 7, *DOM Utilities*, on page 135.

- Similarly, dijit.getEnclosingWidget(nodeVariable) will get the "nearest" widget surrounding it, if you have a DOM node *inside* the widget.

- You can read an attribute or call a method on another object that returns a widget. For example, the attribute adjacent of dojo.layout. StackContainer gives you back a widget.

Now, back to the task of setting the AccordionPane URL. When turning your ideas into widget code, the Book of Dojo at http://www.dojotoolkit.org is your road map. This book contains an entire reference catalog of all the Dijit widgets.

Using the catalog, we find that dijit.layout.AccordionContainer's read-only property selectedChildWidget gets the pane, a dijit.layout.AccordionPane object. From the AccordionPane, the method setHref method changes the URL and reloads the content.

We'll use those elements in the following code:

`widgets/DeclarativePortal.js`

```
dojo.provide("dojobook.widgets.DeclarativePortal");

dojobook.widgets.DeclarativePortal.setUrl = function() {
    // returns back the div tag of the selected AccordionPane
    var paneList = dijit.byId("ups");

    // Get the selected dijit.layout.AccordionPane.  This is
    // kept in selectedChildWidget
    var chosenPane = paneList.selectedChildWidget;

    // Now, get the value from the textbox.  Note we can use
    // dojo.byId() here because the .value property is a property of Node
    var newUrl = dojo.byId("newUrl").value;

    // Change the URL from which the content comes.  Using setHref
    // changes the content right away.
    chosenPane.setHref("services/pure_proxy.php?url=" + newUrl);
}
```

Now wire it into the button:

`widgets/declarative_portal_settable.html`

```
    <label for="newUrl">New URL:</label>
    <input type="text" length="50" id="newUrl">

    <button dojoType="dijit.form.Button" />
        Set
        <script type="dojo/method" event="onClick" args="evt">
            dojobook.widgets.DeclarativePortal.setUrl();
        </script>
    </button>
</body></html>
```

You'll recognize the type=*dojo/method* from Chapter 3, *Connecting to Outside Services*, on page 31. We'll explain the details in Section 12.4, *Extension Points*, on page 329.

Now the user can dynamically change UPS content without a page reload. And from the programmer's side, it's a mere ten lines of Java-Script, neatly tucked away in a module, ready to use for other projects.

```
        // Read the data from our JSON portal data file
        dojo.xhrGet({
            url: "portal_data.json",
            timeout: 1000,
            handleAs: "json",
            // This is the callback used when data arrives
            load: function(objResponse) {
                // Loop once for each array element in tiles, putting the object
                // in portalUrl
                dojo.forEach(objResponse.tiles, function(portalUrl) {
                    // Construct the AccordionPane for that tile
                    var ap = new dijit.layout.AccordionPane({
                        title: portalUrl.title,
                        href: "services/pure_proxy.php?url="+portalUrl.url
                    });
                    // And put it in the AccordionContainer
                    accContainer.addChild(ap);
                });
            },
            error: function(text) {
                // A Toaster will catch this error and display it
                dojo.publish("xhrError",
                    { message: text, type: "error", duration: 0 }
                );
                return text;
            }
        });
}


dojobook.widgets.ProgrammaticPortalDynamic.newPane = function() {
    // Get the value from the form
    var newUrl = dojo.byId("newUrl").value;
    var newTitle = dojo.byId("newTitle").value;

    // Set up the new AccordionPane and insert it at the end
    var ap = new dijit.layout.AccordionPane(
        {
            title: newTitle,
            href: "services/pure_proxy.php?url="+newUrl
        }
    );
    dijit.byId("ups").addChild(ap);
}

dojobook.widgets.ProgrammaticPortalDynamic.deletePane = function() {
    // First get the selected pane, just like we did in declarative example
    var accContainer = dijit.byId("ups");
    var chosenPane = accContainer.selectedChildWidget;

    // And remove it
    accContainer.removeChild(chosenPane);
}
```

Most of the action happens in drawPortal, where an XHR request gets the portal data and the load method turns each row into an AccordionPane widget. Finally, the newPane and deletePane methods call the addChild and removeChild methods of AccordionContainer.

These functions are called from the HTML, now slimmed down to a svelte thirty-five lines:

```
widgets/programmatic_portal.html
```

```html
<!DOCTYPE HTML PUBLIC "-//W3C//DTD HTML 4.01//EN"
          "http://www.w3.org/TR/html4/strict.dtd">
<html>
<head>
<title>Portal Application</title>
    <style type="text/css">
        @import "/dojoroot/dijit/themes/tundra/tundra.css";
        @import "/dojoroot/dojo/resources/dojo.css"
    </style>
    <script type="text/javascript" src="/dojoroot/dojo/dojo.js"
            djConfig="parseOnLoad: true"></script>
    <script type="text/javascript">
        dojo.registerModulePath("dojobook","../../dojobook");
        dojo.require("dojo.parser");
        dojo.require("dijit.layout.AccordionContainer");
        dojo.require("dijit.layout.ContentPane");
        dojo.require("dojox.widget.Toaster");
        dojo.require("dojobook.widgets.ProgrammaticPortalDynamic");
        dojo.addOnLoad(dojobook.widgets.ProgrammaticPortalDynamic.drawPortal);
    </script>
</head>
<body class="tundra">
    <div id="ups" dojoType="dijit.layout.AccordionContainer"
        style="width:500px;height:500px">
        <!-- Initially Empty -->
    </div>

    <label for="newUrl">New URL:</label>
    <input type="text" length="50" id="newUrl">
    <label for="newUrl">Title:</label>
    <input type="text" length="50" id="newTitle">

    <button dojoType="dijit.form.Button"
        onclick="dojobook.widgets.ProgrammaticPortalDynamic.newPane();">
        Add</button>
    <button dojoType="dijit.form.Button"
        onclick="dojobook.widgets.ProgrammaticPortalDynamic.deletePane();">
        Remove Selected</button>

    <div dojoType="dojox.widget.Toaster" duration="0"
        messageTopic="xhrError" positionDirection="tr-left" />
</body></html>
```

This illustrates yet again how Dojo and Dijit help partition your application cleanly. The HTML, the JavaScript, and the data are separated instead of being lumped together in a big multilanguage glob. When your programs get large, this becomes even more important.

One more thing. Just as any widget can be created programmatically, it can also be destroyed programmatically like so:

```
ap.destroy()
```

destroy removes the DOM node, erases it from the screen, and then frees the underlying object. In UPS, removeChild calls destroy so we didn't have to worry about it.

If you're building a one-page app with lots of widgets, it's a good habit to destroy widgets when you're finished. When Dijit creates a widget, it places a reference to it in a global registry. Even if the DOM node is removed and the visual portion of the widget disappears, the global registry entry remains. As long as it does, JavaScript can't garbage collect the widget. Calling destroy takes care of the erasure and removing the object from the registry.

So, we've been through the entire widget cycle from creation to method calling to destruction. By calling methods, you can change widget attributes. Similarly, *extension points* allow you to attach widget *code*, as we'll see next.

12.4 Extension Points

In good object-oriented frameworks, some built-in methods are meant for the programmer to call, and some are meant for the programmer to override. A good example of the latter is compare in Java. This method is defined at the root of the class tree (Object) and overridden in most of the built-in classes. After all, comparing two strings, two numbers, two points on a plane, and so on, are all computationally different. Rather than trying to write Object.compare to handle all the types, this method is coded in each subclass. Then you can have one Array.sort method calling the appropriate compare for each pair of values.

Widget classes are like that. Dijit classes have *extension points*, which you can override in JavaScript. The function you write is called the *handler*. If you don't provide a handler for the extension point, the Dijit class uses its own default.

Client-Side vs. Server-Side Widget Creation

If you come from a server-side web programming environment—JSP, ASP, PHP, or what have you—you might be tempted to script widget creation through it. If we were storing the UPS page URLs in a database, you could loop through the values and create widgets like this:

```php
<?php foreach ($urlArray as $url) { ?>
    <div dojoType="dijit.layout.AccordionPane"
        url='<?= $url ?>'></div>
<?php } ?>
```

Now say the user wants to add new panes, like with Ajax. So, you write some JavaScript to draw and add new Accordion-Panes.

There are two problems here. The first is redundancy—you end up writing essentially the same code in the PHP and JavaScript. After all, both take as input a list of URLs, and both output an AccordionContainer of pages.

The second is performance. The more you rely on server code to output the widgets, the more HTML you send through the wire, which in turn makes the browser parser work harder.

You would be better off using the server to query the database and send the UPS data in JSON. This is a much smaller and easily parsed set of packets. Then your JavaScript code can transform the data into panes, and you can reuse this code to create new panes on the fly. So, it's more compact code-wise and data-wise. It's hard to beat that!

That's a bit abstract, so let's add a handler to dijit.form.Button's onClick extension point. To use an extension point, you first need to know the *signature*—which is the name of the handler and its parameters. These are all listed in the Dijit catalog at http://www.dojotoolkit.org.

We find the signature for onClick in dijit.form.Button is as follows:

```
onClick(/* dojo.Event */ evt)
```

When the user clicks the button, Dijit catches the event object and passes it to our handler. As we learned in Section 6.1, *Programming DOM Events with Dojo*, on page 95, dojo.Event events are standard DOM Level 2 events. We will make use of that fact in a second.

We stub out the click handler like so:

```
<div dojoType="dijit.form.Button">
    <script type="dojo/method" event="onClick" args="clickEvent">
        // Code which can use clickEvent
    </script>
</div>
```

event= denotes the name of the extension point, and here it's onClick. But this extension point is not an event in the same way mouseover is. Rather, it's a user event that we first saw in Section 6.2, *Hooking JavaScript Functions*, on page 111. In particular, it's the name of a widget class method, in this case dijit.form.Button.onClick. With extension points, usually the method is empty—it's present but doesn't do anything.

There are two type= attributes you can use here:

- dojo/method replaces the widget class method with your own code. So in the previous case, our onClick handler runs, but dijit.form. Button.onClick does not.

- dojo/connect connects the widget class method with your own code. If we had changed the previous type to dojo/connect, our onClick handler would run before or after the dijit.form.Button.onClick method. Recall that in user-defined event connections, we don't control the order of execution.

If the class method does nothing, dojo/method and dojo/connect act identically. So, which do you use? We tend to use dojo/method unless we know the class method does something.

The args= attribute takes a list of JavaScript variable names and connects these with the signature parameters. You can consider them the formal parameters of our method. So when Dijit calls the handler code, it will put the event into the variable clickEvent, which you can then use in the body of the handler.

Now let's fill in the stub:

widgets/dojo_method.html

```
<div dojoType="dijit.Toolbar">
    <div dojoType="dijit.form.Button" id="deleteButton" label="Delete">
        <script type="dojo/method" event="onClick" args="evt">
            if (evt.shiftKey) {
                console.debug("SHIFT-CLICK = Delete Permanently");
            } else {
                console.debug("CLICK = Send to Trash");
            }
        </script>
        <script type="dojo/method" >
            console.debug(dijit.byId("deleteButton").label + " button loaded");
        </script>
    </div>
</div>
```

Because Dijit passes the handler a full-fledged Dojo event, you can use properties like shiftKey. That alone puts this handler miles ahead of the DOM 0 onclick= attribute.

What about that second dojo/method without an event? Scripts defined this way are executed when the widget is drawn. So, it's a good place to tuck some initialization code.

Let's leave the portal example and look at a pantry shelf display using Dijit.Tree. getIconClass is a handy extension point for the dijit.Tree component. We'll cover trees in detail in Chapter 13, *Tree*, on page 339, but here's a brief introduction. Trees often contain different kinds of items, and many GUI applications indicate this with different icons to the left. For example, Windows Explorer uses a tree to model folders and files, and it displays different icons for different file types. Our pantry application will arrange food by shelves, but each shelf can contain different kinds of food items. Trees are built with data from a dojo.data data store, so we meet our old friend from Chapter 10, *dojo.data*, on page 257: the JSON-backed dojo.data.ItemFileReadStore. Here's one with the pantry data:

widgets/services/pantry.json

```
{
    identifier: 'id',
    label: 'name',
    items: [
        {  type: 'shelf', name: 'Top Right', id: "tr",
           children: [
             {  type:'fooditem', id:'pnkbns', name:'Pink Beans',
                foodType: 'Canned' },
```

```
            { type:'fooditem', id:'olvs', name:'Olives',
              foodType: 'Canned' },
            { type:'fooditem', id:'rstt', name:'Risotto',
              foodType: 'Grain' }
          ]
      },
      { type: 'shelf', name: 'Bottom Right',  id:"br",
        children: [
            { type:'fooditem', id:'ktchp', name:'Ketchup',
              foodType: 'Condiment' },
            { type:'fooditem', id:'sysac', name:'Soy Sauce',
              foodType: 'Condiment' }
          ]
      },
      { type: 'shelf', name: 'Top Left', id:"tl",
        children: [
            { type:'fooditem', id:'mthrnlwstng',
              name:'Mother in Laws Tongue', foodType: 'Grain'
            },
            { type:'fooditem', id:'xxxhthrsrdsh',
              name:'XXX-Hot Horseradish',
              foodType: 'Condiment'
            },
            { type:'fooditem', id:'pckldoctps',
              name:'Pickled Octopus',
              foodType: 'Canned'
            }
          ]
      }
    ]
}
```

In the left side of Figure 12.3, on the following page, you can see our first cut at the tree. It's OK, but the different food items are hard to distinguish. We'd like to put a food type icon next to each: Grain, Condiment, or Canned Good.

Our goal is to provide a getIconClass handler. This code will be invoked on each item of the tree. If you provide no handler, Dijit does the default thing and displays no icon at all. The getIconClass extension point's signature is String getIconClass(/*dojo.data.Item i */). So, already it's a bit different from onClick—you must *return* a value as well. In this case, we return a CSS class containing the icon as a background image.

Inspired by Ruby on Rails, "convention over configuration" will be our motto. Since each icon corresponds one-to-one to a food type, we'll name our CSS classes the same as the foodType properties, suffixing each with Icon.

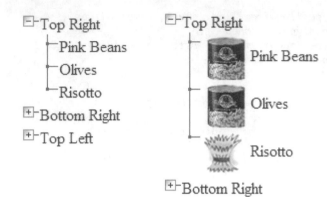

Figure 12.3: A SPARSE TREE AND A SPRUCED-UP TREE USING GETICON-CLASS

It looks like this:

```
widgets/dojo_method_iconClass.html
<style>
    .GrainIcon {
       background-image: url(grain.gif);
       width: 45px;
       height: 45px;
    }
    .CannedIcon {
       background-image: url(canned.jpg);
       width: 45px;
       height: 45px;
    }
    .CondimentIcon {
       background-image: url(condiment.jpeg);
       width: 45px;
       height: 45px;
    }
 </style>
```

Then the getIconClass handler is straightforward. Using the techniques in Chapter 10, *dojo.data*, on page 257, we extract the foodType property from each item as it passes by, turning it into a CSS class name and passing it back.

`widgets/dojo_method_iconClass.html`

```
<div dojoType="dojo.data.ItemFileReadStore" jsId="pantryData"
     url="services/pantry.json" />

 <div dojoType="dijit.Tree" id="panTree" store="pantryData"
     query="{type:'shelf'}"  >
     <script type="dojo/method" event="getIconClass" args="foodItem">
         // Returns Canned, Grain or Condiment, each of which
         // corresponds to a CSS class suffixed by "Icon".  Note
         // that the root node is not an item, so we must test
         // for a valid item each time
         if (pantryData.isItem(foodItem)) {
             return pantryData.getValue(foodItem, "foodType") + 'Icon';
         }
     </script>
 </div>
```

The result is the right side of Figure 12.3, on the facing page. The icons definitely make it easier to find things.

Our extension handler is easy, but you can make some pretty interesting and complex ones too. Say, for example, you have a tree of news feed items. You can display the tree and use getIconClass to fill in read/unread, new/out-of-date, or category icons next to each item, loaded asynchronously so the user can browse the items before the icons load.

As you get more sophisticated with handlers, you'll want to separate them more from your HTML. Dijit can handle that. You simply define your handlers in JavaScript and then link them into your widget. So, for our getIconClass example, you can write the handler like this:

`widgets/programmatic_iconClass.html`

```
function getFoodIcon(foodItem) {
     if (pantryData.isItem(foodItem)) {
         return pantryData.getValue(foodItem, "foodType") + 'Icon';
     }
}
```

Of course, you may place this code in a module to keep it away from the HTML. Then you connect it into the widget declaratively like this:

`widgets/programmatic_iconClass.html`

```
<div dojoType="dijit.Tree" id="panTree" store="pantryData"
     query="{type:'shelf'}"  >
     <script type="dojo/method">
         // This method runs after the widget is created
         this.getIconClass = getFoodIcon;
     </script>
</div>
```

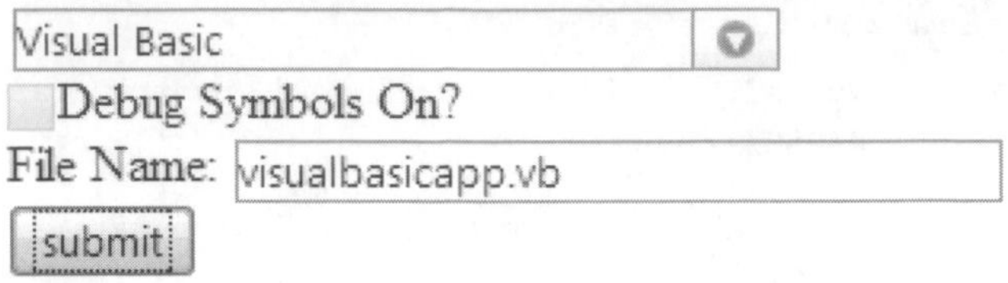

Figure 12.4: LIVE FORM FOR CODE GENERATION

Again, placing the code in a dojo/method script without an event= makes the code run at initialization. We can also use dojo.connect here, which works the same as a dojo/connect script. But it won't work in this particular case because getIconClass must return a value. Connected methods can't send a return value back through the call chain.

As you start extending the widgets, you will eventually find a need to make the same extension over and over again. In that case, you will want to build or extend a widget class. You do this by combining some techniques here with dojo.declare, and that's something we pick up with in Chapter 17, *Creating and Extending Widget Classes*, on page 455. But first, given what we know now about widget creation, methods, and extension points, we can create some really useful Ajax-style behavior. Let's take a moment to see how.

12.5 Example: Live Forms

Michael Mahemoff's book *Ajax Design Patterns* [Mah06] describes coding and functionality patterns for modern web applications. One pattern is called *Live Form*. A live form's controls adjust to the choices made so far.

In Figure 12.4, you see an example live form for a code generation program. Each control potentially affects the other controls:

- The choice of language determines whether the Include Debug Symbols checkbox is disabled—specifically, C is the only language with debug symbols.

- The choice of file name can affect the programming language. If the file extension is .vb, .c, or .java, we can change the programming language based on that. This should, in turn, enable or disable the Include Debug Symbols box.

If you've built a live form using straight JavaScript, you've seen how it gets complex very quickly. Soon the controls start reading and writing the form's other controls, and you have to control the order of execution and updates.

This is a perfect application for publish-subscribe events, which we saw in Chapter 6, *Asynchronous Programming*, on page 95. Instead of connecting code by hardwiring object calls, we use Dojo's central dispatcher. Widgets whose values change announce to the dispatcher "My value has changed" with an event topic. Widgets that are interested in this topic subscribe to it. This creates a sort of enlightened self-interest: widgets need to specify only what they're interested in. They do not need to change, or even know about, other controls that depend on them. They only need to keep the dispatcher informed.

Now for the design. First we create a topic roster:

- The /formchange/gencode/language topic will be published when the language box changes. Naming the topic after the form and control name ensures uniqueness.

- Likewise, the /formchange/gencode/filename topic will fire on file-name changes.

First, we'll build the filename box:

widgets/connected_buttons.html

```
<label for="filename">File Name:</label>
<div dojoType="dijit.form.ValidationTextBox" length="50" name="filename">
   <script type="dojo/method" event="onChange" args="newFile">
      dojo.publish("/formchange/gencode/filename",[newFile]);
   </script>
</div>
```

When the filename field changes, the change is communicated through the appropriate topic. We also communicate the filename so that interested widgets don't need to query the box directly—an extra nicety. Note the array notation in dojo.publish's second parameter. That's necessary, even when passing one variable over the topic.

Next, we build the debug symbols box:

widgets/connected_buttons.html

```
<div dojoType="dijit.form.CheckBox" name="debugSymbols"
    id="debugSymbols" value="Y">
  <script type="dojo/method">
      dojo.subscribe("/formchange/gencode/language",this,function(language) {
      var debugSymAvailable = language=='c' || language=='java';
          this.setDisabled(!debugSymAvailable);
      });
  </script>
</div><label for="debugSymbols">Debug Symbols On?</label>
```

Remember the dojo/method handler with no event executes right after the widget is created. Here, it simply hooks in to the filename change topic and starts listening.

Finally, the language box uses both publishes and subscribes:

widgets/connected_buttons.html

```
<select dojoType="dijit.form.FilteringSelect" name="language" id="language">
    <option value="c">C</option>
    <option value="java">Java</option>
    <option value="vb">Visual Basic</option>

    <script type="dojo/method" event="onChange" args="newLang">
        dojo.publish("/formchange/gencode/language", [newLang]);
    </script>

    <script type="dojo/method">
        // Danger: heavy use of regular expressions!  Consult your
        // favorite JavaScript reference for details
        dojo.subscribe("/formchange/gencode/filename",this,function(filename) {
          // Change language based on extension, if c, vb, or java
          if ((extension = /\.(java|c|vb)$/.exec(filename)) != null) {
            this.setValue(extension[1]);
          }
        });
    </script>
</select>
```

And now we have three independent, yet connected, widgets. Using publish-subscribe effectively encapsulates the widgets, turning them into black boxes. That makes debugging much easier.

Connecting JavaScript to widgets makes them richer, fuller, and more dynamic. This is going to be essential in using the Tree widget, which we met briefly here and discuss fully in the next chapter.

Tree

In Chapter 10, *dojo.data*, on page 257, we looked at flat data stores where the items have only primitive attributes. But dojo.data can work with complex data too. For example, XML data sources may have nested elements, and JSON data stores may have nested arrays and hashes.

Humans seem to prefer the *tree* for visualizing hierarchical data. User interfaces in email programs and the file manipulation portion of an operating system use trees to show items within folders, in turn within other folders, and so forth. Dijit's tree widget, dijit.Tree, makes this visual display simple. Its tight integration with dojo.data nested data sources ensures an accurate onscreen depiction at all times. By tapping into dijit.Tree's many extension points and drag-and-drop functionality, you can create a powerful user experience.

13.1 A Simple Tree

We are going to build a web application for Return Material Authorizations (RMAs) to demonstrate the flexibility of Trees. The contractee, Gag-ool, specializes in gag gifts and rarely gets returns, but it wants to make the return process speedy and painless. Gag-ool pays all shipping costs of the return using its preferred shipping supplier. This shipper has a web service to arrange pickup and generate shipping labels. The shipper has certain restrictions, most notably a 15-pound limit on packages.

Gag-ool will handle the shipper integration; our job is to create the UI. A customer will log on to the site, see a list of their orders and serial numbers, and choose items to RMA.

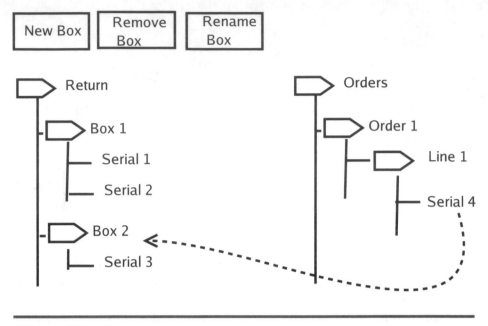

Figure 13.1: Cocktail napkin drawing of the return application

We'll design this with two trees. The right tree, called the *order tree*, will contain recent orders, their items, and the serial numbers. The left tree, called the *box tree*, will contain boxes of serial numbers to return. The user drags items they want to return from the order tree to the box tree. The application should prevent the user from creating boxes heavier than 15 pounds. The user can create, update, and delete boxes as they move the product around to fit their own packing list. In Figure 13.1, you can the cocktail napkin view.

It's best to start simple, so first we'll model the main nodes of the order tree. The tree itself is a dijit.Tree widget requiring a dojo.data store to feed it.[1] Each item in the data store becomes a node of the tree. The topmost node is called the *root* and has no corresponding item in the data store—instead, you provide the root label in the dijit.tree.ForestStoreModel tag. (You can also have a rootless tree by setting showRoot="false" in the dijit.Tree widget.)

---

1. That's not entirely true. You can embed static Tree nodes into a Tree with the dijit._TreeItem widget. But static Trees are comparatively rare, and you can create one with dojo.data and a static file anyway.

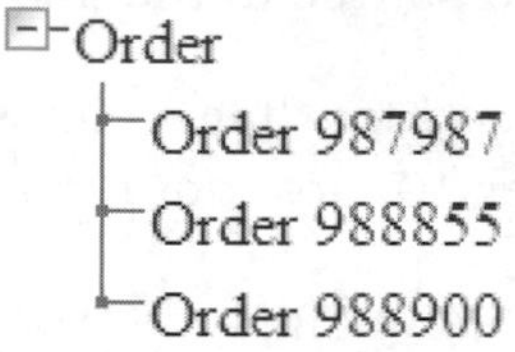

```
⊟ Order
    ├ Order 987987
    ├ Order 988855
    └ Order 988900
```

Figure 13.2: A DIJIT.TREE WIDGET

You can use any dojo.data driver to feed the Tree, but we'll use the familiar ItemFileReadStore. As with other examples, a static file will provide the sample data, later to be replaced by a dynamic service. Here is datasource/order.json:

`tree/datasources/order_header.json`

```
{
    identifier: 'id',
    label: 'description',
    items: [
        { id: 987987, description:"Order 987987",
          priority:"Next Day Air"
        },
        { id: 988855, description:"Order 988855",
          priority:"2nd Day Air"
        },
        { id: 988900, description:"Order 988900",
          priority:"2nd Day Air"
        }
    ]
}
```

With this data source, these five lines of code produce Figure 13.2:

`tree/simple_tree.html`

```html
<div dojoType="dojo.data.ItemFileReadStore" url="datasources/order_header.json"
    jsId="ordJson"></div>

<div dojoType="dijit.tree.ForestStoreModel" rootLabel="Order" store="ordJson"
    jsId="ordModel"></div>

<div dojoType="dijit.Tree" id="ordTree" model="ordModel"></div>
```

The data flows from the data source to the Tree in three steps:

1. The dojo.data.ItemFileReadStore tag defines the data source, just like we used in Chapter 10, *dojo.data*, on page 257.

2. A *model* acts like a pipe adapter between the data source and the tree. Its input comes from the jsId= of the data store and outputs through its own jsId=. Here you can filter data through the familiar dojo.data query. Tree comes bundled with two adapters. dijit.tree.ForestStoreModel, the more popular of the two, takes a multiitem store, makes the items children and adds an artificial root node. You specify the label of this root node in the attribute rootLabel=. dijit.tree.TreeStoreModel takes the root from the store, and it expects the query dojo.data store to return one item, presumably with plenty of child items.

3. The dijit.Tree tag connects to the model's jsId= through its model= attribute.

13.2 Hierarchical Data Stores

Our first example was a one-level tree. If the backing data store supports hierarchical data, as ItemFileReadStore and XmlStore do, a Tree can go down any number of levels. This nesting lessens the number of trips to the server. An order, for example, has header information (containing orderNumber, customer) and zero to many lines (containing sku, quantity). Rather than fetching a header and the associated lines in two separate requests, you can include the lines within the header.

ItemFileReadStore and Trees

An ItemFileReadStore can nest JSON hashes within JSON hashes, a technique we saw in Section 3.2, *Literals and Hashes*, on page 33.[2] That structure translates directly to a tree—a nested hash will display as a "folder" node that you can expand.

---

2. This kind of nesting is called *native nesting*. ItemFileReadStore also supports reference nesting, allowing more complex relationships such as assigning multiple parents to a child. These relationships cannot be modeled with a Tree anyway, but if you're interested, the Book of Dojo at http://dojotoolkit.org has details.

For example, here is an ItemFileReadStore showing line nesting within an order:

`tree/datasources/order_combined.json`

```
{
    identifier: 'id',
    label: 'description',
    items: [
        { id: 987987, description:"Order 987987",
          priority:"Next Day Air",
          line: [
              { id: '987987-1', qty:1,
                sku:11761, description: 'Yodeling Pickle'},
              { id: '987987-2', qty:3,
                sku:11798, description: 'Gummy Tapeworm'}
          ]
        },
        { id: 988855, description:"Order 988855",
          priority:"2nd Day Air" ,
          line: [
              { id: '988855-1', qty:4,
                sku:11753, description: 'Gummy Haggis'}
          ]
        },
        { id: 988900, description:"Order 988900",
          priority:"2nd Day Air",
          line: [
              { id: '988900-1', qty:15,
                sku:11824, description: 'Worlds Largest Inflatable Heart'},
              { id: '988900-2', qty:1,
                sku:11548, description: 'Deluxe Librarian Action Figure'}
          ]
        }
    ]
}
```

When fed into a Tree with this code...

`tree/tree.html`

```
<div dojoType="dojo.data.ItemFileReadStore"
    url="datasources/order_combined.json"
    jsId="ordJson"></div>

<div dojoType="dijit.tree.ForestStoreModel"
    rootLabel="Order" store="ordJson"
    childrenAttrs="line"
    jsId="ordModel"></div>

<div dojoType="dijit.Tree" id="ordTree"
    model="ordModel"></div>
```

the data store looks like Figure 13.3, on the next page.

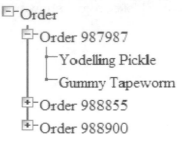

Figure 13.3: A HIERARCHICAL TREE

Note the childrenAttr= property, a comma-separated list of data store properties. The previous code says all properties named line will hold nested elements. If you don't specify childrenAttr=, Tree assumes the property children specifies which properties hold nested elements. But for data store readability, it's a good idea to explicitly state childrenAttr=. children is simply not descriptive enough—a property name like line tells what the nested items are. It's also a good idea to name them differently at different levels, for example, line at the first level and lineDetail at the second with childrenAttr="line,lineDetail".

ItemFileReadStore has a few caveats when used with Trees. Each item, whether parent or child or grandchild, must have a single identifier attribute. In our example, id is the identifier. Furthermore, identifier values must be unique within the JSON document.

Accessing Complex Data from JavaScript

Tree's extension points require access to your hierarchical data. But how does that work? Earlier, in Section 10.4, *Calling Read Methods from JavaScript*, on page 272, you saw how to get an item with fetch and extract values from it with getValue. The JSON data stores hand you back JavaScript primitives as values. dojox.data.XmlStore hands you back an XmlItem, which you can pass to toString to convert.

getValue can also return a nested item. In this case, you treat the return value as you would any other item—you use getValue to retrieve its values and so forth.

Data stores can also have *multivalues*. A multivalued property has zero-to-many values assigned to it. Most often these values are themselves nested items, but they could be any kind of value. If you try to retrieve a multivalue with getValue, the data driver may throw an exception or may simply hand you the first value (as ItemFileReadStore does). Neither option is very good. You really want *all* the values here, and to get them, you must use getValues.

getValues returns a JavaScript array of values for that property. These values may themselves by primitives, like a JavaScript primitive or an XmlItem, or nested items. Conveniently, getValues will work for any attribute. It may return a zero-element array if the attribute doesn't exist or an array of one element or many elements.

How you write an multivalue in the data source depends on the data driver. In ItemFileReadStore, a JavaScript-like array bracketed with [...] indicates a multivalue. In XMLStore, any two or more sibling elements with the same tag name become a multivalue. So in our previous examples, the *<order>* tags and the *<line>* tags become multivalues.

All this machinery makes accessing complex data uniform across data drivers. An example shows how this all works together. Here's our sample order data again, but this time formatted in XML:

tree/datasources/order_combined.xml

```xml
<orders>
   <order>
      <orderNumber>987987</orderNumber>
      <description>Order 987987</description>
      <priority>Next Day Air</priority>
      <line>
         <lineId>987987-1</lineId>
         <qty>1</qty>
         <sku>11761</sku>
         <description>Yodeling Pickle</description>
      </line>
      <line>
         <lineId>987987-2</lineId>
         <qty>3</qty>
         <sku>11798</sku>
         <description>Gummy Tapeworm</description>
      </line>
   </order>
   <!-- More Orders Here -->
</orders>
```

The following code extracts the description attribute from the first line of the first order in both JSON and XML data stores.

Here are the data store definitions, written the programmatic way:

```
tree/using_heirarchies.html
dojo.require("dojo.data.ItemFileReadStore");
var ordJson = new dojo.data.ItemFileReadStore( {
    url: "datasources/order_combined.json",
    childrenAttr: "line"
});
dojo.require("dojox.data.XmlStore");
var ordXml = new dojox.data.XmlStore( {
    url: "datasources/order_combined.xml",
    rootItem: "order",
    keyAttribute:"orderNumber",
    label:"description"
});
```

This is the first XmlStore definition we've seen, but it's pretty much like the ItemFileReadStore. The two properties keyAttribute and label are the analogues of ItemFileReadStore's identifier and label properties. The rootItem property gives the tag name of the main elements.

And here's the extraction code:

```
tree/using_heirarchies.html
function commonComplete(storeDescription, dataStore, items, request) {
    // Get the first order
    var firstOrder = items[0];

    // Get array of each line from the lines list
    var lineList = dataStore.getValues(firstOrder,"line");

    // Get description of the first item.  The +"" applies toString()
    // to the value, necessary for XmlStore
    console.debug(
        storeDescription,
        dataStore.getValue(lineList[0],"description")+
        ""
    );
}

// Example 1: ItemFileReadStore and JSON
ordJson.fetch({
    query: { id: '*' },
    onComplete: function(items, request) {
        commonComplete("JSON Native Nesting: ", ordJson, items,request);
    }
});
// Example 2: XmlStore
ordXml.fetch({
    query: { orderNumber: '*' },
```

```
    onComplete: function(items, request) {
        commonComplete("XML: ", ordXml, items, request);
    }
});
```

Note that in both cases the extraction code is commonComplete, and the extracted values are identical. That's dojo.data making things easy for you.

13.3 Extension Points

Like most widgets, Trees have extension points in which to hook your own code. Back in Chapter 12, *Scripting Widgets*, on page 317, we saw the getIconClass extension point in action. Another extension point, onClick, will be useful in the RMA app, as we'll see in a second.

The Box Tree

The tree needs one box to start, and the user will add, remove, and rename boxes as needed. Trees are backed by data stores, but now Item-FileReadStore isn't enough. We need a store implementing dojo.data.Write, and ItemFileWriteStore is the natural choice here, using the same format as ItemFileReadStore.

The initial data store, kept in datasources/rma_boxes.json, defines one initial box with no items in it. It looks like this:

tree/datasources/rma_boxes.json

```
{
    identifier: 'id',
    label: 'name',
    items: [
        { id: 1, name: "Box 1", type:"box", weight:0 }
    ]
}
```

This looks pretty trivial; does it need to be in a file? Not really. We could as easily put this initial store in a string and pass it to the data= property of the store tag. But by using a URL, we can easily convert the static file to a server-based process later.

Our app will look like a split screen, a simple thing to achieve with a dijit.layout.BorderContainer and two dijit.layout.ContentPanes. Later, in Chapter 16, *Dijit Themes, Design, and Layout*, on page 427, you'll learn all the details of both, but for now here's a brief explanation. The screen is split into two halves, each delineated by a ContentPane. The entire

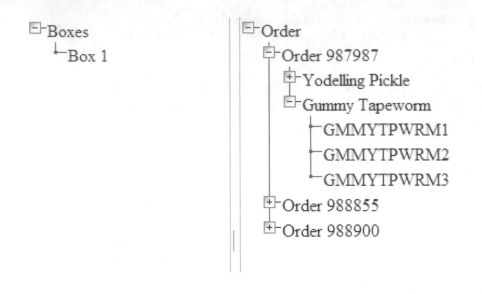

Figure 13.4: LAYING OUT THE BOX TREE AND THE ORDER TREE

BorderContainer box is 400 by 600 pixels, and initially each tree takes up half as shown in Figure 13.4.

Laying out the page takes a few ContentPanes pushed into a BorderContainer. Here's the skeleton:

tree/on_click.html
```
<div dojoType="dijit.layout.BorderContainer" style="width:600px; height:400px"
>
    <div dojoType="dijit.layout.ContentPane" region="leading">
    Box Tree
    </div>

    <div dojoType="dijit.layout.ContentPane" region="trailing">
    Order Tree
    </div>
</div>
```

The onClick Extension Point

The box tree's Remove and Rename buttons will require the user to select a box first. So, somehow the program needs to keep track of the last-selected box. dijit.Tree provides the extension point onClick that'll work well in this case. Though onClick is also an event, Tree's onClick extension point works a little differently. Tree passes the *underlying data item* to the handler rather than the DOM event object.

The onClick handler itself simply remembers the last item clicked. The extension point receives the entire item, not just the label, the identifier, or the DOM node, making it easier to retrieve properties later.

`tree/on_click.html`

```
<div dojoType="dijit.layout.ContentPane" region="leading"
    splitter="true" style="width:200px"
>
    <div dojoType="dojo.data.ItemFileWriteStore"
        url="datasources/rma_boxes.json"
        jsId="boxJson"></div>

    <div dojoType="dijit.tree.ForestStoreModel" store="boxJson"
        jsId="boxModel" rootLabel="Boxes"></div>

    <div dojoType="dijit.Tree" id="boxes" model="boxModel">
        <script type="dojo/method" event="onClick" args="item">
            // Given item, the backing dojo.data.Item backing this node,
            // save it for later deleting and/or renaming
            lastBoxSelected = item;
        </script>
    </div>
</div>
```

With boxes now selectable, we're ready to manipulate them.

13.4 Manipulating the Tree

The Dijit Tree design is a slice of Model-View-Controller heaven, with dojo.data providing the model and Tree providing the view and controller. To manipulate the tree, you don't call methods on the Tree object. Instead, you simply change the model, and the onscreen Tree changes accordingly. The in-memory data store representation and the Tree display are always in sync.

Adding, Removing, and Modifying Tree Nodes

So to change the Tree, you change the data store, and that means using the dojo.data.Write API. Write contains methods for creating, modifying, removing, and saving items. But instead of calling the Write methods directly, you call them on the Tree model. The Tree model then passes them back to the data store.

You create items with newItem:

`newItem(Hash obj, [, Hash parentInfo])` → `dojo.data.Item`

newItem creates an item in the data store. The properties of obj will become properties in the new item. newItem is data-store-agnostic—obj is a plain ol' JavaScript hash whether the store type is ItemFileWriteStore or XmlStore.

parentInfo is used to inject nested items into existing items. It's a hash of the following form…

`{ parent: anItem, attribute: "attributeName" }`

where anItem is the data store item that will become the parent and where attributeName is the attribute to place it. attributeName will be one of the childrenAttr attributes you've listed for the store.

The Add button calls newItem to add a box—very straightforward. A newItem call without parent information creates the new item underneath the root, which is what we want:

`tree/writing_model.html`

```
<div dojoType="dijit.form.Button">
    Add Box
    <script type="dojo/method" event="onClick" args="evt">
        highestBoxId++;
        boxJson.newItem({
            id: highestBoxId,
            name: "Box "+highestBoxId,
            type: "box",
            weight:0
        });
    </script>
</div>
```

Remember, for Trees, you call the Write methods on the model, not the store itself. deleteItem does what you think:

`deleteItem(dojo.data.Item i)`

i must be an actual dojo.data.Item object, not just a plain ol' JavaScript hash as in newItem. The same is true for setValue and setValues.

`setValue(dojo.data.Item i, String attributeName, Object value)`
`setValues(dojo.data.Item i, String attributeName, Object[] value[])`

setValue(s) is the flip side of Read's getValue(s), writing an attribute to an item. It has an interesting side effect: using setValue on the designated store label changes the label on the Tree node. That's exactly how to do the Rename button.

So, onto the buttons... First set up the dojo.require statements and housekeeping variables. highestBoxId will keep track of the last-assigned box ID. Allocation is sparse; that is, if a box is deleted, there will be a "hole" in the IDs. That's fine.

`tree/writing_model.html`

```
dojo.require("dijit.form.Button");

// This is a dummy counter until the real one is in place.
var highestBoxId = 1;
```

The Remove button passes lastSelectedItem to deleteItem, and the box disappears:

`tree/writing_model.html`

```
<div dojoType="dijit.form.Button">
    Remove Box
    <script type="dojo/method" event="onClick" args="evt">
        if (!lastBoxSelected || !boxJson.isItem(lastBoxSelected)) {
            alert('You must select a box first');
            return;
        }
        boxJson.deleteItem(lastBoxSelected);
    </script>
</div>
```

Rename uses lastSelectedBox and the Write method setValue to set a label on the box:

`tree/writing_model.html`

```
<div dojoType="dijit.form.Button">
    Rename Box
    <script type="dojo/method" event="onClick" args="evt">
        if (!lastBoxSelected || !boxJson.isItem(lastBoxSelected)) {
            alert('You must select a box first');
            return;
        }
        // Low-tech solution.  Would be better as a Dijit Dialog
        if (newName = prompt("What would you like to call it?")) {
            boxJson.setValue(lastBoxSelected,"name",newName);
        }
    </script>
</div>
```

Note in all three buttons, the code touches only the data store. The internal representation of the store is always up-to-date with the visual Tree. That's nice, but it gets the data only halfway to its destination. How do you get it the rest of the way—to the server?

Saving the Tree Back to the Server

In the traditional web world, you could save data only upon form submission. In the Ajax world, you have more options. You can save one field at a time as the user enters it. You can save a record as the user moves from one record to another. You can save at certain time intervals, like a word processor's autosave feature, or you can save upon form submission. There are advantages to each strategy. For example, saving data more frequently avoids the "all-or-nothing" pitfall, while saving data less frequently is easier to script.

dojo.data allows these options and those in between—a continuum between coarse granularity (saving more data less frequently) and fine granularity (saving less data more frequently). And because changing Tree involves changing only the model, this goes on without the knowledge of Tree.

For fine granularity, you plug your save routine (usually using XHR or JSONP) into the dojo.data.Notification API. Notification is like the mirror image of Write. When each Write method completes, it fires the corresponding Notification event: Write's setValue fires Notificaton's onSet event, delete fires onDelete, and newItem fires onNew. Tree itself works by plugging handlers into these events. For instance, its onNew handler adds the new item as a Tree node. If you wanted to perform a save at that point, you plug your handler into onNewItem as well. Both handlers—from Tree and your own code—execute.

Dojo.data drivers implementing Notification, such as ItemFileWriteStore, define the following extension points:

```
onNew(dojo.data.Item i)
onDelete(dojo.data.Item i)
onSet(dojo.data.Item i, String attributeName, Object value, Object newValue)
```

The signatures match their counterparts in dojo.data.Write with one exception: onSet adds the oldValue parameter. This is useful because if oldValue==newValue, it probably doesn't need saving back to the server. Your handler must check for this condition.

Using this in our example, the onNew event runs our handler, sending the new box data back to the server through dojo.xhrPost:

`tree/writing_model_fine_granularity.html`

```
<div dojoType="dojo.data.ItemFileWriteStore"
    url="datasources/rma_boxes.json"
    jsId="boxJson">
```

```
<script type="dojo/connect" event="onNew" args="newItem">
    dojo.xhrPost({
        url: "datasources/rma_boxes.json",
        content: {
            id: this.getValue(newItem,"id"),
            description: this.getValue(newItem,"name"),
            operation: "insert"
        },
        timeout: 1000,
        error: function() {
            alert('Uh oh.  The box wasn\'t saved.');
        },
        load: function() {
            console.debug("new box saved");
        }
    });
</script>
</div>
```

Since we're not dealing with server programs in this book, this example posts to a static URL. But you can watch the action in Firebug, as shown in Figure 13.5, on the following page. The server program can translate these packets into database operations.

Coarse-grained saving is similar. The dojo.data.Write API's save routine serializes the store and posts it back to the URL, which is essentially fetch in reverse. The following code places a Save button next to the other buttons:

tree/writing_model_coarse_granularity.html

```
<div dojoType="dijit.form.Button">
    Save
    <script type="dojo/method" event="onClick" args="evt">
        // Turns JavaScript object into JSON.  Like dojo.objectToJSON, but
        // respects dojo.data Type Maps
        var newFileContentString = boxJson._getNewFileContentString();
        dojo.xhrPost({
            url: "datasources/rma_boxes.json",
            // The boxes parameter name is arbitrary
            content: {
                boxes: newFileContentString
            },
            timeout: 1000,
            load: function() {
                console.debug("all boxes saved");
            },
            error: function() {
                alert('Uh oh.  The boxes weren\'t saved.');
            }
        });
    </script>
</div>
```

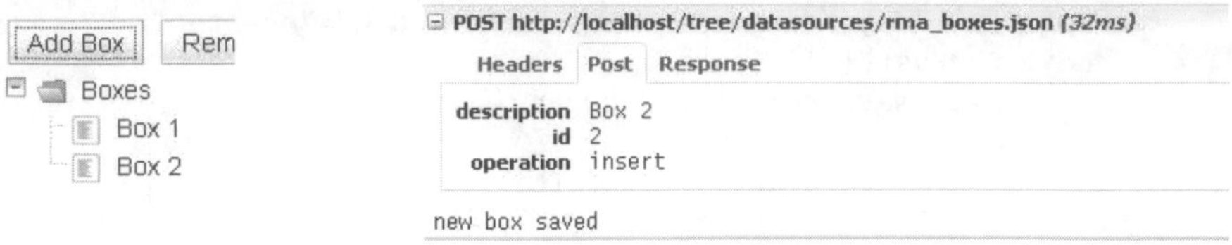

```
Add Box    Rem        POST http://localhost/tree/datasources/rma_boxes.json (32ms)
⊟ 🗀 Boxes             Headers   Post   Response
    📄 Box 1         description  Box 2
    📄 Box 2                 id  2
                     operation  insert

                     new box saved
```

Figure 13.5: CLICKING ADD SENDS XHR PACKET

Again, the routine posts to a static URL, but you can watch the activity in Firebug.

You may be asking, "Why use the extension points? You could just as easily attach the code right to the button." By using the extension points, you ensure the routines run no matter how the data gets in. For example, in the next section, the drag-and-drop controller will manipulate the data store.

When it does, it'll use our onNew, onSet, and onDelete handlers. So, there's no new code to write!

13.5 Drag and Drop

The last ingredient we need for the RMA app is drag-and-drop functionality. Users will drag items from the order tree to the box tree, and the code must change the display and the data stores appropriately.

We will cover low-level drag and drop in Chapter 19, *Adding Dynamic Content to an RIA*, on page 507. dijit.Tree builds drag and drop right into its core, covering the low-level details and initialization so you don't have to.

A Little Refactoring

Before continuing, notice how our app is getting a bit chunky. Some refactoring is in order. The box tree, which contains the bulk of the code, would fit nicely in an object.

Since the box tree represents an RMA, we'll name the object class dojo-
book.tree.objects.rma. RMA methods would include adding, removing,
and renaming a box; checking that an item can fit in a box; and adding
an item to a box.

Some skeleton code starts the object:

`tree/objects/rma.js`

```
dojo.provide("dojobook.tree.objects.rma");

dojo.require("dijit._tree.dndSelector");
dojo.require("dojo.dnd.Manager");

dojo.declare("dojobook.tree.objects.rma", null, {
    // Data store associated with the return, will contain boxes
    // and serial numbers
    store: null,

    // Keep the dndSource controller for this tree.
    dndController: null,

    // Generator for unique box id's
    highestBoxId: 1,

    // For use in Delete and Rename
    lastBoxSelected: null,

    // Serial numbers already in the return
    allRMASerials: [ ],

    // Box weight limit, imposed by our shipper
    MAX_WEIGHT: 15,

    // Constructor
    constructor: function(dataStore, inDndController) {
        this.store = dataStore;
        this.dndController = inDndController;
    },
```

Back in the HTML page, we declare an instance of this object:

`tree/rma.html`

```
// Object tree uses
dojo.require("dojobook.tree.objects.rma");
var rma = null;
```

We also create the actual object inside the tree widget.

It's necessary to do it here because the constructor needs parameters
that were created along with the tree:

tree/rma.html

```
<div dojoType="dijit.Tree" id="boxes"
    model="boxModel"
    dndController="dijit._tree.dndSource"
    onDndDrop="dndDrop"
    checkItemAcceptance="itemAccept"
    >
    <script type="dojo/method">
        // Executed when the widget is created
        rma = new dojobook.tree.objects.rma(boxJson, this.dndController);
    </script>

    <script type="dojo/event" event="onClick" args="item">
        rma.lastBoxSelected = item;
    </script>
</div>
```

Then the button-backing code moves over to the object class:

tree/objects/rma.js

```
addBox: function() {
    this.highestBoxId++;
    this.store.newItem({
        id: this.highestBoxId,
        name: "Box "+this.highestBoxId,
        type: "box",
        weight:0
    });
},

removeBox: function() {
    if (!this.lastBoxSelected || !this.store.isItem(this.lastBoxSelected)) {
        alert('You must select a box first');
        return;
    }
    this.store.deleteItem(this.lastBoxSelected);
},

renameBox: function() {
    if (!this.lastBoxSelected || !this.store.isItem(this.lastBoxSelected)) {
        alert('You must select a box first');
        return;
    }
    if (newName = prompt("What would you like to call it?")) {
        this.store.setValue(this.lastBoxSelected,"name",newName);
    }
}
```

And method calls are left in its place:

`tree/rma.html`

```
<div dojoType="dijit.form.Button">
    Add Box
    <script type="dojo/event" event="onClick">
        rma.addBox();
    </script>
</div>

<div dojoType="dijit.form.Button">
    Remove Box
    <script type="dojo/event" event="onClick" args="evt">
        rma.removeBox();
    </script>
</div>

<div dojoType="dijit.form.Button">
    Rename Box
    <script type="dojo/event" event="onClick" args="evt">
        rma.renameBox();
    </script>
</div>
```

That's much better. The more JavaScript code we can remove from the HTML, the clearer the user interface design will be.

_TreeNodes and Associated Objects

To operate on the tree, we need a little background on its contents. From the discussions on widgets, you'll recall that each widget is really two objects: the widget object and the DOM node for the onscreen representation. The former responds to Dijit method calls, and the latter responds to DOM operations such as setting the style.

A Tree is a container widget, which means it's meant to contain other widgets. In this case, the contained widgets are always of type dijit._TreeNode. You don't create these widgets—Tree does that for you—but you do need to access them. Because _TreeNodes are widgets, they have a backing widget instance and DOM node. But they also have a third representation: a dojo.data.Item. In MVC parlance, the dojo.data.Item is the model object, the DOM node is the view, and the _TreeNode is the controller.

The good news is there's a one-to-one-to-one correspondence here. One _TreeNode always has exactly one associated DOM node and one associated Item. That never varies. The trouble is you may have only one of these objects, and you need information from another object. For example, the getIconClass extension point gets the item, but not the widget or DOM node. So, conversion between these three objects is essential. Here's a handy list of conversions:

- Use treeObject._itemNodeMap[itemId] to convert from the item to the widget. _itemNodeMap maps identity values to _TreeNode objects.[3]

- Use dijit.getEnclosingWidget to convert from the DOM node to the widget. We saw this in Chapter 12, *Scripting Widgets*, on page 317.

- To convert from the widget to an item, use widget.item.

Combinations of these three conversions cover the other cases. For example, this method converts a DOM node to an item:

`tree/objects/rma.js`

```
// Handy method for computing dojo.data item connected to a DOM node
domToItem: function(domNode) {
    return dijit.getEnclosingWidget(domNode).item;
},
```

Checking Drop Operations

Enabling a Tree with drag and drop requires just one property: dndcontroller=. All of the tree items then become drag sources and drop targets. So first, hook up the order tree:

`tree/rma.html`

```
<div dojoType="dijit.Tree" id="ordTree"
    model="ordModel"
    dndController="dijit._tree.dndSource"
    checkAcceptance="never">
</div>
```

In most drag-and-drop Tree cases, the bundled controller dijit._tree. dndSource works fine. If you need extra functionality, you can always subclass dndSource or write your own controller.

Among other things, dndSource checks the legality of a drop. Or, more accurately, it calls *our* code that checks the legality of a drop. This code plugs into Tree's checkAcceptance or checkItemAcceptance extension point. The difference between the two is scope.

---

3. This is why identity values need to be unique in the data store, even at differing nesting levels—if they weren't, you'd have collisions in the _itemNodeMap array.

checkAcceptance answers "Can you drop this item anywhere in this tree?" checkItemAcceptance answers "Can you drop this item on this particular tree node?" If you don't provide a handler, the answer is assumed "yes."

An example will clarify. The order tree should not accept any dragged objects, no matter which node the user attempts to drop it on. Therefore, we plug a function into checkAcceptance:

`tree/rma.html`

```
<div dojoType="dijit.Tree" id="ordTree"
    model="ordModel"
    dndController="dijit._tree.dndSource"
    checkAcceptance="never">
</div>
```

And in this case the function is trivial:

`tree/rma.html`

```
function never() { return false; }
```

Nodes of the box tree, on the other hand, *do* accept dropped items, but not in all cases. The checkItemAcceptance extension point is more appropriate here. We need to check three rules. First, you can drop a serial number only on a box, not a root node or another serial number. Second, you cannot drop a serial number onto the box tree more than once. Third, each box must observe the 15-pound box limit.

The checkItemAcceptance extension point has the signature checkItemAcceptance(dojo.dnd.Target target, dojo.data.source[] sources). Tree passes over the drop target, and an *array* of drag sources—though our tree allows dragging only one source at a time, so we'll need only the first element. The Tree tag points to our checkItemAcceptance function (and the onDndDrop function, which we'll cover in the next section):

`tree/rma.html`

```
<div dojoType="dijit.Tree" id="boxes"
    model="boxModel"
    dndController="dijit._tree.dndSource"
    onDndDrop="dndDrop"
    checkItemAcceptance="itemAccept"
    >
```

It would be nice if checkItemAcceptance could directly call a dojobook. tree.objects.rma method declaratively, but it's not possible with Dojo 1.1.

So, instead, it calls a utility function in the HTML file:

```
tree/rma.html
```

```
// functions that actually call methods
function itemAccept(target, source) {
    return rma.itemAccept(target, source);
}

function dndDrop(source, nodes, copy) {
    rma.boxDrop(source, nodes, copy);
};
```

And the utility function in turn calls the item acceptance method in the
rma. class. This is where the rubber meets the road.

```
tree/objects/rma.js
```

```
itemAccept: function(target, source) {
    // First make sure we're dropping on a box, not another serial #
    targetBoxItem = this.domToItem(target);

    // There is no item connected with the root
    if (! targetBoxItem) {
        return false;
    }

    // Only boxes have a type attribute
    if (! boxJson.hasAttribute(targetBoxItem, "type")) {
        return false;
    }

    // Loop through all the dragged nodes.  See the DnD chapter
    // for details on the .selection property
    var draggedSerials = source.selection;
    var draggedWeight = 0;
    for (thisSerial in draggedSerials) {
        // If any serial number has already been moved, don't let it
        // be moved again.
        if (dojo.indexOf(this.allRMASerials, thisSerial) > -1)
            return false;

        // Get the item weight, and add it to the dragged item weight
        var serialItem = this.domToItem(draggedSerials[thisSerial]);
        var thisSerialWeight = parseInt(ordJson.getValue(serialItem,"weight"));
        draggedWeight += thisSerialWeight;
    }

    // Finally, add up all the weights and make sure they're OK
    if (parseInt(this.store.getValue(targetBoxItem,"weight"))
        + draggedWeight > this.MAX_WEIGHT) {
        return false;
    }
```

```
    // Everything is fine
    return true;
},
```

Checking the first rule (drop only on a box) is straightforward. Even though the extension point passes a DOM node, the handy domToItem translator retrieves the data behind it. Only boxes have the type= property of that data item, so that check is quick. The second rule checks for "double dragging," and to make this easy, a flat list of all serials in the box tree resides in allRMASerials, which the drop operation manipulates as items are dropped. If the item has already been dropped, it'll appear in here.

Weight checking needs to consult the order data source. The code loops through all dragged nodes, converting them to their dojo.data.Item counterparts. The item contains the weight, and we add that to a running total. Add this to the box weight, which is kept in the boxes' weight property (also updated when items are dropped), and make sure it's less than 15 pounds. If it is, the drop can proceed.

Dropping and Adding Items

The checkItemAcceptance method relies on some housekeeping operations performed as items are dropped: it expects the box weight to be correct and the allRMASerials list to be up-to-date. These go into Tree's onDndDrop extension point. The chain of events on a drop goes like this:

1. The user lets go of the mouse.

2. checkAcceptance and checkItemAcceptance are called. If they both return true, the drop proceeds.

3. Tree updates the display and the data store.

4. Lastly, Tree calls the onDndDrop extension point. If no method is connected there, the drop operation ends.

The signature for onDnDDrop is onDndDrop(dojo.dnd.source source, dojo.dnd.source[] nodes, boolean copy). It's like most other drag-and-drop extension points, but it adds the copy parameter, which is set to true if the user holds down Shift while dragging.

This doesn't matter in our app.

`tree/objects/rma.js`

```
boxDrop: function(source, nodes, copy) {
    // The DnD controller contains the drop target (the box).
    // For convenience, convert this to an item
    var targetBoxItem = this.domToItem(this.dndController.current);

    // The weight is init'ed to zero and we add weight as items
    // are dropped into it.
    var currentBoxWeight = this.store.getValue(targetBoxItem, "weight");

    // Handle more than 1 serial number, if needed
    for (var i=0;i<nodes.length;i++) {
        // Convert to an item
        var draggedItem = this.domToItem(nodes[i]);
        // Remember the serial number
        this.allRMASerials.push(ordJson.getValue(draggedItem,"id"));

        // Add the weight of this serial, obtaining the weight from
        // the order item
        var thisSerialWeight =
            parseInt(ordJson.getValue(draggedItem,"weight"));
        currentBoxWeight += thisSerialWeight;
    }
    this.store.setValue(targetBoxItem, "weight", currentBoxWeight);

    // Store it back in the item store.
    if(this.dndController.containerState == "Over"){
        // Stop dragging
        this.dndController.isDragging = false;

        // Create a new dropped item in the target
        var items = this.dndController.itemCreator(
            nodes,
            this.dndController.current
        );

        // Create a data store item for each dragged serial number
        // The tree then changes to match it.
        for(var i = 0; i < items.length; i++){
            pInfo = {parent: targetBoxItem, attribute: "children"};
            var newItem = this.store.newItem(items[i], pInfo);
        }
    }

    // Cancel all other event handlers
    this.dndController.onDndCancel();
},
```

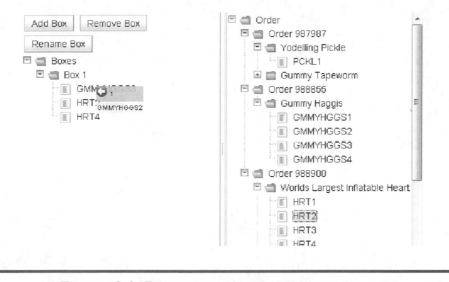

Figure 13.6: THE TRAGIC RETURN OF GUMMY HAGGIS

Similar to checkItemAcceptance, the drop operation loops through all dropped items, adds the weights to the current box total, and stores the serial numbers in allRMASerials. At this point, the drop operation ends, and the user can drag another item. All of these operations happen in a controlled, intuitive fashion, and to the user, it's one fluid motion. In Figure 13.6, you can see the action in progress.

Between the two source files, there are about 250 lines of source code including comments. That's not too bad for an application with drag and drop, access to outside services, validation, and tree control!

Other JavaScript toolkits have tree widgets, but none has the clean MVC architecture of Dijit. Because dojo.data is flexible and standard, reading/writing hierarchical values is a breeze, no matter what the server data format is. And the tree display update is automatic. If you've ever tried writing data to the browser and then "screen-scraping" it back off to do calculations, you realize how important that integration is. It's a real time-saver. In the next chapter, we'll see another widget that integrates tightly with dojo.data: Grid.

Grid

As we saw in Chapter 3, *Connecting to Outside Services*, on page 31, the Grid widget is a spreadsheet-like "supertable." Grids are *de rigueur* in client-server application land, but web application land hasn't adopted them very quickly. The technology to build them just wasn't there: in a regular fill-and-submit form, it's impossible to make a grid that feels interactive.

But the big bang of JavaScript, Dynamic HTML, and XHR makes browser-based grids possible, and the Grid widget is the state-of-the-art. It gives client-server grids a run for their money in features, performance, and stability. Dojo's Grid widget began life as TurboGrid, built independently on top of early Dojo releases by Scott Miles and Steve Orvell. In late 2007, their company, TurboAjax, was purchased by ActiveGrid, which in turn contributed TurboGrid technology to the Dojo Foundation.

Despite its inclusion in Dojox, Grid is more than just a Dojo extension. It's a powerful display environment on its own, popular among Dojo users, and very feature-rich:

- A Grid's data elements can span multiple columns or multiple rows, just like an HTML table. And you can freeze particular columns while the rest of the Grid scrolls.

- Rows can contain multiple subrows working together as a unit. Subrows can be selectively hidden on certain rows, making it useful for grouping and aggregation.

- Even with thousands of rows, Grid performs well. Rows are lazy-rendered as the user moves down the Grid.

- Grid has a large assortment of extension points to hook in your own code. Many extension points act on standard DOM Level 2 events, adding Grid-specific properties to the standard event object. This makes for easier coding.

- Grid supports rich data editors, some custom-made for Grid and some based on existing Dijit form controls.

- Grid works with all bundled dojo.data drivers. Data synchronization is built in: changing the data changes the display, and vice versa.

That's a lot of functionality, and it's accessible through the Dojo idioms you've come to know and love.

14.1 Grid Display and Design

Let's briefly review what we learned in Chapter 3. A Grid is fed data through a model, which in all our examples will be a dojo.data data source.[1] The Grid widget looks like a table with one row, and you use *<th>* tags to define columns, their widths, and the attributes that provide them with data.

Data-wise, Grid is similar to its data-enabled brethren widgets Tree, FilteringSelect, and ComboBox. The store= attribute connects the Grid to its store. The query= and queryOptions= attributes define which items initially feed the Grid. You can also specify an initial sort order, but unlike the other data-enabled widgets that use the sort= property, in Grid the property is sortFields=. The sort criteria format is the same.

Now, onward to bigger and better Grids. In this chapter, we'll follow the evolution of a Grid-based ice cream rating system. (Life is too short to waste on mediocre ice cream!) The user will get a prepopulated Grid of ice cream flavors, calorie and fat information, and ingredient summaries. They can then add their own ratings.

Every Grid begins with data. Our data store is in the familiar JSON format using the ItemFileReadStore data driver.

---

1. You can also use straight two-dimensional arrays as models. This was the only way to feed data to the Grid in the days before dojo.data. Its use has been deprecated, so these days *data store* and *model* are fairly synonymous. But a thin model class remains tied to Grid, and the term *model* lives on in Grid's properties, attributes, and method names.

The items, one per ice cream flavor, look like this:

`grid/datastores/ice_cream.json`

```
{  identifier: "name",
   label: "name",
   items: [
         { name: "banana split",baseFlavor:"banana",
           mixins:"fudge, strawberries, cherries",
           calories:280,fat:16 ,source:1,rating:3 },
         { name: "black raspberry chip",
           baseFlavor:"black raspberry and vanilla",
           mixins:"chocolate chips",
           calories:280,fat:18 ,source:1,rating:3 },
           // Lots more...
```

It looks simple enough to put into a Grid:

`grid/grid_1_subrow.html`

```
<span dojoType="dojo.data.ItemFileReadStore"
    jsId="icStore" url="datastores/ice_cream.json">
</span>

<table id="grid" dojoType="dojox.grid.Grid"
           store="icStore"
           clientSort="true"
           style="width: 35em; height: 15em;">
    <thead>
      <tr>
          <th field="name">Flavor</th>
          <th field="baseFlavor" >Base Flavor</th>
          <th field="calories" >Calories</th>
          <th field="fat" >Fat</th>
          <th field="mixins">Mixins</th>
      </tr>
    </thead>
</table>
```

Note: One nice shortcut comes courtesy of Grid. Every data-enabled widget uses a dojo.data query to do the first fetch. With FilteringSelect and Tree, you placed that query in the tag. You can with Grid too, but if you don't specify the query, it uses the default: { name: '*' }. Since the identifier in our data store is called name and we want Grid to list all items, the default is perfect, and we don't need to specify our own query. Many Dojo programmers use this convention when designing data stores for Grid.

But the results are not quite what we wanted, as shown in Figure 14.1, on the next page. The word wrapping in the larger columns mixins and flavor cause a lot of whitespace in the others. And when you try to fix

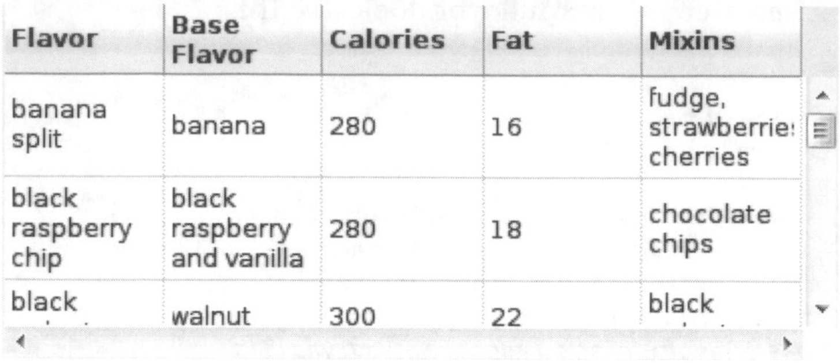

Flavor	Base Flavor	Calories	Fat	Mixins
banana split	banana	280	16	fudge, strawberrie: cherries
black raspberry chip	black raspberry and vanilla	280	18	chocolate chips
black	walnut	300	22	black

Figure 14.1: COLUMNS ARE UNBALANCED

the column sizes, the results don't look right. You're trying to fit too much text in one line.

Besides adding width to a Grid, you can give the data some breathing room using either *subrows* or *views*. Let's take up subrows first.

Subrows

A subrow is simply a horizontal subdivision of a row onto different physical lines. Each row is like a *<tr>* tag. In fact, the declarative version of Grid uses *<tr>* tags to group *<th>* tags into subrows. We've been using subrows all along, but only one of them per row.

Since the mixins column is the largest, we'll put it on its own subrow like this:

```
grid/grid_2_subrows.html
<tr>
    <th field="name" width="10em">Flavor</th>
    <th field="baseFlavor" >Base Flavor</th>
    <th field="calories" >Calories</th>
    <th field="fat" >Fat</th>
</tr>
<tr>
    <th field="mixins" width="15em" colspan="4" >Mixins</th>
</tr>
```

Notice the *<th>* tags need no changes except the mixins field's colspan= attribute. Just like in HTML, colspan="4" means the field will span the four columns defined above it.

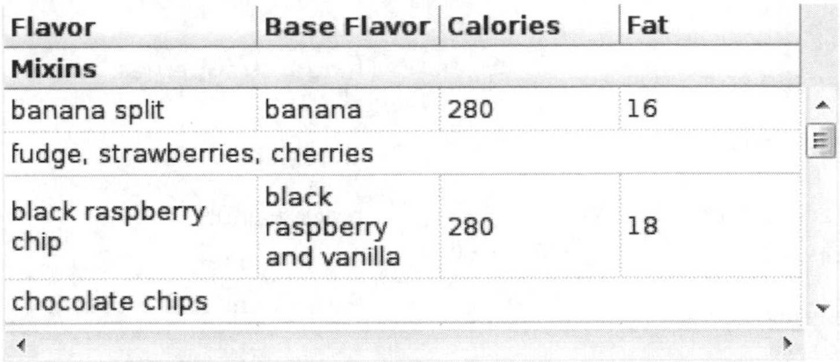

Flavor	Base Flavor	Calories	Fat
Mixins			
banana split	banana	280	16
fudge, strawberries, cherries			
black raspberry chip	black raspberry and vanilla	280	18
chocolate chips			

Figure 14.2: GRID WITH ROWS SPLIT INTO TWO SUBROWS

As you can see in Figure 14.2, the subrows stay together as a group. All of a row's subrows share the same odd or even coloring. And when you click one data element, all the subrows are selected as a group.

Subrows are not only good for design but also for grouping and aggregating, which come up later in this chapter. But first, an alternative to subrows called *views* can also give your data more breathing room.

Views

Looking vertically, subrows make up rows, and rows make up a Grid. Horizontally, columns make up *views*, and views make up a Grid. A view is a set of contiguous columns. One view can scroll independently of other views horizontally but will always scroll vertically in lockstep with other views. In other words, a row spans all the Grid views, and its subrows always stay together.

In Figure 14.3, on the next page, you can see our data with one subrow per row and two views. The left view holds just the ice cream flavor name, while the right view holds the remaining fields. The scroll bar on the right view's bottom border moves the columns left and right, while the other view stays fixed. (You could have the left view scroll left and right too, but it's not very interesting with one column.) This conveniently leaves the ice cream name in place while you browse the other view's fields. The right scroll bar moves both views up and down in lockstep so that "banana split" is always on the same line as its mixins "fudge, strawberries, cherries."

To split columns into views, you use the HTML-standard (though not very popular) <*colgroup*> tag. Its HTML use is to apply attributes to several contiguous columns. In Grid, each <*colgroup*> defines one view.

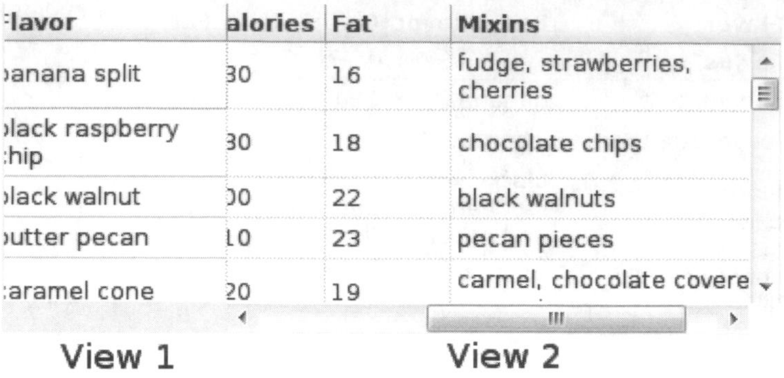

Flavor	alories	Fat	Mixins
banana split	30	16	fudge, strawberries, cherries
black raspberry chip	30	18	chocolate chips
black walnut	00	22	black walnuts
butter pecan	10	23	pecan pieces
caramel cone	20	19	carmel, chocolate covere

View 1   View 2

Figure 14.3: MULTIPLE VIEWS

Through its span= attribute, <*colgroup*> gets the number of columns to put in the view. Additionally, the Grid-specific noscroll= attribute removes the scroll bars on the bottom and right sides of the view. This code implements the Grid in Figure 14.3:

grid/grid_2_views.html

```
<span dojoType="dojo.data.ItemFileReadStore"
    jsId="icStore" url="datastores/ice_cream.json">
</span>

<table id="grid" dojoType="dojox.grid.Grid"
        store="icStore"
        clientSort="true"
        style="width: 35em; height: 15em;">
    <colgroup span="1" noscroll="true"></colgroup>
    <colgroup span="4"></colgroup>
    <thead>
      <tr>
        <th field="name"  width="15em">Flavor</th>
        <th field="baseFlavor"  width="10em">Base Flavor</th>
        <th field="calories" width="5em">Calories</th>
        <th field="fat" width="5em">Fat</th>
        <th field="mixins" width="7em">Mixins</th>
      </tr>
    </thead>
</table>
```

If a <*colgroup*> tag leaves out the span= attribute, it's assumed span="1".

So in the example, the first view gets the first row and removes the scroll bar. The second view picks up the remaining four columns.

Remember, rows span views. And views do not change that each row is fed by one dojo.data item. In other words, you cannot feed one view from a data source and another view from a different one.

14.2 Programmatic Structures

Like all widgets, you can create a Grid programmatically. But you can also create just the *structure* of the Grid programmatically. A structure is the set of cell and view definitions making up a Grid. In other words, it's the Grid minus the model. Although we don't use the term *structure* with declarative Grids, you can think of a structure as the set of <colgroup>, <tr>, and <th> inside the <table> tag.

Grid Structure Definitions in JavaScript

As a structure gets more complex, it makes more sense to move it to JavaScript. For one thing, it keeps the HTML smaller and more manageable. It allows you to reuse the Grid structure in many different pages. Most important, a programmatic structure has extension points where declarative tags don't. Keeping the Grid tag declarative and moving the structure to JavaScript is a nice compromise between ease and flexibility. The general form of a Grid structure looks like this:

```
var s = [  // A structure is an array of views
    {  // A view is an array of cells
      cells: [
          {
              name: '«Column Display Name»',
              field: '«Field in Datastore»',
              «other properties»
          },
          «more cells»
      ]
    },
    «more views»
];
```

You then pass it to the Grid's structure= property. The Grid no longer needs <thead>, <tr>, or <th> tags, and the dojoType="dojox.grid.Grid" attribute can go in a <div> instead of a <table>.

To see this in action, we'll go back to our basic ice cream–fueled Grid. We've seen how to use both subrows and views to get more space, but subrows seem to look better, so we'll go that route.

So, here's the result:

`grid/grid_definitions/programmatic.js`

```
Line 1   dojo.provide("dojobook.grid.grid_definitions.programmatic");

         (function() {
           dojobook.grid.grid_definitions.programmatic.structure = [
    5        {
               cells: [
                 [
                     {name: 'Flavor', field:"name", width:'10em'},
                     {name: 'Base Flavor', field:"baseFlavor"},
   10                {name: 'Calories', field:"calories"},
                     {name: 'Fat', field:'fat'}
                 ],
                 [
                     {name: 'Add-Ins', field:"mixins",
   15                 width:'15em', colSpan:4}
                 ]
               ]
             }
           ]
   20    })();
```

The indentation clarifies the element nesting. Reading from the inner-most to the outermost, the hash in line 8 defines a *cell*. Probably a more apt name for a cell is a *column definition*, since it defines one column's properties: the column heading, the associated field, and so on. Spreadsheets use *cell* to mean an actual data element—the intersection of a row and a column. But here, we'll follow Dojo Grid terminology.

The cell property names match the attribute names you use in <*th*>. The column name you'd normally put in <*th*>'s body goes in the property name. Subrows in lines 7 and 13 are arrays of cells, just like a <*tr*>. Subrows are kept in the cells array, which functions like <*thead*>. View definitions normally kept in <*colgroup*> are now hashes with the cells property, as in line 6. A structure, the outermost array, functions like a <*table*> tag. For the most part, a programmatic structure is the declarative structure with { ... } and [...] substituted for tags.

Finally, you pass the structure into the Grid tag's structure= attribute.

`grid/grid_programmatic_structure.html`

```
<div id="grid" dojoType="dojox.grid.Grid"
    jsId="icGrid"
    store="icStore"
    clientSort="true"
    style="width: 35em; height: 15em;"
    structure="dojobook.grid.grid_definitions.programmatic.structure">
    </div>
```

The result is a modularized Grid, with more maintainable code. And now more options are open to us, like extension points and row bars.

Row Bars

Programmatic structures allow a special view called a *row bar*, used for row selection. You may already have noticed that clicking a data element highlights its entire row. This works in read-only data elements, as ours have been. But once you enable editing, as we will in Section 14.4, *Cell Editing*, on page 384, clicking will start up the cell editor. How does a user select rows under these conditions?

A row bar contains no data but lives only for users to click and select rows. You can see it on the left in Figure 14.4, on the following page.[2] Clicking the row bar selects an entire row, and you can select multiple noncontiguous rows with Ctrl +click and multiple contiguous rows with Shift +click.

This definition adds the row bar, which is always of type dojox.grid. GridView. Note this view has no subrows and no cells. Its noscroll property prevents an unnecessary scroll bar on the right (row bars never have a bottom scroll bar).

`grid/grid_definitions/rowbar.js`

```
dojo.provide("dojobook.grid.grid_definitions.rowbar");

(function() {
    dojobook.grid.grid_definitions.rowbar.structure = [
        { // View #1: rowbar
            type: dojox.grid.GridView, width:"20px", noscroll:true
        },
        { // View #2: data
          cells: [
              [
                  {name: 'Flavor', width:'10em', field:"name"},
                  {name: 'Base Flavor', width:'7em',
                        field:"baseFlavor"},
                  {name: 'Calories', width:'5em',
                        field:"calories"},
                  {name: 'Fat', width:'5em', field:'fat'}
              ]
              // Other subrow removed for this example only
          ]
        }
    ];
})();
```

---

2. For some reason, the row bar appears on the right in Internet Explorer 6. This bug

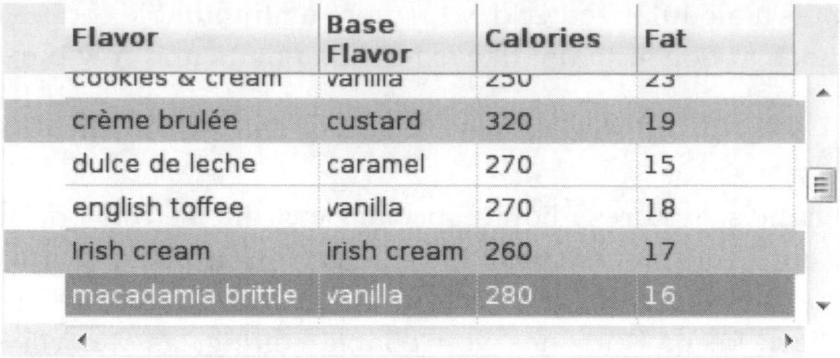

Flavor	Base Flavor	Calories	Fat
cookies & cream	vanilla	250	23
crème brulée	custard	320	19
dulce de leche	caramel	270	15
english toffee	vanilla	270	18
Irish cream	irish cream	260	17
macadamia brittle	vanilla	280	16

Figure 14.4: A ROW BAR ALLOWS EASIER ROW SELECTION.

14.3 Extension Points

As has been a constant theme throughout the book, extension points allow JavaScript-based handlers to add or change widget behavior. In a Grid, extension points exist at the cell, view, and Grid levels.

Cell-Level Extension Points: Derived Values with get

The cell provides a very useful extension point: get. You are already familiar with one way a cell gets data: from a dojo.data data store field, specified in the field property. There are two other ways:

- The value= property, which populates a constant value to each cell in a column

- The get= extension point, where you may plug a handler to calculate the data element

get= makes *derived cells* possible. Derived cells are so named because they derive their values from other data. You can add, subtract, and concatenate fields together to create a new value this way. And although it's true you can do this on the server and send the results down, using get saves the bandwidth of doing so.

As an example, the handler on the next page calculates the total calories per fat gram of a particular ice cream flavor.

---

should be cleared up in a later release.

```
grid/grid_definitions/derived.js
```

```
Line 1   dojo.provide("dojobook.grid.grid_definitions.derived");

         (function() {
            var gd=dojobook.grid.grid_definitions.derived;
5
            gd.getCaloriesPerFatGram = function(inRowIndex) {
               // This is standard for many grid handlers
               if (!icGrid) { return; }

10             var currentRow = icGrid.model.getRow(inRowIndex);
               if (! currentRow)  // Skip header rows
                   return;

               return currentRow.calories / currentRow.fat;
15          };
         })();
```

The code in line 8 will appear often in our examples, so it's worth picking it apart. In our main HTML, we will include the class like this:

```
grid/grid_derived.html
```

```
dojo.registerModulePath("dojobook","../../dojobook");
dojo.require("dojox.grid.Grid");
dojo.require("dojo.data.ItemFileReadStore");
dojo.require("dojobook.grid.grid_definitions.derived");
icGrid = null;
```

Eventually the Grid widget will be placed in the icGrid, but we initialize it to null to prevent reference errors. The parser creates the Grid widget before it can be assigned to variable named in jsId. In our case, jsId is icGrid. But get is called while the widget is being created and icGrid has not been filled yet. Although there are clever tricks to get a Grid reference in its half-finished state, luckily you don't have to resort to them. Grid makes a preliminary pass over the rows, then instantiates the object icGrid, and then makes another pass. With icGrid properly initialized, the second pass's calls to get work fine.

Line 10 is another common idiom. The goal is to get the data in the current row. You start from icGrid, the Grid widget. icGrid.model designates the entire Grid model, in other words, all the data. A model's getRow function returns a hash whose properties match the data store item. Since getCaloriesPerFatGram is also called on the column header where there is no associated item, getRow returns **null** in this case, and the function returns without a value. Otherwise, it returns the calculation, which is then displayed.

With the function written, you plug it into the get property:

`grid/grid_definitions/derived.js`

```
[
    {name: 'Mixins', field:"mixins",colSpan:3},
    {name: 'Cal / Fat g',
     get: gd.getCaloriesPerFatGram
     }
```

Everything is hunky-dory. With this technique, you can derive all kinds of formulas on the fly. And as we see in the next section, that includes formulas running across multiple rows.

Aggregate Functions and the onBeforeRow Extension Point

An *aggregate function* is a derived value function calculated over a set of rows. Summing, averaging, or finding the maximum value are popular examples. The challenge with aggregates isn't computing them properly. The function itself is easy. Displaying the aggregates in the right places requires a few tricks.

Suppose you want to average the calorie count over base flavors. Are chocolate-based ice creams more fattening than vanilla-based? Here's your chance to find out. Your first thought might be, "Just sort the data by base flavor, define another row type for subtotals, and stick those in between the regular rows." The trouble is you can't just invent row types and stick them in willy-nilly.

So, how do you pull it off? It turns out you can easily *hide* subrows at will. So if you define a subrow holding the cumulative totals for each row and then hide the subrows that are not on group boundaries, you end up with the grid you want.

Let's take those tasks one at a time. First, you'll insert the subrows with cumulative averages. A cumulative average means "What is the average calories for base flavor X that we have seen so far?"

Grouping by base flavor makes sense only when the rows are sorted by base flavor. That's easy in the Grid tag:

`grid/grid_subtotals.html`

```
<div id="grid" dojoType="dojox.grid.Grid" jsId="icGrid"
            store="icStore"
    sortFields='[ {attribute: "baseFlavor"} ]'
            clientSort="false"
            style="width: 35em; height: 15em;"
    structure="dojobook.grid.grid_definitions.subtotals.structure"
    >
</div>
```

Averages require a cumulative sum and an item count, and that's where the view's onBeforeRow extension point comes in. The handler you provide is called once for each row before anything is drawn. The signature is as follows:

```
onBeforeRow(Integer inRowIndex, Hash[] inSubrows )
```

inRowIndex is the current row number, just like in get. The inSubrows array will be important in a bit. For now, we provide our own handler to do the averages. Note that the subtotaling row is the *first* subrow. That's necessary because you don't know that whether you've hit a group boundary until the group changes. So if rows 6 and 7 contain cotton candy and row 8 contains custard, then:

- Row 6's first subrow will average the group before cotton candy.

- Row 7's first subrow will average the cotton candy group so far, which is just one element in row 6.

- Row 8's first subrow will again average the cotton candy group so far: rows 6 and 7.

- Row 9's first subrow will begin averaging the custard group so far: row 8.

Having the plan spelled out, here's the code:

grid/grid_definitions/subtotals.js

```
dojo.provide("dojobook.grid.grid_definitions.subtotals");

(function() {
    var gs=dojobook.grid.grid_definitions.subtotals;

    // Here are our running totals
    gs.baseFlavorAveraged = null;
    gs.currentBaseFlavor = null;
    gs.flavorTotalCal = 0;
    gs.flavorGroupCount = 1;

    gs.runningAverage = function(inDataIndex, inSubrows) {
        if (!icGrid) { return; }

        var currentRow = icGrid.model.getRow(inDataIndex);
        if (! currentRow) { // Return on header row
            return;
        }

        // Calculate stats for the group to this point
        gs.flavorAvg = gs.flavorTotalCal / gs.flavorGroupCount;
        gs.baseFlavorAveraged = gs.currentBaseFlavor;
```

```
          // If we're not on a new base flavor, increment the counts
          if (gs.flavorGroupCount==0  //
              || gs.currentBaseFlavor == currentRow.baseFlavor) {
              gs.flavorGroupCount++;
              gs.flavorTotalCal += currentRow.calories;
          } else {
              // Reset stats
              gs.flavorTotalCal = currentRow.calories;
              gs.flavorGroupCount = 1;
              gs.currentBaseFlavor = currentRow.baseFlavor;
          }
      };
```

The first few lines of runningAverage look just like a get handler. The last few do the actual averaging and resetting the totals.

onBeforeRow is a view extension point, so it belongs in the view definition. The cells define two get handlers that merely return the current running average and group name computed by runningAverage:

grid/grid_definitions/subtotals.js
```
// View #2: The data
{
  onBeforeRow: gs.runningAverage,

  cells: [
      [
          { name: 'N/A', width:'10em', value:'<b>Avg for </b>'},
          { name: 'N/A', width:'7em',
            get: function() { return gs.baseFlavorAveraged;  } },
          { name: 'N/A', width:'5em',
            get: function() { return gs.flavorAvg;  } },
          { name: 'N/A', width:'5em', value:'' }
      ],
      [
          {name: 'Flavor', width:'10em', field:"name" },
```

Note that when doing subtotals like this, it's best to specify all the column widths outright. In Figure 14.5, on the next page, you can see the results so far, with averages printing on each subrow.

That's looking good so far. Now we just need to hide the averages in between group boundaries. You can do this through the inSubRows array passed to the onBeforeRow handler. inSubRows closely mirrors the cell definitions for this view. So, inSubRows[0] will contain the averages subrow, and inSubRows[1] contains the data subrow. Then you just set the subrow's hidden to true to hide the subrow.

N/A	N/A	N/A	N/A
Flavor	Base Flavor	Calorie:	Fat
Avg for	chocolate	265	
triple chocolate	chocolate	300	21
Avg for	chocolate	288	
chocolate	chocolate	270	18
Avg for	chocolate	285	

Figure 14.5: Averaging calories per base flavor, printed every row

So as we loop through rows, it's a matter of setting inSubRows(0).hidden to false. Here's the doctored-up runningAverage with the code inserted in lines 4 and 23:

grid/grid_definitions/subtotals.js

```
Line 1   gs.runningAverage = function(inDataIndex, inSubrows) {
    -        if (!icGrid) { return; }
    -        // Turn off the subrow initially, making rendering a bit faster.
    -        inSubrows[0].hidden = true;
    5
    -        var currentRow = icGrid.model.getRow(inDataIndex);
    -        if (! currentRow) { // Return on header row
    -            return;
    -        }
    10
    -        // Calculate stats for the group to this point
    -        gs.flavorAvg = gs.flavorTotalCal / gs.flavorGroupCount;
    -        gs.baseFlavorAveraged = gs.currentBaseFlavor;
    -
    15       // If we're not on a new base flavor, increment the counts
    -        if (gs.flavorGroupCount==0  //
    -                || gs.currentBaseFlavor == currentRow.baseFlavor) {
    -            gs.flavorGroupCount++;
    -            gs.flavorTotalCal += currentRow.calories;
    20       } else {
    -            // Unhide the row, except for the very first one
    -            // (which totals nothing)
    -            if (gs.currentBaseFlavor)
    -                inSubrows[0].hidden = false;
    25
    -            // Reset stats
    -            gs.flavorTotalCal = currentRow.calories;
    -            gs.flavorGroupCount = 1;
    -            gs.currentBaseFlavor = currentRow.baseFlavor;
    30       }
    -    };
```

Now the Grid, shown in Figure 14.6, on the facing page, looks just right.

Grouping and aggregate computation is tremendously useful. Besides doing averages and such, onBeforeRow can selectively expand and collapse groups by setting the hidden property on or off accordingly. You can tie these expando buttons at each group boundary. This helps users scan a smaller list and then drill down into the groups they want.

Row Selection

Working our way up from cell-level extension points like get to view-level extension points like onBeforeRow, we arrive at Grid-level extension points. Two of these, onSelect and onDeselect, act at the Grid level because a row may span multiple views. Recall that users can select rows one of two ways: by clicking a read-only cell or by clicking a row bar (provided you added one). onSelect helps implement the popular spreadsheet edit cycle: select your rows and then do something to them.

You will put onSelect to use in an ice cream calorie counter. The user selects their favorite flavors, and a combined calorie count appears at the bottom of the screen.

The approach is to start the counter at zero, then add calories when a user selects a row, and subtract calories when a user deselects a row. Like our other extension points, onSelect and onDeselect get passed a rowIndex for the row selected or deselected. But unlike our other extension points, the handlers will be placed on the HTML side where the Grid widget lives. In our case, we put as little code in the HTML as possible, delegating the addition task to a JavaScript method:

`grid/grid_actions.html`

```
<div id="grid" dojoType="dojox.grid.Grid"
    jsId="icGrid"
    store="icStore"
    clientSort="false"
    style="width: 35em; height: 15em;"
    structure="dojobook.grid.grid_definitions.actions.structure">
    <script type="dojo/method" event="onSelected" args="inRowIndex">
        dojobook.grid.grid_definitions.actions.updateCalories(inRowIndex, +1);
    </script>
    <script type="dojo/method" event="onDeselected" args="inRowIndex">
        dojobook.grid.grid_definitions.actions.updateCalories(inRowIndex, -1);
    </script>
</div>

<h3>You have selected <span id="numberCalories">no</span> calories so far.</h3>
```

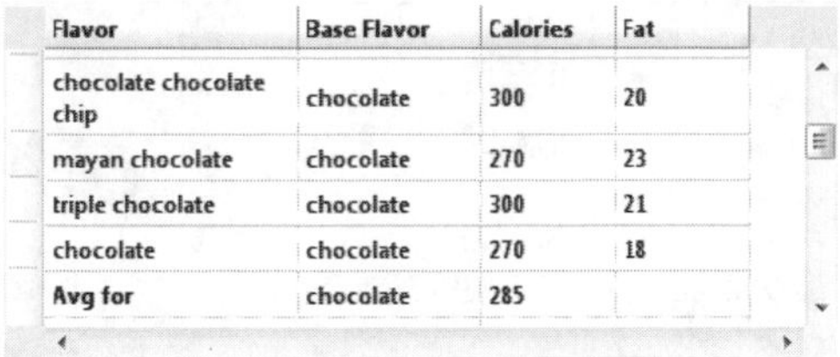

Flavor	Base Flavor	Calories	Fat
chocolate chocolate chip	chocolate	300	20
mayan chocolate	chocolate	270	23
triple chocolate	chocolate	300	21
chocolate	chocolate	270	18
Avg for	chocolate	285	

Figure 14.6: WITH SUBROW HIDING, AVERAGES APPEAR ONLY WHERE THEY SHOULD.

The addition function, then, is fairly straightforward:

`grid/grid_definitions/actions.js`

```
dojo.provide("dojobook.grid.grid_definitions.actions");

(function() {
   var ga=dojobook.grid.grid_definitions.actions;

   ga.numberCalories = 0;

   ga.updateCalories = function(rowIndex, direction) {
      var gridRow = icGrid.model.getRow(rowIndex);
      ga.numberCalories += direction * gridRow.calories;
      dojo.byId("numberCalories").innerHTML = ga.numberCalories;
   };
})();
```

The result is shown in Figure 14.7, on the next page. Note that unlike our other handlers, we don't have to check for icGrid's definition. Since these extension points are always called on user input, which can't happen until everything has been initialized, icGrid is always populated.

Mouse and Keyboard Events

For finer control, Grid defines extension points for many of the common DOM mouse and keyboard events (Chapter 6, *Asynchronous Programming*, on page 95, gives the full scoop on Dojo events). They pass an event object to the handler, just like the general DOM extension points do.

So, why would you want to use them? First, they're more granular. You can catch a MouseOver event at the cell level using the onCellMouseOver extension point, at the Row level with the onRowMouseOver extension point, or at the Grid level with the onMouseOver extension point. The

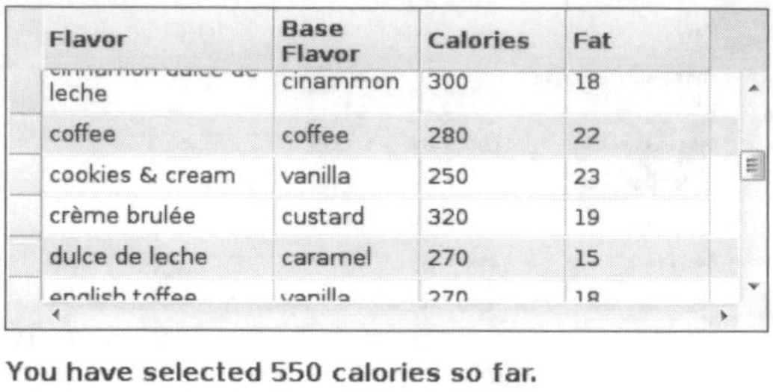

You have selected 550 calories so far.

Figure 14.7: ROW SELECTION AND DYNAMIC UPDATE

MouseOver event bubbles to the top, executing onCellMouseOver first, then onRowMouseOver, and then onMouseOver. You can place your code at the level that makes most sense.

Second, Grid *decorates* the event object with Grid-specific information. So if you write the handler for onMouseOver(evt), evt will have the following properties besides the normal target, and so forth:

- evt.grid is the underlying Grid.
- evt.rowIndex is the row number in the Grid.
- evt.cell is the cell information with field name and styles.

That saves you from having to translate target's coordinates into a usable location. evt.grid.model.getRow(evt.rowIndex) gives you all the data used in that row, from which you can derive information to display or use.

Here are all the extension points available. There are five variations of each handler: plain (which applies to the entire Grid), Row, Header, Cell, or HeaderCell:

```
on[Header | HeaderCell | Cell | Row]MouseOver(Event evt)
on[Header | HeaderCell | Cell | Row]MouseDown(Event evt)
on[Header | HeaderCell | Cell | Row]MouseOut(Event evt)
on[Header | HeaderCell | Cell | Row]Click(Event evt)
on[Header | HeaderCell | Cell | Row]DoubleClick(Event evt)
on[Header | HeaderCell | Cell | Row]ContextMenu(Event evt)
on[Header | HeaderCell | Cell | Row]Focus(Event evt)
```

As a small example, here's another space-saving alternative for the Grid. Instead of placing the Mixins field on the Grid, have the user click the flavor name. The mixins will pop up in a Toaster off to the left.

First, place the Toaster widget and onCellClick extension point handler in the Grid:

grid/grid_mouse_events.html

```
<div id="grid" dojoType="dojox.grid.Grid"
    jsId="icGrid"
    store="icStore"
    clientSort="false"
    style="width: 35em; height: 15em;"
    structure="dojobook.grid.grid_definitions.mouse_events.structure">
    <script type="dojo/method" event="onCellClick" args="evt">
        dojobook.grid.grid_definitions.mouse_events.showMixins(evt);
    </script>
</div>

<div dojoType="dojox.widget.Toaster" duration="1000"
    messageTopic="toasterInfo" positionDirection="tr-left" />
```

Then, the handler can interpret the location of the click, relative to the Grid. In order to make sure the user is in the right column, it checks evt.cell.name to make sure we're in the correct column. Finally, you can use the Grid and rowIndex to look up the actual data in the customary fashion:

grid/grid_definitions/mouse_events.js

```
dojo.provide("dojobook.grid.grid_definitions.mouse_events");

(function() {
   var gme=dojobook.grid.grid_definitions.mouse_events;

   gme.showMixins = function(evt) {
      // Only display when clicking a flavor
      if (evt.cell.name != 'Flavor')
          return;
      var gridRow = icGrid.model.getRow(evt.rowIndex);
      dojo.publish("toasterInfo",["Contains "+gridRow.mixins]);
   };
})();
```

In this section, we sampled the most popular extension points at all levels of the Grid. There are more listed in the API guide at http://dojotoolkit. org. They permit almost limitless freedom in bending the Grid to match your needs.

14.4 Cell Editing

Just as trees allow you to add, edit, or remove nodes, Grid allows on-the-fly data changes. Cell editing requires the data driver to implement dojo.data.Write and dojo.data.Notification. The edits come from two sources:

User-initiated edits By attaching an editor property to a cell, you make it user-editable. Users can double-click the cell;[3] change its data; and then ⎡Tab⎤, ⎡Enter⎤, or click out of the cell to save changes. Pressing ⎡Esc⎤ cancels the edit. Grid writes the new value back to the data store and fires a dojo.data.Notification event.

JavaScript-initiated edits You can call the dojo.data.Write methods to add, remove, or edit data store rows. Grid picks up these changes via dojo.data.Notification and writes them to the browser.

We won't have much to say here about JavaScript-initiated edits since the dojo.data.Write was covered in Chapter 13, *Tree*, on page 339. But there's much to say about user-initiated edits.

Using Cell Editors

Making a cell user-editable requires filling in its editor property with a Dojo class. You choose an editor based on the type of data and its ease of use for the data set. Some are simply Grid-compatible versions of Dijit form controls. The others were built especially for Grid and are called *native cell editors*. Grid bundles the following:

- dojox.grid.editors.Input (Native): A garden-variety textbox. Its property keyFilter is a regular expression you can fill in to disallow certain key presses in the box.

- dojox.grid.editors.Bool (Native): A garden-variety checkbox. Unlike all other cell editors, this one does not require double-clicking to invoke. You can click the checkbox on or off at any time.

- dojox.grid.editors.Select (Native): A garden-variety <select>. This accepts the properties options and values, two identically sized arrays holding the visible and passed-back values.

- dojox.grid.editors.ComboBox (Dijit): Like Select, but ignores the values array and can accept entries not in the options array.

---

3. Or you can single-click if the singleClickEdit= is set to **true** in the Grid tag.

- dojox.grid.editors.DateTextBox (Dijit): Accepts dates with a drop-down calendar.

- dojox.grid.editors.Editor (Dijit): Rich text editor.

- dojox.grid.editors.Dijit (Dijit): Uses the property editorClass to specify an arbitrary Dijit form control as an editor. If a constraint property is used (as in validation boxes), this is passed to the form control as a constraint.

Onscreen, you cannot tell the Dijit and native cell editors apart. But programmatically it's important to know the difference.

Dijit cell editors accept any properties that the corresponding Dijit control accepts. You place these properties in a hash and then place the hash in the editorProps cell property. We'll cover the details more fully in Chapter 15, *Form Controls*, on page 393. On the other hand, native cell editors have their own properties, which you use directly by name in the cell properties.

First we'll look at a Dijit cell editor. Ratings will be a number from 1 to 5, and we want to make sure only those legal values are used. Here's the cell definition:

`grid/grid_definitions/editors.js`
```
{ name: 'Rating', field:"rating",
  editor: dojox.grid.editors.Dijit,
  editorClass: "dijit.form.NumberTextBox",
  constraint: {min:1, max:5},
  editorProps: {required:true}
},
```

The editor property signals that the cell is editable. editorClass is set to the class of the form widget, in this case dijit.form.NumberTextBox, which ensures only numbers go in the box. We'll learn about the details in Section 15.4, *Numbers*, on page 411, but for now the constraint property sets the upper and lower bounds. The required property is familiar. We saw it back in Section 2.5, *Improved Form Controls*, on page 24 to require an entry in a field. By placing it in editorProps, it gets passed to the NumberTextBox as well.

Next, we'll look at a native cell editor. dojox.grid.editors.Select requires options to be passed in one or two arrays: a required options array and an optional value array.

grid/grid_definitions/editors.js

```
{ name: 'Source', field:'source',
  editor: dojox.grid.editors.Select,
  options: ['Restaurant', 'Qwik-E Mart', 'Wegmans' ],
  values: [ 1, 2, 3 ],
  formatter: function(inDatum) {
    return this.options[inDatum - 1];
  }
}
```

This code sets up the element <select>. The result looks like Figure 14.8, on the next page.

Cell editing is an addictive feature. Once users get used to it, they don't want to go back to the view-page/edit-page/view-page cycle of page refreshes. A spot change is quick and easy.

Cell Formatters: The format Extension Point

Hmmmmmm. What is that formatter property? It turns out Select needs a little help in displaying its data value. For example, if the source is 1, we want the value Restaurant displayed onscreen. Without some help, Grid will display 1. It will edit and save OK, though—the Select still shows the Restaurant choice, and if the user picks Wegmans, 3 is sent back to the data store. But now the display will say 3.

To fix this, you provide a handler for formatter that translates the number to a displayed value. This handler, unlike most other Grid extension points, receives only the raw data. No rowIndex- or Grid-specific context is sent.

In our case, we simply take the data value and use it as an index back into the options array (less 1, since the array is 0 based). For more sophisticated Selects, you may need to loop through all the value elements and then pick the corresponding entry from options.

The formatter extension point isn't just for Select. It's also handy for formatting currency, displaying tooltips, or truncating long values to fit in a column.

Data Synchronization

Cell editors all write changed values back to the data store. To prove this to yourself, you can hook into the onSet extension point provided by your driver's dojo.data.Notification feature.

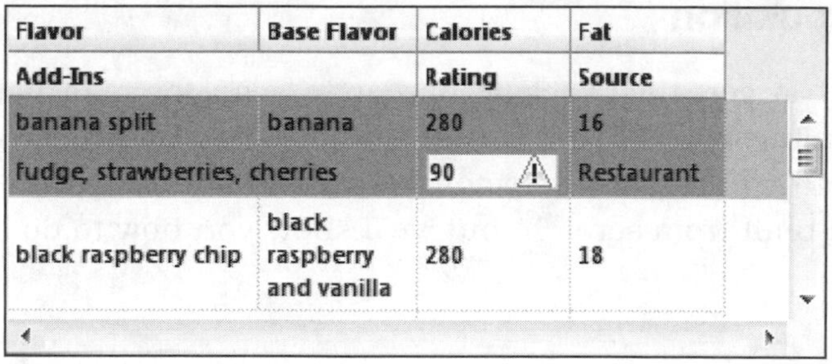

Figure 14.8: ENTERING RATINGS OUTSIDE THE RANGE YIELDS AN ERROR.

Here's a handler for our example:

grid/grid_editors.html

```
<span dojoType="dojo.data.ItemFileWriteStore"
    jsId="icStore" url="datastores/ice_cream.json">
    <script type="dojo/connect" event="onSet"
            args="item,attribute,oldValue,newValue">
        console.debug(attribute+" changed from "+oldValue+" to "+newValue);
    </script>
</span>
```

Now when you make an editing change, the console will display the corresponding item and the details.

Although editing changes are written to the in-memory copy of the data store, they are not automatically written back to the server. To do that, you need to write your own code for the onSet, onDelete, and onNew extension points. We covered this in Section 13.4, *Saving the Tree Back to the Server*, on page 352.

For convenience, Grid also defines the extension points...

```
onStartEdit(Hash inCell, Integer inRowIndex)
onApplyCellEdit(Object inValue, Hash inCell, Integer inRowIndex)
onCancelEdit(Integer inRowIndex)
```

which allow you to weave in custom code before the editing begins and after it ends. All of these are more Grid-centric than dojo.data-centric, passing the row index rather than an item. These are still good for doing display updates or UI work before the Notification extension points fire.

14.5 Grid Manipulation

As grids get larger, they become harder to scan for information. Two ways for dealing with that are sorting and filtering. Sorting comes built-in to Grid, but you can add some hints to make it more useful. Filtering needs to be built from scratch, but we'll show you how to do it.

Sorting

Sorting happens automagically in Grid. The user clicks a Grid column, and the rows sort accordingly. If the field contents are numbers, the sort is numerical, and if they are strings, it is alphabetical. Pretty straightforward.

There are two instances where you might need to change this behavior. The first is multikey sorts. In our example, clicking the Base Flavor column sorts fine, but the names within each group appear in no particular order. It'd be nice to sort each group by name as well. The second instance is where your sort criteria don't appear in the selected column. For example, suppose you display employees in a company by ranking so that the CEO appears at the top. But the rankings are kept in another data store field that is not displayed on the Grid. Since the default sort lists all employees in alpha order, you need some way to substitute the ranking as the sort column.

You can do either by replacing the Grid model's sort method. It's not as difficult as it sounds. sort is passed a column index—that is, the index of the clicked cell within the model (fields are assigned numbers in the same order they appear in the first record of your data source). Your sort routine will transform this into dojo.data sort criteria, as in [{attribute:'baseFlavor'}]; place it in the sortFields property; and redisplay the Grid. The dojo.data driver does the heavy lifting.

To change the baseFlavor column sorting behavior, you replace the sort routine like this:

```
grid/grid_sorting.html

Line 1  <div id="grid" dojoType="dojox.grid.Grid"
    -       jsId="icGrid"
    -       store="icStore"
    -       clientSort="true"
    5       style="width: 35em; height: 15em;"
    -       structure="dojobook.grid.grid_definitions.sorting.structure">
    -       <script type="dojo/method">
    -           this.model.sort = function(colIndex) {
    -               var col = Math.abs(colIndex) - 1;
```

```
10      var colNameToSort = this.fields.values[col].name;
        var sortDescending = (colIndex > 0);
        if (colNameToSort == 'baseFlavor') {
            this.sortFields = [
                {attribute: 'baseFlavor', descending: sortDescending},
15              {attribute: 'name', descending: sortDescending}
            ];
        } else {
                this.sortFields = [
                {'attribute': colNameToSort, 'descending': sortDescending}
20              ];
            }

                this.refresh();
        }
25  </script>
    </div>
```

Normally you replace methods by subclassing. In our case, it's easier just to replace the method for one JavaScript instance. In line 8, we replace the model's sort routine wholesale. When you click a column name, this sort routine will be called in lieu of the prototype. This method is sent a column index as a positive number if the sort is ascending and as a negative number if the sort is descending. Line 10 converts this to an attribute name. Then you simply replace the sort-Fields property with the right criteria. For base flavor sorts, our routine substitutes the multikey criteria at line 13. All other sorts go through unchanged. Finally, line 23 refreshes the model data, causing a refetch with the new sort criteria.

Filtering

Like sorting, *filtering* makes it easier to find interesting data in a large Grid. Popular in spreadsheet programs, a filter is a drop-down with a particular column's values in sorted order. Choosing an option filters the Grid down to just the rows whose value fits the filter. Usually you have one filter for each "interesting" column—that is, every column that has more than a few values, but not too many. (The identifier is not a good candidate for filtering.)

Grid does not have a native filtering mechanism, but you can bolt one on. Our job here will be adding a base flavor filter to our own grid. It'll look something like Figure 14.9, on the next page when finished.

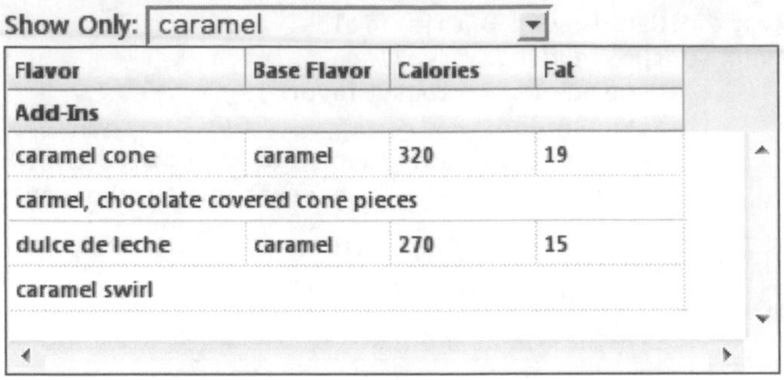

Figure 14.9: FILTERING A GRID BY BASE FLAVOR

The Grid itself remains unchanged, but we add a placeholder for the *<select>* above the grid:

```
grid/grid_filters.html
Show Only:
<select id="filterContainer"><option value="">[No Filter]</option></select>

<div id="grid" dojoType="dojox.grid.Grid"
    store="icStore"
    clientSort="true"
    jsId="icGrid"
    structure="dojobook.grid.grid_definitions.filters.structure"></div>
```

The most challenging part is filling the box with filter values. Here, you can take advantage of the data store that the Grid uses, since you are dipping from the same data pool.

loadFilter fetches all the items from the Grid's data store. (For a refresher course on fetch, see Section 10.4, *fetch and Pagination*, on page 272.) This routine and the actual Grid may be fetching at the same time. dojo.data drivers are usually smart enough to consolidate these requests, thus eliminating an unnecessary trip to the server. As you read in values, you store them in a hash. This gets rid of duplicates. At the end, you simply read and sort the values, constructing an *<option>* tag for each.

```
dojobook.grid.grid_definitions.filters.loadFilter = function() {
    // Store our filter values in a sorted set to automatically take
    // care of duplicates
    var filterHash = {};
    // The store is already set, so do a fetch on it

    icStore.fetch({
        query: { name: "*" },
        onItem: function(theItem) {
            // Fires on each item.  Set filterHash["vanilla"]
            // to true on seeing a vanilla baseFlavor
            filterHash[theItem.baseFlavor[0]] = true;
        },
        onComplete: function() {
            // Fires at the end of all loading.  First push the
            // baseFlavors into an array
            var sortedFilters = [];
            for (baseFlavorName in filterHash) {
                sortedFilters.push(baseFlavorName);
            }

            // Sort them
            sortedFilters.sort();

            // And create an option for each one
            var filterBox = dojo.byId("filterContainer").options;
            dojo.forEach(sortedFilters, function(bf) {
                filterBox[filterBox.length]= new Option(bf);
            });

            // And finally, connect it to a filtering event
            dojo.connect(dojo.byId("filterContainer"), 'change',
                dojobook.grid.grid_definitions.filters.applyFilter);
        }
    });

};

dojo.addOnLoad(dojobook.grid.grid_definitions.filters.loadFilter);
```

At the end of the load process, you connect the onChange event to your
filter handler. Doing the filtering is the easy part. You simply tell the
Grid model the new query and to refetch its contents. It's very similar to
our sort example.

A Grid is tremendously useful, and in most cases it's no more difficult
than building a table. Yet it's flexible and handles large amounts of data
with ease.

grid/grid_definitions/filters.js

```
dojobook.grid.grid_definitions.filters.applyFilter = function () {
    var currentValueBox = dojo.byId("filterContainer");
    var currentValue =
        currentValueBox.options[currentValueBox.selectedIndex].text;
    icGrid.model.query = { baseFlavor: currentValue || '*' };
    icGrid.model.refresh();
}
```

Sometimes, however, you need a traditional form and lots of editing power. As you will see in the next chapter, Dijit has got you covered there too.

Form Controls

We started our Dijit journey back in Chapter 2 with form controls. They were easy to pop in, and they did amazing things: enforcing field requirements, trimming and capitalizing strings, and popping up a calendar for easy date entry. Now that we've added Ajax magic, event-driven scripting, and other Dojo tools to our toolbelt, it's time to revisit form controls. When your application is a one-page Ajax-enabled form, the considerations are much different: you need to save space, make things more intuitive, and mirror the controls people use in word processors and spreadsheets. And since the world you can reach is much larger, you want controls that'll reach people in different countries and different physical circumstances.

Dijit has you covered. In this chapter, we'll fill in some details, introduce new widgets, and show you some things to watch out for.

15.1 Form Control Features

Dijit contains form controls for numbers, dates, and various forms of text. But no matter what they look like, they are all designed to make data input easy and then validate it, provide feedback, and ship it back to the server. So first we'll look at their commonalities.

Dijit Form Controls and Their HTML Counterparts

Every HTML form control has a Dijit counterpart. A form can mix and match Dijit form controls and plain HTML form controls, but the plain HTML controls won't follow the design theme and will look out of place. Also, using all-Dijit controls and boxing up your form in a dijit.form.Form tag, you can take advantage of form-wide validation.

Here are drop-in replacements for all the HTML controls:

HTML Control	Dijit Form Control
<input type="checkbox"/>	<div dojoType="dijit.form.Checkbox">
<input type="radio"/>	<div dojoType="dijit.form.RadioButton">
<select>...</select>	<div dojoType="dijit.form.FilteringSelect">
<input type="text"/>	<div dojoType="dijit.form.TextBox">
<textarea>...</textarea>	<div dojoType="dijit.form.SimpleTextArea">
<button/>	<div dojoType="dijit.form.Button">

You can use the same HTML attributes in the Dijit replacement with no problems. Generally, the widget version is used in a <*div*> or <*span*> tag. They *can* be used in their native tag as well—so you can put a dojoType="dijit.form.ValidationTextBox" attribute in an <*input*> tag. This allows *degradation*, meaning a browser can still render the form if JavaScript is unavailable. The minus is you can't define extension point handlers inside an <*input*> tag, since most browsers don't accept a <*input*></*input*> pair.

Common Methods

Form controls in Dijit are descendents of the class dijit.form._FormWidget (itself a subclass of dijit._Widget). This bestows the following properties:

- Given that formWidget is a form widget, formWidget.value is the current value. Even though form controls are often written in <*div*> tags, they act mostly like an <*input*> box in that respect. However, you *cannot* set this property. Instead, you must use formWidget.setValue to set it.

- Every form widget responds to the following...
  ```
  formWidget.setAttribute("disabled", «Boolean»)
  formWidget.setAttribute("readOnly", «Boolean»)
  ```
  to disable the widget or set it to read-only mode. To the user they act the same, but disabled controls are not submitted with the form and read-only ones are.

- Every form widget can include the attributes name=, alt=, value=, type=, and tabindex=, which act exactly like their HTML counterparts.

- formWidget.focus() sets the focus on that widget.

- The extension point formWidget.onChange exists universally. Unlike the DOM Level 0 onchange event, the onChange handler receives the new value as a parameter.

- formWidget.undo restores the original value upon entering the field (for example, the value at the last onChange event).

Form Submission

You can submit a Dijit form one of two ways: by a normal HTML form submit or by XHR. The former method is fairly straightforward. You simply add dojoType="dijit.form.Form" to the <*form*> tag, and all validations will be checked when the user clicks the submit button. If you try to submit an invalid form, as in Figure 15.1, on the next page, the Form widget will highlight all the invalid fields and set the focus on the first invalid control.

Using XHR requires a manual step. Before calling the dojo.xhr* method in an extension point like onChange or onClick, you need to make sure the form elements meet their validation criteria. To do this, simply call the form widget's validate method like this:

```
form_controls/isvalid.html
<form dojoType="dijit.form.Form" name="mojoform" id="mojoform">
    <p style="margin-top:200px;width:300px;">
    Got my Mojo workin' but it just don't work on
    <span dojoType="dijit.form.ValidationTextBox"
          required="true" name="who"></span>
    </p>

    <button dojoType="dijit.form.Button">
        Submit
        <script type="dojo/method" event="onClick">
            if (dijit.byId("mojoform").validate()) {
                dojo.xhrPost({
                    url: "controller.html",
                    form: "mojoform",
                    load: function() {
                        console.log("Form successfully submitted");
                    },
                    error: function() {
                        console.error("Error on submission");
                    }
                });
            }
        </script>
    </button>
</form>
```

A **false** return value means some fields are invalid. Like using a submit button, validate highlights all the invalid fields for you.

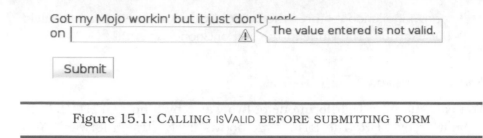

Figure 15.1: CALLING ISVALID BEFORE SUBMITTING FORM

15.2 Streamlined Editing

In a traditional web application, the view and add/edit modes usually have distinct pages. A view page can cram more information than an add/edit form. Form controls take up more room than text.

In the Ajax world, where you typically stay on one page, you've got a space problem. If you turn all the changeable elements into HTML form elements, you crowd out all the useful view page information.

Dijit has two space-saving methods to help: dialog boxes and inline editing. The former overlays a form on top of the existing page, while the latter switches parts of the page from view mode to edit mode with a simple click.

Dialog and TooltipDialog

A dialog box acts like a web form on a sticky note. By overlaying the view page underneath it, the dialog box can use room for more form controls. Dijit has two kinds of dialog boxes:

- dijit.Dialog is a modal, user-closable dialog box. It must be opened through a JavaScript method call.

- dijit.TooltipDialog connects to a DropDownButton (which we'll look at in detail in Section 15.5, *Action Buttons, Toolbars, and Menus*, on page 417). When the user clicks the button, the dialog box appears underneath. Unlike the modal dijit.Dialog, this dialog box cannot be opened or closed programmatically. The user may close it by clicking anywhere outside the dialog box.

Because dialog boxes often submit their own form data, most of them have *<form>* tags on the inside (hopefully using dojoType="dijit.form.Form" to take advantage of validation). It's tempting to place the dialog box close to the control invoking it. But if the dialog box's form is itself in a main page form, you'll have problems submitting the main form. HTML form tags, as you probably know already, cannot be nested. For this reason, it's best to place all dialog boxes toward the bottom of your HTML page.

In Figure 15.2, on the next page, you can see a modal dialog box, drawn from the following code:

form_controls/dialog_box.html

```
<div dojoType="dijit.form.Button">
    Guess the Singer
    <script type="dojo/method" event="onClick">
        dlg.show();
    </script>
</div>

<div dojoType="dijit.Dialog" jsId="dlg">
    <div>
        <label for="singer">Singer:</label>
        <span dojoType="dijit.form.TextBox" id="singer"></span>
    </div>

    <div>
        <label for="singer">Date of Guess:</label>
        <span dojoType="dijit.form.DateTextBox"></span>
    </div>

    <div dojoType="dijit.form.Button">
        Go
        <script type="dojo/method" event="onClick">
            // Do a submit here
            dlg.hide();
        </script>
    </div>
</div>
```

Note that this dialog box can be moved by the title bar, as is common with dialog boxes in windowed operating systems. The background is shaded with an opaque gray—you can see the underlying data, but you cannot move the focus to it without dismissing the dialog box first.

A dijit.TooltipDialog is a little less obtrusive. As soon as you click outside of it, the dialog box will disappear without action.

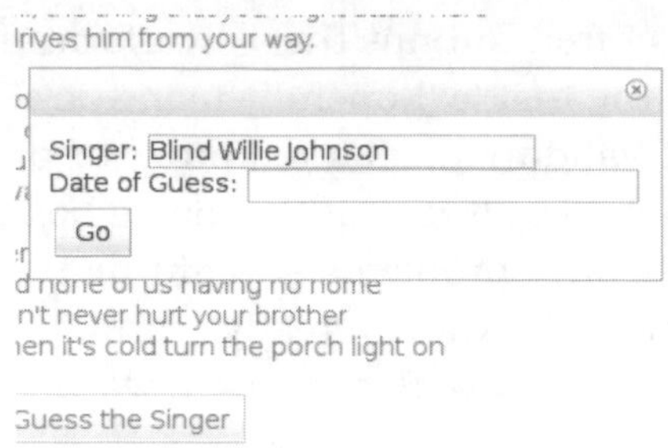

Figure 15.2: A DIJIT.DIALOGBOX CONTROL

In Figure 15.3, on the facing page, you can see a TooltipDialogin action. The code that draws it is a lot like a Dialog:

`form_controls/tooltip_dialog_box.html`

```
<div dojoType="dijit.form.DropDownButton">
    <span>Print</span>
    <div dojoType="dijit.TooltipDialog" jsId="dlg">
        <div>
            <label for="copies">Copies:</label>
            <span dojoType="dijit.form.NumberSpinner"
                id="copies" value="1"></span>
        </div>
        <div dojoType="dijit.form.Button" type="submit">
            Go
        </script>
        </div>
    </div>
 </div>
```

The dijit.form.NumberSpinner is a simple integer textbox. It's frequently a good alternative to full-blown validating controls when the numbers are likely to be small.

There are two things to remember with TooltipDialog:

- You must *always* use it inside a dijit.DropDownButton. It looks like a dijit.Button widget, but it requires the button text to be inside an HTML tag—usually a <*span*> tag. (We'll cover this in detail in Section 15.5, *Action Buttons, Toolbars, and Menus*, on page 417.)

- You must use the line dojo.require("dijit.Dialog"); to include it. This is one of those rare times that the control name does not match the module name.

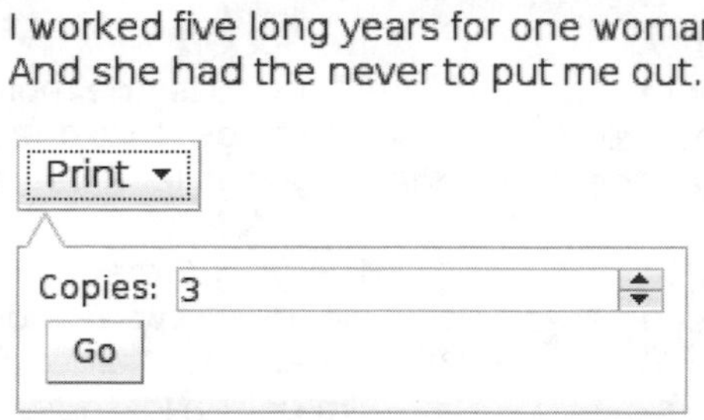

I worked five long years for one woman
And she had the never to put me out.

Print ▾

Copies: 3 ⬍
Go

Figure 15.3: A DIJIT.TOOLTIPDIALOG CONTROL

Inline Editing

As we saw in Chapter 14, *Grid*, on page 365, dijit.Grid has a nice inline cell-editing system. You tell Grid which editor control to use in a particular column, and Grid then allows the user to double-click the cell, edit it, and then save it back. The Grid-editing paradigm was so useful, it inspired a more general inline editing widget that works in any kind of form.

dijit.InlineEditBox is more of a container widget than a stand-alone widget. InlineEditBox hands most of the work off to a Dijit form control. You wrap a piece of text, a date, a number, or whatever with an InlineEditBox widget like this:

`form_controls/inline_number_edit.html`

```
<div style="width:350px">
    I've got
    <span dojoType="dijit.InlineEditBox"
        editor="dijit.form.NumberSpinner"
        width="100px">
        99
    </span>
     
    <span dojoType="dijit.InlineEditBox"
        editor="dijit.form.FilteringSelect"
        editorParams="{store: genderStore, autocomplete: true}"
        width="150px"
        >women</span>.
    </span>
    <br/>
    All I need is one more<br/>
    When I get that one, pallie <br/>
    Gonna let the other ones go<br/>
</div>
```

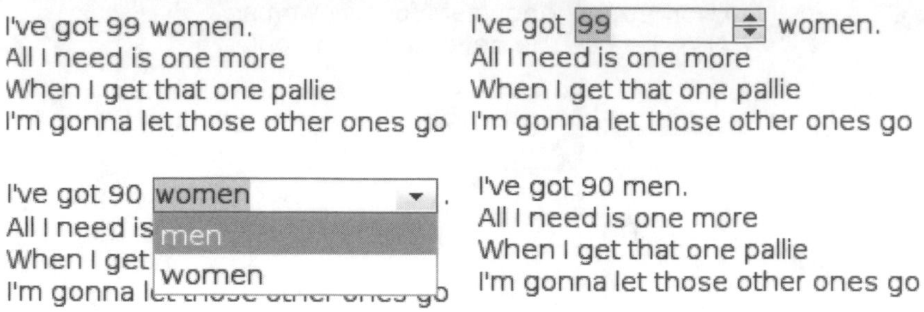

I've got 99 women.
All I need is one more
When I get that one pallie
I'm gonna let those other ones go

I've got 99 ⬍ women.
All I need is one more
When I get that one pallie
I'm gonna let those other ones go

I've got 90 women ▼ .
All I need is men
When I get women
I'm gonna let those other ones go

I've got 90 men.
All I need is one more
When I get that one pallie
I'm gonna let those other ones go

Figure 15.4: Using InlineEditBox to update an old blues tune

The two inline boxes are independently editable, as you can see in Figure 15.4. A couple of things are worth nothing:

- To change the width of the inline editor, you must use the width= attribute. Width specified in a CSS style is ignored.

- The editor= attribute specifies the Dijit control class. You must remember to dojo.require that control class in the page.

- editorParams= specifies attributes to send to the editor control. It is a hash, just like you would use in a programmatic widget constructor call.

Text Editing

While we're on the topic of inline editing, it's also a good time to talk about multiline text editing. Dijit provides two widgets for this: dijit.form.SimpleTextarea, which emulates a fixed-height fixed-width textbox, and dijit.form.Textarea, which is a box that expands at the bottom as you fill it with text. The latter widget is useful for saving screen real estate, since you use only the editing area you need to fit the text.

dijit.form.SimpleTextarea and dijit.form.Textarea

SimpleTextarea takes the same standard HTML attributes as <textarea>. TextArea does too except for rows= and cols=. Since Textarea= expands at the bottom, the rows= attribute doesn't make sense.

And because Dijit uses proportional fonts, the cols= attribute is meaningless as well. Instead, you should specify the width in the style or CSS class of the widget.

Viewing
    The woman I love took from my best friend
    Some joker got lucky stole her back again
    You better come on in my kitchen

Editing
    The woman I love took from my best friend
    Some joker got lucky stole her back again
    You better come on in my kitchen
    It's going to be raining outdoors

Figure 15.5: TURNING DISPLAYED TEXT TO EDITABLE TEXT

Finally, TextArea works very well in conjunction with an InlineEditBox, as you can see in Figure 15.5. You can rope off a section of text with an inline edit using dijit.form.Textarea as the editor and turn a paragraph of displayed text into an editable field, as shown in this example:

form_controls/textarea.html

```
<div style="width:350px">
    <div dojoType="dijit.InlineEditBox"
        editor="dijit.form.Textarea">
        The woman I love took from my best friend<br/>
        Some joker got lucky stole her back again<br/>
        You better come on in my kitchen<br/>
    </div>
</div>
```

Like all inline edits, you can read the TextArea's getValue property to send the contents back to the server when editing ends.

Rich Text Editor

For more industrial-strength text editing, Dijit includes the rich text editor dijit.Editor. This widget offers HTML-backed editing with a handy toolbar and keyboard shortcuts. It's like embedding a little word processor in a form field, as you can see in Figure 15.6, on the next page.

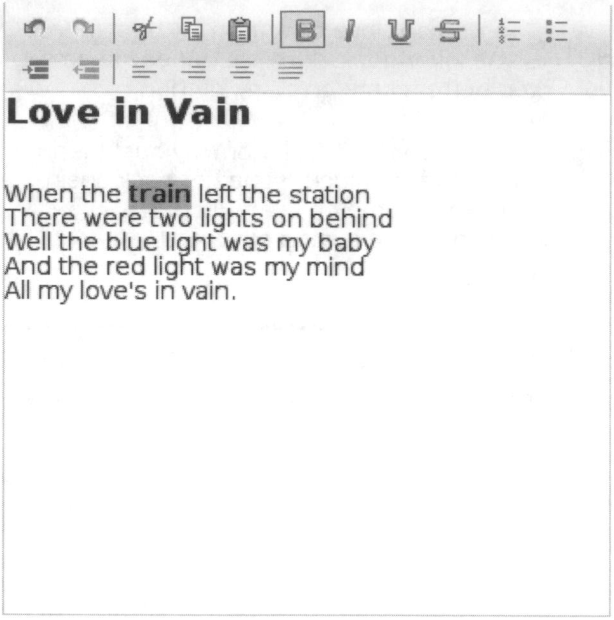

Figure 15.6: DIJIT'S RICH TEXT EDITOR

There are two ways to embed the editor. The first is with a fixed width and height box:

`form_controls/fixed_editor.html`

```
<div style="width:350px;height:500px">
    <div dojoType="dijit.Editor"
    >
        <h2>Love in Vain</h2>
        <br/>
        When the train left the station<br/>
        There were two lights on behind<br/>
        Well the blue light was my baby<br/>
        And the red light was my mind<br/>
        All my love's in vain.
    </div>
</div>
```

The second is a slight variant that marries the download-expanding dijit.form.Textarea widget with a rich text palette. This is achieved by adding the height="" attribute and then loading the dijit._editor.plugins. AlwaysShowToolbar plug-in (we'll discuss plug-ins in a bit).

```
form_controls/fixed_editor.html
```

```
<div dojoType="dijit.Editor"
    height=""
    extraPlugins="['dijit._editor.plugins.AlwaysShowToolbar']"
    ></div>
```

Note the toolbar on top of Figure 15.6, on the facing page. This has standard icons for (in order) undo and redo, cut, copy and paste, bold, italic, underline and strikethrough, numbering and bullets, left and right indentation, and left/right/center justification. Since these are pretty familiar in modern GUI applications, users will recognize them right away.

Occasionally, though, you may want to customize the editing toolbar. For instance, you might want to limit the toolbar choices to Bold and Italic. You can use the attribute to specify exactly which plug-ins to load:

```
<div dojoType="dijit.Editor" plugins="['bold','|','italic']" />
```

Here the pipe symbol (|) creates a separator bar between buttons. The complete set of toolbar buttons, as they need to appear in the plugins= attribute, are as follows:

- undo and redo
- cut, copy, and paste
- bold, italic, underline, and strikethrough
- insertOrderedList and insertUnorderedList
- indent and outdent
- justifyLeft, justifyRight, justifyCenter, and justifyFull

In addition, you can add the following optional plug-ins. Unlike the standard buttons mentioned earlier, these plug-ins need a dojo.require to make them work. Each plug-in has optional properties, so include them as hashes within your plugins= attribute like this:

```
plugins="['bold','italic','|', {
        name:'dijit._editor.plugins.FontChoice',
        command:'fontName', generic:true
    }]"
```

dijit._editor.plugins.FontChoice

> fontName: A drop-down box for choosing a font. If you set the generic property to true, the generic HTML font families (monospace, serif, and so on) are listed. Otherwise, the common web font families (Arial, Times New Roman, and so on) are listed.

>>> fontSize: A drop-down box for standard relative font sizes 1–7.
>>>
>>> formatBlock: A drop-down box for standard paragraph-level styles (p, h1, h2, and so on).

dijit._editor.plugins.AlwaysShowToolbar

Use this plug-in when planning for potentially large textboxes. It keeps the toolbar at the top of the window no matter where the editor is. Without it, if the edit box expands to a height larger than the browser window, the toolbar will scroll offscreen, and you won't be able to use it for sentences at the bottom of the box.

dijit._editor.plugins.EnterKeyHandling

Used primarily for Internet Explorer so each new line does not become a new paragraph. Its property blockNodeForEnter defines the HTML tag used when the user presses Enter. This defaults to br but can also be div or p.

dijit._editor.plugins.LinkDialog

>>> createLink: Inserts a hypertext link
>>>
>>> insertImage: Adds an image tag

dijit._editor.plugins.TextColor

>>> foreColor: Sets the foreground color
>>>
>>> hiliteColor: Sets the background color

One last note: To enable cut, copy, and paste from other windows to Firefox, see http://www.mozilla.org/editor/midasdemo/securityprefs.html.

15.3 Feedback

Besides streamlining, one-page applications have another challenge. If the browser is doing something in the background, how do you signal this? And if something changes on the page, how do you indicate that it happened? In traditional apps, these are both communicated through a page change.

One technique for indicating change is the Yellow Fade Technique, which you saw on Section 7.5, *Animating with dojo.animateProperty*, on page 165. This technique indicates something has changed by turning the changed element to a background yellow (like a highlighter) and fading the yellow down to white over a matter of seconds.

Sometimes for the user's sake, you must be more specific about what's happening. In those cases, you can use Dijit tooltips, progress bars, and toasters.

Tooltips

Tooltips and balloon help have become pervasive user interface elements in web and client-server applications.

Dijit tooltips are like the title= attribute, but unlike title=, you can display large amounts of text with HTML inside. To make them more visible, you can place them in other places relative to the mouse pointer.

There are two kinds of tooltips. An *anchored* tooltip uses the widget class dijit.Tooltip. The anchor means you're tying it to a particular element, and the tooltip is visible only when hovering over that element. The following code...

```
form_controls/anchored_tooltip.html
```

```html
<p style="margin-top:200px;width:300px;">
What's that making your tongue flippy-flop?
When you drink a <span style="color:purple" id="def">NuGrape</span>
you don't know when to stop.
I got your ice cold
<span style="color:purple" id="def2">NuGrape.</span></p>

<span dojoType="dijit.Tooltip" connectId="def,def2"
      style="display:none;">NuGrape is a
      <span style="color:purple">grape soda</span>.
      <p style="width:150px">First bottled in 1921, its
      strange, barrelhouse- inspired jingle <em>I Got Your
      Ice Cold NuGrape</em> is
      a favorite among roots music snobs.</p>
      </span>
```

produces the tooltip shown in Figure 15.7, on the following page. Note that dijit.Tooltip widgets can appear anywhere in the page, but like dijit. Dialog tags, they are best placed at the bottom so as not to disrupt the document flow. Setting the style to display:none keeps them invisible when drawing the page.

What anchors them to elements is the id= attribute of the anchors and the connectId= attribute of the Tooltip tag. In our case, connectId= connects to two anchors: the two instances of "NuGrape."

Anchored tooltips cannot be turned on and off from JavaScript. A *master tooltip* solves this problem. As the name implies, there is one master

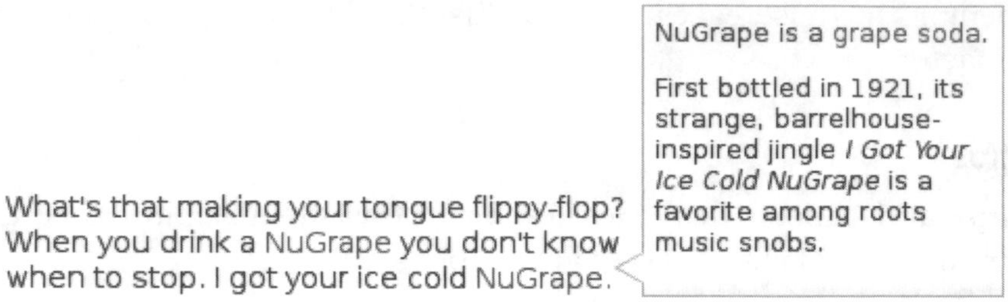

NuGrape is a grape soda.

First bottled in 1921, its strange, barrelhouse-inspired jingle *I Got Your Ice Cold NuGrape* is a favorite among roots music snobs.

What's that making your tongue flippy-flop? When you drink a NuGrape you don't know when to stop. I got your ice cold NuGrape.

Figure 15.7: AN ANCHORED TOOLTIP STAYS BY ITS ANCHOR.

tooltip per page, but the good news is you can move it anywhere at will. You create and hide the master tooltip through the JavaScript methods:

```
dijit.showTooltip(String htmlContents, DOMNode aroundNode, [, String[] position])
dijit.hideTooltip(DOMNode aroundNode)
```

Here, the DOM node aroundNode functions as the anchor. The position parameter is interesting—it holds an array of positions to try for the tooltip. The possible values are above, below, after, and before.[1] The positions are tried in order until the tooltip fits within the page boundaries. That ensures tooltips are never cut off. The default position is ['after','before'], meaning it will try after first and then before.

There is one caveat: master tooltips are not a11y-compatible like Dijit widgets are. So, they should be used sparingly and always be accompanied by some other accessible mechanism.

Progress

When long operations happen, the user needs to be informed at the beginning and at regular intervals. At the very least, they need to know there's time for a cup of coffee. But they also need to be reassured the process is continuing and that the browser, server, and network are still working. In the traditional web model, long operations always happen between pages, so the browser's spinning logo tells you things are happening.

---

1. After and before are more accurate terms since right-to-left languages like Arabic will put an after tooltip to the left.

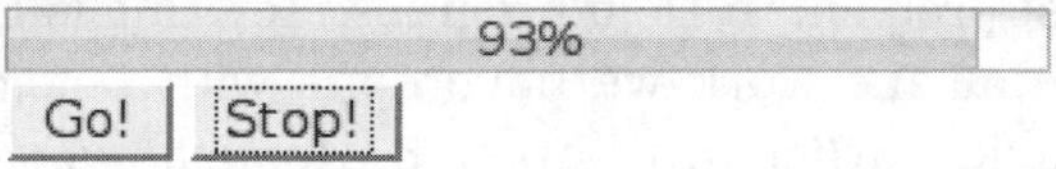

Figure 15.8: A PROGRESS METER IN FLIGHT

In the Ajax world, operations happen without a page request, so you must provide your own feedback. Fortunately, Dijit has a widget for you! It's called dijit.ProgressBar, and it looks like Figure 15.8.

You set up the bar like this:

`form_controls/progress_bar.html`

```
<div dojoType="dijit.ProgressBar" style="width:300px"
    jsId="jsProgress" id="downloadProgress"></div>
<input type="button" value="Go!"
    onclick="dojobook.form_controls.objects.progress_bar.download();" />
<input type="button" value="Stop!"
    onclick="clearInterval(_timer);_timer=null;" />
```

Without any pushing, the progress bar will sit at 0% forever. You must communicate progress through a JavaScript method call, update({ maximum: numParts, progress:0 });. Since we're being server agnostic, we will simulate a long operation through the standard JavaScript setInterval method and a random time interval between progress reports:

`form_controls/objects/progress_bar.js`

```
dojo.provide("dojobook.form_controls.objects.progress_bar");

(function() {
    dojobook.form_controls.objects.progress_bar.download = function(){
        // Split up bar into 7% segments
        numParts = Math.floor(100/7);
        jsProgress.update({ maximum: numParts, progress:0 });

        for (var i=0; i<=numParts; i++){
            // This plays update({progress:0}) at 3nn milliseconds,
            // update({progress:1}) at 6nn milliseconds, etc.
            _timer = setTimeout(
                "jsProgress.update({ progress: " + i + " })",
                (i+1)*300 + Math.floor(Math.random()*300)
            );

        }
    }
})();
```

Often the biggest problem in Dojo progress metering is getting progress reports. Despite all the work we have done with Deferreds and asynchronous callbacks earlier in Chapter 6, *Asynchronous Programming*, on page 95, JavaScript is still single threaded. And often the things you want to monitor work in one statement. Say you need to pull down 100,000 records to the browser through an XHR request. If you issue dojo.xhr* for the entire set, the method seems to work asynchronously in the sense that you can scroll up and down the page, enter form elements, and so on. But you can't ask "How many records have you downloaded so far?"

The most common way around this is to get data in chunks, updating the progress meter in the onLoad callback of dojo.xhr*. For dojo.data loads, using QueryReadStore helps partition the work so you can call the progress meter in stages.

Notifications with Toaster

Sometimes you don't need all the detail of a progress meter. For example, suppose you just want to tell a user you're saving a document in the back group. The widget dojox.widget.Toaster is good for that. You can set up a Toaster like this:

form_controls/save_toaster.html
```
<div dojoType="dojox.widget.Toaster" duration="0" jsId="saveToaster"
    messageTopic="/saving" positionDirection="tr-left"></div>
```

Then invoke it in some background, possibly long-running process. We'll simulate that here with some buttons:

form_controls/save_toaster.html
```
<div dojoType="dojox.widget.Toaster" duration="0" jsId="saveToaster"
    messageTopic="/saving" positionDirection="tr-left"></div>
```

Setting the timer to 0 in the widget means "keep onscreen until it's clicked." You publish the topic at the beginning of your operation to set the Toaster in motion. Then at the end, you call _setTimer(1), meaning keep the Toaster onscreen for 1ms longer and disappear. The user can also dismiss the Toaster manually by clicking it.

15.4 Dates, Numbers, and i18n

In Section 2.5, *Improved Form Controls*, on page 24, we learned about regular expression validation, which can handle your text validation needs. But numbers, currency, dates, and times need extra care. Valid examples are different depending on the country you're in. In other words, you need to pay attention to internationalization, or i18n (which means "i and n with 18 letters in between").

For example, if you're asked for a date in the DateTextBox, you would be correct typing 1/31/2008 in the United States, but not in England. (England puts the month after the day, and there is no 31st month!) So, validating input depends on a *locale*, that is, the customs of a particular country or language, and you must validate within that context. Locales greatly affect the formatting of four things in particular: numbers, currency, date, and time.

The good news is Dijit takes care of many of the details invisibly, for the most part. Dojo reads the browser's installed locale (the only i18n-specific information available to JavaScript) as part of its startup process and makes it available to all JavaScript code. Dijit in turn reads the locale and retrieves information about its formatting patterns and uses them to display and interpret things in the widgets. The Dojo source version bundles the entire Unicode CLDR localization database, and you can pick which locales to support as part of a custom build. The Dojo binary version contains a subset of the most common locales.

The following controls are i18n-enabled:

- dijit.form.NumberTextBox
- dijit.form.CurrencyTextBox
- dijit.form.NumberSpinner
- dijit.form.DateTextBox
- dijit.form.TimeTextBox

Standard Form

Although Dojo knows your locale and can format dates based on it, if you get the following item in ItemFileReadStore...

```
[ "5/10/2003", "Frank", "Stokes", ... ]
```

how does Dojo know whether the 5/10/2003 is May 10 or November 5? Dojo could force you to send the server locale information with each response, but it seems bandwidth-wasteful to do so. So, Dojo requires specifying dates and numbers in a clear, well-defined standard form.

For numbers, standard form is the same as JavaScript number literals. So, the number 92367.45 is in standard form because you can say var

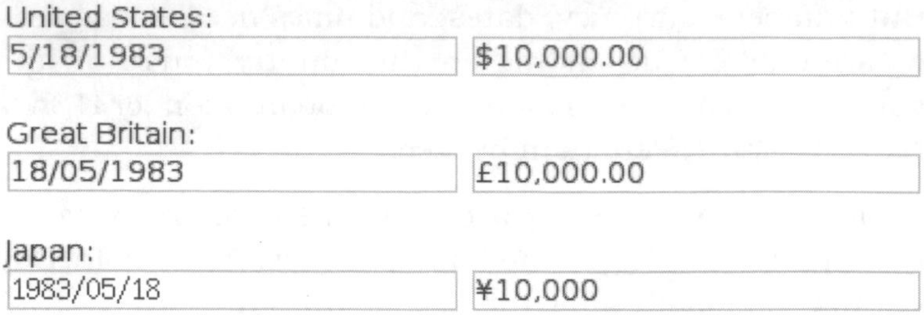

United States:

5/18/1983	$10,000.00

Great Britain:

18/05/1983	£10,000.00

Japan:

1983/05/18	¥10,000

Figure 15.9: THE STANDARD FORM VALUES 1983-05-18 AND 10000.001 RENDERED IN DIFFERENT LOCALES

x=92367.45;. And 92.367,45 is not in standard form, even though it's a legal number in locales where . is the digit group separator and , is the decimal point.

Dates are trickier. You can unambiguously create a Date object in JavaScript, and that's good for programmatic widgets. But programmatic widgets need a text-based standard form. Dojo uses ISO 8601, whose form is as follows:

`yyyy-mm-dd«Thh:mi:ss»`

The string 2003-10-05T06:30:00 is November 5, 2003, at 6:30 a.m. The "T" and time can be left off if it's not applicable. Dates sent in this format will always be translatable by the DateTextBox and TimeTextBox implementations.

In Figure 15.9, you see how the standard form date 1983-05-18 and the number 10000.001 are rendered using different locales and currency formats.

Constraints and Formatting

Although you could validate numbers, times, and dates with a ValidationTextBox and regular expressions, Dijit provides specialized subclasses of ValidationTextBox that are much easier. Rather than specifying a regular expression, these controls use *constraints* that are specialized and easier to read. The constraint is used both to format a standard form number or date into a readable, localized form *and* to parse it from a localized form back to standard form.

There are two forms of constraints: property-based and pattern-based. A property-based constraint specifies the characteristics (number of places after the decimal point, and so on) in a JavaScript hash, while a pattern-based constraint encodes them in a string like #.##. Pattern-based constraints are sort of the printf in Dojo. You can write all constraints in either form, so it's your choice.

Numbers

Let's examine constraints in number validation—property-based first. The widget dijit.form.NumberTextBox deals with numeric input.

You place all constraints, whether property or pattern-based, in the constraint= attribute. For instance, this property-based constraint prints a number as a percent (that is, multiplied by 100) with two decimal digits, rounding all values with a third decimal digit from 0–5 downward and from 6–9 upward.

```
{type: 'percent', places: 2 }
```

The properties min, max, type (which is one of percent, currency, or decimal), and places (the number of digits after the decimal point) are all legal for number constraints.

The equivalent pattern-based constraint says it more succinctly:

```
{pattern: '#.##%' }
```

Pattern-based constraints for numbers are based on the standard Unicode TR35 language. It is the same pattern language that Java uses for numbers... a nice benefit. Rather than go through it in full here, we refer you to the specification itself at http://www.unicode.org/reports/tr35/#Number_Format_Patterns.

Here are a few common use cases with pattern-based and property-based constraints:

form_controls/constraints.html

```
<!-- Displays 1.01 -->
<div dojoType="dijit.form.NumberTextBox" name="n1"
    value='1.007' constraints="{ places: 2 }"
    ></div>

<!-- Displays 1.00 -->
<div dojoType="dijit.form.NumberTextBox" name="n2"
    value='1.004' constraints="{ pattern: '#.##' }"
    ></div>
```

```
<!--  Displays 110%, but reverts to 1 when the box gets focus,
      and expects you to input the % sign -->
<div dojoType="dijit.form.NumberTextBox" name="n3"
    value='1.1' constraints="{ type: 'percent', places: 0 }"
  ></div>

<!--  Displays 1,005.0 -->
<div dojoType="dijit.form.NumberTextBox" name="n4"
    value='1005' constraints="{ pattern: '#,##0.0' }"
  ></div>
```

So, constraints help you on the output side; now let's look at the input side. If someone enters 1.116 in a box with two decimal places, Number-TextBox will reformat it as 1.12 when the box loses focus. Occasionally constraints can cause user confusion. A percent type box will always expect a % in the input. If you don't provide the user a good prompt message, they won't know they must enter the % sign, leading to frustration. That's never a good thing.

Mapped Textboxes

The percentage constraint brings up a good question. Server programs don't like input with commas and percent signs—they prefer numbers with only digits and a decimal point, in other words: standard form. But if the NumberTextBox forces the user to enter a percent sign, how do we make the server swallow it?

Dijit uses a neat trick called *mapped textboxes* to take care of this. Each NumberTextBox actually gets expanded into two *<input>* tags: one that's displayed and one that isn't. The displayed one contains the "user-friendly" version with the percent sign, and the hidden one contains the standard form. *Only the standard form is submitted.* So after entering 50% and leaving the field, the hidden field contains 0.5, and that's what is submitted.

In Figure 15.10, on the next page, you can see what goes on. In Firebug, you can see how the widget becomes two input boxes. When the form submits, as shown at the bottom, only the n3 parameter is submitted.

Dijit's four special validation widgets—NumberTextBox, CurrencyTextBox, DateTextBox, and TimeTextBox—are all mapped textboxes. Later we'll see how to exploit mapped textboxes to submit other forms of numbers or dates besides standard form.

```
                    50%

 ⊟ <div class="dijitReset dijitInputField">
       <input id="dijit_form_NumberTextBox_2" class="dijitReset" type="t
           <input type="text" value="" style="display: none;" name="n3"/>
       </div>
   </div>
              POST /dojobook/form_controls/constraints.html HT
              Host: localhost
              User-Agent: Mozilla/5.0 (X11; U; Linux i686; en-US
              Accept: text/xml,application/xml,application/xhtml
              Accept-Language: en-us,en;q=0.5
              Accept-Encoding: gzip,deflate
              Accept-Charset: ISO-8859-1,utf-8;q=0.7,*;q=0.7
              Keep-Alive: 300
              Connection: keep-alive
              Referer: http://localhost/dojobook/form_controls/co
              Content-Type: application/x-www-form-urlencoded
              Content-Length: 27
               └n1=1.01&n2=1&n3=0.5&n4=1005
```

Figure 15.10: A MAPPED TEXTBOX IS REALLY TWO TEXTBOXES.

Currency

Currency carries a bit more complexity than numbers. With numbers, you have only one locale to deal with—that of the browser—and a number can be translated to any other locale by using standard form.

The dijit.form.CurrencyTextBox is like a NumberTextBox, but it throws in the local currency symbol for free. If you're in the United States, for example, it pops in a dollar sign when the box loses focus. But if someone in Papua New Guinea uses that same page, they will enter a number and the kina symbol will appear. Because of the mapped tax boxes, only the number will be passed, so how does the server know the currency is in kinas?

One way is to decode the locale in your server program and format the currency accordingly. Another, which is much clearer and easier to program, is to embed the currency symbol in a constraint. The constraint looks like this:

form_controls/constraints.html

```
<!-- Displays 1.01 -->
Amt to Charge (in Japanese Yen)
<div dojoType="dijit.form.CurrencyTextBox" name="c1"
    value='1.007' constraints="{ currency:'JPY' }"
  ></div>
```

Here, currency is the standard ISO 4217:2001 three-character code. Then you set up one box for each currency you'll accept. This makes things quite unambiguous.

The currency also carries some standards for fractions. For example, U.S. dollars (USD) go to two decimal places, while Japanese yen (JPY) use none. You can override this for a particular currency by specifying fractional as true or false. This is necessary for micropayments or per-unit costs for very small items.

Dates and Times

We've already used DateTextBox with its handy drop-down calendar. By default, this control always displays the date in the locale-specific format. But because it's a mapped textbox, only the standard form date is sent back to the server.

If the default onscreen format is not to your liking, you can use one of the following constraints:

- formatLength can be set to short, medium, long, or full, which displays the date in various degrees of terseness.
- pattern specifies a full date pattern string, conforming to the Unicode TR-35 Date Pattern format specification (http://www.unicode.org/reports/tr35/#Date_Format_Patterns). As with number patterns, this standard is the same standard Java uses for dates.

dijit.form.TimeTextBox does for times what DateTextBox does for dates. This control uses formatLength or pattern just like a DateTextBox. In addition, it adds the following constraints:

- clickableIncrement specifies the granularity of time that a user can select. This is specified in Dojo common format, as in "T00:10:00", which means a user can choose 1:10, 1:20, 1:30, and so on.
- visibleIncrement specifies when printed labels occur on the time chart. For example, "T01:00:00" means list 1:00, 2:00, and so on.
- visibleRange tells how much time is visible on the scale at any time.

The control, as shown in Figure 15.11, on the facing page, uses the constraint {formatLength:'short',clickableIncrement:'T00:15:00', visibleIncrement: 'T01:00:00', visibleRange:'T02:00:00'}.

Bypassing Standard Form

Servers can be very stubborn about date formats. A DateTextBox accepts ISO 8601 dates, but it may be difficult for the server to send them in

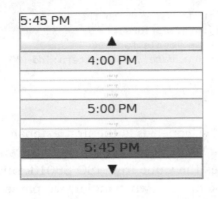

Figure 15.11: A DIJIT.FORM.TIMETEXTBOX

that format. Making it worse, the server may have a hard time accepting ISO 8601 dates. Fortunately, you can get around this restriction by making your own DateTextBox, and you don't have to do it from scratch.

By default, the Oracle database accepts and returns dates of the form dd-MMM-yyyy, as in 15-MAY-2008. Here we'll write a subclass of Date-TextBox that will short-circuit the parsing and formatting process:

form_controls/widgets/OracleDateTextBox.js
```
dojo.provide("dojobook.form_controls.widgets.OracleDateTextBox");
dojo.require("dijit.form.DateTextBox");

dojo.declare("dojobook.form_controls.widgets.OracleDateTextBox",
        [dijit.form.DateTextBox], {

    postMixInProperties: function() {
        this.inherited(arguments);
        if(this.srcNodeRef) {  // If the widget was created declaratively

            // The postMixInProperties in superclasses have ISO parsing built
            // in.  So here we overwrite the parsed value.
            var unparsedValue = this.srcNodeRef.getAttribute('value');
            if(unparsedValue) {
                var dateFromOracle = dojo.date.locale.parse(
                    unparsedValue,
                    {selector:'date', datePattern: 'dd-MMM-yyyy'}
                );
                this.value = dateFromOracle;
            }
        }
    },
```

```
        // Returns date in dd-MMM-yyyy to the server
        serialize: function(d, options) {
            return dojo.date.locale.format(
                d, {selector:'date', datePattern:'dd-MMM-yyyy'}
            );
        }
});
```

In a nutshell, postMixInProperties is the first extension point run during widget construction. We delegate the duties to the superclass DateTime-TextBox first. It parses the value from ISO 8601 format to a date. When control passes back to our own handler, we parse the original value according to Oracle specs, overwrite the value, and return.

The serialize extension point runs when the value changes. Here, we do the reverse step and format the date in Oracle format, which gets placed in the hidden text field of a mapped textbox. When the form is submitted, the Oracle format gets sent. Meanwhile, onscreen, all you see is the date in locale-specific format. It's like magic!

Then you can use the widget as a drop-in replacement for DateTextBox, like so:

form_controls/form_OracleDateTextBox.html

```
<input dojoType="dojobook.form_controls.widgets.OracleDateTextBox"
       name="mydate" value="04-MAR-2008"/>
```

Subclassing widgets is such a useful technique that we'll see much more of it later in Chapter 17, *Creating and Extending Widget Classes*, on page 455.

Feedback

When constraining the input, sometimes it's not clear what you expect from the user. And sometimes, despite warnings, users make a mistake and enter bad input. Dijit's design philosophy is to give the user feedback early yet inobtrusively.

You give Dijit a boost by providing the text. The promptMessage= attribute text displays in a tooltip when the control gets focus, as in the following:

```
<div dojoType="dijit.form.ValidationTextBox"
     promptMessage="Enter a date before 8/20/1974"
>
```

As you've seen in the examples in Chapter 3, the prompt appears as a tooltip after the control. You can change the position of this tooltip by using the position= attribute, with the same values as dijit.MasterTooltip.

The prompt appears when the focus arrives on that control and the control has no value. As soon as the user enters something, that something is validated against the constraints. If the value is invalid, the attribute invalidMessage= is displayed:

```
<div dojoType="dijit.form.ValidationTextBox"
    invalidMessage="The date must be before 8/20/1974"
>
```

This too is displayed as a tooltip and can be positioned with the position= attribute.

15.5 Action Buttons, Toolbars, and Menus

Over the past few chapters, dijit.Button has come in handy for all kinds of action initiation. It requires only a label, an iconClass= that points to a style with a icon, or both, and an onClick handler.

In a Rich Internet Application, you could presumably make one button for each command. But that would be a dreadful waste of real estate and would be confusing besides. So, Dijit provides two containers for compacting a set of buttons. dijit.Menu stacks its contents vertically. A menu doesn't use buttons per se, but it uses dijit.MenuItems, which are essentially borderless buttons with menu-closing authority. The other container, dijit.Toolbar, displays its contents, which are always buttons, horizontally.

dijit.Menus and dijit.Toolbars can live in the following habitats:

- dijit.form.DropDownButton is a button that, when clicked, displays the menu or toolbar inside. This button always has two children: a label, usually in a *<span>* tag, and a menu or toolbar.

- dijit.form.ComboButton is like a combination Button and DropDown-Button. It has an arrow to the side, which when clicked displays the submenu. Clicking the ComboButton itself performs its own button-like action.

- With no parent menus, the menu or toolbar displays onscreen all the time. In a Menu, you can also set the contextMenuForWindow= to **true** and make it a context (right-click) menu.

Note that dijit.form.Button includes both dijit.form.DropDownButton and dijit.form.ComboButton types, so you need to dojo.require that module only.

A menu can contain the following items:

- dijit.MenuItem is a menu's leaf node. All of your onClick handlers go here.
- dijit.PopupMenu is like a MenuItem, but it always has two children: a label, usually in a *<span>* tag, and another menu. It does not have an onClick extension point because clicking always displays its subordinate menu.
- dijit.MenuSeparator is not selectable but draws a line between elements.

The module dijit.Menu includes all these widgets.

A toolbar is like a menu but contains Buttons that make it function like the traditional software toolbar. You can also add DropDownButtons and ComboButtons to make a menu bar. Lastly, there is a button separator, dijit.ToolbarSeparator.

To see how this all works, let's start with a basic menu:

`form_controls/buttons.html`

```
<div dojoType="dijit.Menu">
    <div dojoType="dijit.MenuItem">Disaster Menu</div>
    <div dojoType="dijit.MenuSeparator"></div>
    <div dojoType="dijit.PopupMenuItem">
        <span>Natural</span>
        <div dojoType="dijit.Menu">
            <div dojoType="dijit.MenuItem">Boll Weevils</div>
            <div dojoType="dijit.MenuItem">Flood</div>
        </div>
    </div>
    <div dojoType="dijit.PopupMenuItem">
        <span>Emotional</span>
        <div dojoType="dijit.Menu">
            <div dojoType="dijit.MenuItem">Spouse Left You</div>
            <div dojoType="dijit.MenuItem">Spouse Caught You Cheating</div>
            <div dojoType="dijit.MenuItem">
                Spouse Caught You Cheating and Left
            </div>
            <div dojoType="dijit.MenuItem">Spouse With Best Friend
                <script type="dojo/method" event="onClick">
                    console.log("Now that is REALLY bad!");
                </script>
            </div>
        </div>
    </div>
</div>
```

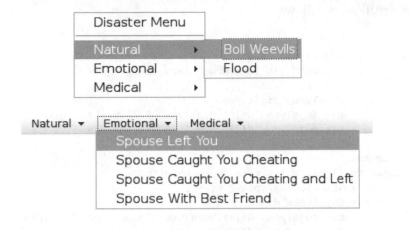

Figure 15.12: A MENU AND A TOOLBAR MASQUERADING AS A MENU

```
<div dojoType="dijit.PopupMenuItem">
    <span>Medical</span>
        <div dojoType="dijit.Menu">
        <div dojoType="dijit.MenuItem">TB</div>
        <div dojoType="dijit.MenuItem">Rheum-y-tism</div>
    </div>
</div>
</div>
```

Normally, you'd have onClick handlers for each menu item, but this example includes just one for brevity. Placing this on its own in a page, this menu will display a vertical list of the items, as shown in Figure 15.12

To make this a context menu, you simply add the attributes contextMenuForWindow="true" and style="display:none" to the tag. You can also then hide the menu in a DropDownButton:

```
<div dojoType="dijit.DropDownButton">
   <span>Disasters</span>
   <div dojoType="dijit.Menu">
      ...
   </div>
</div>
```

Or you can make it into the traditional menu bar by changing the PopupMenu elements to DropDownButtons and changing the outer widget to a toolbar.

The result is as follows:

`form_controls/buttons.html`

```
<div dojoType="dijit.Toolbar">
    <span dojoType="dijit.form.DropDownButton">
        <span>Natural</span>
        <div dojoType="dijit.Menu">
            <div dojoType="dijit.MenuItem">Boll Weevils</div>
            <div dojoType="dijit.MenuItem">Flood</div>
        </div>
    </span>
    <span dojoType="dijit.form.DropDownButton">
        <span>Emotional</span>
        <div dojoType="dijit.Menu">
            <div dojoType="dijit.MenuItem">Spouse Left You</div>
            <div dojoType="dijit.MenuItem">Spouse Caught You Cheating</div>
            <div dojoType="dijit.MenuItem">
                Spouse Caught You Cheating and Left
            </div>
            <div dojoType="dijit.MenuItem">Spouse With Best Friend
                <script type="dojo/method" event="onClick">
                    console.log("Now that is REALLY bad!");
                </script>
            </div>
        </div>
    </span>
    <span dojoType="dijit.form.DropDownButton">
        <span>Medical</span>
        <div dojoType="dijit.Menu">
            <div dojoType="dijit.MenuItem">TB</div>
            <div dojoType="dijit.MenuItem">Rheum-y-tism</div>
        </div>
    </span>
</div>
```

The result looks like the bottom half of Figure 15.12, on the previous page.

15.6 A11y

Accessibility, often abbreviated *a11y* to mean "a plus 11 letters plus y," refers to making pages accessible to everyone. From its beginning, Dijit has made accessibility a priority, and all bundled Dijit components are a11y compliant.

If you are unfamiliar with a11y and its relation to web browsing, http://www.w3.org/WAI/ provides a good primer. But here is the 50,000-foot view. People with impaired vision or motor disabilities might have problems using your web app. Those with impaired vision such as color blindness or fuzzy or cloudy vision may have trouble picking up cues communicated through color and shape. Those with no vision may rely on screen readers to communicate text and feedback. Finally, motor disabilities may prevent someone from using the mouse, instead relying on keyboards, switches, or voice recognition to generate input.

With JavaScriptless fill-and-submit web pages, you could rely on the browser and the OS to handle many of the a11y concerns. As long as you used *<label>* tags and alt= attributes on controls, the a11y APIs could pick them up. Screen readers could read the text and control state information—for example, a checkbox could read "Vegetarian Meal checkbox checked."

Ajax throws a wrench into things. All of sudden controls may be implemented with *<div>* tags, and their state may live in JavaScript variables. How can the browser tell which *<div>* tags mark text and which mark controls? From Dojo's point of view, there are three main accessibility issues to solve:

Images and color Dijit relies heavily on background images because they are portable, they are easily blendable into a theme, and they live in the style sheet where they're easy to maintain. But if a person with low or no vision has images turned off, this is no longer a reliable way to communicate state or progress. We'll talk about this along with general design in Chapter 16, *Dijit Themes, Design, and Layout*, on page 427.

Keyboard usage HTML controls automatically handle [Tab] navigation and selection. If Dijit controls do not at least emulate this, they risk making the page unable to be navigated. Furthermore, Dijit controls have many options that HTML controls don't have, and the challenge is to make these work seamlessly for a keyboard user. Part of this can be solved with Dojo's rich keyboard event system, described earlier in Section 6.1, *Keyboard Event Objects*, on page 99. We'll see how to assign tab order to individual controls in the next section.

Conveying role and state While checkboxes are easy to present, sophisticated Dijit controls require some thought. Let's say you've focused onto a tree node with label "Gummy Haggis, Order 23199" as its parent and with five serial numbers listed beneath. Pretend you are talking to someone at that same page in their own browser and where they need to be to match yours. You could communicate the role "Tree Node" and the state as "Parent label Order 23199, label Gummy Haggis, open, number of children: 5," for example. Obviously, Dijit needs some help in this area, which we'll talk about in the next section.

Tab Order

Intuitively, the Tab key should move to the next control on the form in some natural order. With Dijit form controls, you set tab order in the same manner as HTML—with the tabindex= attribute. The possible values are as follows:

tabindex=	Meaning
-1	The user cannot tab into this control. It can be focused only through a JavaScript widgetObject.focus() call.
0	Visit this control in the order the controls appear in the markup. This is the default, and generally you make either all controls 0 or none of them 0.
1–32767	Order in which this control should be visited. To make form rearrangement easy, using increments of 10 is a good strategy.

Conveying Roles and States in Extension Points

So, now a widget has focus. How does the screen reader convey the information there? For regular old HTML controls, the problem is pretty straightforward. Each control has a role and a state for which to convey information. For example, in a checkbox like this...

```
<label to="gone">My baby's gone</label>
<input id="gone" type="checkbox" value="y" />
```

the screen reader would say: "My baby's gone; pressed is true" or "My baby's gone; pressed is untrue." (And if your baby is gone, that mechanical voice won't reassure you much.) That functionality is built into the accessibility feature of browsers. But what about this widget?

```
<label to="gone">My baby's gone</label>
<div dojoType="dijit.form.Checkbox"
    id="gone" value="y" />
```

First, browsers don't know about dijit.form.Checkbox, so how do they know the state will be checked or unchecked? Second, as you know about declarative widgets, they almost never stay intact. The source <div> tag is replaced with a bunch of other tags by the Dojo parser. So, how will the browser and the screen reader know what type of control this is?

This is where the Web Accessibility Initiative comes in. A standards body that looks at accessibility in web applications, WAI is developing the Accessible Rich Internet Application (ARIA) standard. ARIA defines information *dimensions*, which describe things happening on the page. These dimensions answer certain questions like "What is this object?" (the ARIA dimension called the *role*) and "What meaningful properties does this object have it this time?" (the *state*) and "What object am I working on?" (the *focus*). The focus is covered by the taborder= attribute, but the role and state need some explanation.

Let's take the role first. The role essentially answers the question "What does this control act like?" Typical values include row, gridcell, button, tooltip, directory, img, and so forth. The role usually affects what actions the user may take and what states are kept with the control. role= is an attribute of the XHTML 1.1 standard, and Firefox 1.5 (and newer) recognizes it. So, you *could* identify the previous checkbox with the following:

```
<label to="gone">My baby's gone</label>
<div dojoType="dijit.form.Checkbox"
    role="checkbox"
    id="gone" value="y" />
```

At least you could do this if widgets carried over the role= attribute. But as we'll see in Chapter 17, *Creating and Extending Widget Classes*, on page 455, attributes that the widget doesn't explicitly use or pass on are quietly dropped. Instead, the widget class sets the role attribute.

A widget may actually have several controls with distinct roles. For example, a ComboButton combines an action button with a drop-down menu button. Each of these has the ARIA role button. In the drop-down menu itself, each menu item has an ARIA role option.

And that brings us to the *state*, which is settable through Dojo. State is important to get right when you're adding extension point handlers, since your handler may actually be changing the state of the control. Or you may want to add extra state information to make navigation a little easier. To do this with a Dijit control, you follow these steps:

1. Locate the template for that Dijit control. These are usually in /dojoroot/dijit/templates or a templates directory underneath and are named after the Dijit class with the extension .html.

2. Find existing WAI roles, WAI states, and dojoAttachPoint attributes.

3. Construct a call to dijit.setWaiState.

So, suppose you want to set a state called importance in ComboBox. You first find the template /dojoroot/dijit/form/templates/ComboBox.html. Here's what it looks like:

```
form_controls/ComboBox.html
```

```
Line 1  <div class="dijit dijitReset dijitInlineTable dijitLeft"
  -       id="widget_${id}"
  -       dojoAttachEvent="onmouseenter:_onMouse,onmouseleave:_onMouse,\
  -         onmousedown:_onMouse"
  5       dojoAttachPoint="comboNode" waiRole="combobox" tabIndex="-1"
  -       ><div style="overflow:hidden;"
  -             ><div
  -           class='dijitReset dijitRight dijitButtonNode dijitArrowButton\
  -             dijitDownArrowButton'
  10          dojoAttachPoint="downArrowNode" waiRole="presentation"
  -           ><div class="dijitArrowButtonInner"> </div
  -           ><div class="dijitArrowButtonChar">&#9660;</div
  -         ></div
  -         ><div class="dijitReset dijitValidationIcon"><br></div
  15        ><div class="dijitReset dijitValidationIconText">&Chi;</div
  -         ><div class="dijitReset dijitInputField"
  -         ><input type="text" autocomplete="off" name="${name}" class='dijitReset'
  -         dojoAttachEvent="onkeypress:_onKeyPress, onfocus:_update, compositionend"
  -         dojoAttachPoint="textbox,focusNode"
  20        waiRole="textbox" waiState="haspopup-true,autocomplete-list"
  -         /></div
  -       ></div
  -     ></div>
```

Don't worry about understanding all this—we'll cover the Dijit template language in Section 17.1, *Widget Classes Using dijit.Declaration*, on page 456. The important thing is finding the WAI attributes and the dojoAttachPoint= attributes.

You notice there are three waiRole= attributes in the tags here: combobox, presentation, and textbox. presentation is a special role that says "This node does not hold any state information." These nodes are for design purposes only. The one we really want is textbox. For sighted users, this box will be colored green, orange, or red depending on the importance level, but we'll set a WAI state for screen readers to pick up.

The textbox node has a dojoAttachPoint="textbox,focusNode" attribute. You need this as a location to set the state—in this case you can use either textbox or focusNode in your method call:

```
dijit.setWaiState: function(widget.textbox, 'importance', 'very important');
```

Now when the browser focuses on that element, the screen reader will speak the importance information we also have encoded as a textbox color.

Once you have the process down, it's fairly straightforward to take the few extra steps to make your controls a11y compliant. Dijit is far beyond other JavaScript toolkits in this area, and as browser manufacturers add more ARIA-compliant features, you can be sure Dijit will evolve accordingly.

Dijit Themes, Design, and Layout

A cramped, poorly colored, or inconsistent page can kill user enthusiasm as much as poor functionality. So like it or not, you must pay attention to the visual details. That takes a good eye (which you may not have) and lots of time (which you *definitely* don't have).

Dijit provides themes and layout widgets to help you. Themes apply color, icons, and font choices to your page's widgets. Out of the box the themes bundled with Dijit provide balanced color, readability, and elegance. But if you need to add or change the design, Dijit's well-thought-out structure makes it easy to change everything from individual elements to whole widget classes. A good understanding of theme structure, which we'll cover in the first part of the chapter, will make the change process straightforward.

Layout widgets separate, group, and align elements. If themes are Dijit's paint box, layout widgets are its X-acto knife and rubber cement. Layouts are made of *panes*, which function like pastable elements. Their content can come from the same page or different pages. You lay panes beside each other in a dijit.layout.BorderContainer, which acts like a paste board. Or you can lay panes on top of one another with *stack containers*, which act like flip charts pasted on the top with one pane showing at a time. The second part of the chapter will cover all of these elements.

16.1 Theme Structure

OK, suppose you've placed a nice green widget on your page, only to find it displays as blue. Where did the widget gets its blue color? And how do you change it? To answer those questions, you must know where to

Figure 16.1: BUNDLED THEMES: NIHILO, SORIA, TUNDRA, AND TUNDRA IN A11Y MODE

look in the Dijit theme style sheets. So, let's talk about what makes a theme and how it's organized.

Up until now we've been using the bundled Tundra theme, and that's a good choice for applications you build from scratch. In all, Dijit comes with three prepackaged themes:

- Nihilo (/dojoroot/dijit/themes/nihilo/nihilo.css): Greenish tint with very bright buttons
- Soria (/dojoroot/dijit/themes/soria/soria.css): Dark blue tabs with lighter buttons
- Tundra (/dojoroot/dijit/themes/tundra/tundra.css): Very inobtrusive light gray and blue

In Figure 16.1, you can see these together for comparison. (If this is the printed book, the differences are less noticeable.)

They not only look good, but Dijit themes are also easy to apply. You just include the appropriate style sheet and add a class to the *<body>* tag, as we saw in Section 2.3, *Adding Dojo and Dijit to a Page*, on page 15. This comes courtesy of a Dijit theme's meticulous structure, which uses Cascading Style Sheets (CSS) principles to the hilt.

Each theme can also display in a11y mode. When people with low vision or no vision use the application, particular design element choices may mean a lot. By detecting whether the computer's high-contrast setting is on (wherever that is in the operating system), Dijit in effect adjusts the theme for the high-contrast colors.

Most look-and-feel decisions are coded in the theme. You may want to review or override those decisions in these cases:

- A Dijit element doesn't look quite right, and you want to see the styles used in creating it. For example, you may need to change a widget's z-order to properly position your nonwidget elements.
- You want to change the look of an individual widget or an entire Dijit class. For example, you may be placing your logo next to an element whose colors clash.
- You are creating your own Dijit class, and you need to add styles for it.
- An element looks correct in one browser, say Internet Explorer, and not in another, such as Firefox, and you need to analyze why. As we'll see, Dijit has facilities for applying different styles to different browser types.

So first, we'll go over the styles and CSS elements that make up a Dijit theme. Then we'll see how to change theme styles at the HTML element or style sheet level. Finally, we'll look at the a11y theme, how it helps users with low vision, and how you can tap into its functionality. An understanding of the rules and extensions will make you an uber widget developer, loved and respected by one and all!

Files That Make Up a Theme

A theme, code-wise, is simply CSS and some matching background images. Like good object-oriented design, good CSS design uses patterns to prevent redundancy and improve readability.[1] Fortunately, learning to navigate those patterns will go a long way toward making themes work the way you want.

All themes load the "super style sheet" dojoroot/dijit/themes/dijit.css. This file defines very few visual elements but instead factors out common elements among all style sheets. In addition, the a11y theme is defined here so developers don't need to include it on every page (the a11y theme is autoselected, as we'll see in Section 16.3, *A11y and Themes*, on page 439).

The tundra directory includes tundra.css and a directory of images used for rendering the components. You may wonder why Dijit components

---

1. For some background on good CSS design, I recommend Eric Meyer's *CSS: The Definitive Guide* [Mey06] and Jeffrey Zeldman's *Designing with Web Standards* [Zel06].

use images for arrows, colored backgrounds, and other things. Why not use plain HTML styles or wingdings? First, it allows you to better match the graphic with the theme. Second, images look consistent across platforms. With regular controls, the width of a <*select*> box, for example, could cause wrapping on a Mac but not on Windows. Third, you can include images as part of the background elements. That way you can keep your design variations segregated to the style sheet.

Style Namespaces

Tundra.css has more than 300 styles. That requires some enterprise-level organization. At the very least, you want to prevent CSS name collisions since these cause hard-to-find style problems with no error messages. For example, you may want a tag with class="SaveButtonSmall" to look different in a big dialog box than in a small one. Many JavaScript toolkits try to distinguish the two by cramming on prefixes. So, in a toolkit called EnRoute with a dialog box component BigDialogBox, you might see a class name EnRouteBigDialogBoxSaveButtonSmall. Now *that's* a typing accident waiting to happen. What's worse is that in a BigDialogBox you end up typing the prefix EnRouteBigDialogBox in all your classes—a lot of useless repetition.

Other languages solve this problem with namespaces. For example, Java classes form a namespace where com.pragprog.foo.Bar is a different class than com.pragprog.open.Bar. Through Java's **import** statement, you can say "whenever you see Bar in this class, assume it's com.pragprog.open.Bar." That's much easier on your typing hand. And because Java namespaces are guaranteed unique by the file system, you can mix classes from different vendors freely, even if they use the same class names.

Although CSS does not have a native namespace feature, Dijit simulates one with *compound selectors*. A compound selector is just a string of selectors that match a hierarchy of tags. For example, here's a selector used for the dijit.TitlePane widget:

```
.tundra .dijitTitlePaneTitle .dijitOpenCloseArrowOuter {
      margin-right:5px;
}
```

This says "match any tag with class dijitOpenCloseArrowOuter that sits inside a tag with class dijitTitlePaneTitle, which in turns sits inside a tag with class tundra." So in Figure 16.2, on the next page, you can see how CSS matches each part of the selector. That selector does look longish.

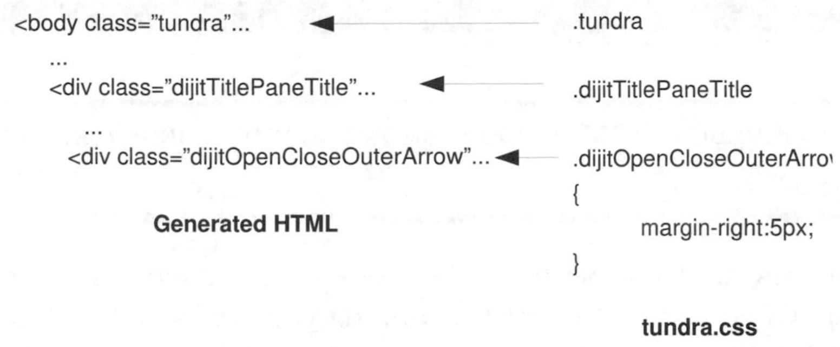

```
<body class="tundra"...        ◀─────────────        .tundra
  ...
  <div class="dijitTitlePaneTitle"...   ◀───────      .dijitTitlePaneTitle
    ...
    <div class="dijitOpenCloseOuterArrow"...  ◀──   .dijitOpenCloseOuterArro\
                                                    {
              Generated HTML                            margin-right:5px;
                                                    }

                                                       tundra.css
```

Figure 16.2: MATCHING COMPOUND SELECTORS TO HTML CLASSES

But now the widget needs to place only class="dijitOpenCloseArrowOuter" in the tag and rely on parent nodes to match the rest. Hence, the class names are shorter, and you save bytes in your HTML. Furthermore, other widgets can reuse class="dijitOpenCloseArrowOuter" without accidentally applying TitlePane's margin-right:5px;.

What does that mean for you? Suppose you want to know "why is this arrow green and not blue?" Firebug's inspect mode tells you the arrow has class="dijitOpenCloseArrowOuter". If tundra.css has two selectors that end with .dijitOpenCloseArrowOuter, you just follow the parent tags up. If you find a class="dijitTitlePaneTitle", then you match our earlier selector. Note also that the selector does not use .titlePane. If it did, an open/close arrow inside a TitlePane's button would also match that selector, which we don't want to happen.

"Hey!" you might say, "My code uses dijit.TitlePane, but I never used a dijitTitlePaneTitle class in it." Good point. It's not there in original HTML or in the View Source window. Instead, a *<div>* with that class was created after the page was loaded by dojo.parser. (See the sidebar on page 17 for details.) This is yet another case where Firebug is indispensable. As you can see in Figure 16.3, on the next page, Firebug shows the HTML as it exists on the screen now, that is, after dojo.parser had finished with it. View Source shows only the untouched, pristine downloaded copy of the HTML.

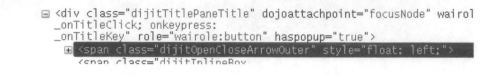

Figure 16.3: FIREBUG DOM WINDOW SHOWS ELEMENT INSERTED BY
DIJIT

The descendents need not be direct descendents to match, which is
a good thing. Often you find yourself wrapping your widgets in <*div*>
tags or HTML tables or in other structures. For example, you might
introduce a tag between the tables or in other structures; specifically,
you might introduce a tag between the tag with class="tundra" and the
tag with class="dijitTitlePaneTitle". But the selector .tundra .dijitTitlePaneTitle
will still match. This bit of magic allows you to have one class="tundra"
in your entire document.

Style Inheritance

That covers matching rules to nodes. A totally separate issue, style
inheritance, also benefits from this namespace-like structure. Because
.one is contained in .tundra, then .one inherits the styles of .tundra and
may override them for themselves and their children.

Word processors often do this in their own style sheets. You may have
a Normal style that defines text as Times 11 pt, 7" lines, and so on.
A quote style, then, may be defined as Normal + 5" lines indented 1"
on the left. If you want to change the entire paper to Helvetica, you
need to change only the Normal style. This is a simple object-oriented
inheritance applied to a nonprogramming language.

Let's take an example from Dijit. The following rule...

```
.tundra .dijitTitlePaneTitle .dijitOpenCloseArrowOuter {
        margin-right:5px;
}
```

has a parent rule:

```
.tundra .dijitTitlePaneTitle {
    background: #cccccc; background:#fafafa
    url("titleBarBg.gif") repeat-x bottom left;
    border:1px solid #bfbfbf;
    padding:4px 4px 2px 4px;
    cursor: pointer;
}
```

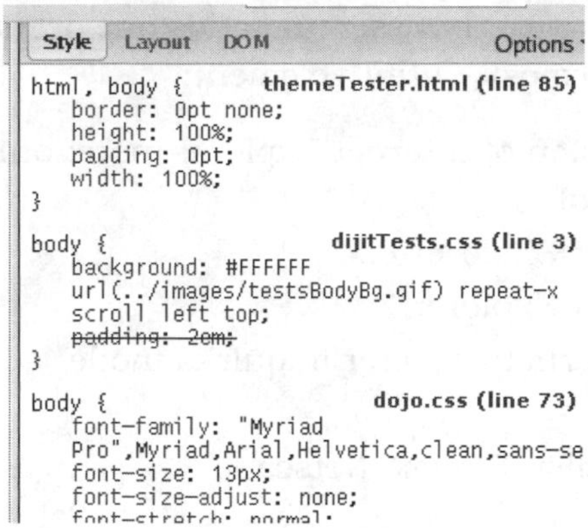

```
 Style   Layout   DOM                    Options
html, body {              themeTester.html (line 85)
    border: 0pt none;
    height: 100%;
    padding: 0pt;
    width: 100%;
}

body {                      dijitTests.css (line 3)
    background: #FFFFFF
    url(../images/testsBodyBg.gif) repeat-x
    scroll left top;
    padding: 2em;
}

body {                         dojo.css (line 73)
    font-family: "Myriad
    Pro",Myriad,Arial,Helvetica,clean,sans-se
    font-size: 13px;
    font-size-adjust: none;
    font-stretch: normal;
```

Figure 16.4: FIREBUG CSS WINDOW

Because .tundra .dijitTitlePaneTitle .dijitOpenCloseArrowOuter has no cursor attribute, it inherits the one in .tundra .dijitTitlePaneTitle, in this case, a pointer.

Firebug also shows you the inheritance rules at work, as you can see in Figure 16.4. In this right window, the most specific rules appear on top and go down to least specific at the bottom. If a more specific rule overrides a style of a less specific one, Firebug crosses out the overridden style. That's very helpful in debugging.

Browser-Specific Styles

Styles do not always render the same in Internet Explorer, Firefox, and Safari. This is an annoying problem, but Dijit themes make life easier. Certain styles are applied only in a specific browser, and finding these styles can help you debug design inconsistencies. They can also help you with your own theme extensions. In most cases, design incompatibilities can be solved by a small change to the style. For example, a style that renders fine in Mozilla may require a position:absolute to work in Internet Explorer.

In tundra.css, a few styles break the "all selectors begin with the theme name" rule. Here are some examples:

```
.dj_ie6 .tundra .dijitInputField,
```

The module dijit._base.Sniff is part of Dijit Base (meaning it's automatically included anytime you load a widget; you don't need to dojo.require it). Sniff detects the user's browser and adds one or more of the following classes to the outermost <*html*> element:

- dj_ie: Any version of Internet Explorer (note: only 6 and 7 are supported by Dojo)
- dj_ie6: Internet Explorer 6.*x*
- dj_ie7: Internet Explorer 7.*x*
- dj_iequirks: Internet Explorer in quirks mode
- dj_safari: Safari
- dj_gecko: Mozilla, Firefox, Netscape

For example, an Internet Explorer 6 browser running in quirks mode will have its <*html*> element changed to the following:

```
<html class="dj_ie dj_ie6 dj_iequirks">
```

Now any selectors in tundra.css beginning with .dj_ie6 will apply. The Dijit designers use these selectors to fix any browser "mistakes" with styles. For example, if Internet Explorer 6 needs a style foo: bar but this style makes Firefox render incorrectly, then they write the rule .dj_ie6 { foo: bar }. This guarantees the rule will be applied only in Internet Explorer 6. It's seamless and much cleaner than using CSS hacks—styles that deliberately break CSS processing in certain browsers.

But what about the .tundra .dijitInputField selectors? Will they fire too? Fortunately, no. Under the rules of CSS, if there is more than one matching selector, the most specific will apply. Since .dj_ie6 .tundra .dijitInputField is more specific than .tundra .dijitInputField, it alone will be applied in Internet Explorer 6.

Dijit uses compound selectors and inheritance to improve the serviceability of a style. Now that you understand the structure, you can debug a style with ease.

16.2 Changing Look and Feel

Now that you've found the offending style, what does it take to change it? By "change it," you can either do it statically, meaning that when the page renders the look and feel is fixed, or do it dynamically through JavaScript events or user actions. Well, if you're like us, you will be tempted to do the following:

- Hack the theme style sheet (static changes).

- Change the style properties directly through JavaScript like this: document.getElementById("errorMsg").style.backgroundColor = 'red'; (dynamic changes).

Don't do it! Hacking theme style sheets is bad because the next Dojo upgrade will overwrite your changes. And don't delude yourself into thinking "I'll remember to keep my copy of that file." You won't. Trust me. And changing the styles directly from JavaScript violates the separation of concerns: keep the content in the HTML, the code in Java-Script modules, and the design in CSS. After all, CSS was invented to convey style and design decisions. JavaScript was not.

But no worries here. There are nice, safe ways to change the look and feel of elements. We'll see how to make static changes to individual elements and whole classes of elements. We'll cover a little about how to design your own theme. Lastly, we'll see how to change elements dynamically by manipulating classes.

Individual Elements

You can override the design settings of a theme by filling in the style= attribute of a tag. For example, you could change a button tag directly like this:

```
<body class="soria">
...
<input type="button" dojoType="dijit.Button"
      style="background-color:red" />
```

But then it will always be red, no matter what the Soria theme states. In keeping with our theme of putting elements in their proper files, it's preferable to write this in the button:

```
<body class="soria">
...
<input type="button" dojoType="dijit.Button" id="soreThumb" />
```

and in your application style sheet:

```
#soreThumb { background-color: red; }
```

Element Classes

If you wanted to make all the Soria theme buttons red, you wouldn't want to change each and every button. To change a theme style over all pages, there are two methods.

You could simply add a style with the same selector as the theme style. So if soria.css has this...

```
.soria .dijitButton {
    height:30px;
    padding:0px;
    border-width:0px;
    background-color:transparent;
    background-repeat:no-repeat;
    margin:5px;
}
```

then you would place this in your application style sheet:

```
.soria .dijitButton {
    height:30px;
    padding:0px;
    border-width:0px;
    background-color:red;
    background-repeat:no-repeat;
    margin:5px;
}
```

There are two issues here:

- You must make very sure to load your style sheet after soria.css, since the last style with the same selector wins.
- If soria.css changes, you may have to make corresponding changes to your application style sheet.

If you can guarantee the browser is Firefox, Safari, or Internet Explorer 7 and newer, there's a more "dijit-friendly" method: introduce your own outer class. For example, you can make a mySoria selector and place it in the <*body*> element:

```
<body class="mySoria soria">
```

Then your application style sheet elements will be as follows:

```
.mySoria.soria .dijitButton {
    height:30px;
    padding:0px;
    border-width:0px;
    background-color:red;
    background-repeat:no-repeat;
    margin:5px;
}
```

Notice how .mySoria and .soria are smooshed together, meaning these two classes must be applied to the same tag. This technique doesn't suffer from the earlier first problem and requires only a little extra HTML. The downside is versions of Internet Explorer 6 and older do not handle these multiple-class selectors properly.

Sections

Perhaps you need even more radical surgery. Say you need Soria's form elements but Tundra's text style. No problem!

Simply surround any section with *<div>* tags, and give them the theme you want as a class. For example:

```
<div class="tundra">
Lorum ipsum dolor...
</div>
<div class="soria">
<input type="button" dojoType="dijit.Button"    />
</div>
```

The bottom line is that as long as the theme class is outside the dijit components, they can go in any HTML tag. They don't need to go into body. But if you use this method, make sure your theme sections don't overlap; a section with two overlapping themes will pick the last-loaded theme. Such effects can be difficult to diagnose.

Themes from Scratch

For the mother of all modifications, you can write your own theme. Although we don't normally recommend copy and paste, in this case it makes good sense to copy an established Dijit theme to one of your own and then modify it. After all, there are 300 styles to change.

Here are a few tips to make this process easier:

- Place design decisions as far up the tree as you can. If you find yourself repeating the same style decision in peer classes with the same ancestor, push the style up to the ancestor.
- If you have an existing style sheet, use it as a rough guide for coding styles in your theme. You may want to place your theme styles directly in the existing style sheet and use inheritance there.

Dynamic Changes

After the previous three sections, the following rule shouldn't be surprising: *you change an element's look by changing its class.* This is the way that Dijit changes the look of its own elements. Replacing a class in JavaScript is straightforward: domElememnt.className = 'newStyle". And don't forget about the Dojo functions addClass, removeClass, hasClass, and toggleClass discussed in Section 7.1, *Core Dojo DOM Utility Functions*, on page 135. For example, /dojroot/dijit/Menu.js has this...

```
dojo.addClass(this.arrow, "dijitMenuRightArrowEnabled");
```

which, when combined with the style (this one from tundra.css), effectively makes arrowRight.png magically appear:

```
.tundra .dijitMenuRightArrowEnabled {
    margin-top:4px;
    background:url('images/arrowRight.png') no-repeat bottom center;
    display:inline;
}
```

CSS classes work really well for recording state. Say you have an electrical switch whose icons are switchon.png and switchoff.png. Rather than using a Boolean variable to keep track of the on/off state, we can use classes dijitOn and dijitOff to keep track. First place these icons in the styles:

```
.tundra .dijitLightSwitch {
    // The light switch cover is brown, no matter what the state
        background-color: brown;
}
.tundra .dijitLightSwitch.dijitOn {
    url("images/switchon.png");
}
.tundra .dijitLightSwitch.dijitOff {
    url("images/switchoff.png");
}
```

Notice how .dijitOn is crammed up next to .dijitLightSwitch in the selector. That means both classes must appear in the same element, though they could be listed in either order.

You could then change the className attribute to either dijitOn or dijitOff. Note also that the .tundra .dijitLightSwitch selector matches in either case, so the background of the image (which will show through any transparent colors) will always be brown. Dojo helper functions help change the state of these icons without disturbing other classes:

```
dojo.toggleClass("livingRoomSwitch", "dijitOff");
dojo.toggleClass("livingRoomSwitch", "dijitOn");
```

Using a class name for the control state ensures that the data and the visual state are always in sync. Yet again, we have followed the DRY (Don't Repeat Yourself) rule, and our agility is assured.

To sum up, changing the look and feel of elements can be accomplished cleanly and without redundancy. You can change the look of individual elements with an overriding *<style>*. You can change the look of an entire element by overriding the theme style in your own CSS. You can start with a new theme altogether. And you can change the look of elements programmatically by adding, subtracting, and querying the classes attached to an element.

16.3 A11y and Themes

In Chapter 15, *Form Controls*, on page 393, we introduced a11y as an integral part of Dijit. Its keyboard alternatives make navigating widgets possible for users with low mobility or users with screen-reading programs. Now we'll look at using Dijit a11y for users with impaired vision. At first you might think, "Why would someone with low vision care about colors and fonts?" At the level of choosing between Lucida Sans and Verdana, they probably wouldn't. But the difference between orange and black could be the difference between reading everything and nothing.

Low-vision users correct for this by using high-contrast color schemes bundled with Windows, Gnome, KDE, or Mac OS. These schemes map foreground colors to white and background colors to black, or vice versa. Modern browsers detect this and adjust their default style sheets to match this setup. However, most web sites don't use the default—they use their own style sheets. If that style sheet is not a11y-friendly, the user can turn it off altogether in the browser and substitute their own. The trouble here, especially for Dijit users, is the styles contain layout and size information critical to proper display.

Background images are also ineffective for low-vision users, so many opt to turn images off altogether. For a11y design, this rule is key: never convey information in background images and colors only. For example, simply turning a textbox red is not a11y-friendly. Adding a tooltip to display the error message, as Dijit's ValidatingTextBoxes do, makes it acceptable to both audiences.

The trouble is while a11y discourages the use of background images, Dijit's CSS-based design philosophy *encourages* the use of background images. That's because you specify background images as part of a CSS style. A11y design traditionally uses HTML foreground images with a title= attribute like this:

```
<img src="images/uparrow.gif" title="Go up" />
```

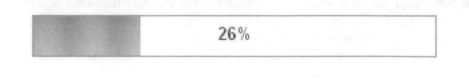

Figure 16.5: PROGRESS BAR IN TUNDRA

The title "Go up" is read out loud by a screen reader. Unfortunately, CSS has no provision for a title attached to a background image. We can partially get around this with keyboard handling and Web Accessibility Initiative (WAI) rules. This, however, limits low-vision users to the keyboard.

Dijit solves this knotty problem in a clever way. Whenever you load the base Dijit classes, which happens anytime you use dojo.require to load a Dijit component, Dijit performs a small test:

1. It constructs a small red and green bordered box outside of the browser limits. Because of its coordinates, the user will never actually see it.
2. Dijit then tests to see whether the *actual* colors of the box borders are green and red. If they're not, Dijit takes that to mean its own style sheet is off.
3. Then, exactly like setting the dj_ie and dj_gecko styles, it tags the document with a dijit_a11y class.
4. Whenever a component needs an a11y alternate, the Dijit style sheet, dijit.css, has overriding rules with selectors beginning with dijit_a11y.

One widget that capitalizes on this is ProgressBar, which we'll learn about in Chapter 15, *Form Controls*, on page 393. Tundra shades the completed portion differently than the uncompleted portion, as shown in Figure 16.5. The dijit_a11y class shifts the style rules to make it look like Figure 16.6, on the next page. Now the bar border conveys the progress information clearly.

So, what does this mean to you as a theme designer? Actually, not a lot. The whole point of a11y mode is to prevent you from having to code style sheets in two versions. However, just as you test your design changes in various browsers, so you should test them in a11y mode. It's

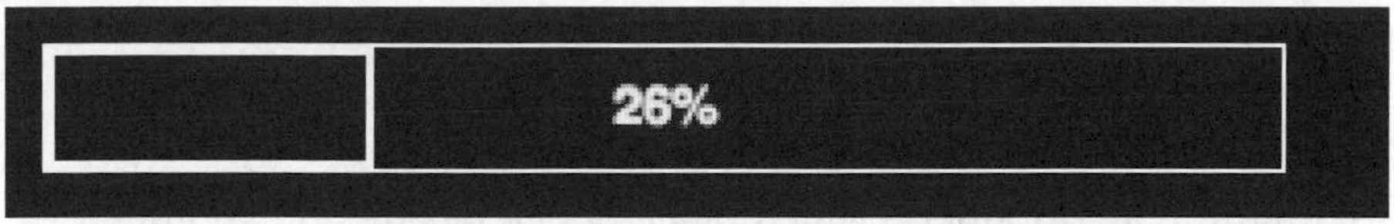

Figure 16.6: PROGRESS BAR IN A11Y MODE

easy to do this without changing your color scheme to high contrast. Simply add this...

```
dojo.addClass(dojo.body(), "dijit_a11y");
```

to your header code. This activates the dijit_a11y mode artificially.

In summary, the Dijit theme system brings order to the chaos of look and feel. By grouping rules into a CSS style sheet with hierarchical structure, you apply the DRY rule to color, shape, and layout. Making sweeping changes is as easy as changing a style close to the hierarchical top. Yet it's flexible enough to allow overriding at any level for exceptional cases.

Dijit themes also help you make sense of different browser needs, by allowing browser-specific styles to accommodate different interpretations of the CSS standards. And a11y styles accommodate the needs of those with low vision or no vision.

Though design decisions in these instances may require thought, having the places to plug in those changes gives you a sizable head start. The Dijit themes provided are well commented and structured, so you can use them as guidelines for your own work. This is a far cry from the days of black backgrounds with purple, blinking text!

16.4 Panes: ContentPane and TitlePane

For the next three sections, we'll take a look at the layout widgets. If themes manage the color in your application, you could say layout widgets manage the whitespace. They align elements, stack elements on each other, or pull content from other sources, among other tasks.

You can group layout elements into three classes:

- Panes, which define blocks of content

- Alignment containers, which place panes beside one another

- Stack containers, which stack panes and alignment containers on each other, revealing one pane at a time

So first we'll look at the pane widgets dijit.layout.ContentPane and dijit.TitlePane,[2] which are like Dijit layout "atoms." ContentPane is a general-purpose blank pane, while TitlePane adds an expando button to show or hide the content.

The easiest form of ContentPane simply renders the content between the tags. This code displays a slot machine:

themes_and_design/content_panes.html

```
<div dojoType="dijit.layout.ContentPane"
    style="width:100px;height:200px;float:left"
    id="slot1">
    <div dojoType="dijit.form.Button">
        cherry
    </div>
</div>

<div dojoType="dijit.layout.ContentPane"
    style="width:100px;height:200px;float:left"
    id="slot2">
    <div dojoType="dijit.form.Button">
        cherry
    </div>
</div>

<div dojoType="dijit.layout.ContentPane"
    style="width:100px;height:200px;float:left"
    id="slot3">
    <div dojoType="dijit.form.Button">
        bar
    </div>
</div>
```

It's not very exciting so far... this does little more than a plain <div> tag. It gets more interesting, though, when you programmatically modify content.

---

2. Note this is the only layout widget *not* in dijit.layout.

The click of a button pulls the slot machine arm to get a new triple:

`themes_and_design/content_panes.html`

```
<div dojoType="dijit.form.Button">
    Pull Arm
    <script type="dojo/method" event="onClick">
        var slotValues=["cherry", "lemon", "orange", "bar", "seven"];
        function randomSlotButton() {
            var thisSlot = slotValues[Math.floor(Math.random()*5)];
            return "<div dojoType='dijit.form.Button'>" + thisSlot + "</div>";
        }
        dijit.byId("slot1").setContent(randomSlotButton());
        dijit.byId("slot2").setContent(randomSlotButton());
        dijit.byId("slot3").setContent(randomSlotButton());
    </script>
</div>
```

ContentPane's setContent method takes care of the widget parsing automatically. Remember that Dojo's parser turns tags with dojoType into real HTML tags. Just setting an innerHTML property on a DOM node is not enough.

setContent has one caveat, however—code in <script> tags will not run. In particular, that means you can't use dojo.require in the content tag; you must make sure to do it in the main HTML file. If you absolutely need to run script tags, we do have a solution for that in a little bit.

Where ContentPane gets really interesting is in loading external content. You can simply call setHref, give it a URL, and you're done. So, put the following code in spinner_try1.html:

`themes_and_design/spinner-try1.html`

```
<div dojoType='dijit.form.Button'>
    <script>document.write(slotValues[Math.floor(Math.random()*5)]);</script>
</div>
```

Then you can load it in with setHref:

`themes_and_design/content_panes.html`

```
<div dojoType="dijit.form.Button">
    Pull Arm Remotely
    <script type="dojo/method" event="onClick">
        //var includeUrl="spinner-try1.html";
        // This one works:
        var includeUrl="spinner-try2.html";
        dijit.byId("slot1").setHref(includeUrl);
        dijit.byId("slot2").setHref(includeUrl);
        dijit.byId("slot3").setHref(includeUrl);
    </script>
</div>
```

Uh-oh. If you actually ran this content, you'd see three blank buttons. That's because as with setContent, setHref does not run the <script> tags. Fortunately, there's an easy workaround—simply use dojo/method scripts, as we did in Section 12.4, *Extension Points*, on page 329. Recall that code in a dojo/method script nested in a widget and having no event property executes when the widget is created. So, this simple rewrite does the job:[3]

themes_and_design/spinner-try2.html

```
<div dojoType='dijit.form.Button'>
   <script type="dojo/method">
       alert("hello!");
       var slotValues=["cherry", "lemon", "orange", "bar", "seven"];
       this.setLabel(slotValues[Math.floor(Math.random()*5)]);
   </script>
</div>
```

This trick works well if you control the code. But if you must use plain <script> tags, dojox.layout.ContentPane (note the dojox) overcomes those limitation, if somewhat imperfectly. Dojox's ContentPane applies liberal rewriting to the incoming content, so the URLs are executed relative to the including HTML. That rewriting can cause hard-to-diagnose problems. Nevertheless, the option is available if you need it.

A couple more tips are in order. First, the included content must form legal HTML when plopped into the page. This point also holds true for setContent, but you must especially watch out for it in external content because it's easy to include peripheral tags like <html> if you're not careful.

Finally, because setHref uses XHR to load content, it's subject to the same-domain rule. If you want to aggregate off-site content, you can always use the proxy technique shown in Section 12.2, *Finding and Manipulating Declarative Widgets*, on page 320.

If you're used to server-side programming in ASP, JSP, PHP, and so on, you probably recognize ContentPane as a modularization technique. Absolutely! If your HTML documents share a common snippet of code, you can factor that out into its own file and use ContentPane to include it in multiple pages. It's good for cutting long HTML pages into manageable pieces, even if the pieces are not reused.

---

3. This trick, unfortunately, does not seem to work in Internet Explorer 6 as of Dojo 1.1.

Increasing Perceived Performance

In addition to separating content and making replacement easy, ContentPanes can also "look" fast. Imagine a content-laden page. It sounds like rendering everything instantly would be a big advantage, but it's not. Humans can take in only so much information, and it's just as good to render the parts they want first and fill in the other details later. ContentPane can help you increase this perceived performance in three ways:

- *Simultaneous loading* maximizes throughput by loading separate pieces with separate, simultaneous server requests.

- *Lazy loading* defers loading long-running web requests until the user asks for it.

- *Pane reloading* refreshes only the parts of the screen that need refreshing, rather than refreshing the entire page.

To use simultaneous loading, you place the major web page pieces into ContentPanes, each loaded from a different URL. Modern browsers make many HTTP connections at once, each of which communicates with the web server. Usually there's one grabbing the HTML itself, while others grab images, causing the page to shift and rerender as images fill in. ContentPane allows this with any content. Of course, there is a risk that certain pieces don't render, and you are left with an 80% complete page. But this risk usually is small.

Lazy loading involves tying a setHref to a user event like onClick. For example, if one of your page sections takes a long time to run, you can simply leave that as a blank ContentPane and use setHref when the user requests the information.

A common mistake developers make in lazy loading is to set the href property of ContentPane in the tag and then set the style to display:none:

`themes_and_design/title_panes.html`

```
<div dojoType="dijit.layout.ContentPane" style="width:200px;height:200px"
    style="display:none"
    id="contentPane" href="spinner-try2.html">
</div>
```

This still executes the content load, and in fact ContentPane ignores the display:none altogether. So unless you need the content right away, you should leave the href property blank.

Lazy loading is such a popular paradigm that Dijit offers a variant of ContentPane named TitlePane. TitlePane adds a border, a title bar on the top, and an expando button on the top-right corner. Clicking the expando toggles between hiding and showing the content.

TitlePane uses the same options as ContentPane and adds two more: title, which specifies the title on the top bar, and open, which you can set to false to initially hide the content, leaving only the title bar and expando button visible. In a TitlePane, you can set the href in the properties to some content. It will not be loaded until the user clicks the expando button. To illustrate this, the following example uses TitlePane to show a bar:

themes_and_design/title_panes.html

```
<div dojoType="dijit.TitlePane" style="width:200px;height:200px"
    title="Open to see the spinner"
    id="titlePane" href="spinner-try2.html" open="false">
</div>
```

Even with href=, the open="false" tells Dijit not to load the URL contents until the user opens the pane. This works great for portals, where each portlet can use its own TitlePane and slow ones can be initially closed.

Finally, you can refresh a section of the page with pane reloading. Here you set a ContentPane to a URL and then reload content as it changes. The URL must be a server-side program whose contents could change with the data environment. There's one caveat. Let's say you ask for personlist.php and then issue a setHref to load it again. Dojo caches pages and will hand back the same content without calling the server. You disable this with preventCache="true" in the ContentPane. preventCache= also adds a random hash mark to the URL, which effectively disables server-side caching.

16.5 The Alignment Container: BorderContainer

If panes are the one-dimensional points of layout, then an *alignment container* is a two-dimensional plane of layout. Dijit has one alignment container named dijit.layout.BorderContainer whose sole purpose is to keep panes next to each other.[4] It's a more readable alternative to CSS's positioning and floating attributes.

---

4. In releases 0.9 and 1.0, Dijit provided two alignment containers: dijit.layout. LayoutContainer with fixed boundaries and dijit.layout.SplitContainer with user-movable boundaries. In 1.1, their functionality has been merged into dijit.layout.BorderContainer.

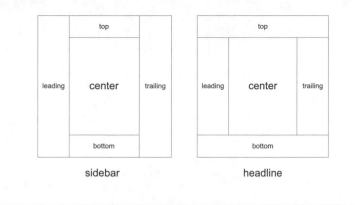

sidebar   headline

Figure 16.7: BORDERCONTAINER DESIGNS: HEADLINE AND SIDEBAR

A BorderContainer looks like this:

```
<div dojoType="dijit.layout.BorderContainer"
    style="width:«width»; height:«height»">
    <div dojoType="dijit.layout.ContentPane" region="center"
        style="height:«region height»">
        Center content Pane content
    </div>
    <div dojoType="dijit.layout.ContentPane" region="top"
        style="height:«region height»">
        Top content Pane content
    </div>
... panes for leading, trailing and bottom regions
    </div>
```

A BorderContainer consists of five *regions*: top, bottom, leading, trailing, and center, as shown in Figure 16.7. leading and trailing are synonyms for left and right in left-to-right languages like English, and vice versa for right-to-left languages.

Each region's content is in a ContentPane with a region= attribute on each. BorderContainer requires only one region—the center one—and all others are optional and may be specified in any order.

Width and height are very important in a BorderContainer and its ContentPanes. The BorderContainer itself requires a fixed width and height. The regions top and bottom must have a height, which may be either a fixed size or a percentage. Similarly, the leading and trailing regions must have a width, either a fixed size or a percentage. The center region *must not* have dimensions, however. The center region area is what's leftover from the other regions.

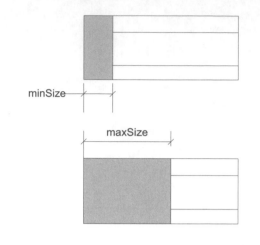

Figure 16.8: A SPLITTER ALLOWS USER-RESIZABLE REGIONS.

BorderContainers come in two designs—headline and sidebar—specified in the design= attribute. The difference between them is which regions get priority. In the headline design, shown on the left of Figure 16.7, on the previous page, the top and bottom regions have top priority and get all the space between the left and right borders. It looks like a newspaper with a headline in the top region. The sidebar design gives more weight to the leading and trailing regions, and they grab all the space from top to bottom.

What if the user disagrees with your region sizing choices? You can put the sizing power in their hands with *splitters*. A splitter is a draggable border between two panes, and you add one to a ContentPane with the splitter="true" attribute. This makes the center-facing border draggable. If you want to keep the user in reasonable bounds, you can specify minSize= and/or maxSize= attributes on the ContentPane, as shown in Figure 16.8. These sizes constrain the area of that particular region and default to 0px and Infinity, respectively, to mean "no constraints."

The following example places the programmer questionnaire of Chapter 7 in a tidy layout with a headline and help on the side (although the Help will probably not help anybody here). The result is shown in Figure 16.9, on the next page.

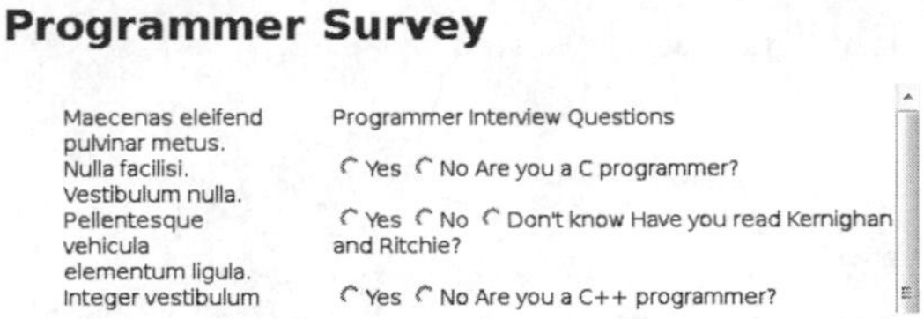

Programmer Survey

Figure 16.9: A BORDERCONTAINER IN ACTION

```
themes_and_design/border_container.html
```

```
<div dojoType="dijit.layout.BorderContainer" design="headline"
    style="width:600px; height:400px" liveSizing="true">

    <div dojoType="dijit.layout.ContentPane" region="top"
        style="height:75px">
        <h1>Programmer Survey</h1>
    </div>

    <div dojoType="dijit.layout.ContentPane" region="leading"
        splitter="true" style="width:200px">
        <div dojoType="dojobook.creating_widgets.widgets.GreekingWidget"
            paragraphs="1" tag="blockquote">
        </div>
    </div>

    <div dojoType="dijit.layout.ContentPane" region="center"
        href="../dom/questions4.htm">
    </div>
</div>
```

The liveSizing= attribute of BorderContainer controls whether panes are redrawn during dragging. Setting it to **true** helps the user by giving visual feedback on how the resizing will look. But it can be slow if your ContentPanes have a great deal of HTML in them.

Finally, like dijit.Tree, BorderContainer can save the state of the sliders in a browser cookie. Just set persist= to **true**, and everything is done automagically. Users will love not having to tinker with the borders every time they use your app.

Now we've covered the first and second dimensions of layout, so naturally stack containers are next.

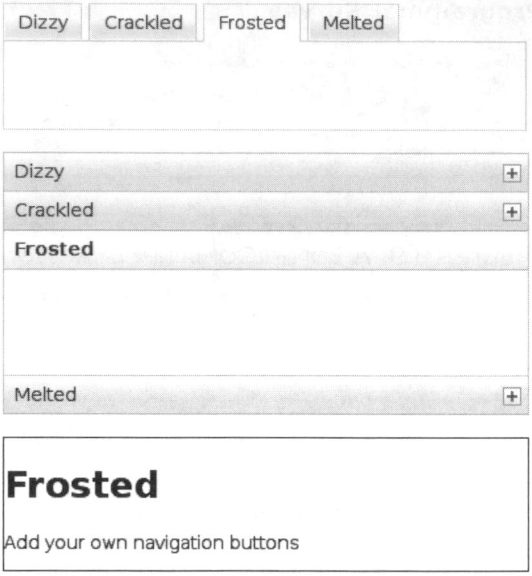

Figure 16.10: STACK CONTAINERS (TOP TO BOTTOM): TABCONTAINER, ACCORDIONCONTAINER, STACKCONTAINER

16.6 Stack Containers

Stack containers extend layouts into the third dimension. They contain an ordered series of panes stacked on top of one another like equally sized pieces of paper. Only one pane is visible at a time. Stack containers are useful when you need to fit a lot of information into a little space and you can naturally divide that information into groups. It's also nice for presenting ordered series of questions, as in a wizard.

Dijit has three stack containers. dijit.layout.StackContainer is the most generic and requires you to provide navigation and control code. The other two, dijit.layout.AccordionContainer and dijit.layout.TabContainer, provide their own navigation controls. AccordionContainer buttons appear inline with the panes, while TabContainer buttons fit along the top, as shown in Figure 16.10.

Because pane widgets are nested right inside the stack container, they are called *children* or *child panes*. StackContainer and TabContainer allow

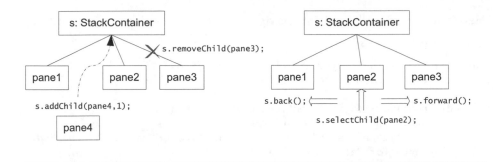

Figure 16.11: STACK CONTAINER MODIFICATION AND NAVIGATION APIS

ContentPanes as their child pages, while AccordionContainers allow only AccordionPanes. Attributes are the same in both ContentPane and AccordionPane, but in an AccordionPane, the title= attribute accepts widgets, while ContentPanes do not.

We already saw an example of TabContainer in Chapter 2, *Powerful Web Forms Made Easy*, on page 13 and an example of AccordionContainer in Section 12.2, *Finding and Manipulating Declarative Widgets*, on page 320. The StackContainer is especially useful in wizards, where there's a well-defined sequence of viewing the pages.

Dijit has a common stack container API. All StackContainer objects respond to these calls, and you use them to add or remove panes from the stack or navigate in between stack pages. On the left side of Figure 16.11, you can see the stack modification methods addChild and removeChild. All panes in a stack are numbered from 0 to numberOfPanes - 1, and you can use addChild's second parameter to insert a pane in a particular spot. All panes from that point move up one in the sequence. Consequently, removeChild removes a particular pane from the list and pushes elements down one to fill the gap.

When the user views a stackContainer, there is always one pane on top and fully viewable. You can move to a particular pane with selectChild, as shown on the right side of Figure 16.11. Or you can move forward or backward one pane with forward and back. These methods are essential for building wizards and other StackContainer widgets, and you usually wire them to the onClick extension point of a button.

Here's a wizard with multiple navigation paths based on user input:

themes_and_design/wizard.html

```
Line 1  <div dojoType="dijit.layout.StackContainer" jsId="sc"
    -       style="width:300px;height:300px">
    -
    -       <div dojoType="dijit.layout.ContentPane" jsId="start">
    5           <p>Did you eat your meat?</p>
    -           <input type="radio" name="ateIt" id="ateItY" value="Y" checked>
    -           <label for="ateIt">Yes</label>
    -           <br/>
    -           <input type="radio" name="ateIt" id="ateItN" value="N">
   10           <label for="ateIt">No</label>
    -           <br/>
    -           <div dojoType="dijit.form.Button">
    -               Next &gt;&gt;
    -               <script type="dojo/method" event="onClick">
   15                   // If they chose Y goto pane "pudding", otherwise "noPudding"
    -                   sc.selectChild(
    -                       dojo.byId("ateItY").checked ? pudding : noPudding
    -                   );
    -               </script>
   20           </div>
    -       </div>
    -
    -       <div dojoType="dijit.layout.ContentPane" jsId="pudding">
    -           <p>Choose Your Pudding</p>
   25           <select name="puddingType">
    -               <option>Chocolate</option>
    -               <option>Vanilla</option>
    -               <option>Blood (in England only)</option>
    -           </select>
   30           <br/>
    -           <div dojoType="dijit.form.Button">
    -               &lt;&lt; Previous
    -               <script type="dojo/method" event="onClick">
    -                   sc.back();
   35               </script>
    -           </div>
    -           <div dojoType="dijit.form.Button">
    -               Finish &gt;&gt;
    -               <script type="dojo/method" event="onClick">
   40                   sc.selectChild(done);
    -               </script>
    -           </div>
    -       </div>
    -
   45       <div dojoType="dijit.layout.ContentPane" jsId="noPudding">
    -           <p>
    -               You can't have any pudding.
    -               How can you have any pudding if you don't eat your meat?
    -           </p>
```

```
50          <br/>
            <div dojoType="dijit.form.Button">
                &lt;&lt; Previous
                <script type="dojo/method" event="onClick">
                    sc.selectChild(start);
55              </script>
            </div>
            <div dojoType="dijit.form.Button">
                Finish &gt;&gt;
                <script type-"dojo/method" event="onClick">
60                  sc.forward();
                </script>
            </div>
        </div>

65      <div dojoType="dijit.layout.ContentPane" jsId="done">
            All in all, we're all just bricks in the wall, y'all!
        </div>
    </div>
</div>
```

This Pink Floyd–inspired wizard has four panes in its StackContainer. Each has a jsId= attribute to create a JavaScript variable pointing to the widget. That makes them easily accessible by selectChild, which is helpful for leaping around to various panes according to the input.

The first pane starts at line 4 and displays a radio button. When the user clicks the Next button, the code at line 14 fires, branching to either the pudding or noPudding pane according to the radio button. The other three panes follow the same pattern, using selectChild for most pane switching except for a back in line 34 and a forward in line 60.

Note that the entire wizard acts as a form, not just the visible pane. That makes it very nice for gathering a large amount of input and submitting it in one shot.

You're probably thinking, "That's a lot of code. I think I'll build a wizard widget to handle all that button stuff automagically." You're such an overachiever! An easier way is to use the dojox.widget.Wizard widget, which wires up Next, Previous, Done, and Cancel buttons for you and is more style-aware than our example.

Using Dijit is like getting your own open source art studio. From adding dots of color to creating page-sized layouts, Dijit provides scalable and easy-to-use tools for your creative side.

Creating and Extending Widget Classes

Up until now, we've been pretty content using the bundled Dijit components. They're pretty flexible in themselves: you can change the look and behavior of individual widgets easily. But what about changing an *entire class* of widgets? On the look-and-feel side, you can override a widget-level style with style= or a widget class-level style through CSS, as we saw in Chapter 16, *Dijit Themes, Design, and Layout*, on page 427. It'd be nice to have the same flexibility on the code side.

Recall (from Section 12.1, *What Exactly Is a Widget?*, on page 317) that a Dijit class is an object class whose methods call Dojo and native JavaScript libraries. You already know how to create a Dojo-based object class—you use dojo.Declare, as we saw in Chapter 9, *Defining Classes with dojo.declare*, on page 221. Dijit classes are no different. You can use dojo.declare to define new widget classes, or you can subclass existing widget classes to create new ones with different behavior. The whole power of object orientation is there to use.

You have more options in defining widget classes than regular classes. In addition to using dojo.declare, you can define them declaratively through dijit.Declaration. The way you declare widget classes and the way you use them do not have to match: you can declare a widget class programmatically and create instances of it declaratively, or vice versa. Which method should you use? The trade-off is pretty much the same as for widgets themselves: the declarative way is easier, and the programmatic way is more flexible.

Naturally, we'll survey the easy way first: dijit.Decaration. At the same time, we'll cover the Dijit template language, used in both methods. Templates are the basis for most of the bundled Dijit components. Then we'll contrast the programmatic method. Next we'll cover the life cycle of a Dijit component, in which you can hook your own behavior. We'll finish with the notes on extending classes and building a fairly sophisticated widget class.

17.1 Widget Classes Using dijit.Declaration

So, here's the widget story so far. A programmer adds a dojoType= attribute to a tag. Upon starting the page, the Dojo parser picks up this tag and calls the widget constructor on it. That's the declarative method. Alternatively, the programmer calls the widget constructor directly from JavaScript—the programmatic method. Either way the widget begins life as a single DOM node. Then the constructor expands this DOM node into a larger snippet of HTML. Most of the time this snippet comes from a *template*, and that's where our journey begins.

Templates are nothing new. The venerable C language has macros, and even Microsoft Word's mail merge facilities are just a template mechanism. Whatever the case, the idea is to provide some constant text and some placeholders so the template interpreter can fill in the dynamic things later.

We've already used a "lite" version of templates, dojo.string.substitute, in Section 3.2, *Function Literals*, on page 36. Dijit uses the same ${} syntax and extends it. Dijit classes are not required to use templates—they may generate HTML from string or DOM functions. But templates are so useful that most widgets use them.

Dijit provides placeholders for straight text or for whole snippets of HTML:

${arbitraryName}
> Is replaced with a property from the widget class. Note this can be *any* property in the widget class or any superclass. A special case of this, ${id} is a property assigned to every widget—you can specify it yourself or let Dijit generate a unique one for you.

<div dojoAttachPoint="containerNode" />
> Is replaced with the body of the widget. Nested widgets are allowed.

<div dojoAttachPoint="arbitraryName" />

Is replaced with nothing. Instead, arbitraryName becomes a property of your widget class, holding the DOM node for the div tag. That way you can write things like this.arbitraryName.addChild(aContainedNode) and this.arbitraryName.className = 'enabledClass'. Note there is an implied attach point called domNode that holds the root DOM node—for example, the node with the dojoType in it.

<div dojoAttachEvent="evt1:handler1,evt2:handler2,..." />

Is also replaced with nothing but does a dojo.connect from this node, event evt1, to handler name handler1, which is expected to exist as a widget method. Connecting events this way saves you from having to retrieve the node later for a manual dojo.connect.

A special event called ondijitclick is a nice shortcut. It is fired on a click, the downstroke of Enter, or the upstroke of the spacebar. By combining all the standard browser control activation events into one, you write just one handler and one event connection. That's it!

Say, for example, you're typing up your Christmas card list:

creating_widgets/pre_dijit_declaration.html

```
<style>
td {
    border: 1pt solid black
}
</style>
<table>
    <tr>
        <td>
        Donald Trump<br/>
        590 Trump Tower<br/>
        New York, NY 55555<br/>
        <br/>
        <strong>Open immediately!</strong>
        </td>
    </tr>
    <tr>
        <td>
        Martha Stewart<br/>
        Club Fed<br/>
        Attica, NY 11111<br/>
        </td>
    </tr>
</table>
```

It seems wasteful to repeat the *<td>* and *
* tags in each label. So, we'll build a simple widget that encapsulates it. To do this declaratively, you use a dojoType="dijit.Declaration" attribute. Our label will look like this:

`creating_widgets/dijit_declaration.html`

```
Line 1  <style>
   -    td {
   -       border: 1pt solid black
   -    }
   5    </style>
   -    <div dojoType="dijit.Declaration" widgetClass="CardLabel"
   -        defaults="{name: 'Nobody', address: 'Nowhere', csz: 'Nowhere'}">
   -      <tr>
   -         <td>
   10         ${name}<br/>
   -          ${address}<br/>
   -          ${csz}<br/>
   -          <br/>
   -          <div dojoAttachPoint="containerNode"></div>
   15     </tr>
   -    </div>

   -    <table>
   -      <div dojoType="CardLabel" name="Donald Trump" address="590 Trump Tower"
   20        csz="New York, NY 55555">
   -         <strong>Open immediately!</strong>
   -      </div>
   -      <div dojoType="CardLabel" name="Martha Stewart" address="Club Fed"
   -        csz="Attica, NY 11111"></div>
   25   </table>
```

In line 6, we open the declaration and name the new widget class Card-Label. You must define the widget before any uses of it—think of it as a variable declaration of sorts.

Line 7 defines the attributes of the new class. Note the JavaScript hash literal here—each property of this hash essentially becomes an attribute of each widget. Because the object is called defaults, you might think you can omit properties that don't have a default. Not true. You *must* specify every property here; otherwise, it will not be replaced properly in the template.

Now for the template elements. In line 10, ${name} is substituted with the name=property. In line 14, the body of the tag will be substituted verbatim.

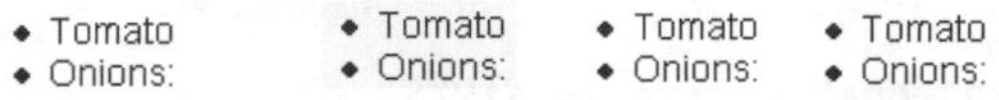

- ◆ Tomato   ◆ Tomato   ◆ Tomato   ◆ Tomato
- ◆ Onions: ◆ Onions: ◆ Onions: ◆ Onions:

Figure 17.1: THE YELLOW FADE TECHNIQUE IN ACTION

The Donald Trump label at line 20 will have "Open Immediately" here, while the Martha Stewart one, which has no body, will quietly ignore it.

The space savings are not obvious in our two-address example, but the more addresses you add, the more bandwidth you save. More important, the widget makes a clearer separation between data and design.

CardLabel is an application-specific widget class, one that's not very useful beyond its page. Now we'll use templates to create a more general widget class.

Example: The Yellow Fade Technique

People are not accustomed to dynamically changing web pages. Therefore, if small bits change on the screen, the user may easily overlook them. The book *Ajax Design Patterns* describes a pattern named One-Second Spotlight, where the changing portion of the screen is highlighted for a second or two. Figure 17.1 illustrates the method. This visual indicator is intuitive and helpful yet unintrusive since the highlight disappears after a bit. (An alert box saying "Look! You have new info!"—that's intrusive.)

We're going to implement a kind of one-second spotlight called the Yellow Fade Technique. Pioneered by 37signals, the YFT has become a widespread Ajax user interface idiom. The idea is to color the background pane yellow and fade it gently back to the original color over a few seconds. This gives the effect of running a highlighter pen over that pane. Our YFT widget, Changebox, will be a container widget. That means it's there only to hold other widgets in a group, much like dijit.layout.ContentPane. Changebox will use dijit.Declaration and templates, and in particular, the template's containerNode attach point to render all the widgets inside.

`creating_widgets/yft.html`

```
<div dojoType="Changebox" boxId="supply">
    <h2>Supply Chain</h2>
    <ul>
        <li>Tomato Price: $0.735 per pound</li>
        <li>Onions: $0.466 per pound</li>
    </ul>
</div>

<div dojoType="Changebox" boxId="majoracct">
    <h2>Major Accounts</h2>
    <ul>
        <li>McDonald's: +3.11% </li>
        <li>Burger King: -1.29%</li>
        <li>Wendy's: unchanged</li>
    </ul>
</div>

<div dojoType="Changebox" boxId="stock">
    <h2>Competitor Stock</h2>
    <ul>
        <li>Heinz: $5.99 per share</li>
        <li>Hunt Wesson: $8.12 per share</li>
        <li>Wal Mart: $10.51 per share</li>
    </ul>
</div>

<div id="toolbar1" dojoType="dijit.Toolbar">
    <div dojoType="dijit.form.Button" id="toolbar1.supply"
        onClick="dojo.publish('/changebox/supply');">Supply Change</div>
    <div dojoType="dijit.form.Button" id="toolbar1.majoracct"
        onClick="dojo.publish('/changebox/majoracct');">Major Acct Change</div>
    <div dojoType="dijit.form.Button" id="toolbar1.stock"
        onClick="dojo.publish('/changebox/stock');">Stock Change</div>
</div>
```

Like the widgets in Section 12.5, *Example: Live Forms*, on page 336, the publish-subscribe event system comes in handy here. Generally, you will publish events from an asynchronous process like the load callback of dojo.getXhr. But here, a toolbar button click will fire the topic—that's a good technique for unit testing the widget.

dijit.Declaration defines a template, writes a heading, and places the inner HTML in the containerNode attach point:

`creating_widgets/yft.html`

```
<div dojoType="dijit.Declaration" widgetClass="Changebox"
    defaults="{boxId: 'None'}">
    Changebox for ${boxId}
```

```
<div dojoAttachPoint="containerNode"></div>

<script type="dojo/method">
    // Define YFT animation.  The domNode is different for
    // each widget, so we define a different animation fn for each.

    this.animationFn = dojo.animateProperty({
        node: this.domNode,
        duration: 2000,
        properties: {
            backgroundColor: { start: "#FFFF00", end: "#FFFFFF" }
        }
    });

    // Fire it whenever the event /changebox/boxId is published
    dojo.subscribe("/changebox/"+this.boxId, this, function() {
        this.animationFn.play();
    });
</script>
</div>
```

The interesting thing here is the load extension point. You will recall
from Section 12.4, *Extension Points*, on page 329 that an extension
point is a method the widget allows you to override. Like extension
points filled in for a particular widget (cf. Section 12.4, *Extension Points*,
on page 329), extension points here are filled in with <*script*> tags of
type *dojo/method*. And they apply to each widget created by this class.

Although the code is shared among instances, the properties are not.
Each instance of YFT needs a different animation function since the
root nodes are different. That is perfectly fine, and assigning this.
animationFn separately for each instance ensures this is true.

Now you can use this widget anywhere, right?

Well, er...as long as you stay in the same HTML page, you're fine.
But copying the dijit.Declaration from file to file isn't such a good idea.
And even if you do it smartly, such as through server-side includes,
it's simpler and cleaner just to use a programmatically defined widget
class. That's what we'll cover next.

17.2   Widget Classes Using dojo.declare

So, the Yellow Fade Technique was easy to define with dijit.Declaration.
Declaring it programmatically is quite similar. Because every widget
class is a Dojo object class, we use dojo.declare to define it. The result
will be functionally equivalent to the dijit.Declaration version.

creating_widgets/yft_prog.html

```
Line 1   dojo.declare("Changebox",
    -        [dijit._Widget, dijit._Templated],
    -        {
    -        // Holds the id attribute of the box on which to use YFT
    5        boxId: 'None',
    -
    -        // Template
    -        templateString: "<div>Changebox for ${boxId}"+
    -            "<div dojoAttachPoint='containerNode'></div></div>",
    10
    -        // Holds subscription handle
    -        changeboxSub: null,
    -
    -        // postCreate is called after the widget has been constructed.
    15       postCreate: function() {
    -            this.animationFn = dojo.animateProperty({
    -                node: this.domNode,
    -                duration: 2000,
    -                properties: { backgroundColor: {
    20                   start: "#FFFF00",
    -                    end: "#FFFFFF"
    -                } }
    -            });
    -
    25           changeboxSub = dojo.subscribe(
    -                "/changebox/"+this.boxId,
    -                this,
    -                function() {
    -                    this.animationFn.play();
    30               }
    -            );
    -        },
    -
    -        destroy: function() {
    35           // Unsubscribe from the event
    -            dojo.unsubscribe(changeboxSub);
    -            this.inherited(arguments);
    -        }
    -   });
```

Every programmatically defined widget class uses dojo.declare, as in line 1. By the very definition of a Dijit class, we must subclass from dijit._Widget, as in line 2. Either dijit._Widget or a subclass of dijit._Widget must always be listed first. Templated widgets must also mix in the class dijit._Templated.

Unlike declaratively defined widget classes, you don't need to specify a defaults attribute. Instead, you just define the properties right in the class. So, line 5 defines the boxId= attribute.

The template can be embedded in the templateString property, as we've done here in line 9. There are actually three ways to define a template:

templateString

The template is specified directly in the string. This requires you to escape certain characters, as you must do with all JavaScript string literals. This can make the code a little awkward.

templatePath

The template is read from templatePath. Since the template needs to be legal HTML only, not a JavaScript string, escaped characters are unnecessary. During execution, it requires an extra XHR fetch to get the template. If this is too much of a performance drag, the build system described in Chapter 11, *The Dojo Loader and Build System*, on page 283 can turn these into embedded templateStrings for you.

templateNode

The template is in a DOM node and its descendents. Note templateNode must be a DOM node, not an ID—in other words, you should pass dojo.byId("n") and not "n". This creates a "template island" in your document, similar to data islands in Internet Explorer. Remember to hide it with a display:none style.

Our initialization code goes into the postCreate property at line 15. postCreate= is one of the essential extension points of all widgets, which we'll cover later in this chapter. To be nice, we unsubscribe to the topic in the destroy= extension point handler at line 34. Don't wanna leave anyone hanging on the line, right?

So, the template language is essentially the same as dijit.Declaration, but there are two subtle differences:

- The template must have only one outer node; for example, a template like The end is not legal, but <div>The end</div> is fine.
- The template itself may have widgets, but only if you set the property widgetsInTemplate to **true**. This property is always true for dijit.Declaration-defined widget classes.

Example: Greeking Widget

Another example will illustrate creating widget classes *without* a template. We'll call this widget class GreekingWidget, and its purpose in life will be to generate meaningless sentences. That in itself may sound meaningless, but "Greek" text is good for the design stage of application building. It'll generate arbitrary amounts of sentences for you, rather than trying to think of some yourself. And since the text will be different each time, you can rerun the app a few times to make sure arbitrary text flows properly.

creating_widgets/widgets/GreekingWidget.js

```
// dojo programmatic Greeking Widget
// Thank you, Agent Zlerich for 0.4 code!  Adapted for Dojo 1.0 by authors.
// See http://agentzlerich.blogspot.com
//                /2007/06/programmatic-greekingwidget-for-dojo.html
// for original post and usage examples
dojo.provide("dojobook.creating_widgets.widgets.GreekingWidget");

dojo.require("dijit._Widget");

dojo.declare(
'dojobook.creating_widgets.widgets.GreekingWidget',
[dijit._Widget],
{
    // Number of paragraphs to generate
    paragraphs: 3,

    // Length of each paragraph in sentences
    sentencesPer: 7,

    // If true, always start with "Lorem Ipsum..."
    loremIpsum: false,

    // CSS class to apply to each paragraph
    addClass: "",

    // Tag to use for surrounding each paragraph
    tag: "p",

    // The heart is in the postCreate extension pt.

    postCreate: function () {

        // Rudimentary error checking
        if (this.paragraphs < 1) {
            throw new Error("paragraphs < 1");
        } else if (this.sentencesPer < 1) {
            throw new Error("sentencesPer < 1");
        }

        // The sentences[] array has Greek sentences.  Pick
        // a random starting place, or start at 0 for
        // the classic "Lorem Ipsum..."
        var sentenceOffset;
```

```
        if (this.loremIpsum) {
            sentenceOffset = 0;
        } else {
            sentenceOffset = Math.floor(Math.random() * this.sentences.length);
        }

        // Create each "paragraph" as a DOM node
        for (var p = 0; p < this.paragraphs; p++) {
            var paraNode = dojo.doc.createElement(this.tag);

            // Print sentencesPer sentences sequentially, wrapping
            // to the first of the array if necessary
            for (var s = 0; s < this.sentencesPer; s++) {
                paraNode.appendChild(document.createTextNode(
                    this.sentences[sentenceOffset] + "  "
                ));
                sentenceOffset = (sentenceOffset + 1) % this.sentences.length;
            }

            // Attach a CSS style, if needed, then add to the page
            if (this.addClass.length > 0) {
                dojo.addClass(paraNode, this.addClass);
            }
            this.domNode.appendChild(paraNode);
        }
    },

    sentences: [
        "Lorem ipsum dolor sit amet, consectetuer adipiscing elit.",
        "Donec eleifend.",
        "Morbi tincidunt, neque ac consequat condimentum, nibh purus bibendum.",
        // Download code sample to get the entire set of sentences!
```

We'll look at the properties and the purpose of postCreate in a moment, but for now just concentrate on postCreate's body. Because we allow the user so many customizations, including the surrounding tag name, it makes little sense to use a template. Instead, the standard DOM creation functions build the pieces for us. So now when you need some random paragraphs, you just drop in this widget like so:

creating_widgets/GreekingWidgetDemo.html

```
<div dojoType="dojobook.creating_widgets.widgets.GreekingWidget"
    paragraphs="1"
    sentencesPer="1"
    loremIpsum="true"
    style="width:200px"
></div>
```

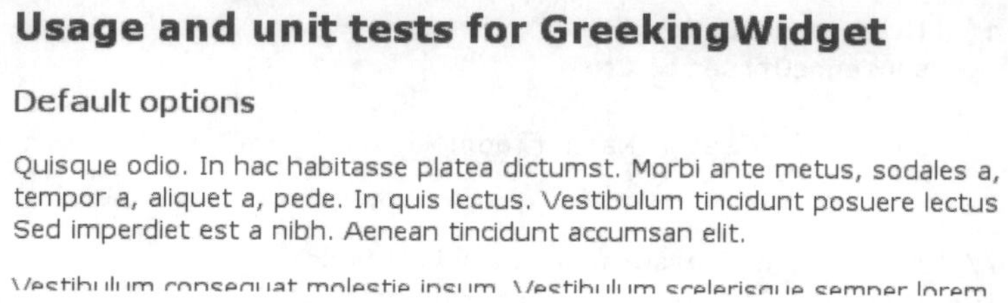

Usage and unit tests for GreekingWidget

Default options

Quisque odio. In hac habitasse platea dictumst. Morbi ante metus, sodales a, tempor a, aliquet a, pede. In quis lectus. Vestibulum tincidunt posuere lectus Sed imperdiet est a nibh. Aenean tincidunt accumsan elit.

Vestibulum consequat molestie ipsum. Vestibulum scelerisque semper lorem

Figure 17.2: WE CAN'T RESIST SAYING. . . IT'S ALL GREEK TO US

You can see a sample run of the demo in Figure 17.2. It shows the beautifully random text. (Your mileage may vary—after all, it's random.)

Now that we have a widget with lots of properties, it's a good time to revisit dojo.parser. We've used it for declarative widgets throughout the book, but how does it actually work?

17.3 The Widget Life Cycle

In the Greeking widget class, the action happens in postCreate. But how does Dijit know which method to call, and when? This is part of the widget life cycle—all widgets have specifically named methods called in a specific order by their base class dijit._Widget. So, a good understanding of that cycle will tell you where to place your code and how to debug it later.

Dojo.parser and Widgets

When programmatically creating widgets, as we saw in Section 12.3, *Creating Instances Programmatically*, on page 325, the birth process is pretty straightforward. You call the **new** keyword, and the parameters are assigned to attributes of the widget. But in declaratively created widgets, the birth is handled by dojo.parser.

One of the main jobs of dojo.parser is to set properties in a widget instance. Let's see how this works in GreekingWidget. dojo.parser activates when the entire page is finished downloading. It searches the entire DOM tree for dojoType= attributes. When it finds one, it instantiates an object with that type and then maps the other attributes on whatever properties it finds in the class.

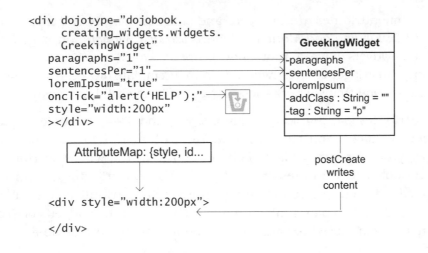

Figure 17.3: DOJO.PARSER COPIES ATTRIBUTES TO PROPERTIES.

So, for our GreekingWidget:

1. A new dojobook.creating_widgets.widgets.GreekingWidget object is created.

2. dojo.parser places the attribute paragraphs into the widget property paragraphs. It does the same for sentencesPer and loremIpsum.

3. The widget properties addClass and tag are left with their default values since there are no matching attributes.

This copying process is shown in Figure 17.3. It doesn't seem so magical anymore, does it?

The Attribute Map

What happens to attributes in the tag without analogous properties in the class? We need to consider this for our declarative widget attributes style= and onclick= earlier. But it also could happen with programmatically created instances, for example:

creating_widgets/GreekingWidgetDemo.html

```
var greek = new dojobook.creating_widgets.widgets.GreekingWidget({
      paragraphs: 1,
      sentencesPer: 1,
      loremIpsum: true,
      style: 'width:200px'
  }, dijit.byId("whereGreekShouldGo")
);
```

Well, some attributes are dropped, and some are not. Recall from Section 12.2, *Finding and Manipulating Declarative Widgets*, on page 320 that all widgets have a root node property called domNode. All the markup the widget creates, whether from a template or not, lives inside this node. And that's where these extra attributes will be copied.

The attributes id=, dir=, lang=, class=, style=, and title= are copied in all widget instances. You can define more attributes in the attributeMap property of your own widget class. In short, all the widget attributes and attributeMap attributes are kept, and all other attributes are quietly dropped. So in our previous example, the onclick= attribute is not copied over. That's not so bad, really. Adding a handler to the widget's onClick extension point does the same thing, and it's much more flexible.

Rendering the Widget

The widget rendering job is handled through extension points, which we learned about in Section 12.4, *Extension Points*, on page 329. You provide the handlers, and dijit._Widget calls them in order.

1. postMixInProperties is called after the properties have been initialized. You can override default values here, as we'll see in Section 17.4, *Extending Widgets*, on the next page.

2. buildRendering gets the template (if present) and fills in the details. Generally, you will *not* override this unless you know what you're doing—like you've built a new templating system.

3. postCreate usually contains the interesting work. At this point your widget has been turned into HTML and inserted into the page, and you can access properties like this.domNode. However, none of the child widgets has been taken care of yet.

4. startup is the last extension point called, after all of the child widgets have been drawn.

The widget rendering process is illustrated in Figure 17.4, on the facing page. Here, notice that YourWidget has a nested widget inside the template. That means the YourWidget class should set the widgetsInTemplate property to **true**.

Knowing this process helps you plug your code into the right places. For example, suppose you're building a container widget and need to know the combined size of its contained widgets. Since the widgets aren't built until startup, you'll put your code in the startup handler.

```
<div dojoType="yourWidget"
    style="width:200px">
  <div dojoType="anotherWidget">
  </div>
</div>
        ↓
    yourWidget constructor          ┌──────────────────────────┐
                                    │ anonymous : yourWidget   │
        ↓                           ├──────────────────────────┤
    mixin parameters                │ id : String = yourWidget-1│
                                    └──────────────────────────┘
  ┌ ─ ─ ─ ─ ─ ─ ─ ─ ─ ─ ─ ─ ┐
  │   postMixinProperties()  │         Dijit._Templated
  └ ─ ─ ─ ─ ─ ─ ─ ─ ─ ─ ─ ─ ┘
        ↓
    assign id, if not provided    <div id="yourWidget-1">
                                     <div dojoType="anotherWidget">…
  ┌ ─ ─ ─ ─ ─ ─ ─ ─ ─ ─ ─ ─ ┐       <!-- Expanded yourWidget -->
  │     buildRendering()     │    </div>
  └ ─ ─ ─ ─ ─ ─ ─ ─ ─ ─ ─ ─ ┘

                                  <div id="yourWidget-1" style="width:200px">
        ↓                            <div dojoType="anotherWidget">…
    copy attribute map               <!-- Expanded yourWidget -->
                                  </div>

  ┌ ─ ─ ─ ─ ─ ─ ─ ─ ─ ─ ─ ─ ┐    <div id="yourWidget-1" style="width:200px">
  │       postCreate()       │       <div id="anotherWidget-1">
  └ ─ ─ ─ ─ ─ ─ ─ ─ ─ ─ ─ ─ ┘          <!-- Expanded anotherWidget -->
        ↓                            </div>
    Expand child widgets             <!-- Expanded yourWidget -->
                                  </div>
  ┌ ─ ─ ─ ─ ─ ─ ─ ─ ─ ─ ─ ─ ┐
  │        startup()         │
  └ ─ ─ ─ ─ ─ ─ ─ ─ ─ ─ ─ ─ ┘
```

Figure 17.4: BIRTH OF A WIDGET: A SOUL-STIRRING SIGHT INDEED

That covers the beginning of the widget life. You then manipulate and destroy widgets using techniques in Chapter 12, *Scripting Widgets*, on page 317.

17.4 Extending Widgets

As we've said, widgets are objects. We know how to override the behavior of a widget instance through extension points. But what if you want to override the behavior of an entire widget class? It should be obvious that you *don't* change widget behavior by changing the source code, although it's tempting. So, how do you make changes safely?

You do it by using the object-oriented tricks you saw in Section 9.6, *Resolving Property Name Clashes*, on page 248. Here's a trivial example involving properties. Dijit.TitlePane components open and close by pushing an arrow button at the top-left corner. They are open by default. Suppose your application uses many dijit.TitlePane components, but in this case each must start in a closed state to save screen space. After adding the attribute open="false" over and over, you realize it'd be much easier if open= defaulted to false.

You can create a subclass of dijit.TitlePane to do just that. We'll call the component dojobook.creating_widgets.widgets.ClosedTitlePane. The corresponding file dojoroot/dojobook/widgets/ClosedTitlePane.js looks like this:

`creating_widgets/widgets/ClosedTitlePane.js`

```
dojo.provide("dojobook.creating_widgets.widgets.ClosedTitlePane");

dojo.require("dijit.TitlePane");

dojo.declare(
"dojobook.creating_widgets.widgets.ClosedTitlePane",
[dijit.TitlePane],
{
    open: false
}
);
```

Here's the trick. If you define a subclass property with the same name as a superclass property, the subclass property takes precedence. That is good for us. We merely define open= with a different default. Even though we don't use that property in the class, every time dijit.TitlePane reads or writes open=, it uses the ClosedTitlePane copy.

As you might expect, the same thing goes for methods. After all, this is JavaScript, and all methods are just data of type Function. You can define a subclass and then specify the extension points and methods to override.

Having learned how to create and extend a widget and all the things that happen afterward, we'll end with a useful example.

17.5 Example: A Yahoo Answers Widget

The pleasantly addictive Yahoo Answers site is Web 2.0 at its finest: someone asks a question about any subject, and others contribute answers. The answers themselves are rated by others. After a fixed amount of time, the question closes, and the question asker selects the "best" answer, which may or may not reflect the given ratings. And that question and answer are kept for posterity. Being a question answerer is like trolling around a cocktail party, eavesdropping on conversations, and leaping into ones that interest you. And everything is recorded!

This collaborative filtering aspect makes it a nifty search engine. If the term *relativity* appears in your text, hopping on Yahoo Answers and typing "relativity" will yield the most popular questions about relativity.

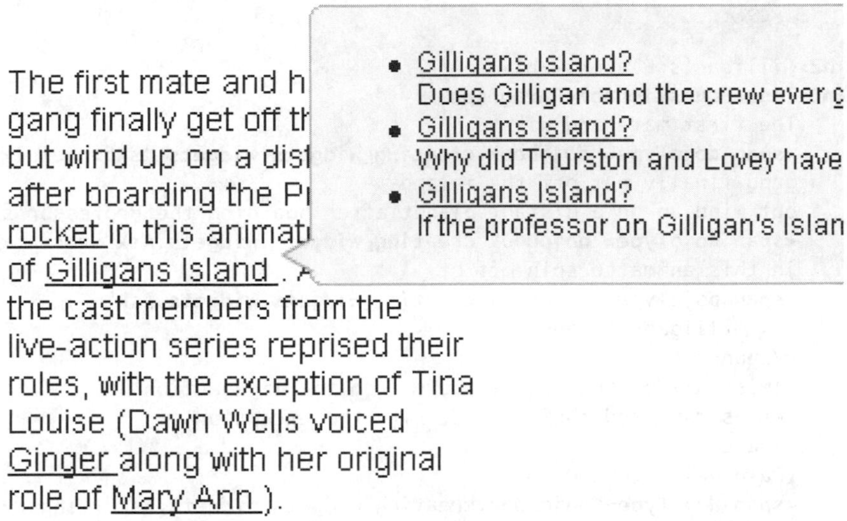

The first mate and h
gang finally get off th
but wind up on a dist
after boarding the Pr
rocket in this animati
of Gilligans Island . A
the cast members from the
live-action series reprised their
roles, with the exception of Tina
Louise (Dawn Wells voiced
Ginger along with her original
role of Mary Ann).

- Gilligans Island?
  Does Gilligan and the crew ever g
- Gilligans Island?
  Why did Thurston and Lovey have
- Gilligans Island?
  If the professor on Gilligan's Islan

Figure 17.5: CLICK A WORD TO LOOK AT SOME YAHOO QUESTIONS.

That's a good place to start your research. Fortunately, Yahoo Answers is also available through a web service. It would be nice to do a quick lookup on Yahoo Answers for certain terms that we think may cause the user to stumble. By calling the web service, we can actually get some Yahoo Questions without leaving the page. Figure 17.5 shows what we want the user to see.

The "bubble" is easily done with a Dijit *master tooltip*. Recall from Section 15.3, *Tooltips*, on page 405 that only one master tooltip can be displayed at a time, and it does not go away when you leave the underlying area. That makes it easy to create the Yahoo Answers as links. If one of the questions looks relevant, the user just clicks it.

We want this widget class to be easy to use. The widget "consumer" need only wrap a possibly difficult term with the Ask widget definition.

It's done like this.

creating_widgets/yahoo-answer-demo.html

```
<h2>Gilligan's Planet:</h2>
<p class="questionableParagraph">
    The first mate and his
    <span dojoType="dojobook.creating_widgets.widgets.Ask">woeful</span>
    gang finally get off the island---
    but wind up on a distant planet after boarding the Professor's
    <span dojoType="dojobook.creating_widgets.widgets.Ask">rocket</span>
    in this animated spin-off of
    <span dojoType="dojobook.creating_widgets.widgets.Ask">
        Gilligans Island
    </span>.
    Almost all of the cast members from the live-action
    series reprised their roles, with the exception of
    Tina Louise
    (Dawn Wells voiced
    <span dojoType="dojobook.creating_widgets.widgets.Ask">Ginger</span>
    along with her original role of
    <span dojoType="dojobook.creating_widgets.widgets.Ask">Mary Ann</span>).
</p>
```

Where do you start? The user interface is pretty straightforward, so let's get an early win. A little CSS takes care of the formatting for the terms:

creating_widgets/css/ask.css

```
.ask {
    text-decoration: underline;
    cursor: pointer;
}
.questionableParagraph {
    width: 200px;
    /* Next two effectively center the paragraph in the browser */
    margin-left: auto;
    margin-right: auto;
}
```

The template, kept in templates/Ask.html, references this style and adds some wiring:

creating_widgets/templates/Ask.html

```
<span class="ask"
      dojoAttachEvent="ondijitclick:_getQuestions">
<span dojoAttachPoint="containerNode"></span>
</span>
```

Recall that Dijit fills containerNode with the tag contents. In this case, we want to repeat the term the user wrapped. Also, the ondijitclick event will fire whenever the user clicks, presses Enter , or presses the space-bar on that term. The _getQuestions method will fire in this case, and we provide its implementation in the widget. The prefix _ implies a private method, which is nice for our case because we make assumptions about the input the ordinary users might not.

Now for the widget class itself. Because we'll be using this on many pages, it's best to create it programmatically. The interesting thing here is we don't need any extension points like postCreate. We give an empty postCreate body here just so future viewers of our code don't say "Where is postCreate?"

creating_widgets/widgets/Ask.js

```
dojo.provide("dojobook.creating_widgets.widgets.Ask");

dojo.require("dijit._Widget");
dojo.require("dijit._Templated");
dojo.require("dojo.io.script");
dojo.require("dijit.Tooltip");


dojo.declare(
"dojobook.creating_widgets.widgets.Ask",
[dijit._Widget, dijit._Templated],
{
    templatePath: dojo.moduleUrl("dojobook",
            "creating_widgets/templates/Ask.html"),

    postCreate: function(){
        // Don't do anything because all the magic happens in _getQuestions
    },
```

The bulk of the good stuff is in _getQuestions. Here you'll notice the variable hookedTo carries the widget object into the body of _getQuestions through a closure. You can also use dojo.hitch to do this—it's largely a matter of taste.

creating_widgets/widgets/Ask.js

```
_getQuestions: function() {
    // Through JavaScript closures, this variable allows us to reference the
    // surrounding object from within the get(...) methods.
    var hookedTo = this;

    // Go to Yahoo Answers for relevant questions
    dojo.io.script.get({
        // URL for Yahoo Relevant Questions
        url: "http://answers.yahooapis.com/AnswersService/V1/questionSearch",
```

```
                    // Send search term parameters.  The appid is the one you obtained for
                    // chapter 3's example.
                    content: {
                        appid: "DEMO",
                        /* The search term we're sending is the body of the tag */
                        query: hookedTo.containerNode.innerHTML,
                        output: "json",
                        results: 3,
                        /* Look only in the questions for the term, not the answers */
                        search_in: "question"
                    },

                    // If the response takes longer than 10000ms (= 10 seconds), error out
                    timeout: 10000,

                    // Yahoo API requires you to send the callback function name in the
                    // parameter "callback"
                    callbackParamName: "callback",

                    // Function run when Yahoo returns with the answer
                    load: function(results) {
                        // Build the tooltip text
                        var questionTooltipHtml = "<ul>";
                        dojo.forEach(results.all.questions, function(question) {
                            questionTooltipHtml +=
                                dojo.string.substitute(
                                    "<li><a href='${Link}'>${Subject}</a>"+
                                    "<br/>${Content}</li>",
                                    question
                                );
                        });

                        // Create a tooltip
                        questionTooltipHtml += "</ul>";
                        dijit.showTooltip(
                            questionTooltipHtml,
                            hookedTo.domNode
                        );
                    },

                    // And this is the callback used when a web service communication
                    // error or timeout occurs.  Note that errors returned from Yahoo
                    // in the response are still handled with load()
                    error: function(text) {
                        alert("An error has occurred.");
                        return text;
                    }
                });
        } // End of _getQuestions
```

The Yahoo Answers service, like the Yahoo Search service we saw in Section 3.4, *Researching Cigars Using JSONP*, on page 49, uses JSONP. We attach to it through dojo.io.script. From there, we retrieve the input and format it into a list. dojo.showTooltip displays this in a tooltip bubble. And that's pretty much it.

Through our four examples, you can see how Dijit provides a solid structure for reusing visual components. You can both use and define the classes through HTML markup or through JavaScript. Templates and CSS provide an easy way to change the visual layout without touching the code and are reusable across many different pages. Finally, you can extend components through the same ways you extend regular classes. There are many JavaScript toolkits out there, but none of them has this amount of flexibility and power.

Part IV

Rich Internet Applications

Chapter 18

Building a Rich Internet Application

In Figure 18.1, on the following page, you can see a Rich Internet Application (RIA) being hosted in Firefox. The application includes a menu, a resizable multiple-pane workspace, and a status bar—just like so many native applications. Unlike typical web pages, the menu is anchored at the top, and the status bar is at the bottom. Also, there is no URL navigation; it is a "single-page" application. If you hate markup, you'll love this app since it includes a grand total of fifty lines of HTML.

Instead of crafting many pages of massive markup, we're going to leverage Dojo to build a browser-based application framework and then use that framework to sketch the application shown. Along the way, we'll touch on just about every aspect of Dojo we've discussed elsewhere. Even if you're never going to build an RIA, you'll use most of the Dojo described in this chapter during the normal course of building modern web pages. And, if you fancy yourself a "real" programmer who doesn't "do" JavaScript or HTML, then this chapter is for you. You're going to see just how powerful Dojo and JavaScript really are.

18.1 The Big Picture

Before we start, let's discuss why building an RIA is a good idea. We'll also look at the high-level design of the framework and application we're going to build.

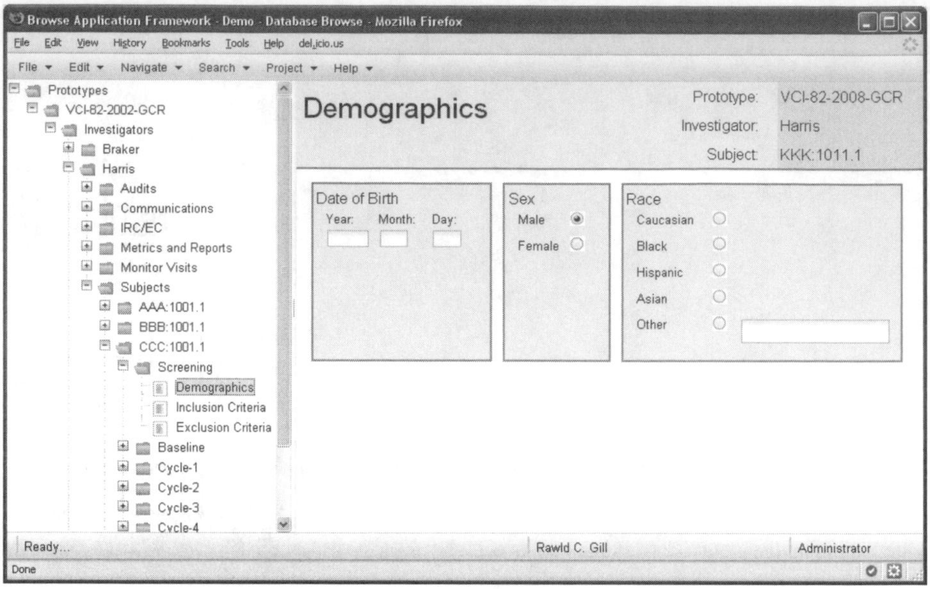

Figure 18.1: THE BROWSE SINGLE-PAGE APPLICATION

The Browser Is the UI Platform

Broadly speaking, there are two classes of browser-based applications. First, traditional web pages follow the browser application paradigm that's been dominant since the beginning of the Web. These pages are constructed in HTML (statically or dynamically) and are served to the user's browser from an off-host HTTP server. They include hyperlinks to other pages and may collect information through HTML form controls. All of the cool Ajax stuff that has been discussed here and elsewhere makes these pages more dynamic and functional, but the basic use paradigm is unchanged: get a page, do a *little* something, get another page.

The second class of browser-based application takes form as the so-called single-page application: the user navigates to a URL that then presents a complete application—akin to a native desktop application—*without ever leaving the page*. The document managed by the browser is really a complete GUI program. At a minimum, such a program will display the GUI through HTML and CSS and implement logic through JavaScript. The program may also communicate with some off-host HTTP server, but this is not a requirement.

Indeed, such a program could just as easily communicate with the local host through Java applets, Google Gears, or any number of other technologies. The browser becomes the UI platform.[1]

The idea of the browser as a UI platform is quite powerful. First, the browser is ubiquitous. All desktop environments include a browser. Increasingly, other devices such as phones also include browsers. In cases where the RIA is backed by off-host HTTP servers, the application will have *zero* installation footprint. This is truly a case of "write once, run anywhere."

The second reason the idea has power is that it can be used to enforce a clear separation of concerns. The browser-side application is concerned only with implementing the GUI—the machinery required to present information to the user and gather input from the user. All other computational activity (that is, the machinery that actually makes the program do something useful) takes place somewhere else. Contrast this architecture to most web app frameworks that dynamically generate presentation and handle several other UI tasks at the server. No matter how careful you are, computational logic and presentational logic inevitably leak into each other. And these dependencies increase complexity, which makes the whole thing harder to get right.

In the design presented here, all presentation logic is handled in the browser. This logic is delivered to the browser in a set of *static* scripts and *static* presentation data. The server returns raw data (often JSON, but sometimes scripts with executable code) and is strictly forbidden from executing any presentation logic. Of course, the data presented by the UI may be dynamic.

The Browser Application Framework

We're going to build two things:

- A browser application framework

- A sample application that uses the framework

---

1. *Rich browser application* describes the architecture more accurately, but we'll stick with RIA because this moniker is so pervasive.

An Important Caveat

The RIA design and framework sketched in this and the next chapter is opinionated. It assumes a certain view of the world in which it lives. For example, it assumes the user is going to spend a lot of time within the application without navigating away to another web page—much like a native application such as a word processor or spreadsheet. Also, it makes the value judgment that all of the UI should be implemented in the browser. These and other assumptions and judgments may not be optimal for some kinds of applications. This is but one way to solve one class of problems. We are not claiming it's the only way; and we're certainly not claiming that there is only one class of RIA problem. While Dojo works beautifully in this example, it's just as powerful in any other design that leverages client-side JavaScript.

The framework is named Browser Application (BAF).[2] Since this is a book about Dojo and not about designing frameworks, we're not going to spend time discussing the design trade-offs encountered when building an application framework. Suffice it to say that there are alternatives to the design presented, each with different strengths and weaknesses. And we're not going to describe every last gory detail of a particular framework. We'll show enough to get the idea across but leave some details incomplete. But, before we can start building, we need *some* design. So, without further ado...

The Workspace Object Abstraction

The core abstraction used by the application is a container for widgets termed a *workspace object* (WSO). A WSO is the thing that the user interacts with to get information and provide input. Often it will look like a form, as shown in Figure 18.1, on page 480, but WSOs come in all shapes and sizes. Here are some examples:

- A word processor (a WSO that contains a single rich text editor widget)

---

2. This example is loosely based on the framework being developed at Vista Information Technologies (see http://www.vistainfotech.com). Wavemaker, built by Dojo core contributors Scott Miles and Steve Orvell, is another popular Dojo-based framework (see http://www.wavemaker.com/).

- A control panel that requests a report
- A static or dynamic report or dashboard
- A form that presents and collects data for a standard create-read-update-delete (CRUD) database application

The point of these is examples is that the WSO abstraction is not just another form-based framework, but rather a general abstraction for just about anything you can build in a GUI. The widgets may be initialized with data from the server and/or collect input to send to the server. But the key idea is this: the definition of a particular WSO type is given by a set of widget types together with their layout and behavior properties, and this definition is *static* (the definition is completely independent of the data ultimately presented by the WSO).

For example, let's say a particular WSO displays a list of contacts in a grid. The WSO definition would include the name of the particular JavaScript class that implements the grid widget together with layout and behavior properties that describe how an instance of the grid widget should work in the WSO. When the user demands an instance of the WSO, the application requests the WSO definition and queries the server for the list of contacts. Then the application instantiates a grid instance as directed by the WSO definition, fills it with the data, and displays the WSO instance to the user. Contrast this to the way a more-traditional web app works where the server takes the contact list data and dynamically constructs HTML that presents the list and then sends the whole monolithic mess to the browser.

Implementing the WSO concept is the job of the framework. It's a class that takes a WSO definition and some data and returns an object that's convenient to display inside the rest of the UI framework.

A WSO definition is provided by a JSON object that lists all the widgets and their properties. Since this definition is static, there is no need to keep asking the server for the same definition. Instead, the framework provides a manager that caches WSO definitions.

The data interface can range from simple to complex. At the simple end, the server could return a set of (name, value) pairs as JSON, and the WSO definition could include properties that describe how to map these pairs to widgets; writing new/changed data back to the server could be implemented by returning the JSON object, updated with changed values. This design falls down when the application includes the ability to have several WSO instances open at the same time. For example, if the user had the contact list open as well as a particular contact on that list and then edited and saved the contact name, care should be taken to ensure the contact list is refreshed with the changed name. This can be implemented by binding widgets to dojo.data data stores and then implementing a data store manager in the framework. The manager ensures that data requests that reference the same data are connected to the same data store.

So, at this point, our framework should be capable of something like this:

```
Line 1    function getWsoInstance(
            wsoDefId, //identifier for the type of WSO to return
            dataQuery //the data to fill the WSO
          ){
     5      var wsoDef= WsoDefinitionManager.get(wsoDefId);
            var data= DataManager.get(dataQuery);
            return new WSO(wsoDef, data);
          }
```

The Command System

Most applications have a system where a user can issue a command (for example, "open a file" or "save the current object"). The UI for issuing the command almost always comes in the form of a menu or context menu, a toolbar, or an accelerator key.

Although the idea of a menu is often considered independent of a toolbar, they are really the same concept. A set of items is presented to the user that he can select. When an item is selected, a command is issued. In the case of a menu item that displays a submenu, the command can be thought of as "display submenu." With this in mind, the framework implements the menu in terms of a dijit.Toolbar instance and submenus in terms of dijit.Menu. Although the example doesn't implement context menus, they could be implemented using the same techniques we'll use when implementing the menu.

As you saw in Chapter 15, *Form Controls*, on page 393, toolbars/menus and submenus can be implemented in markup. BAF takes a different approach by providing machinery to dynamically build toolbar/menus and submenus from data. This has a couple of benefits:

- The content of the toolbar/menus and submenus can be easily changed based on current user and/or current context.

- The presentation (language, icons, layout, and the rest) of individual items can be easily changed, independent of content.

The framework defines two abstractions:

Command items

The text, accelerator, icon, tooltip, and other attributes of a particular command. Here's a few examples:

```
Line 1    var fileCommandItem= {
   -          id: "file",
   -          type: baf.commandType.submenu,
   -          order: 100,
   5          group: baf.commandGroup.top,
   -          text: "File"};

   -       var saveCommandItem= {
   -          id: "save",
   10         type: baf.commandType.command,
   -          order: 160,
   -          group: baf.commandGroup.save,
   -          text: "Save"};

   15      var saveAsCommandItem= {
   -          id: "saveAs",
   -          type: baf.commandType.command,
   -          order: 170,
   -          group: baf.commandGroup.save,
   20         text: "Save As..."};
```

Actual command items have a few more properties. Notice the order and group properties; they can be used to automatically organize a submenu and insert menu separator bars.

Command menus

A hierarchy of command items that make up a menu. For example:

```
Line 1    var menu= {
   -          file: {
   -             save: 0,
   -             saveAs: 0,
   5             saveAll: 0,
   -             close: 0,
   -             closeAll: 0,
   -             logoff: 0,
   -             switchUser: 0,
   10         },
   -          edit: 0,
   -          //etc...
   -       };
```

Note how this structure cleanly captures the hierarchy of a menu; this compares quite favorably to markup. It's also very easy to edit both statically (that is, in a file) and dynamically while the program is running.

The framework includes the class baf.dijit.Menuband that manages a dojo.toolbar, a command menu object, and a set of command items.

When a user issues a command through any means (menu, toolbar, accelerator), the command subsystem simply broadcasts the command through dojo.publish. Any other subsystem that's interested in the command can receive this message by connecting with dojo.subscribe. One of the cool side effects of this design is that subscribers can easily change the way menu items and submenus are presented. For example, before a submenu is presented by the manager, it broadcasts that a submenu was "commanded." A client can add or subtract items from the submenu before it's displayed. And with the simple command menu data structure shown earlier, this is quite easy to do.

Accelerator keys could be implemented by catching keyboard events, then dojo.publishing a command when an accelerator key is detected.

The Status Bar

Putting a stylized div at the bottom of a page with a few children that display status items isn't rocket science. The key idea is to abstract the status bar to its true functional purpose: define a set of panes and allow client components to send content to those panes. The framework includes the class baf.dijit.Statusbar that implements this functionality.

Data-on-Demand Data Stores

Tree-based navigation is almost as common as the browser. However, when the number of items in the tree is large—thousands or even millions—it is clearly not practical to download all this data in one chunk. Fortunately, dijit.Tree was designed to demand tree items only when needed; unfortunately, Dojo 1.1 doesn't include a data store that provides this functionality. So, BAF includes a data store that requests items only as demanded. The actual configuration of the tree navigation widget is left to the application.

Mock Services

Since the server's only responsibility is to return data (remember, there is no need to generate dynamic markup), it's easy to build a mock service in JavaScript. The idea is to construct an object that is initialized with a set of response objects. The mock service provides an interface that mimics whatever real interface would be used to communicate with a real service (for example, like the dojo.xhr* interface). When a request is given, the mock service sets a timer that fakes the time required to hit a real server; when the timer expires, the response object is returned.

The framework includes mock services that return navigation items and WSO definitions. These mocks can be initialized with various sets of data required to execute different tests. This is fairly powerful in the real world. The team responsible for the UI component can be provided with a working (but fake) service on day one—long before the real server is available. Heck, sales teams could be provided with demo products that work off the mock servers, greatly increasing the probability they'll give a good demo! This is yet another example of the power behind the RIA architecture.

The Browse Application

So much for the framework. Let's spec out an application. We're going to build an application that retrieves and displays WSOs as provided by some service. We'll name the application OBE, which stands for object browser and editor.

As shown in Figure 18.1, on page 480, OBE contains a main menu bar at the top, a status bar at the bottom, and a workspace that occupies all the remaining space available in the browser window. The workspace is further divided by a splitter bar into two panes—a navigation pane on the left and an object pane on the right; the splitter bar can be used to resize the two panes. The navigation pane presents the hierarchy of objects. The object pane displays the object currently selected in the navigation pane.

The application is built on top of the BAF framework described earlier. It includes a top-level object that instantiates the main menu, navigator pane, status bar, WSO definition manager, and workspace manager. The navigator pane includes a dijit.Tree instance that's backed by an on-demand navigation data store provided by the framework. The workspace manager catches a demand for a new workspace object and coordinates the construction of a new WSO instance and the destruction of the existing instance (if any). Finally, all the visual components are arranged in a dijit.layout.BorderContainer that's created and managed by the application.

We'll build this application in steps. Let's get started.

18.2 Step 1: Create the Application Skeleton

The goal of the first step is to get organized and get something minimally running.

Organization

The work is divided into two projects: BAF (the browser application framework) and OBE (the object browser and editor application). Each of these projects defines a top-level module. Since we hate typing capital letters, these top-level modules are named baf and obe.

The BAF project implements several subsystems that are defined as child modules of baf:

baf.command

> This is the command subsystem. It defines a class that manages command items, baf.command.ItemManager.

baf.data

> This is the data subsystem. It defines customized dojo.data drivers and other machinery to handle sending/receiving/caching data with a service including the following:
>
> - baf.data.LazyTreeStore: A dojo.data driver retrieving tree items on demand from some service
> - baf.data.WsoDefinitionsManager: Machinery that retrieves and caches WSO definitions from some service

baf.dijit

> Custom Dijit-based components, including:
>
> - baf.dijit.LazyTreeModel: A subclass of dijit.tree.TreeStoreModel that interfaces with baf.data.LazyTreeStore
> - baf.dijit.MenuBand: Dijit-based component that manages a menu
> - baf.dijit.Statusbar: Dijit-based component that implements a status bar
> - baf.dijit.StaticText: Dijit-based widget that displays a stylized block of static text
> - baf.dijit.Pair: Dijit-based widget that positions and displays a related pair of widgets; intended to be used to display (label, value) pairs
> - baf.dijit.Wso: Dijit-based widget that contains a hierarchy of other widgets

baf.test

This is the machinery to help test applications; all mock services are included here:

- test.mocks.services.Base: A base class for mock services that includes the basic functionality to simulate a dojo.xhr* call
- test.mocks.services.WsoDef: A mock service that delivers a WSO definition
- test.mocks.services.Navigator: A mock service that delivers navigator tree items

Since most of the implementation details are factored out into the BAF framework, OBE is quite simple. Test data is located in the obe.test module tree, but there are no subsystems.

Here's what the directory tree looks like:

```
/<document-root>
  /baf
    /command
    /data
    /dijit
    /test
      /mocks
        /services
    /wso
  /obe
    /test
```

This organization factors the project into a set of small, tightly defined, largely independent classes and modules that helps control complexity. Different parts of the project can be worked on by different people, independently. And with the Dojo build system, all of these tiny scripts can be aggregated and compressed to optimize download performance when it's time to release the application to production.

Building the Main Program

The goal of step 1 is to load and execute a function that initializes the application and draws the UI with menu, navigator, workspace, and status panes. The navigator and workspace panes should be resizable along their widths with a draggable resize bar separating the two panes.

The HTML document that hosts OBE is trivial. The head element loads the style sheets, dojo.js, and the top-level module that starts the application. The body element simply displays "loading."

Here's the complete file:

`baf/step1/obe/main.htm`

```
Line 1  <!DOCTYPE HTML PUBLIC "-//W3C//DTD HTML 4.01//EN"
   -      "http://www.w3.org/TR/html4/strict.dtd">
   -    <html>
   -      <head>
   5        <title>Mastering Dojo - Object Browser and Editor</title>
   -
   -        <style type="text/css">
   -          @import "/dojoroot/dojo/resources/dojo.css";
   -          @import "/dojoroot/dijit/themes/tundra/tundra.css";
   10         @import "/obe/obe.css";
   -        </style>
   -
   -        <script type="text/javascript" src="/dojoroot/dojo/dojo.js">
   -        </script>
   15
   -        <script type="text/javascript" >
   -          dojo.require("obe.main");
   -          dojo.addOnLoad(function(){
   -            //e.g., given: location.search == ?test=run001
   20           //        then: dojo.require(obe.test.tests.run001)
   -            var testId= location.search.match(/(\?test\=)(\w+)/);
   -            if (testId) {
   -              dojo.require("obe.test.tests." + testId[2]);
   -            } else {
   25             obe.main.startup();
   -            }
   -          });
   -        </script>
   -      </head>
   30     <body class="tundra">
   -        <div id="bafLoading">
   -          <p>Loading</p>
   -        </div>
   -      </body>
   35   </html>
```

Notice that dojo.js is loaded from /dojoroot/dojo/dojo.js, which causes *dojo-module-path* to be calculated as /dojoroot/dojo. Since no other module paths are set, top-level modules will be loaded as siblings to /dojoroot/dojo. For example, the loader will try to load /dojoroot/obe/main.js when the module obe.man is dojo.required. We solved the problem on our development box by aliasing the path /dojo/obe to /obe in the development directory tree on the local HTTP server (/dojo/baf must also be aliased to /baf). This technique eliminates the need for module paths as well as different development and release versions of main.htm.

In the future, the div.bafLoading element (line 31) could be replaced with a simple logon form that collects a user identifier and password. Then, if the cross-domain loader was employed, the application could be downloading scripts while the user is typing his logon information. This would give an illusion of extra speed.

In a moment we'll see that the application begins executing by calling the function obe.main.startup; if the URL contains the query parameter "?test=*testModule*", then the module obe.test.tests.*testModule* is loaded and expected to start the application. This technique provides a convenient way to control how the program is started during development; we'll use it later. That's it for the one-and-only HTML document used in the application; next let's look at the JavaScript that makes things happen.

The module obe.main holds the "main program"; the function obe.main. startup is the entry point for the program. OBE utilizes dijit.layout. BorderContainer to handle the top-level layout. At this point, no real functionality is going into the panes, so each pane is stuffed with a dijit.layout.ContentPane that holds a single p element that names the pane. Here's the code:

`baf/step1/obe/main.js`

```
Line 1  dojo.provide("obe.main");
        dojo.require("dijit.layout.BorderContainer");
        dojo.require("dijit.layout.ContentPane");
        (function(){
   5      //define the main program functions...
          var main= obe.main;
          main.startup= function() {

            //create a fake menu...
  10        main.menu= new dijit.layout.ContentPane({
              id: "menu",
              region: "top",
              //height must be given for top/bottom panes...
              style: "height: 2em;"
  15        });
          main.menu.setContent('menu');

            //create a fake navigator...
          main.navigator= new dijit.layout.ContentPane({
  20          id: "navigator",
              region: "left",
              //width must be given for left/right panes...
              style: "width: 20%; overflow: auto",
              splitter: true
  25        });
```

```
          main.navigator.setContent('navigator');

          //create a fake workspace...
          main.workspace= new dijit.layout.ContentPane({
30          id: "workspace",
            region: "center"
            //note, no sizing!
          });
          main.workspace.setContent('workspace');
35
          //create a fake status bar...
          main.status= new dijit.layout.ContentPane({
            id: "status",
            region: "bottom",
40           //height must be given for top/bottom panes...
            style: "height: 2em;"
          });
          main.status.setContent('status');

45        //create the main application container....
          var appContainer= main.appContainer= new dijit.layout.BorderContainer({
            //fill up the viewport...
            style: "width: 100%; height: 100%",
            design: "headline"
50        });

          //finally, destroy the loading message and show it all...
          dojo._destroyElement(dojo.byId("bafLoading"));
          dojo.place(appContainer.domNode, dojo.body(), "first");
55        appContainer.addChild(main.menu);
          appContainer.addChild(main.status);
          appContainer.addChild(main.navigator);
          appContainer.addChild(main.workspace);

60        //tell the container to recalculate its layout...
          appContainer.layout();

          window.onresize= function(){
            appContainer.layout();
65        };
        };
      })();//(function(){
```

We've seen this before in markup in Section 16.5, *The Alignment Container: BorderContainer*, on page 446. Once again, the code is trivial. Notice the call to lay out the display after it's first initialized (line 61) and after each viewport size change (line 63).

Lastly, we need a little style sheet magic. The html and body elements should be set to 100% height and width; this forces the top-level dijit. layout.BorderContainer to use the entire browser viewport. The style sheet also includes some coloring and borders to help test the panes for correct sizing and positioning:

baf/step1/obe/obe.css

```css
html, body {
  height: 100%;
  width: 100%;
}

#menu {
  border: 1px solid black;
  background-color: #D00000;
}

#navigator {
  border: 1px solid black;
  background-color: #00D000;
}

#workspace {
  border: 1px solid black;
  background-color: #A0A0D0;
}

#status {
  border: 1px solid black;
  background-color: yellow;
}
```

That is it for step 1. Start your localhost HTTP server and navigate to obe.htm. You should see something like Figure 18.2, on the next page. When the browser window is resized, the panes should adjust correctly, and the drag bar between the navigator and workspace panes should cause these panes to resize correctly.

18.3 Step 2: The Main Menu and Command System

The goal of the this step is to create the main menu and supporting command item manager. We'll also demonstrate starting the application with test data.

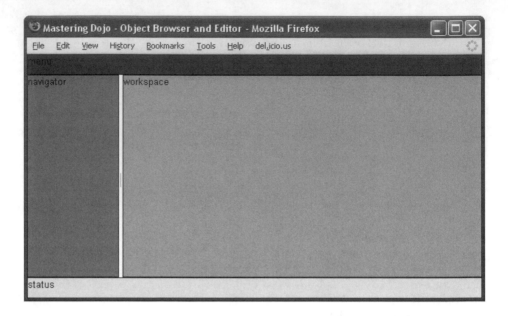

Figure 18.2: BASIC APPLICATION LAYOUT

The Command Item Store

Recall from the design discussion that menus, toolbars, and context menus are filled with command items. Command items hold the display properties of a command. So before we can implement a menu, we need a local cache of command items. Hmmm, sounds like a dojo.data data store might do the trick. If command items are delivered to the program as JSON data, then dojo.data.ItemFileReadStore will work.

Unfortunately, there are a couple of potential problems. Menus, submenus, and context menus are going to be built dynamically. For example, the File submenu is not filled with items until the user clicks the File submenu button. We'll see in a moment that this design is quite powerful. But, it has the drawback that the menu machinery can't wait around for an asynchronous fetch of command item data. Instead, when a menu demands a command item, it needs something—immediately. Since dojo.data.ItemFileReadStore.fetch operates asynchronously, a little modification is required.

The other problem is the dojo.data getValue interface is fairly verbose. For example, say item is a command item. To get its order property,

we have to write something like commandItemStore.getItem(item, "order").
Certainly, item.order would be much more convenient.

Both of these problems can be solved simply by deriving from dojo.data.
ItemFileReadStore and adding a function that guarantees to immediately
return an item (solves the first problem) and further converts the item
to a hash before returning it (solves the second problem). Here's the
code:

`baf/step2/baf/command/ItemManager.js`

```
Line 1   dojo.declare("baf.command.ItemManager", dojo.data.ItemFileReadStore, {

           getItem: function(id) {
             //   summary:
    5        //       Returns a command item as a hash; guaranteed to return immediately

             var theItem;
             function onItem(item) {
               theItem= item;
   10        }

             this.fetchItemByIdentity({
               identity: id,
               onItem: onItem
   15        });

             if (theItem) {
               var result= {};
               for (var p in defaultCommandItem) {
   20            if (defaultCommandItem.hasOwnProperty(p)) {
                   result[p] = this.getValue(theItem, p, defaultCommandItem[p]);
                 }
               }
               return result;
   25        } else {
               return dojo.mixin({}, defaultCommandItem, {text: id});
             }
           }
   30   });
```

If the demanded item is in the store, then theItem will always be filled
with a value (line 9) before fetch returns (line 16); otherwise, the function just creates a default command item with minimal information.
Before the item is returned, it's converted to a hash (line 19).

The store can be filled as usual. We'll provide some test JSON data.

Here's a sample:

`baf/demo.js`

```
Line 1   obe.test.data.command.set001.commandItems= {
  -        identifier: "id",
  -        label: "text",
  -        items: [{
  5          id: "file",
  -          type: baf.commandType.submenu,
  -          text: "File",
  -          order: 1000
  -        },{
  10         id: "save",
  -          type: baf.commandType.command,
  -          text: "Save",
  -          order: 1520,
  -          group: "save"
  15       }
  -        //et cetera....
  -        ]
  -      };
```

Since a single command item store is used by all menus (regular and context) and toolbars in a program, it should be a property of obe.main. Typically, it would be filled during program startup with all the items needed for the lifetime of the application. This is accomplished by passing in some startup data to obe.main.startup and then passing the data on to the command item store. Here's how the modified obe.main.startup looks so far:

`baf/step2/obe/main.js`

```
Line 1   main.startup= function(args) {

  -        main.commandItemStore= new baf.command.ItemManager({
  -          data: args.commandItems
  5        });
```

Now we can leverage the machinery we have put in main.htm to call obe.main.startup with some test data. First, we need a startup script that calls obe.main.startup with the test data. Here's an example:

`baf/step2/obe/test/tests/run001.js`

```
Line 1   dojo.provide("obe.test.tests.run001");
  -      dojo.require("obe.test.data.command.set001");
  -      dojo.addOnLoad(function(){
  -        var startupArgs= {
  5          commandItems: obe.test.data.command.set001.commandItems,
  -          menu: obe.test.data.command.set001.mainMenu
  -        };
  -        obe.main.startup(startupArgs);
  -      });
```

The actual data is brought in from another module (line 2); it's just plain ol' JSON objects. We'll need the menu (line 6) in the next section.

Now, pointing the browser to ./main.htm?test=run001 causes obe.test.tests. run001 to be dojo.required, which calls obe.main.startup with the appropriate test data. Pretty cool! Next, let's build the menu.

The Main Menu

Part of the design said that the contents of (sub)menus is specified by nested hashes of command item identifiers; we'll call these hashes *menu objects*. This makes menus very easy to configure. Here's an example menu object:

`baf/demo.js`

```
Line 1   obe.test.data.command.set001.mainMenu= {
    -      file: {
    -        save: 0,
    -        saveAll: 0,
    5        saveAll: 0,
    -        close:0,
    -        closeAll: 0,
    -        send: {
    -          sendToContact: 0,
    10         sendToList: 0
    -        },
    -        logoff: 0,
    -        switchUser: 0
    -      },
    15     edit: {
    -        //et cetera....
    -      }
    -      //et cetera....
    -    };
```

The top-level menu is simply a dijit.Toolbar that's populated by the top-level command items of a menu object. So, we'll derive the BAF menu class baf.dijit.MenuBand from dijit.Toolbar. A menu needs both a menu object and access to a command item store; these are expected in the constructor arguments:

`baf/step2/baf/dijit/MenuBand.js`

```
Line 1   dojo.declare("baf.dijit.MenuBand", dijit.Toolbar, {
    -      constructor: function(args) {
    -        this.commandItemStore= args.commandItemStore;
    -        this.menu= args.menu;
    5        this.sort= args.sort || function(lhs, rhs){return lhs.order-rhs.order;};
    -      },
```

The top-level objects are sorted and grouped before they are inserted into the toolbar; separators are automatically inserted between groups. Here's how that looks:

baf/step2/baf/dijit/MenuBand.js

```
Line 1    _prepareList: function(menu){
    -       var contents= [];
    -       for (var p in menu) if (menu.hasOwnProperty(p)) {
    -         contents.push(this.commandItemStore.getItem(p));
    5       }
    -       contents.sort(this.sort);

    -       var result= [];
    -       if (contents.length) {
    10        result= [contents[0]];
    -         var group= contents[0].group;
    -         for (var i= 1; i<contents.length; i++) {
    -           if (contents[i].group!=group) {
    -             result.push({id:"separator", type: baf.commandType.separator});
    15            group= contents[i].group;
    -           }
    -           result.push(contents[i]);
    -         }
    -       }
    20      return result;
    -     },
```

Next, we need to insert the objects returned by _prepareList into the toolbar. These objects will be commands, separators, or submenus. Submenus require a little more attention since part of the design said that submenus could be configured dynamically before they are displayed. The idea is to broadcast (via dojo.publish) that a submenu is being displayed and let other program objects add/subtract/manipulate the submenu as required by program semantics. So, the submenu is populated *just* before it is displayed. This is easy to do by subclassing dijit.Menu and overriding the onOpen function to call a function that builds the submenu. Here's what that looks like:

baf/step2/baf/dijit/MenuBand.js

```
Line 1    dojo.declare("baf.Submenu", dijit.Menu, {
    -       onOpen: function(){
    -         this.onOpenSubmenu();
    -         this.inherited(arguments);
    5       },
    -       onClose: function(){
    -         this.inherited(arguments);
    -         dojo.forEach(this.getChildren(), function(child){
    -           this.removeChild(child);
```

```
10        child.destroy();
  -     }, this);
  -   }
  - });
```

As long as any instance of baf.Submenu.onOpenSubmenu is hooked up to
a function that populates the menu, the menu will be populated before
it is opened. dijit.Menu.onClose is also overridden to remove and destroy
all the children; that way when a submenu is repeatedly opened and
closed, duplicates don't appear. With this in place, we can write the
function baf.dijit.MenuBand._build, which initializes a new instance:

baf/step2/baf/dijit/MenuBand.js

```
Line 1  _build: function() {
  -       var contents= this._prepareList(this.menu);
  -       this._publish(["beforeDisplay", this, contents]);
  -       dojo.forEach(contents, function(commandItem){
  5         this._publish(["beforeDisplayItem", this, commandItem]);
  -         var item= null;
  -         switch (commandItem.type){
  -           case baf.commandType.command:
  -             item= new dijit.form.Button({
  10              label: commandItem.text,
  -               onClick: dojo.hitch(this, "_exec", commandItem)
  -             });
  -           break;
  -
  15          case baf.commandType.separator:
  -             item= new dijit.ToolbarSeparator();
  -           break;
  -
  -           case baf.commandType.submenu:
  20          case baf.commandType.menu:
  -             var popup= new baf.Submenu();
  -             popup.onOpenSubmenu= dojo.hitch(
  -               this,
  -               this._onOpenDropDown,
  25              this.menu[commandItem.id], popup);
  -             item= new dijit.form.DropDownButton({
  -               label: commandItem.text,
  -               dropDown: popup
  -             });
  30          break;
  -
  -           default: break;
  -         }
  -         if (item) {
  35          this.addChild(item);
  -         }
  -       }, this);
  - },
```

First, the function constructs the menu items using _prepareList (line 2). Then any interested code can inspect and optionally edit the menu items (line 3). Next, each item is added to the toolbar. Notice that submenus instances hook their onOpenSubmenu property (a function) to this._onOpenDropDown (line 22). When a submenu is opened, _onOpenDropDown is called upon to populate that submenu. _onOpenDropDown looks much like _build except that command items are dijit.MenuItems rather than dijit.form.Buttons:

`baf/step2/baf/dijit/MenuBand.js`

```
Line 1    _onOpenDropDown: function(menuObject, menu){
   -        var contents= this._prepareList(menuObject);
   -        dojo.publish(["beforeDisplaySubmenu", this, contents]);
   -        dojo.forEach(contents, function(commandItem){
   5          dojo.publish(["beforeDisplayItem", this, commandItem]);
   -          var item= null;
   -          switch (commandItem.type){
   -            case baf.commandType.command:
   -              item= new dijit.MenuItem({
   10               label: commandItem.text,
   -                 onClick: dojo.hitch(this, "_exec", commandItem)
   -              });
   -            break;

   15           case baf.commandType.separator:
   -              item= new dijit.MenuSeparator();
   -            break;


   -            case baf.commandType.submenu:
   20           case baf.commandType.menu:
   -              var popup= new baf.Submenu();
   -              popup.onOpenSubmenu= dojo.hitch(
   -                this,
   -                this._onOpenDropDown,
   25               menuObject[commandItem.id],
   -                popup);
   -              item= new dijit.PopupMenuItem({
   -                label: commandItem.text,
   -                popup: popup
   30             });
   -            break;


   -            default: break;
   -          }
   35         if (item) {
   -            menu.addChild(item);
   -          }
   -       }, this);
   -    },
```

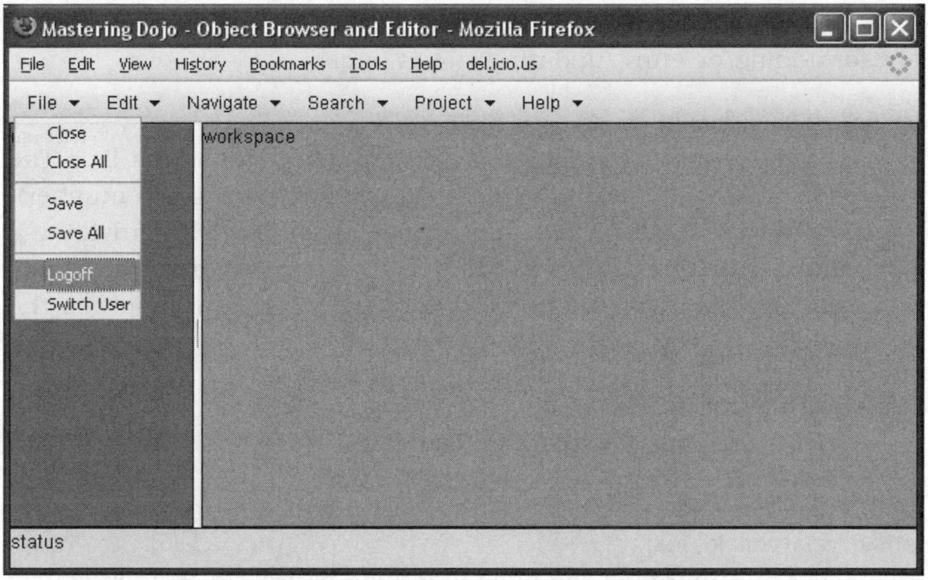

Figure 18.3: APPLICATION WITH A MENU

That completes the BAF menu. Next, obe.main.startup needs to be modified to use the new menu:

`baf/step2/obe/main.js`

Line 1 `main.menu= new baf.dijit.MenuBand(args);`

The startup data shown at the end of the previous section already had a menu item. That's it for step 2.

Start the HTTP server, navigate over to ./main.htm?test=run001, and you should see something like Figure 18.3. As the menu is navigated, it publishes "beforeDisplay", "beforeDisplayItem", and "execute" events to "baf.dijit.MenuBand". Other program machinery can choose to subscribe and then react to these events.

18.4 Step 3: A Custom Statusbar Widget

BAF includes the Dijit-based component baf.dijit.Statusbar, which provides status bar functionality. The idea is to create a widget class that manages its own layout, can be inserted in other container widgets (for example, dijit.layout.BorderContainer), and includes a super-simple interface for adding/deleting/updating status panes:

createTextPane(paneId, args)
> Inserts a pane that holds text at the end of the status bar. The pane is associated with the identifier paneId (a string or a number). args (a hash) controls the appearance of the pane by providing a value for the property class (the HTML class attribute of the pane) and/or a value for the property style (HTML styles to apply to the pane).

deleteTextPane(paneId)
> Deletes the pane identified by paneId and previously created with createPane.

setTextPane(paneId, text)
> Sets the contents of the pane identified by paneId and previously created with createPane.

baf.dijit.Statusbar can be used inside obe.main.startup like this:

`baf/step3/obe/main.js`

```
Line 1  main.statusbar= new baf.dijit.Statusbar();
   -    main.statusbar.createTextPane("message");
   -    main.statusbar.createTextPane("userName", {style: "width: 20em"});
   -    main.statusbar.createTextPane(
   5      "role",
   -      {"class": "statusPaneRed", style: "width: 10em"});
```

After a status bar is created (line 1), panes are added (lines 2–6). Typically, all panes except the leftmost pane (the first pane added) will include a width style as in the previous example. When the status bar layout is calculated, the panes are placed next to each other, right-to-left, and any leftover space is given to the first pane. The pane's rendering is usually controlled by including an HTML class value and associating that value with a style in the style sheet. Panes automatically include the class bafDijitStatusStaticPane. An example of providing an additional class is shown on line 6.

Implementing baf.dijit.Statusbar is quite straightforward—particularly because it's built on top of Dijit's layout widget framework. A great example of this is dijit.layout.BorderContainer. This widget can contain up to five other widgets, and its sole purpose is to size and position the contained widgets. A status bar does exactly the same thing.

baf.dijit.Statusbar is derived from dijit.layout._LayoutWidget, which is in turn derived from dijit._Widget with dijit._Container and dijit._Contained mixed in. dijit._Contained gives children the ability to traverse their siblings and report their parent; dijit._Container gives containers the ability to insert, remove, and traverse their children. The widgets that baf.dijit.Statusbar contains are the status bar panes. Usually a status bar contains just text panes; the class dijit._widget has all the functionality needed. With this much information, we can start implementing baf.dijit.Statusbar:

`baf/step3/baf/dijit/Statusbar.js`

```
Line 1  dojo.declare("baf.dijit.Statusbar", [dijit.layout._LayoutWidget], {

          postCreate: function(){
            this.inherited(arguments);
5           dojo.addClass(this.domNode, "bafDijitStatus");
          },

          createTextPane: function(paneId, args){
            args= args || {};
10          this[paneId]= new dijit._Widget(args);
            dojo.addClass(this[paneId].domNode, "bafDijitStatusStaticPane");
            this.addChild(this[paneId]);
          },

15        deleteTextPane: function(paneId){
            var pane= this[paneId];
            if (pane) {
              removeChild(pane);
              pane.destroy();
20          }
          },


          setTextPane: function(paneId, text){
            var pane= this[paneId];
25          if (pane) {
              pane.domNode.innerHTML= text;
            }
          },

30      //more to follow...
```

The only thing baf.dijit.Statusbar does special during the construction process is add the HTML class bafDijitStatus to the root DOM node (line 5); any processing that needs the DOM node must be done in postCreate after the base class postCreate has been called (line 4) since the node won't exist prior to this point. createTextPane creates a widget and adds it to the set of children widgets the baf.dijit.Statusbar instance contains (line 8); deleteTextPane removes a previously added child (line 15). Both of these routines leverage the addChild/removeChild methods provided by the mixin dijit._Container (lines 12 and 18). Finally, setTextPane simply sets the innerHTML on the div node that _widget created.

Layout is accomplished by ensuring all of the children have the value of absolute for the style position and then setting the margin boxes of each child. dijit._Container.addChild is overridden to set the style each time a child is added:

`baf/step3/baf/dijit/Statusbar.js`

```
Line 1    addChild: function(/*Widget*/ child){
     -        this.inherited(arguments);
     -        this._setupChild(child);
     -        if(this._started){
     5            this._layoutChildren();
     -        }
     -    },
```

`baf/step3/baf/dijit/Statusbar.js`

```
Line 1    _setupChild: function(/*Widget*/child){
     -        var node= child.domNode;
     -        if (node) {
     -            node.style.position = "absolute";
     5        }
     -    },
```

The function _layoutChildren sets the margin boxes of the children. It finds the right content edge of the status bar DOM node and then lays one child next to the other, right to left:

`baf/step3/baf/dijit/Statusbar.js`

```
Line 1    _layoutChildren: function(){
     -        var
     -            thisDomNode= this.domNode,
     -            children= this.getChildren(),
     5            totalWidth= 0,
     -            e1= dojo._getPadBorderExtents(thisDomNode),
     -            e2= dojo._getMarginExtents(thisDomNode),
     -            rightEdge= dojo.marginBox(thisDomNode).w - (e1.w - e1.l) - (e2.w - e2.l);
     -
     10       for (var i= children.length-1; i>0; i--){
     -            var node= children[i].domNode;
     -            rightEdge-= dojo.marginBox(node).w;
     -            dojo.marginBox(node, {l:rightEdge});
     -        }
     15       var l= e1.l + e2.l;
     -        dojo.marginBox(children[0].domNode, {l: l, w: rightEdge - l});
     -    }
```

The private function _layoutChildren is called anytime a child is added or removed as well as when the public function layout is called.

Lastly, baf.dijit.Statusbar includes a function to set its own height. This function is typically called before a baf.dijit.Statusbar is laid out as a child within another container. Here is setHeight:

`baf/step3/baf/dijit/Statusbar.js`

```
Line 1  setHeight: function(){
   -      var
   -        height= 0,
   -        thisNode= this.domNode;
   5
   -      dojo.forEach(this.getChildren(), function(child){
   -        height= Math.max(dojo.marginBox(child.domNode).h, height);
   -      });
   -
  10      height=
   -        height +
   -        dojo._getPadBorderExtents(thisNode).h;
   -
   -      dojo.marginBox(thisNode, {h: height});
  15    },
```

Assuming a baf.dijit.Statusbar was incorporated into obe.main.startup as shown at the beginning of this section, the bar can be used anywhere in the program like this:

`baf/step3/obe/test/tests/run001.js`

```
obe.main.statusbar.setTextPane("message", "Ready...");
obe.main.statusbar.setTextPane("userName", "Rawld C. Gill");
obe.main.statusbar.setTextPane("role", "Administrator");
```

In Figure 18.4, on the next page, you can see the new status bar in the application.

At this point, the application is beginning to look like a native application. It fills up the viewport. It has a menu and status bar that stay anchored at the top and bottom of the viewport. And it has two workspaces that are resizable with a splitter bar. We'll finish the application in the next chapter when we add some content to the workspace.

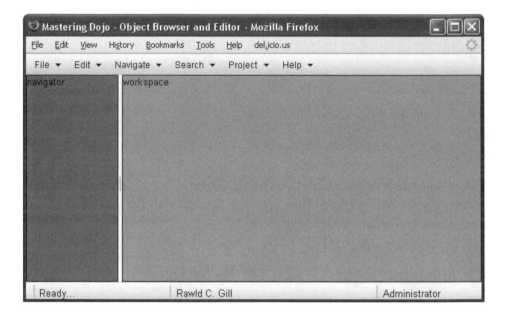

Figure 18.4: APPLICATION WITH A MENU AND STATUS BAR

Chapter 19

Adding Dynamic Content to an RIA

So far the application looks like just about any ordinary native desktop application—which is exactly the point. We'll pick up the application development where we left it and add an object navigator in the left pane and a workspace object in the right pane.

19.1 Step 4: The Navigator Pane and On-Demand Data Store

This step fills the left workspace with a tree widget that is used to navigate a hierarchy of items. The items are delivered by a mock service that provides data on-demand as branches are opened.

Retrieving Tree Data On Demand

None of the stock dojo.data drivers is specialized to handle hierarchical data on demand. This is an important case for a tree-based navigation paradigm because the contents of the tree may be too large to transmit in one bundle and/or simply be unavailable. Typically, this type of interface retrieves the children for a node only when that node is opened. Indeed, dijit.Tree adds a small abstraction layer termed a *model* on top of the data store connected to a tree, and the model demands data from the data store precisely in this mode.

So, the task at hand is to implement a dojo.data driver that returns the children of an item on demand and use this driver to implement a dijit.Tree model. With this in place, the obe.main.startup function can create an instance of the driver, the model, and a dijit.Tree widget; connect them all together; and place the tree widget in the navigator pane. When it's all done, the service behind the tree is hit *only* when a node is opened and then *only* the given node's children are returned.

Currently, the Dijit tree machinery includes two models: on the one hand, dijit.tree.TreeStoreModel models a single-root tree, while dijit.tree. ForestStoreModel models a multiroot tree. BAF includes the class baf.dijit. LazyTreeModel that's derived from dijit.tree.TreeStoreModel. The BAF class overrides the methods mayHaveChildren and getChildren.

mayHaveChildren takes an item from the underlying data store and returns true if the item might possibly have children; it returns false if the item definitely has no children.

getChildren takes an item from the underlying data store as well as onComplete and onError functions. It fetches the children of the item and calls the onComplete function; naturally error conditions call onError. If the children are already present in the store, then the onComplete function is called immediately. Otherwise, it sets up a fetch that retrieves the children and then calls the onComplete/onError functions upon completion of the fetch.

Assuming the underlying data store includes certain capabilities, implementing dijit.tree.TreeStoreModel is super-easy:

`baf/step4/baf/dijit/LazyTreeModel.js`

```
Line 1   dojo.provide("baf.dijit.LazyTreeModel");
    -    dojo.require("dijit.Tree");
    -    (function(){

    5      dojo.declare("baf.dijit.LazyTreeModel", dijit.tree.TreeStoreModel, {
    -        // summary:
    -        //     An optimization of dijit.tree.TreeStoreModel;
    -        //     requires baf.data.LazyTreeStore.

   10        mayHaveChildren: function(item){
    -          return this.store.hasChildren(item);
    -        },

    -        getChildren: function(parentItem, onComplete, onError){
   15          // Calls onComplete() with array of child items
    -          // of given parent item, all loaded.
    -          var store = this.store;
    -          if (!this.mayHaveChildren(parentItem)) {
    -            //no children...
   20            onComplete([]);
```

```
     } else if (store.childrenLoaded(parentItem)) {
       //children already loaded...
       onComplete(store.getValues(parentItem, "children"));
     } else {
25     //need to load the children...
       store.fetch({
         id: parentItem.id,
         getChildren: true,
         onComplete: onComplete,
30       onError: onError
       });
     }
   },

35   //No write functionality...
   newItem: function(){
     throw new Error('baf.dijit.LazyTreeModel: not implemented.');
   },

40   pasteItem: function(){
     throw new Error('baf.dijit.LazyTreeModel: not implemented.');
   }
 });

45 })();//(function(){
```

The model depends on the underlying store including the method has-Children (line 11), and that fetch retrieves the children of an item when the fetch parameter getChildren is true (line 28). The BAF class baf.data. LazyTreeStore includes this functionality.

Implementing a Lazy Tree Data Driver

baf.data.LazyTreeStore is a complete implementation of dojo.data.api. Identity. It makes a few assumptions about the data that's delivered by the service, which simplifies the implementation:

- The service returns items as JSON. Each item has the property id that uniquely identifies the item within the entire hierarchy of items. Further, each item returned also includes the property chil-drenState (an integer) where a childrenState value of childrenNever (==0) indicates that the item does not and will never have children and where a value of childrenMaybe (==1) indicates the item may or may not have children.

- The service returns either a single item (if the query parameter getChildren is false or missing) or the children of an item (if the query parameter getChildren is true). Note that if getChildren is true, only the children of the item are returned; the item itself is not returned, because the store already has the item.

- The root item is retrieved by requesting a single item with an id value of 0. All subsequent requests (for either single items or children of an item) must specify an id received from a previous request. id values don't persist between different instances of a particular store.

The store keeps a map from item id to item. The map is updated as items and children are returned by the service. When a set of children is returned, the map is used to look up the parent, the children are added to that parent, and the parent's childrenState value is set to childrenLoaded (==-1), indicating the children have been loaded.

With this design, determining whether an item has children simply requires inspecting the childrenState property:

`baf/step4/baf/data/LazyTreeStore.js`

```
Line 1   hasChildren: function(item){
   -       return (
   -         item.childrenState==childrenMaybe ||
   -        (item.childrenState==childrenLoaded && item.children.length));
   5     },
```

fetch makes service requests. The service defaults to dojo.xhrGet; however, any function that implements the dojo.xhrGet API can be specified for the service by setting the service property of the store (we'll use this feature later and provide a mock service). Here's fetch:

`baf/step4/baf/data/LazyTreeStore.js`

```
Line 1   fetch:function(/* Object? */ request){
   -       var result= dojo.mixin({}, request);
   -       if (typeof result.id == "undefined") {
   -         //default to get the root...
   5         result.id= 0;
   -       }
   -       result.theDeferred= this.service({
   -         url: this.url,
   -         handleAs: "json-comment-optional",
  10         content: this.requestParams(result),
   -         load: dojo.hitch(this, this.onLoad, result),
   -         error: dojo.hitch(this, this.onError, result)
   -       });
   -       result.abort= function(){
  15         result.theDeferred.abort.apply(result.theDeferred, arguments);
   -       };
   -       return result;
   -     },
```

Finally, when the service calls back the load routine specified by fetch, the new items are processed, and any callbacks specified by the fetch parameters are executed as required by the dojo.data.api.Read read API:

`baf/step4/baf/data/LazyTreeStore.js`

```
onLoad: function(request, data){
  var abort= false;
  request.abort= function() {
    abort= true;
  };

  //data is either a single item or an array of children
  if (!dojo.isArray(data)) {
    //returned a single item; therefore turn it into an array...
    data= [data];
  } else if (this.sort) {
    data.sort(this.sort);
  }

  //set the children of the parent
  if (data.length) {
    this._idToItem[data[0].parentId].childrenState= childrenLoaded;
    this._idToItem[data[0].parentId].children= data;
  }

  //set the _idToItem for each item
  dojo.forEach(data, function(item){
    this._idToItem[item.id]= item;
  }, this);

  var scope= request.scope || dojo.global;

  if(request.onBegin){
    request.onBegin.call(scope, data.length, request);
  }

  if (request.onItem && !abort) {
    dojo.forEach(data, function(item){
      if (!abort) {
        request.onItem.call(scope, item, request);
      }
    });
  }

  if (request.onComplete && !abort) {
    request.onComplete.call(scope, (request.onItem ? null : data), request);
  }
},
```

Line numbers: Line 1, 5, 10, 15, 20, 25, 30, 35, 40

The implementation of the remaining store methods is trivial.

Implementing a Mock Service

This is the point where you usually stop working on the client and open a whole new can of worms on the server. We don't want to do that. Let's finish the client! The idea is to create some machinery that reacts like a real server but isn't. Ideally, it should be rock-solid and easy to configure with different response patterns. It must be *much* easier to implement than a real server; otherwise, it would be foolish to waste time with it. With JavaScript and Dojo, all of this is easy to achieve.

The idea is to initialize the mock server machinery with a bunch of preprogrammed responses. Typically, some kind of JSON map is provided that maps a set of server requests to a set of responses. But other designs are possible, including collecting a response directly from the user. To make the mock server behave like a real server, it should simulate asynchrony. If the mock server were to immediately return the response, then the unpredictability of an asynchronous return would be lost, and the mock server would cause the client program to take quite different execution paths than a real server. Asynchrony is easily simulated with a timer. Let's put this all together an implement a mock server that returns tree items.

The BAF class baf.test.mocks.services.Base implements the asynchronous simulation with a timer. It includes the method call that implements the callback API just like dojo.xhr*:

baf/step4/baf/test/mocks/services/Base.js

```
Line 1   dojo.provide("baf.test.mocks.services.Base");
    -    (function(){
    -      dojo.declare("baf.test.mocks.services.Base", null, {
    -        constructor: function(args){
    5          this.delay= args.delay || 100;
    -        },
    -
    -        getService: function() {
    -          return dojo.hitch(this, "call");
   10        },
    -
    -        call: function(args){
    -          var result= new dojo.Deferred();
    -          if (args.load) {
   15            result.addCallback(args.load);
    -          }
    -          if (args.error) {
    -            result.addErrback(args.load);
    -          }
```

```
20      if (args.handle) {
-          result.addBoth(args.handle);
-        }
-        setTimeout(dojo.hitch(this, "handler", result, args), this.delay);
-        return result;
25      },

-      handler: function(theDeferred, args){
-        throw new Error('baf.test.mocks.services.Base: handler not specified');
-      }
30    });//dojo.declare("baf.test.mocks.services.Base", null, {
-  })();//(function(){
```

call creates a new dojo.Deferred instance just like dojo.xhr*; inserts any load, error, or handle functions into the callback queue; and then connects a timer to the handle method. The default implementation of handle throws an exception; subclasses implement handle to simulate a server response, as we'll see in a moment. The length of the timer is controlled by the property delay (line 23). It can be initialized in construction (line 5) and changed at any time.

The BAF class baf.test.mocks.services.Navigator simulates a service suitable for use with baf.data.LazyTreeStore. The mock server is initialized with an entire tree hierarchy at construction. Then handler simply returns an item or an item's children:

baf/step4/baf/test/mocks/services/Navigator.js

```
Line 1  dojo.declare(
-        "baf.test.mocks.services.Navigator",
-        baf.test.mocks.services.Base, {
-        constructor: function(args){
5          this._delay= 200;
-          this._data= args.data;

-          var idToItem= this._idToItem= [];
-          function walk(item) {
10           idToItem[item.id]= item;
-             dojo.forEach(item.children, walk);
-          }
-          walk(args.data);
-        },
15
-        handler: function(theDeferred, args){

-          function getItemToReturn(item){
-            var result= dojo.mixin({}, item);
20            result.childrenState= (item.children) ?
-               baf.data.LazyTreeStore.childrenMaybe :
-               baf.data.LazyTreeStore.childrenNever;
```

```
            delete result.children;
            return result;
25       }

        if (!args.content.getChildren) {
          var item= this._idToItem[args.content.id];
          if (item) {
30           theDeferred.callback(getItemToReturn(item));
          } else {
            theDeferred.callback({});
          }
        } else {
35         var parent= this._idToItem[args.content.id];
          if (parent && parent.children) {
            var result= [];
            dojo.forEach(parent.children, function(child){
              result.push(getItemToReturn(child));
40           });
            theDeferred.callback(result);
          } else {
            theDeferred.callback([]);
          }
45       }
       }
```

During construction, the tree is walked to build a map from item id to item. This simplifies the handle implementation. When handle looks up the item, if the requested item is not found, then an empty object (line 32) or an empty array (line 43) is returned depending upon whether a single item or an item's children were requested. If the item is found, then the function getItemToReturn creates a copy of the item, sets the childrenState property, and deletes the children. The children are deleted because the contract with the server says the only way to get children is to request them directly. Notice that top-level properties are copied to a new object by the expression dojo.mixin({}. item). It wouldn't work to return a reference to the item in the mock service's data since deleting the children would result in deleting the mock service's data.

All that's left is to construct a JSON object that gives the value of some hierarchy to be simulated. This code is fairly uninteresting so we don't show it.

Connecting All the Parts

Now we have all the parts: a dijit.Tree connects to a baf.dijit.LazyTreeModel, which connects to a baf.data.LazyTreeStore, which connects to a baf.test. mocks.services.Navigator. You can see how you might want to mix and match different implementations of any of these items. For example, maybe some trees can connect to a different model that also writes data. Or, maybe other trees with small amounts of read-only data ignore the model completely and connect to a dojo.data.ItemFileReadStore. With these possibilities in mind, the class obe.Navigator accepts a hash that describes which tree widget, optional model, dojo.data driver, and service to connect:

`baf/step4/obe/Navigator.js`

```
Line 1  dojo.provide("obe.Navigator");
   -    (function(){

   -      dojo.declare("obe.Navigator", null, {
   5        constructor: function(
   -          args //startup parameters passed to main
   -        ){
   -          if (args.navigator.store) {
   -            this.store = new args.navigator.store(args.navigator.storeArgs);
  10            args.navigator.modelArgs.store= this.store;
   -            args.navigator.widgetArgs.store= this.store;
   -          }
   -          if (args.navigator.model) {
   -            this.model= new args.navigator.model(args.navigator.modelArgs);
  15            args.navigator.widgetArgs.model= this.model;
   -          }

   -          this.widget= new args.navigator.widget(args.navigator.widgetArgs);
   -        }
  20      });//;dojo.declare("obe.Navigator", null, {

   -    })();//(function(){
```

Notice how args not only says how to initialize new class instances via the args.navigator.storeArgs, args.navigator.modelArgs, and args.navigator.widgetArgs properties but also which classes to instantiate via the args.navigator.stores, args.navigator.model, and args.navigator.widget properties. obe.main sets defaults for these:

`baf/step4/obe/main.js`

```
Line 1  var defaults= {
   -      navigator: {
   -        store: baf.data.LazyTreeStore,
   -        storeArgs: {
   5          service: dojo.xhr},
   -        model: baf.dijit.LazyTreeModel,
   -        modelArgs: {},
   -        widget: dijit.Tree,
```

```
         widgetArgs: {
10          persist: false,
            region: "left",
            style: "width: 20%; overflow: auto",
            splitter: true,
            id: "navigator",
15          showRoot: false}
         }
     };


     obe.main.startup= function(args) {
20      //mixin defaults to args...
        args= baf.util.setDefaults(args, defaults);
```

baf.util.setDefaults (line 21) takes care of mixing nested objects.

The obe.test.tests.run002 startup module overrides some of these. In particular, the mock service is given:

`baf/step4/obe/test/tests/run001.js`

```
Line 1  dojo.provide("obe.test.tests.run001");
        dojo.require("obe.test.data.navigator.set001");
        dojo.require("obe.test.data.command.set001");
        dojo.require("baf.test.mocks.services.Navigator");
5       (function(){
          var navData= obe.test.data.navigator.set001;
          var navigatorService= new baf.test.mocks.services.Navigator({
            data: navData
          });
10
          var startupArgs= {
            commandItems: obe.test.data.command.set001.commandItems,
            menu: obe.test.data.command.set001.mainMenu,
            navigator: {
15            storeArgs: {
                service: navigatorService.getService(),
                root: navData
              },
              modelArgs: {
20              root: navData
              }
            }
          };
          obe.main.startup(startupArgs);
25
          //fake it for now...
          obe.main.statusbar.setTextPane("message", "Ready...");
          obe.main.statusbar.setTextPane("userName", "Rawld C. Gill");
          obe.main.statusbar.setTextPane("role", "Administrator");
30
        })();
```

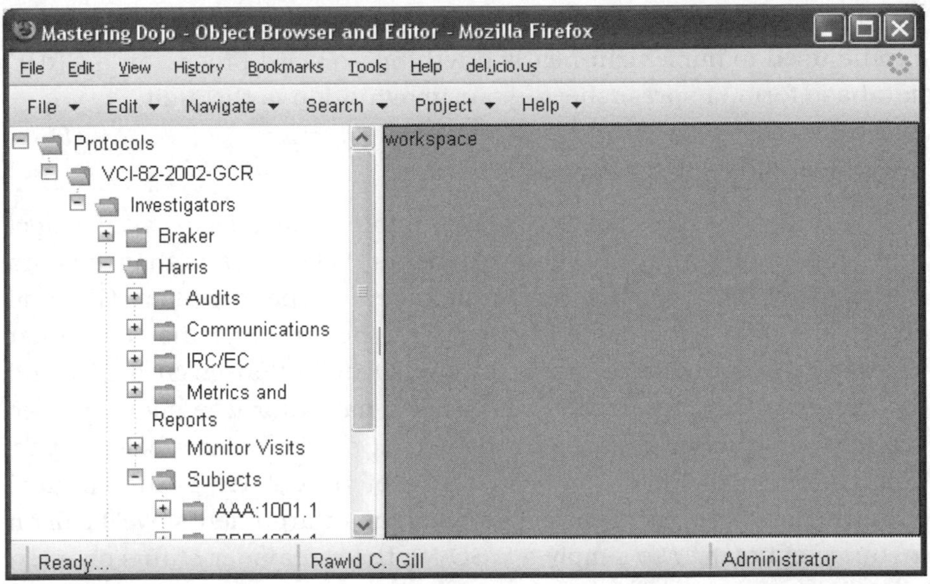

Figure 19.1: APPLICATION WITH A TREE-BASED NAVIGATOR

With that, we're done with step 4. Figure 19.1 shows the navigator in all its glory. We hope you agree that Dojo's tree machinery gives you tremendous power while being quite simple to work with.

19.2 Step 5: Workspace Objects

We're down to the last step—loading and displaying a WSO. Of all the steps, the machinery that's shown in this one is the most powerful; it's also quite simple.

Recall that a WSO is simply a container of widgets. Such a container could hold anything representable in a browser, assuming the necessary components existed. Several design possibilities exist here. One example is a container that prepackages some components and behavior, forming a kind of template in which to put more components. Another example is a design-time container where a WSO definition could be constructed in a WYSIWYG environment. Also, there is no reason the components must be Dijit components. They could be components from other widget systems and/or nonvisual computational components. We mention these possibilities to highlight the extensive capabilities of a WSO. A WSO, and by extension a browser-based UI, can be used to implement nearly anything—a word processor, a CRUD database form, a spreadsheet—your imagination is the limit.

Implementing a WSO Widget

BAF includes the class baf.dijit.Wso that implements a Dijit-based widget that holds a hierarchy of Dijit components. Let's assume that the data returned by the navigator service includes a type-identifier (TID) and object-identifier (OID) for each item. Further assume that two other services are available that return a WSO definition given a TID and data given a OID. When the user clicks a navigator tree node, the two services are queried resulting in two dojo.Deferred objects being *immediately* returned. Then a new instance of baf.dijit.Wso is instantiated with the Deferred objects passed as constructor arguments. We'll call an instance of baf.dijit.Wso simply a WSO for the remainder of this chapter.

When a WSO is first created, the Deferreds that get the WSO definition and data may or may not have completed. So, the WSO displays a message saying that it's loading and then hooks up continuation functions to the callback queues that continue processing when both Deferreds complete. This should sound familiar—it's the same algorithm we used in Section 6.4, *Managing Callbacks with dojo.Deferred*, on page 117. The continuation functions instantiate the hierarchy of Dijit components given by the definition, initialize them with data, and display the result to the user.

baf.dijit.Wso is derived from dijit.form.Form; this provides a few convenience features such as form validation. Since the key abstraction of baf.dijit.Wso *is* a container of widgets, dijit._Container is mixed in. This also helps with duties such as calling the startup method on contained widgets. Here are baf.dijit.Wso's declaration and construction routines:

`baf/step5/baf/dijit/Wso.js`

```
Line 1   dojo.provide("baf.dijit.Wso");
    -    dojo.require("dijit.form.Form");
    -    dojo.require("dijit._Container");
    -    (function(){
    5      dojo.declare("baf.dijit.Wso", [dijit.form.Form, dijit._Container], {
    -        dataResult: null,
    -        wsoDefResult: null,

    -        postscript: function(){
   10          this.inherited(arguments);
    -
```

```
     -        //connect the callbacks...
     -        this.data.addCallback(this, "_continueWithData");
     -        this.data.addErrback(this, "_abortLoad");
    15        this.wsoDef.addCallback(this, "_continueWithWsoDef");
     -        this.wsoDef.addErrback(this, "_abortLoad");
     -      },
     -
     -      buildRendering: function(){
    20        this.inherited(arguments);
     -        //TODO: make this better...
     -        this._loading= document.createElement("p");
     -        var node= this._loading;
     -        dojo.addClass(node, "bafDijitwsoLoading");
    25        node.innerHTML= "Loading...";
     -        dojo.place(node, this.domNode, "last");
     -        //END-TODO
     -      },
```

All arguments passed to the constructor get mixed into the new WSO
instance by the superclass's postscript method called at line 10. As mentioned earlier, the two Deferreds that return the WSO definition and
data are passed to the constructor, so, for example, this.wsoDef holds the
Deferred object that's retrieving the WSO definition. postCreate hooks up
the Deferreds' callbacks starting at line 13. buildRendering adds a single
p element that displays the message "loading"; a real application would
probably put a little animation up to entertain the user. _continueWith-
Data, __continueWithWsoDef, and _abortLoad are unsurprising:

baf/step5/baf/dijit/Wso.js

```
Line 1  _continueWithData: function(data) {
    -     this.dataResult= data;
    -     if (this.wsoDefResult) {
    -       this._finishLoad();
    5     }
    -   },
    -
    -   _continueWithWsoDef: function(wsoDef) {
    -     this.wsoDefResult= wsoDef;
    10    if (this.dataResult) {
    -       this._finishLoad();
    -     }
    -   },
    -
    15  _abortLoad: function() {
    -     if (!this.data) {
    -       return;
    -     }
```

```
20      var
  -       data= this.data,
  -       wsoDef= this.wsoDef;
  -
  -     this.data= null;
 25     this.wsoDef= null;
  -
  -     data.cancel();
  -     wsoDef.cancel();
  -
 30     this._loading.innerHTML= "FAILED!!";
  -   },
```

_continueWithData and _continueWithWsoDef both store their results (lines 2 and 9); when *both* routines have completed (line 3 or 10), _finishLoad is called to load the WSO with widgets and data. _abortLoad marks that an error has occurred by nulling both Deferreds and then notifies the user; nulling the Deferreds gives a way to prevent _abortLoad from being executed more than once.

Before we can discuss _finishLoad, we need to understand what a WSO definition looks like. Broadly speaking, there are two possibilities. First, it could just be a chunk—probably a rather large chunk—of HTML. In this case, the innerHTML property of the root DOM node of the form could be set to the chunk and then the dojo.parser.parse called to parse the subtree. You've seen this time and again in all the declarative widget examples throughout the book.[1] The second possibility is for a WSO definition to be delivered as data, typically a JavaScript object. Then a processor traverses the data and constructs the widgets explicitly.

There are advantages and disadvantages to each method; neither is right or wrong. The second method is convenient for constructing higher levels of abstraction, less verbose definitions, and very fast processors, particularly when matched with a tool (for example, a WYSIWYG editor) for contructing the WSO definition.

baf.dijit.Wso includes a processor that constructs the WSO from data. The processor expects a JSON object that gives a few top-level properties followed by a hierarchy of children objects.

---

1. dojo.parser.parse has been called automatically when the document was loaded by Dojo as a result of setting the djConfig option parseOnLoad to true.

Here's an example:

```
Line 1    {                                 //begin a singe WSO definition
   -        tid: 1,                          //the type identifier
   -        size: ["51em", "25em"],         //the w x h of this WSO
   -        "class": "crf",                 //the HTML class of this WSO
   5        requires: [                     //the classes this WSO uses
   -          "baf.dijit.StaticText"],
   -        children: {                     //the contained widgets
   -          title: [                      //each child is an object in the hash
   -            "baf.dijit.StaticText",     //[0] => the class
  10            {                           //[1] => ctor args
   -              "class": "crfTitle",
   -              posit: {
   -                t: "1em",
   -                h: "5em",
  15                l: "1em",
   -                w: "10em"
   -              },
   -              q: "tl",
   -              text: "Demographics"
  20            }, {                        //[2] => children of this child
   -              //et cetera...            //therefore, forming a hierarchy!
   -            }
   -          ], //end the child named 'title'
   -          someOtherChild: [
  25            //et cetera...
   -          ] //end the child named 'someOtherChild'
   -        }
   -      }
```

The top-level properties include the TID (property tid, line 2), the layout size of the WSO (property size, line 3), HTML attributes to add to the root DOM node for the WSO (line 4 shows the property class, but others such as style could also be included), and an array of modules that the WSO definition needs (property requires, line 5). Lastly, the contained widgets are given in the property children, an object, where each property of the children object names a widget. Widgets are specified by giving an array of two or three elements. The first element gives the widget class, the second gives the constructor arguments to use when creating the particular widget instance, and the optional third element gives the list of children (if any) contained by the widget. Since widgets can contain other widgets, the structure forms a hierarchy.

Given this structure, two steps are required to populate the container with the children. First, the require array must be traversed to ensure that all required modules are loaded.

baf/step5/baf/dijit/Wso.js

```
Line 1  _finishLoad: function() {
   -      dojo.forEach(this.wsoDefResult.require, function(module){
   -        dojo["require"](module);
   -      });
   5      dojo.addOnLoad(dojo.hitch(this, "_buildForm"));
   -    },
```

Notice here how we wrote dojo["require"](module) instead of the usual dojo.require(module). This causes the build system to ignore this dojo. require statement, which is what we want ("module" is not a module; the value of module is a module, and this value isn't knowable at build time). Since the code may be deployed with the cross-domain loader, the require statements will return immediately—before the module is loaded. The dojo.addOnLoad call causes the process to wait until all the requested modules have loaded before continuing with _buildForm. This is a useful pattern for advanced designs.

_buildForm implements the processor that reads the WSO definition and builds the WSO; it's exceedingly simple. After setting the size of the top-level DOM node, it walks the tree, instantiating widgets along the way:

baf/step5/baf/dijit/Wso.js

```
Line 1  _buildForm: function(){
   -      dojo._destroyElement(this._loading);
   -      delete this._loading;

   5      var wsoDef= this.wsoDefResult;
   -      dojo.style(this.domNode, {
   -        position: "absolute",
   -        width: wsoDef.size[0],
   -        height: wsoDef.size[1]
   10     });

   -      function walkChildren(children, parentWidget){
   -        for (var p in children) {
   -          var child= children[p];
   15         var ctor= dojo.getObject(child[0]);
   -          var widget= new ctor(child[1]);
   -          parentWidget.addChild(widget);
   -          if (child[2]) {
   -            walkChildren(child[2], widget);
   20         }
   -        }
   -      }
```

```
   if (wsoDef.children) {
25     walkChildren(wsoDef.children, this);
   }
   this.startup();
}
```

As it stands, the processor is quite powerful: it can generate any hierarchy of classes. The only requirement is that a component that contains children must define the method addChild. Although the design shown (WSO definition + processor) doesn't include the ability to define and hook up event handlers, this could be easily added.

Looking back at Figure 18.1, on page 480, notice that the header is comprised of several blocks of static text. The Dijit-based class baf.dijit. StaticText controls a block of static text. Similarly, the Dijit-based class baf.dijit.Pair implements a pair of children widgets arranged side by side or stacked. These two widget classes make defining form decorations a snap. Let's implement baf.dijit.StaticText.

Implementing a Static Text Widget

baf.dijit.StaticText has three key capabilities:

1. It displays a block of text at an absolute position within its container. The block and text can be styled directly through the HTML style attribute or indirectly through the class attribute associated with a style sheet style.

2. The text can be put in any of the nine locations within the box by specifying the property q (quadrant). q is given by *vertical-location* x *horizontal-location*, where *vertical-location* is one of {'t', 'c', 'b'} and *horizontal-location* is one of {'l', 'c', 'r'}. For example, "bc" means put the text at the bottom-center of the box.

3. It can contain other children widgets and be contained by other widget containers.

4. It's a full Dijit-based widget component.

Does this sound complicated? It actually takes fewer than 100 lines to implement!

Requirements [3] and [4] come nearly free by deriving from dijit._Widget and mixing in dijit._Container and dijit._Contained.

Here's the dojo.declare statement:

`baf/step5/baf/dijit/StaticText.js`

```
Line 1    dojo.declare("baf.dijit.StaticText",
    -       [dijit._Widget, dijit._Container, dijit._Contained],
```

Next we need to build the DOM tree for the element. It's just a div element that contains a p element. The bafDijitStaticText class is added to the element to help with building style sheets. Since this component isn't intended to be used with markup and is very simple, the DOM tree is built directly in buildRendering:

`baf/step5/baf/dijit/StaticText.js`

```
Line 1    buildRendering: function(){
    -       var node;
    -       node= this.domNode= document.createElement("div");
    -       dojo.addClass(node, "bafDijitStaticText");
    5       node= this._textNode= document.createElement("p");
    -       dojo.style(node, {top:0, left:0, position:"absolute"});
    -       node.innerHTML= this.text;
    -       dojo.place(node, this.domNode, "last");
    -     },
```

baf.dijit.StaticText understands the property posit, which defines the properties l, r, t, b, h, and w for left, right, top, bottom, height, and width. The posit property is converted to a style object like this:

`baf/step5/baf/dijit/StaticText.js`

```
Line 1    function positToStyle(posit){
    -       var result= {position: "absolute"};
    -       if (posit.l) {
    -         result.left= posit.l;
    5       }
    -       if (posit.r) {
    -         result.right= posit.r;
    -       }
    -       if (posit.w) {
    10        result.width= posit.w;
    -       }
    -       if (posit.t) {
    -         result.top= posit.t;
    -       }
    15      if (posit.b) {
    -         result.bottom= posit.b;
    -       }
    -       if (posit.h) {
    -         result.height= posit.h;
    20      }
    -       return result;
    -     }
```

The style object is then used to set the style of the div in postCreate:

`baf/step5/baf/dijit/StaticText.js`

```
Line 1   postCreate: function() {
    -        dojo.style(this.domNode, positToStyle(this.posit));
    -     },
```

Lastly, the p element needs to be wrestled into the correct position. If any of the corners are specified, then the left/right and top/bottom styles can be set to zero, and you're done. But to center the text, the div's content box and p's margin box must be calculated. These metrics are not reliable until the elements reside in the displayable document— something that doesn't happen until after construction is complete. This is precisely the point where the startup method comes in handy; it is called after the widget has been displayed. The function getContentPosit calculates the proper position given a q property value and the div and p elements:

`baf/step5/baf/dijit/StaticText.js`

```
Line 1   function getContentPosit(quadrant, parent, contentNode){
    -        var q= quadrant.toLowerCase();
    -        return dojo.mixin(
    -          getContentPosit.calculators[0][q.charAt(0)](parent, contentNode),
    5          getContentPosit.calculators[1][q.charAt(1)](parent, contentNode)
    -        );
    -     }
    -     getContentPosit.calculators= [{
    -        t: function(){
   10          return {top: 0};
    -        },
    -
    -        c: function(parent, contentNode){
    -          return {top:
   15            ((dojo.contentBox(parent).h - dojo.marginBox(contentNode).h) / 2)+"px"};
    -        },
    -
    -        b: function(){
    -          return {bottom: 0};
   20        }
    -     },{
    -        l: function(){
    -          return {left: 0};
    -        },
   25
    -        c: function(parent, contentNode){
    -          return {left:
    -            ((dojo.contentBox(parent).w - dojo.marginBox(contentNode).w) / 2)+"px"};
    -        },
   30
```

```
  r: function(parent, contentNode){
    return {right: 0};
  }
}];
```

Note that the function includes the property calculators that dispatches the required calculation based on the value of q. No if statements, no case statement—this is a nice example of how expressive, parsimonious, and powerful JavaScript can be.

baf.dijit.StaticText.startup clears any positions already placed on the p element and then forces it to the correct position:

```
baf/step5/baf/dijit/StaticText.js
```

```
Line 1   startup: function(){
           if(!this._started) {
             this._started= true;

    5        var style= dojo.mixin(
               {top: "", left: "", bottom: "", right: ""},
               getContentPosit(this.q, this.domNode, this._textNode)
             );
             dojo.style(this._textNode, style);
   10
             dojo.forEach(this.getChildren(), function(child){
               if (child.startup) {
                 child.startup();
               }
   15        });
           }
         },
```

That's it for baf.dijit.StaticText. baf.dijit.Pair is very similar; it's included with the code bundled with the book. Let's get back and finish up displaying a WSO.

Wiring the WSO to the Framework

OBE can be used to test the baf.dijit.StaticText class. We'll create a few WSO definitions that exercise baf.dijit.StaticText, and then we'll put items in the tree that reference these definitions. When the user clicks a tree item, a WSO should be created that shows the instantiated baf.dijit. StaticText widgets. Since there is no data involved, we create a mock data service that returns an empty object.

The first definition includes nine baf.dijit.StaticText widgets that show each of the nine text positions inside a container with a border, the second definition eliminates the border but gives a colorized background, and the third and fourth definitions do the same thing except with an HTML class associated with a style sheet style. Here's part of the first definition:

```
Line 1   obe.test.data.metadata.set002.metadata= [
         {
           tid: 1,
           size: ["51em", "25em"],
     5     "class": "crf",
           requires: [baf.dijit.StaticText],
           children: {
             tl: [
               "baf.dijit.StaticText",
    10         { //ctor args for baf.dijit.StaticText
                 style: "background-color: #D0D0D0;",
                 posit: {t:"1em", h:"5em", l:"1em", w:"10em"},
                 q: "tl",
                 text: "top-left"
    15         }
             ],
             tc: [
               "baf.dijit.StaticText",
               { //ctor args for baf.dijit.StaticText
    20           style: "background-color: #D0D0D0;",
                 posit: {
                   t: "1em",
                   h: "5em",
                   l: "12em",
    25             w: "10em"
                 },
                 q: "tc",
                 text: "top-center"
               }
    30       ],
```

Next, we need a service to deliver WSO definitions. Step 5 includes baf.test.mocks.services.WsoDefinitions, a mock server that works just like baf.test.mocks.services.Navigator. The service is created during startup exactly as we did with the navigator mock service. Step 5 also includes a WSO definition manager (baf.data.WsoDefinitionsManager) that retrieves and caches definitions from a service. obe.main.startup instantiates one of these objects, connecting it to the service provided in the startup arguments.

Similarly, a data manager is provided (baf.data.DataManager). This is *truly* trivial; it just immediately returns an empty object.

`baf/step5/baf/data/DataManager.js`

```
Line 1  dojo.provide("baf.data.DataManager");
   -    (function(){
   -      dojo.declare("baf.data.DataManager", null, {
   -        get: function(oid){
   5          var result= new dojo.Deferred();
   -          result.callback({});
   -          return result;
   -        }
   -      });//dojo.declare("baf.data.DataManager", null, {
  10
   -    })();//(function(){
```

obe.main.startup instantiates a baf.data.DataManager and stores a reference to the new object in obe.main.dataManager. At this point, OBE has everything in place necessary to start creating WSOs: a global WSO definitions manager and data manager available through obe.main.wsoDefinitionsManager and obe.main.dataManager.

WSO creation is handled by a little manager class that removes any existing WSO that's displayed, issues the WSO definition and data requests, creates a new WSO instance, and places the instance in the workspace pane. It subscribes to the focusNavNode event that the navigator tree publishes. When it receives a notification that a new tree item has the focus, it loads the WSO given by the tree item:

`baf/step5/obe/WorkspaceManager.js`

```
Line 1  dojo.provide("obe.WorkspaceManager");
   -    dojo.require("obe.main");
   -    dojo.require("baf.dijit.Wso");
   -    (function(){
   5      var nullObjectValue= {type: 0, oid: 0, form: null};
   -
   -      dojo.declare("obe.WorkspaceManager", null, {
   -        constructor: function() {
   -          this.currentObject= nullObjectValue;
  10          dojo.subscribe("focusNavNode", this, "_showObject");
   -        },
   -
   -        _showObject: function(store, item) {
   -          var
  15            type= store.getValue(item, "type"), //the wsoDefinition type
   -            oid= store.getValue(item, "oid"),    //the object id
   -            nid= store.getValue(item, "id"),     //the navigator id
   -            currentObject= this.currentObject;
   -
  20          if (currentObject.type==type && currentObject.oid==oid) {
   -            //already the current object
   -            return;
   -          }
```

```
25        //TODO: search for non-current, but loaded object

          //load the new current object
          var
            data= obe.main.dataManager.get(oid),
30          wsoDef= obe.main.wsoDefinitionsManager.get(type),
            theNewObject= new baf.dijit.Wso({data: data, wsoDef: wsoDef});

          //destroy the old current object...
          this.destroy();
35
          //display the new current object...
          obe.main.appContainer.addChild(dojo.mixin(theNewObject, {
            region: "center",
            id: nid+"_wso" //"wso" => "workspace object"
40        }));
          obe.main.appContainer.layout();

          //record the current state...
          currentObject.type= type;
45        currentObject.oid= oid;
          currentObject.nid= nid;
          currentObject.form= theNewObject;
        },

50    destroy: function() {
        var currentObject= this.currentObject;
        if (currentObject.form) {
          obe.main.appContainer.removeChild(currentObject.form);
          currentObject.form.destroyRecursive();
55        }
        currentObject= nullObjectValue;
      }

    });
60
})();//(function(){
```

The event is subscribed at line 10. The new WSO is created at line 31, any existing WSO is destroyed at line 34, and the new WSO is placed in the application's workspace pane at line 37.

In Figure 19.2, on the next page, you can see the application running with the test module obe.test.tests.run002 included in step 5.

We're not going to hook up data because there's not much more browser UI insight to be gained by that exercise. Typically, you'll use one or more dojo.data data stores to manage the data. Widgets that can connect directly to the stores may do so; baf.dijit.WSO could also be extended to pull data from stores and push it into controls, and visa versa, for widgets that don't have this capability.

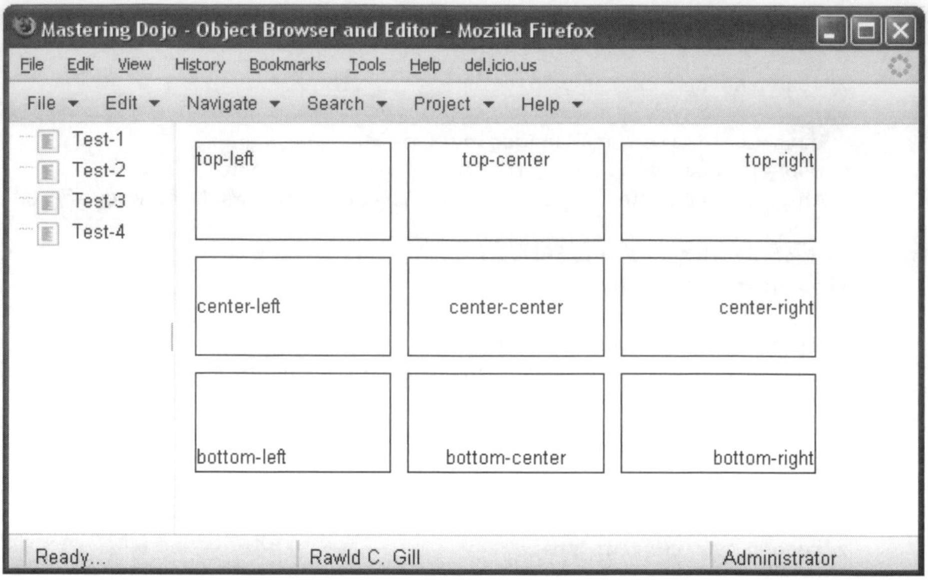

Figure 19.2: OBE TESTING BAF.DIJIT.STATICTEXT

As you can see, the possibilities are limitless. The WSO abstraction could be extended to build nearly any kind of UI. The OBE framework (menu, navigator, workspace, status bar) could be rearranged in countless ways. And of course there's nothing about the BAF framework that's required to build Dojo-based RIAs. Although it's a proven design for certain classes of applications, it is but one example of many design options.

If nothing else, we hope this chapter and the previous one have stimulated your imagination for what can be done in the browser today with Dojo. Although we've covered the most important parts of Dojo extensively, there's a lot more out there, particularly in Dojox. In particular, the graphics framework shows great promise. And Dojo doesn't stop with Dojo. It has been carefully built to play well with others, opening up possible implementation options even further. We look forward to using the great applications you will no doubt create!

Chapter 20

Going Forward

The health of an open source project can be measured by how many contributions its fosters. By this measure, Dojo is very healthy indeed. There are constant additions of new components, widgets, and programming aids to Dojo, especially in the Dojox area.

Unfortunately, all these features won't fit in a reasonably sized book. So for this last chapter, we'll give you an overview of the ones we find interesting and useful and leave the research to you. Think of it as a rough map to new worlds in Dojo. You have your compass handy, so happy trails!

20.1 Foundations

First, we'll cover some modules to make the programming life easier. They extend DOM utility, widget class creation, and agile design tools already in Dojo.

dojo.behavior: **Assigning code to queries**

Behaviors have been part of Internet Explorer since version 4, and now Dojo provides a cross-browser version. Behaviors are an extension of the CSS model, where nodes that fit a certain criteria (the selector) are automatically assigned colors, size, and so on. Behaviors automatically assign *code* to nodes that fit a certain CSS selector. They can dojo.connect a node event with an event handler, for example. Or they can run an arbitrary bit of JavaScript code on the newly created node. It's a little like doing a dojo.query with a forEach.

All this is done by adding rules to the dojo.behavior rule book. It's like a CSS file, except you add rules through JavaScript. One catch is you must call dojo.behavior.apply to apply the rules, where in regular CSS the rules are applied automatically. But even that's not a big problem. For one thing, it allows you to batch node updates and execute them in one shot. For another, apply is smart enough to make only incremental changes to the nodes. It doesn't go through the whole DOM tree to match rules but instead applies only rules to nodes added since the last apply.

dojox.analytics: **Client logging and analysis**

One advantage of the fill-and-submit web model is you can easily track client progress throughout the site. If a particular feature is being used heavily, or not at all, you can detect it. Ajax applications are much tougher to track. Although you can watch data requests on your web server log, they are often short and uninformative. So, dojox.analytics offers a library to hook JavaScript events to data gathering. Its plug-ins work to track specific events in the system: mouse clicks, log messages, and so forth. You can then have the client send these logs back to your web server at regular intervals.

dojox.dtl: **Django template language for Dojo**

The Dijit templating language, described in Section 17.1, *Widget Classes Using dijit.Declaration*, on page 456, provides the minimum language needed for building widgets. Templates, however, are very monolithic. Making a small change to a widget's template requires subclassing the widget and replacing the entire template. Templates have many other uses too, as in dojo.string.substitute. A template language with branching, loops, and more sophisticated expressions would be widely useful.

Django (http://www.djangoproject.com/), a Python framework, has a template language that is so useful that it has been ported to Dojox and called DTL. Django templates have very nice reusability features, so templates feel more object-oriented. Over the next few releases, DTL will gradually replace the older template system in the bundled Dijit components.

dojox.wire: **Wire protocol**

So, Dojo has a flexible data gatherer in dojo.data and fantastic form controls in Dijit. But how do you ship data from one to the other? With what you know now, it's a fairly manual process. But with dojox.wire, you can *bind* data to controls declaratively. When a change occurs in the form control data, it can be wired to write back to the data store, and vice versa.

This sounds vaguely familiar. Both Grid and Tree have data binding built-in, and in fact, Grid's binding is fairly sophsticated. You can think of dojox.wire as an abstraction to this, providing linkage between any Dijit form controls and data.

DOH: JavaScript unit tester

Earlier Dojo releases used various JavaScript unit testing packages. But for the pivotal 0.9 release, the committers decided to build the unit testing system they really wanted. DOH (think what Homer Simpson would say upon finding a bug) is that package. Like most unit testing frameworks, DOH includes assertions, set-up and teardown facilities, and convenient test grouping. And since all Dojo, Dijit, and Dojox unit tests are written with DOH, you have lots of examples to consult!

20.2 Graphics

Dojo has always had an active graphic design subcommunity, making early use of Scalable Vector Graphics (SVG) and other new standards. These modules are fairly well established, and additions have been made through Google's Summer of Code programs in the past few years.

dojox.fx: Animations

The dojox.fx packages adds more animations such as cross-fading, highlighting, and drop shadowing to the standard Dojo Core set. It also adds the popular easing functions, which add pizzazz to the standard transitions.

dojox.gfx and dojox.gfx3d: Low-level graphics

If you're obsessed with graphics—arcs, curves, gradient fills, polygons, and all those other good things—then these packages are for you. The output can be rendered in several formats including SVG and Microsoft Silverlight, depending on what the client has installed. The 3D graph package, in the experimental stage right now, adds the third dimension and lighting.

dojox.charting: **Graphs and charts**

A clear application of the drawing tools, dojox.charting provides tools for drawing 2D and 3D charts. You can plug either dojo.data or simple JavaScript data into one end. Then you can get line graphs, bar graphs, pie charts, and many others with customizable scales and axes.

dojox.image: **Image widgets**

The dojox.image module houses widgets for image collections: a thumbnail picker, some assorted slide show and gallery components, and an image magnifier.

20.3 Dojo Data and Storage

It seems like we never run out of new sources for data. Dojo has been keeping up with this area, keeping it in the forefront of enterprise JavaScript applications.

dojox.off: **Dojo Offline**

With increased client functionality, you can have less dependence on an always-on Internet connection. Dojo Offline is a project that takes advantage of this, providing synchronization services between client and server data stores. A demo application, Moxie, lets you edit web pages offline and then synchronize them with a Java server-side component when you reconnect.

dojox.storage: **Link to Google Gears client-side storage**

Dojo Offline uses Google Gears, a client-side mini-relational database that understands SQL. This storage module serves as the intermediary between the two, but you can use it on its own. It's perfect for storing user preferences and caching oft-used data, saving bandwidth, and increasing performance.

New dojo.data **drivers**

Dojo 1.0 introduced dojo.data drivers for the web services Flickr, Picasa, and SnapLogic. (Yes, there are photography buffs in the Dojo community!) It also included a specialized XML format called OPML, which has a fixed set of tags and the Identity feature, so it's good for using in Dijit components. Dojo 1.1 added an Atom XML format driver, a key-value pair driver (like an INI or Java-style property files), and a driver based on JSONPath.

Part V

Appendixes

Appendix A

Bibliography

[AS96]   Harold Abelson and Gerald Jay Sussman. *Structure and Interpretation of Computer Programs*. The MIT Press, Cambridge, Massachusetts, second edition, 1996.

[BC90]   Gilad Bracha and William Cook. Mixin-based inheritance. In *OOPSLA/ECOOP '90: Proceedings of the European conference on object-oriented programming on Object-oriented programming systems, languages, and applications*, pages 303–311, New York, NY, USA, 1990. ACM.

[Bro95]   Frederick P. Brooks, Jr. *The Mythical Man Month: Essays on Software Engineering*. Addison-Wesley, Reading, MA, anniversary edition, 1995.

[Fla06]   David Flanagan. *JavaScript: The Definitive Guide*. O'Reilly Media, Inc., Sebastopol, CA, fifth edition, 2006.

[GÇH⁺05]   Daniel Glazman, Tantek Çelik, Ian Hickson, Peter Linss, and John Williams. Selectors, W3C Working Draft, 15 December 2005. Technical report, W3C, 2005.

[Mac90]   Bruce J. MacLennan. *Functional Programming, Practice and Theory*. Addison-Wesley, Reading, MA, 1990.

[Mah06]   Michael Mahemoff. *Ajax Design Patterns*. O'Reilly & Associates, Inc, Sebastopol, CA, 2006.

[Mey06]   Eric Meyer. *CSS: The Definitive Guide*. O'Reilly Media, Inc., Sebastopol, CA, third edition, 2006.

[MK08]   Chuck Musciano and Bill Kennedy. *HTML & XHTML: The Definitive Guide*. O'Reilly Media, Inc., Sebastopol, CA, sixth edition, 2008.

[Zel06]   Jeffrey Zeldman. *Designing Web Standards*. Peachpit Press, New York, second edition, 2006.

Index

Web 2.0

Welcome to the Web, version 2.0. You need some help to tame the wild technologies out there. Start with *Prototype and script.aculo.us*, a book about two libraries that will make your JavaScript life much easier.

See how to reach the largest possible web audience with *The Accessible Web*.

Prototype and script.aculo.us

Tired of getting swamped in the nitty-gritty of cross-browser, Web 2.0–grade JavaScript? Get back in the game with Prototype and script.aculo.us, two extremely popular JavaScript libraries that make it a walk in the park. Be it Ajax, drag and drop, autocompletion, advanced visual effects, or many other great features, all you need is write one or two lines of script that look so good they could almost pass for Ruby code!

Prototype and script.aculo.us: You never knew JavaScript could do this!
Christophe Porteneuve
(330 pages) ISBN: 1-934356-01 8. $34.95
http://pragprog.com/titles/cppsu

The Accessible Web

The 2000 U.S. Census revealed that 12% of the population is severely disabled. Sometime in the next two decades, one in five Americans will be older than 65. Section 508 of the Americans with Disabilities Act requires your website to provide *equivalent access* to all potential users. But beyond the law, it is both good manners and good business to make your site accessible to everyone. This book shows you how to design sites that excel for all audiences.

The Accessible Web
Jeremy Sydik
(304 pages) ISBN: 1-934356-02-6. $34.95
http://pragprog.com/titles/jsaccess

Getting It Done

Start with the habits of an agile developer and use the team practices of successful agile teams, and your project will fly over the finish line.

Practices of an Agile Developer

Agility is all about using feedback to respond to change. Learn how to apply the principles of agility throughout the software development process
• establish and maintain an agile working environment • deliver what users really want • use personal agile techniques for better coding and debugging • use effective collaborative techniques for better teamwork • move to an agile approach

Practices of an Agile Developer: Working in the Real World
Venkat Subramaniam and Andy Hunt
(189 pages) ISBN: 0-9745140-8-X. $29.95
http://pragprog.com/titles/pad

Ship It!

Page after page of solid advice, all tried and tested in the real world. This book offers a collection of tips that show you what tools a successful team has to use, and how to use them well. You'll get quick, easy-to-follow advice on modern techniques and when they should be applied. **You need this book if:** • You're frustrated at lack of progress on your project. • You want to make yourself and your team more valuable. • You've looked at methodologies such as Extreme Programming (XP) and felt they were too, well, extreme. • You've looked at the Rational Unified Process (RUP) or CMM/I methods and cringed at the learning curve and costs. • **You need to get software out the door without excuses**

Ship It! A Practical Guide to Successful Software Projects
Jared Richardson and Will Gwaltney
(200 pages) ISBN: 0-9745140-4-7. $29.95
http://pragprog.com/titles/prj

Real World Tools

Learn real-world design and architecture for your project, and a very pragmatic editor for Mac OS X.

Release It!

Whether it's in Java, .NET, or Ruby on Rails, getting your application ready to ship is only half the battle. Did you design your system to survive a sudden rush of visitors from Digg or Slashdot? Or an influx of real-world customers from 100 different countries? Are you ready for a world filled with flaky networks, tangled databases, and impatient users?

If you're a developer and don't want to be on call at 3 a.m. for the rest of your life, this book will help.

Design and Deploy Production-Ready Software
Michael T. Nygard
(368 pages) ISBN: 0-9787392-1-3. $34.95
http://pragprog.com/titles/mnee

TextMate

If you're coding Ruby or Rails on a Mac, then you owe it to yourself to get the TextMate editor. And, once you're using TextMate, you owe it to yourself to pick up this book. It's packed with information that will help you automate all your editing tasks, saving you time to concentrate on the important stuff. Use snippets to insert boilerplate code and refactorings to move stuff around. Learn how to write your own extensions to customize it to the way you work.

TextMate: Power Editing for the Mac
James Edward Gray II
(200 pages) ISBN: 0-9787392-3-X. $29.95
http://pragprog.com/titles/textmate

Leading Your Team

See how to be a pragmatic project manager and use agile, iterative project retrospectives on your project.

Manage It!

Manage It! is a risk-based guide to making good decisions about how to plan and guide your projects. Author Johanna Rothman shows you how to beg, borrow, and steal from the best methodologies to fit your particular project. You'll find what works best for *you*.

• Learn all about different project lifecycles • See how to organize a project • Compare sample project dashboards • See how to staff a project • Know when you're done—and what that means.

Your Guide to Modern, Pragmatic Project Management
Johanna Rothman
(360 pages) ISBN: 0-9787392-4-8. $34.95
http://pragprog.com/titles/jrpm

Agile Retrospectives

Mine the experience of your software development team continually throughout the life of the project. Rather than waiting until the end of the project—as with a traditional retrospective, when it's too late to help—agile retrospectives help you adjust to change *today*.

The tools and recipes in this book will help you uncover and solve hidden (and not-so-hidden) problems with your technology, your methodology, and those difficult "people issues" on your team.

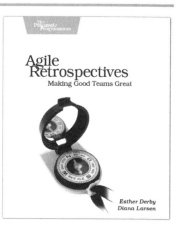

Agile Retrospectives: Making Good Teams Great
Esther Derby and Diana Larsen
(170 pages) ISBN: 0-9776166-4-9. $29.95
http://pragprog.com/titles/dlret

It All Starts Here

If you're programming in Ruby, you need the PickAxe Book: the definitive reference to the Ruby Programming language, now in the revised 3rd Edition for Ruby 1.9.

Programming Ruby (The Pickaxe)

The Pickaxe book, named for the tool on the cover, is the definitive reference to this highly-regarded language. • Up-to-date and expanded for Ruby version 1.9 • Complete documentation of all the built-in classes, modules, and methods
• Complete descriptions of all standard libraries
• Learn more about Ruby's web tools, unit testing, and programming philosophy

Programming Ruby: The Pragmatic Programmer's Guide, 3rd Edition
Dave Thomas with Chad Fowler and Andy Hunt
(900 pages) ISBN: 978-1-9343560-8-1. $49.95
http://pragprog.com/titles/ruby3

Agile Web Development with Rails

Rails is a full-stack, open-source web framework, with integrated support for unit, functional, and integration testing. It enforces good design principles, consistency of code across your team (and across your organization), and proper release management. This is the newly updated Second Edition, which goes beyond the Jolt-award winning first edition with new material on:

• Migrations • RJS templates • Respond_to
• Integration Tests • Additional ActiveRecord features • Another year's worth of Rails best practices

Agile Web Development with Rails: Second Edition
Dave Thomas and David Heinemeier Hansson with Leon Breedt, Mike Clark, James Duncan Davidson, Justin Gehtland, and Andreas Schwarz
(750 pages) ISBN: 0-9776166-3-0. $39.95
http://pragprog.com/titles/rails2

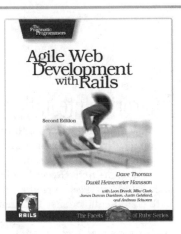

Ruby Everywhere

From day-to-day chores to help you be more productive, to integrating enterprise technologies, Ruby can help.

Everyday Scripting with Ruby

Don't waste that computer on your desk. Offload your daily drudgery to where it belongs, and free yourself to do what you should be doing: thinking. All you need is a scripting language (free!), this book (cheap!), and the dedication to work through the examples and exercises. Learn the basics of the Ruby scripting language and see how to create scripts in a steady, controlled way using test-driven design.

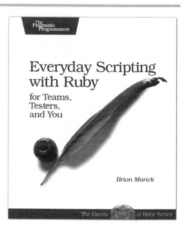

Everyday Scripting with Ruby: For Teams, Testers, and You
Brian Marick
(320 pages) ISBN: 0-9776166-1-4. $29.95
http://pragprog.com/titles/bmsft

Enterprise Integration with Ruby

See how to use the power of Ruby to integrate all the applications in your environment. Learn how to
• use relational databases directly and via mapping layers such as ActiveRecord • harness the power of directory services • create, validate, and read XML documents for easy information interchange • use both high- and low-level protocols to knit applications together

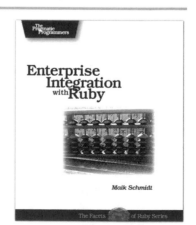

Enterprise Integration with Ruby
Maik Schmidt
(360 pages) ISBN: 0-9766940-6-9. $32.95
http://pragprog.com/titles/fr_eir

Where to Go Next

Take your Ruby on Rails application to the next level, and deploy it effectively.

Advanced Rails Recipes

A collection of practical recipes for spicing up your web application without a lot of prep and cleanup. You'll learn how the pros have solved the tough problems using the most up-to-date Rails techniques (including Rails 2.0 features)

Advanced Rails Recipes
Mike Clark
(300 pages) ISBN: 978-0-9787392-2-5. $32.95
http://pragprog.com/titles/fr_arr

Deploying Rails Applications

Until now, the information you needed to deploy a Ruby on Rails application in a production environment has been fragmented and contradictory. This book changes all of that by providing a consistent, level-headed book containing advice you can trust. You'll get the inside angle from those that have built, deployed, and maintained some of the largest Rails apps in production, anywhere.

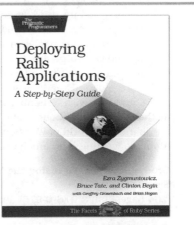

Deploying Rails Applications: A Step-by-Step Guide
Ezra Zygmuntowicz, Bruce Tate, and Clinton Begin
(284 pages) ISBN: 978-0-9787392-0-1. $34.95
http://pragprog.com/titles/fr_deploy

Get Groovy

Expand your horizons with Groovy, and tame the wild Java VM.

Programming Groovy

Programming Groovy will help you learn the necessary fundamentals of programming in Groovy. You'll see how to use Groovy to do advanced programming techniques, including meta programming, builders, unit testing with mock objects, processing XML, working with databases and creating your own domain-specific languages (DSLs).

Programming Groovy Dynamic Productivity for the Java Developer
Venkat Subramaniam
(320 pages) ISBN: 978-1-9343560-9-8. $34.95
http://pragprog.com/titles/vslg

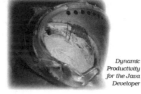

Groovy Recipes

See how to speed up nearly every aspect of the development process using *Groovy Recipes*. Groovy makes mundane file management tasks like copying and renaming files trivial. Reading and writing XML has never been easier with XmlParsers and XmlBuilders. Breathe new life into arrays, maps, and lists with a number of convenience methods. Learn all about Grails, and go beyond HTML into the world of Web Services: REST, JSON, Atom, Podcasting, and much much more.

Groovy Recipes: Greasing the Wheels of Java
Scott Davis
(264 pages) ISBN: 978-0-9787392-9-4. $34.95
http://pragprog.com/titles/sdgrvr

Stuff You Need to Know

From massively concurrent systems to the basics of Ajax, we've got the stuff you need to know.

Programming Erlang

Learn how to write truly concurrent programs—programs that run on dozens or even hundreds of local and remote processors. See how to write high-reliability applications—even in the face of network and hardware failure—using the Erlang programming language.

Programming Erlang: Software for a Concurrent World
Joe Armstrong
(536 pages) ISBN: 1-934356-00-X. $36.95
http://pragprog.com/titles/jaerlang

Pragmatic Ajax

Ajax redefines the user experience for web applications, providing compelling user interfaces. Now you can dig deeper into Ajax itself as this book shows you how to make Ajax magic. Explore both the fundamental technologies and the emerging frameworks that make it easy.

From Google Maps to Ajaxified Java, .NET, and Ruby on Rails applications, this Pragmatic guide strips away the mystery and shows you the easy way to make Ajax work for you.

Pragmatic Ajax: A Web 2.0 Primer
Justin Gehtland, Ben Galbraith, Dion Almaer
(296 pages) ISBN: 0-9766940-8-5. $29.95
http://pragprog.com/titles/ajax

The Pragmatic Bookshelf

The Pragmatic Bookshelf features books written by developers for developers. The titles continue the well-known Pragmatic Programmer style and continue to garner awards and rave reviews. As development gets more and more difficult, the Pragmatic Programmers will be there with more titles and products to help you stay on top of your game.

Visit Us Online

Mastering Dojo's Home Page
http://pragprog.com/ titles/rgdojo
Source code from this book, errata, and other resources. Come give us feedback, too!

Register for Updates
http://pragprog.com/updates
Be notified when updates and new books become available.

Join the Community
http://pragprog.com/community
Read our weblogs, join our online discussions, participate in our mailing list, interact with our wiki, and benefit from the experience of other Pragmatic Programmers.

New and Noteworthy
http://pragprog.com/news
Check out the latest pragmatic developments in the news.

Save on the PDF

Save on the PDF version of this book. Owning the paper version of this book entitles you to purchase the PDF version at a terrific discount. The PDF is great for carrying around on your laptop. It's hyperlinked, has color, and is fully searchable.

Buy it now at pragprog.com/coupon.

Contact Us

Phone Orders:	1-800-699-PROG (+1 919 847 3884)
Online Orders:	www.pragprog.com/catalog
Customer Service:	orders@pragprog.com
Non-English Versions:	translations@pragprog.com
Pragmatic Teaching:	academic@pragprog.com
Author Proposals:	proposals@pragprog.com